RACE IN EARLY

RACE IN EARLY MODERN ENGLAND

A DOCUMENTARY COMPANION

Compiled and Edited by
Ania Loomba and Jonathan Burton

First published in 2007 by
PALGRAVE MACMILLAN™
175 Fifth Avenue, New York, N.Y. 10010 and
Houndmills, Basingstoke, Hampshire, England RG21 6XS.
Companies and representatives throughout the world.

PALGRAVE MACMILLAN is the global academic imprint of the Palgrave
Macmillan division of St. Martin's Press, LLC and of Palgrave Macmillan Ltd.
Macmillan® is a registered trademark in the United States, United Kingdom
and other countries. Palgrave is a registered trademark in the European Union
and other countries.

ISBN-13: 978-1-4039-6167-9

Library of Congress Cataloging-in-Publication Data

Race in early modern England: a documentary companion / edited by Ania
Loomba and Jonathan Burton.
    p. cm.
    Includes bibliographical references and index.
    ISBN 1-4039-6166-2 (alk. paper) – ISBN 1-4039-6167-0 (pbk.: alk. paper)
    1. Racism–England–History–16th century–Sources. 2. Racism–England–
History–17th century–Sources. 3. Historiography–England–History.
4. England–Race relations–History–16th century–Sources. 5. England–Race
relations–History–17th century–Sources. 6. Race in literature. 7. Literature and
society–England–History–16th century. 8. Literature and society–England–
History–17th century. 9. National characteristics, British. I. Loomba, Ania.
II. Burton, Jonathan, 1967–

    DA125.A1R27 2007
    305.800942'09031–dc22

                                                              2007061459

A catalogue record for this book is available from the British Library.

Design by Macmillan India Ltd.

First edition: September 2007

10 9 8 7 6 5 4 3 2 1

Printed in the United States of America.
Transferred to Digital Printing in 2008.

For all students, scholars, and activists fighting against racism.

CONTENTS

LIST OF FIGURES

ACKNOWLEDGMENTS

While a great deal of scholarship is produced in the solitary, contemplative recesses of libraries and studies, this project was launched in the belief that increased collaboration and dialogue is crucial as early modern scholars expand the geographic and temporal scope of their studies. From the beginning, we sought the input of colleagues, and in turn we have benefited from their overwhelming advice and support. Throughout, this project has been an affirmation of the community in which we work, a community that consistently transcends geographic distance with its generosity and intellectual commitment.

Kristi Long, who was then at Palgrave Macmillan, was crucial to launching the project. When it was nothing more than a list of documents, thoughtful letters arrived with suggestions concerning the contents, scope, organization, and rationale of the collection. For this initial boost we thank Bernadette Andrea, Barbara Fuchs, Lisa Lampert, Bob Markley, Patricia Parker, Valerie Traub, and Dan Vitkus. During the publication process Antoinette Burton, Jean Howard, Margaret Ferguson, Cristina Malcolmson, Bob Markley, Patricia Parker, Sarah Rivett, Katherine Rowe, Bill Sherman, Randall Styers, Ayanna Thompson, and Valerie Traub lent us crucial support. Particular points of inquiry were speedily resolved by Terry Hawkes, Gil Harris, Sujata Iyengar, Bill Sherman, David Weston, and Frances Wood. Peter Erickson offered repeated assistance with the illustrations in this volume, while Kellie Robertson, Ayanna Thompson, and Ian Cornelius generously volunteered their skills to translate documents from Middle English and Latin. We got valuable suggestions and learned about rare materials from Kristin Brookes, Peter Erickson, Cristina Malcolmson, and Carla Pestana.

Our greatest debts are to the talented scholars who generously read and commented on our work. Drafts of the introduction benefited enormously from the commentary of Carla Pestana, David Wallace, David Theo Goldberg, Kathleen Wilson, and a faculty research group at West Virginia University that comprised Cari Carpenter, Ryan Claycomb, Donald Hall, John Ernest, and Timothy Sweet. Natalie Zemon Davis read through the entire manuscript, offering both support and constructive criticism. Suvir Kaul commented on several drafts of the project, making crucial suggestions that helped us organize the material and produce a more lucid introduction. These scholars have saved this project from many errors and have helped us think through our basic concepts and arguments; of course, we are responsible for any errors that remain.

Archival work depends on institutions as much as individuals, and we have been especially fortunate in the generosity of several libraries. This project could never have been completed but for the wonderful resources at the University of Illinois. We are especially grateful to Alvan Bregman for help in locating books and rare documents, and to Valerie Hotchkiss for allowing us to reproduce them without permission fees. Bob Kieft of the Haverford College Library and Deborah Silverman at the University of Pittsburgh's Falk Library of the Health Sciences also waived the costs of photography and permissions for materials drawn from their collections, while the photography department at the Folger Library, and especially Bettina Smith, handled the changing requirements of our orders with unflagging patience. Excerpts from Bruno, Bernier, Paracelsus, and Vesualius are reprinted from *Readings in Early Anthropology,* edited by J. Slotkin, by permission of the Wenner-Gren Foundation for Anthropological Research.

For research help, we must thank Kimberly Woosley Poitevin (then at the University of Illinois, Urbana-Champaign) whose own innovative work on race made her a contributor to this collection in its early stages. She located new materials, sifted through existing ones, and tracked down rare sources with diligence and ingenuity. The Research Board at the University of Illinois supported this project with a grant. West Virginia University provided funding for summer research through a Riggle Fellowship. At the University of Pennsylvania, Jeffrey Edwards lent us meticulous and cheerful assistance through many different phases of collecting, transcribing, and editing. During the final months, we benefited from Megan Cook and Stephanie Elsky's research and editorial help. Thanks also to Cathy Nicholson and Urvashi Chakravarty for their inputs, and to Brian Kirk and Ann Marie Pitts for helping us keep many a deadline.

Above all, we are most grateful to our partners, Anita Ravi and Suvir Kaul, who have lived with this project for many years, and whose patience, love, and encouragement make them the most indispensable companions of all.

NOTE ON THE TEXTS

In all the texts transcribed for and printed in this volume, our practice is to modernize capitalization, punctuation, and spelling. Where orthographic variety can help to illuminate the development of racial vocabularies, early modern spelling is retained but in general spelling is modernized, and always in the cases of u/v, i/j, vv/w, and long s (l); words condensed with macrons are expanded; and words spelled with the Middle English thorn (used to represent the voiceless dental fricative) are modernized with the digraph *th*. Where foreign words without conventional English spellings appear (such as proper names and place names), they are kept in their original spelling and italicized. Foreign words, words not found in a standard college English dictionary, as well as archaic words or usages are glossed in footnotes. Additional annotation in footnotes includes information on textual variants suggestive for questions of race and cross-references to related texts not included in the current volume. Where unmistakable printer's errors appear (omissions, obfuscating misspellings), substantial emendations or editorial additions to the text are indicated by square brackets.

In selecting our copy texts, we do not always use the earliest edition available. It is important to clarify that the aim of this documentary companion is not to provide new or authoritative editions of each of these materials, although we hope that it will inspire future projects for the editing of individual texts.

INTRODUCTION

"Race" is one of the most troubling and contentious concepts of our times, one of the most powerful and yet one of the most fragile markers of social difference.[1] In the last few decades, it has become the subject of intense scholarly attention and debate across various disciplines, even as both scientists and humanists have demonstrated that race is not a natural category but a social construct, or, to adapt Stuart Hall's words about blackness, "a narrative, a story, a history. Something constructed, told, spoken, not simply found."[2] Race, as much as the nation, is an "imagined community" that both binds and divides human beings; indeed race is a major factor in the very imagining of the national community.[3] But to say that it is imagined is not to suggest that it can be wished away, for the historical imagining of racial communities and differences has resulted in the formation of social relations and institutions, as well as in structures of thought and feeling, which continue to shape our lives today. And because histories of race, in particular, are mobilized in support of a wide range of social projects, from curricular restructuring to civil legislation, from labor reform to genocide, much is at stake in how they are understood and narrated.

If race can be said to have a history, it is both protracted and erratic. Within its various strands, a range of concepts, themes, and mechanisms for assigning different values to human beings arise and mutate, go dormant, resurface, relocate, and adapt anew. This protean quality complicates the search for origins, definitions, and boundaries. The place of the Renaissance (and particularly the English experience) in these histories is especially contentious. On the one hand, the question of race has in recent years become central to early modern studies. Books and articles, doctoral dissertations, conference programs, and syllabi reflect a growing recognition that sixteenth- and seventeenth-century England cannot be understood without examining the development of ideologies of racial difference at the time.[4] On the other hand, most theorists and historians of race still tend to exclude the sixteenth and seventeenth centuries from extended consideration. Often, they invoke premodern times only as a foil for later, more "racialized" periods. Many early modernists concur, arguing that to speak of "race" in the early modern period is to perpetuate an anachronism, because at that time "race" connoted family, class, or lineage rather than the classifications of modern imperial times, and also because the defining features of racial ideologies—the quasi-biological notion that physical characteristics denoted distinct types of human beings with distinct moral and social features—had not yet come into being.[5]

The Renaissance is widely understood to be an "early modern period" in which our modern world and some of its most cherished as well as problematic ideologies, institutions, and practices (e.g., capitalism, nation formation, the modern family, humanism, individualism, global empires) were engendered. Nevertheless, when it comes to the question of race, the Renaissance is routinely understood as drastically *different,* and indeed as a *pre*modern time when racial ideologies had not taken root. Whereas in other respects the "darkness" of the Middle Ages is routinely contrasted to the "enlightenment" of the Renaissance, with respect to race there is often a fascinating conflation of the two to mark a premodern time before race. Thus the study of race interrogates the principles of conventional periodization. This volume seeks to enable such a study by making visible both the unique characteristics of early modern ideas about racial and cultural difference, and their connections with later ideologies and practices.

The appropriateness of "race" or "racism," "xenophobia," "ethnicity," or even "nation" in describing community identities in early modern Europe has been much debated. Some of these words were coined later, and others, such as "race," did not necessarily convey the same meanings they do now. As the numerous early modern dictionaries cited in this volume show, even when modern-day meanings of words such as "nation" or "race" emerged in the early modern period, older or competing meanings retained a place alongside or in competition with them. But surely this complexity does not suggest that it is anachronistic to study race in the early modern period.[6] After all, "race" is, even today, a confusing word that does not carry a precise set of meanings, but becomes shorthand for various combinations of ethnic, geographic, cultural, class, and religious differences.[7] Similarly, the continually changing notions of difference in early modern England can only be understood by examining a complex amalgam of ideas, vocabularies, and practices. As is the case in the modern world, when we examine early modern notions of racial difference we must consider not only those divisions of humanity that were putatively based on distinctive combinations of physical traits and transmitted through a line of descent, but also the eclectic range of cultural differences that are used to explain, manage, or reorganize relations of power. For this reason, it makes less sense to try to settle upon a precise definition or indeed to locate a precise moment of origin for racial ideologies than to delineate the ways in which they order and delimit human possibilities through a wide range of conjoined discourses and practices.[8]

Race in Early Modern England: A Documentary Companion does not claim to be comprehensive in charting the contours of race as a concept. Rather, by presenting a wide range of sixteenth- and seventeenth-century materials, many of which are not easily available, we hope to open up the question of "race" to sustained critical attention, often from perspectives not considered earlier. The greater part of this volume comprises an array of edited documents from the period 1519–1699. Many of these texts are travelogues or early accounts of global geographies and cultures, since writings on other parts of the world generated some of the most persistent thinking about human difference. We do not include writings on every part of the world, because our goal is not as much to achieve breadth of coverage as it is to make available the ways in which different contact histories generated early classificatory schema and tropes of difference. Different forms of both benign and violent contact meant that notions of geographic difference were in dialogue with questions of religion, nationality, color, conversion, women, sexuality, the human body, lineage, diet, and human nature. Therefore, our extracts include sermons, statutes, medical texts, dictionaries, recipes for cosmetics, atlases, emblem books, religious commentaries, pamphlets, philosophical treatises, and scientific tracts. These selections make available key ideas about skin color, location, religion, rank, and gender and show how older tropes are leavened by recent images and ideas, learned ideas by popular beliefs, and notions of the body by those concerning culture or spirituality. We will point out some of these patterns in this introduction. Together, they indicate that the multiple meanings of the word "race" in early modern England, as well as other terms that seem to be unrelated to this concept, rather than testifying to the *absence* of racial ideologies in the period, illuminate precisely the broad spectrum of discourses and practices of difference that are marshaled by them.

The materials selected for this volume reveal that, from the outset, thinking about difference has involved a variety of ideas regarding animality, environmentalism, kinship, religion, and strangeness. These writings highlight both recurring themes and major breaks or shifts in such ideas, and they also ask us to consider the relationship between precise words and ideologies. For example, Edward Topsell's *The historie of foure-footed beastes* (1607) may not use the word "race" but it nevertheless anticipates later classifications in its discussion of baboons, satyrs, Indians, and Africans, as well as comparisons between Africans and apes. Many other entries will reveal a vocabulary that is substantially transformed or eroded over time, such as that of humoral theory. In his influential *Method for the Easy Comprehension of History* (1566), Jean Bodin employs humoral theory to attribute different dispositions to particular groups of people: "Southerners abound in black bile, which subsides like lees to the bottom when the humors have been drawn out by the heat of the sun and increases more and more through emotions, so that those who are mentally constituted in this manner are plainly implacable." Bodin regards "southerners" as more easily inflamed to passion, more jealous and sinful than "northern people," an association that is calcified by later racial thought, but he simultaneously acknowledges that "from these people letters, useful arts, virtues, training, philosophy, religion, and lastly *humanitas* itself flowed upon earth as from a fountain," an idea that disappears a century later. It is crucial to note that Bodin channels older discourses toward an entirely new division of the "human race" into "three varieties"—Scythians, Southerners, and "men of the middle regions"—each with distinct and hard-to-change mental and physical characteristics.[9]

Another notion that attenuates over time is that of maternal impression, or the belief that what the mother gazed upon at the time of conception or pregnancy shaped the physical characteristics of the child. This idea can be found in the third-century CE Greek romance, Heliodorus's *Aithiopika* or *Ethiopian Story*, as well as in the biblical tale about Jacob waving streaked rods before sheep to ensure a speckled flock; it proliferates in literary texts, including Shakespeare's plays, and is obsessively debated by early modern writers such as Thommaso Buoni, Pierre Boaistuau, and Thomas Browne (to mention but three of the authors included here). Some, like Thomas Lupton in *A thousand notable things, of sundry sortes* (1579), cite the tale of a Spanish woman who, upon producing a black baby and being charged with adultery with a Moor, was exonerated when it was found that a picture of a black man hung in her bedchamber. But others, such as Reginald Scot in his influential *The discoverie of witchcraft* (1584), describe maternal impression as a confidence trick, arguing that blackness could only be the result of black paternity, since black men "never fail to produce black children."[10]

We chose certain writings because they reveal important repetitions, borrowings, and consolidations of key beliefs about human diversity and difference. Thus, readers may note how particular attributes of Turkish women (such as their duplicity and lust) are elsewhere applied to their English or Italian counterparts, or trace how Amazon women are located first in Asia, and then later in Africa and the New World, or collate the various concerns with the degeneracy of English men and women in contact with other cultures. These selections also reveal the range of responses to a single idea, illustrating that in the early modern world, as indeed in later imperial times, there were (often contentious) debates about racial difference. For example, some writers espouse the theory that location and climate produce dark skin, others question this idea, and many (such as Thomas Browne) lay out the entire debate about the causes of blackness. Likewise, the meaning of blackness was subject to debate, as in the five texts collected here that dwell on blackness in the biblical Song of Songs, and help us chart changing views about the relationship of skin color and beauty.[11]

Some of these materials comment quite obviously on the development of race as an idea, such as François Bernier's "A New Division of the Earth, according to the Different Species or Races of Men who Inhabit It" (1684), or a number of passages about the nature and bodies of Indians, Africans, or the Irish. At other times, relevant comments are embedded in a text that seems to be about unrelated issues, such as the seductive dangers of drinking coffee: one author fears that coffee will "bewitch" and then "destroy" English water just as Othello, in Shakespeare's play, killed the white Desdemona; another fears that it will make Christian men "black within." Here coffee becomes emblematic of the widespread fears about English degeneration, an issue that is central to notions of racial identity. George Best's remarks about a black child born to an English mother and an African father (*A True Discourse*, 1578) or Geffrey Whitney's emblem of a blackamoor being washed white in *A choice of emblemes, and other devises* (1586) are well known to early modern scholars, although even these, we should point out, have not been assembled for ready consultation. Other writings are rarely considered in scholarship on race in this period, such as William Rankins's *The English ape* (1588), which argues that the English are created perfect by climate but are tainted by their imitation of foreign manners, an idea that John Bulwer's *Anthropometamorphosis* (1650) later invokes to explain how "moors" turned into "negroes" and to express the fear that English people would also metamorphose into monsters.[12] These lesser-known texts either complicate those that are already well known or open up new lines of inquiry.

Although our own areas of specialization lie primarily in the realm of literary studies, we have chosen to exclude literary materials because their representations of race are less usefully extracted from the whole, and also because they have in recent years been more easily available and more discussed than the materials we include here. The present collection, apart from illuminating many lesser-known discourses, will serve as a very useful companion to literary studies, allowing scholars to locate how early modern poetry, drama, and prose fiction are in conversation with other writing. Our selection of materials is also confined to texts written in English or Latin, or texts translated into English during the early modern period. The latter testify to the important connections between England and the rest of Europe, and to the centrality of Portuguese and Spanish experiences in the development of early modern racial discourses. Of course, England also has a very specific history of racial thought, shaped by its rivalries with other European nations, by its own emergent nationalism and relation with its margins, and by its own sense of its past. An eclectic range of racial markers therefore appears in texts seeking to distinguish the English from the Irish they colonized, the Spanish they battled, the Africans they enslaved, the Turks with whom they traded, and the allegedly barbaric ancient Britons from whom they were descended. In this regard, the documents collected here can help to answer David Theo Goldberg's call for typologies of "regionally prompted, parametered, and promoted racism, linked to its dominant state formation."[13] At the same time, even when self-consciously different, the English discourses of race need to be seen as part of a larger transnational history. Thus, the materials gathered here both challenge the idea of English exceptionalism or belatedness in relation to racial ideologies and suggest how the study of race can interrogate the place of national boundaries in early modern history and literature.

Indeed, what is further needed, but is beyond the scope of this project, is to trace connections between European and non-European texts. After all, the boundaries of what we now call Europe have been shifting and variable, and in the premodern period "continental" divisions as we now understand them simply did not exist.[14] Europe was also formed through intense borrowing and exchange with scholarship from Asia, North Africa, and the non-Christian world, a heritage that has generally been neglected by scholars working on English history and literature.[15] Thus, for example, the idea that blackness as well as the slavery of Africans was the result of Noah's curse upon his disobedient son is shared by Christian, Jewish, and Muslim commentaries from the fourth to the twelfth centuries, a period when black slavery became common in the area now referred to as the Middle East.[16] One fourteenth-century Arab writer, who borrows freely from earlier Arabic sources, cites different versions of the story before suggesting that skin color is instead the effect of geography:

> The historians assert that the cause of the black complexion of the sons of Ham is that he had sexual intercourse with his wife while on the ship and Nūh (Noah) cursed him and prayed to God to modify his seed, so that she brought forth [the ancestor of] the Sudan. Another version is that Hām came upon Nūh asleep with his privy parts uncovered by the wind. He told this to his brothers Sām (Shem) and Yāfath (Japhet) and they rose and covered him, turning their face backward so that they might not see his shame. When Nūh knew of this he said: "Cursed is Hām, blessed is Sām, and may God multiply [the seed of] Yāfath." But in truth, the fact is that the nature of their country demands that their characteristics should be as they are. Contrary to those connected with whiteness, for most of them inhabit the south and west of the earth.[17]

Early modern writings included in this volume also participate in similar discussions. The dense geographical and cultural crossings of the premodern world are useful both in resisting a simple binary opposition between Christian Europe and the rest of the world and in locating how commerce, colonial contact, and European slavery transformed earlier discourses and practices.[18]

The materials in this collection are arranged chronologically, according to the date when a text was first printed in England.[19] Chronological ordering helps trace the (often uneven) trajectory of various ideas; a thematic organization was impossible precisely because each of these writings is not about any single idea but speaks to the thick web of associations that is central to racial thought. However, keywords listed with each entry will help readers trace themes and establish connections between periods and writings, as will the comprehensive index.

We begin with three short sections of classical, biblical, and medieval materials selected to indicate the ways in which the legacy of earlier writings was reworked or engaged with in the early modern period. Thus, for example, a reader may see how Pliny's account of semihuman hybrids in Ethiopia in his *Historie of the World* (finished about 77 CE; English trans. 1601) is adopted in the fourteenth-century *The voyages and travailes of Sir John Mandevile*, strategically relocated in Sir Walter Raleigh's *The Discoverie of the large, rich and bewtiful empire of Guiana . . .* (1596), refuted in George Abbot's *A briefe description of the whole worlde* (1599), and then verified anew in John Pory's introduction to Leo Africanus's *A geographical historie of Africa* (1600). Those reading a play such as *Othello* will be able to detect how these diverse approaches to monstrosity resonate and contend with one another in Shakespeare's text; others will be able to trace connections between early modern versions of the biblical story of Jacob and Laban and its various redactions in writings on blackness, childbirth, witchcraft, and cosmetics, or in Shakespeare's *The Merchant of Venice*.[20] Finally, it is important to emphasize that many of these older texts (such as Mandeville's) can also be thought of as early modern in as much as they are published in later editions, made current, and redeployed for contemporary arguments.[21]

These materials do not indicate unified ideologies-in-the-making, but they do chart early modern conversations about human difference. It is important to remember that even when racial ideologies and racist practices became more entrenched and pernicious, there was no singular approach to or agreement about human difference, something that is often forgotten by those who emphasize only the gap between "fluid" or unformed early modern ideologies and the more rigid modern ones. However, it is true that in the early modern world, there were even more inconsistencies and contradictions in the debates about human difference. Thus, we may find, in the same piece of writing, the beginnings of what we might call a quasi-biological understanding of skin color *and* the language of the Mosaic law of descent. Today, of course, the first is seen as the definitive marker of modern ideologies of race, the latter as evidence that these had not yet taken root. Thus, linkages and ruptures between the past and present go hand in hand, and are found in the same archives. The recent critical tendency to claim that racism could not be said to exist in the early modern period because various non-Europeans were also praised and admired at that time is reductive and unhelpful in tracing the histories of race. Putatively "positive" as well as clearly "negative" traits feed into racialized discourses—the primordial innocence of Native Americans is as important as the supposed bestiality of Africans; the devotion of "Oriental wives" is the flip side of the patriarchy of Eastern societies as well as of the deviance of Eastern women; the Ottomans' political and military organization feed the notion of Oriental despotism as much as they do stereotypes of excessive Oriental luxury and carnality.

To what extent are there qualitative differences between older and newer views? We hope this collection will allow readers to decide for themselves; here we want to emphasize that research into early modern notions of difference does not only give us more "data," it helps us to complicate histories and theories of race in ways that the rest of this introduction will indicate. As recent debates in historiography have highlighted, it is not productive either to survey the past only to confirm that it contains our own world in the making or to look only for "other worlds" marked by their utter difference from the present.[22] Thus, we hope *Race in Early Modern England: A Documentary Companion* will help scholars interpret a crucial period of history both on its own terms and in ways that shed light on racial difference and social inequalities today.

COLONIALISM AND RACIAL IDEOLOGIES

The idea of English belatedness in the formation of racial ideologies, as well as the related marginalization of medieval and early modern periods from histories of race, depends to a large extent upon the definition of race as a post-Enlightenment ideology forged on the twin anvils of colonialism and Atlantic slavery and hinging upon pseudo-biological notions of human differentiation, especially color.[23] *Race in Early Modern England: A Documentary Companion* will question this definition and the assumptions it sustains. First, we suggest that racial ideologies and practices are not just engendered as a simple *consequence* of modern colonialism. Rather, many premodern ideologies and practices *shape* the particular forms taken by modern European colonialism and slavery. This insight does not preclude our ability to distinguish between different kinds of prejudice on the one hand and racism on the other, and to acknowledge in particular the central place of color as well as the history of colonialism in race formation. Second, we show that early modern discourses clearly indicate that ideas about "culture" and "biology" do not occupy separate domains and that they develop in relation to one another. Thus, the bifurcation of "culture" and "nature" in many analyses of race needs to be questioned. As we suggest below, to query both these assumptions is to necessarily emphasize the place of religion, gender, class, and sexuality as central to the formation of and workings of racial ideologies.

In early modern studies, postcolonial theory is often held responsible for a distorted historical focus on race in premodern periods. Edward Said's classic *Orientalism* suggests that an opposition between "the familiar (Europe, the West, 'us') and the strange (the Orient, the East, 'them')" has animated "European imaginative geography" from Greek times to the present.[24] Such a view of difference, some early modernists argue, cannot explain the complexity of international relations in the early modern period, let alone the categories of difference within early modern Europe. They remind us that Europeans desired to re-enter the powerful economic networks of the Mediterranean, the Levant, North Africa, India, and China; feared the military might of the Turks; and were dazzled by the wealth and sophistication of many Asian kingdoms.[25] It is true, of course, that Europe had long and complex engagements with Asia and Africa, and in particular with Islam; indeed the very idea of Europe as an entity is the product of such engagements. At the same time, however, by the end of the seventeenth century, several European city-states and provinces were trading in slaves, plantations were well under way in several parts of the world, and the native populations in the Americas had already been subjected to genocide. Even though European colonialism had not yet fully entrenched itself as a global system, a great many of the material practices and ideological features that came to define modern colonialism began to be shaped at this time.[26] To think of the Renaissance as not only "early modern" but also as "early colonial" is to remember how Western modernity was itself deeply shaped by colonialism.[27] The period covered by this volume is also particularly useful for thinking about the relationship between colonialism and racial ideologies and practices. This relationship is not a linear one, with the latter following the former, but extremely supple, with capitalism and colonialism utilizing, transforming, and expanding the scope of earlier discourses of difference.[28] After all, colonialism did not insert itself upon a blank slate but reshaped

earlier understandings of human differentiation; these in turn prepared the
ground for, and indeed often determined the form of, later racial and colonial perspectives.[29]
    Ivan Hannaford's influential study of race argues that "the human body,
as portrayed up to the time of the Renaissance and Reformation, could not
be detached from the ideas of the *polis* and *ecclesia*. . . ."[30] The idea of a
political sphere in which all able people could freely participate, he insists,
retarded the development of racial ideologies. But Hannaford does not
allow for contradictions or complexities *within* either this concept of the
political sphere or its history. Thus, he never questions why, in the writings
of Aristotle and others, certain groups of people were seen as simply unable
to embrace the values of the Greek polis, or asks why these exclusions were
subsequently rehearsed by early modern and modern writings. As Blackburn
suggests, "By diffusing a greater awareness of the cultural achievement of
antiquity and contributing a sense that late medieval Christendom was its
legitimate heir, the Renaissance nourished a sense of cultural superiority
that dovetailed with the classical Aristotelian doctrine that barbarians were
natural slaves."[31] So, for example, John Mair's 1519 defense of Spain's New
World slavery draws on Aristotle's argument in *The Politics* that certain men
were naturally subordinate to others, while obscuring the philosopher's
acknowledgment that while "[n]ature would like to distinguish between
the bodies of freemen and slaves . . . the opposite often happens." So also
Aristotle's view that the natives of Asia "are wanting in spirit and therefore
always in a state of subjection and slavery" (an opinion shared by Herodotus)
is invoked in Machiavelli's belief that "where the essential institutional forms
of governance are missing, as in Asia and Africa, there can be no politics
and no political *virtù*."[32] Obviously, Herodotus and Machiavelli are not
identical to each other, or to later expressions of Asian or African difference,
but they alert us to sociocultural repetitions that are key to understanding
racial ideologies. A wide range of writings makes visible the way in which
older ideas such as Oriental despotism, African lechery, Southern feebleness,
or the Egyptian reversal of gender roles were invoked and transformed to
demarcate white European Christians from others (and at other times the
English from their neighbors or from Southern Europeans) in the early
modern period.
    At the same time, somewhat contradictorily, the English, at least, often
justified colonialism by invoking their own past colonization by the Romans.
Frequent comparisons were made between ancient Britons and New World
Indians. Thomas Hariot's history of the Roanoke colony strikingly juxtaposed engravings of ancient Picts and Virginia natives (included here from a
1590 Latin edition). Observing that the Indians painted their bodies, William
Strachey also notes that "Britons dyed themselves red with woad." Strachey
defended English plantations by pointing out that Roman colonization had
endowed hitherto barbarous Britons with the "powerful discourse of divine
reason (which makes us only men, and distinguisheth us from beasts . . .)."[33]
Such discourses suggest that Virginians were capable of improvement in

the same way as the Britons themselves were once civilized by the Romans, though in practice no people colonized by the British (whether the Irish or the Native Americans in the early modern period, or Africans and Indians later on) were deemed capable of bridging the gap. Ideologies, as Gramsci reminds us, are never smooth but rather always contradictory, and marshal a range of ideas, both old and new, learned and commonsensical, elite and popular.[34] Thus, the contradictory elements in these writings do not indicate that race is "not yet formed" (or do not prove that the idea had many "false starts," as one theorist claims) but that it is always an amalgam of contradictory, unstable, and evolving ideas; the key is to also consider them within a history of discriminatory *practices*.

Recent work in medieval studies has further complicated the genealogies of race and colonialism by attending to the history of the Crusades as well as the relationships between Muslims, Jews, and Christians within Europe.[35] Indeed, as David Wallace suggests, the "Westward Ho!" tendency in early modern studies has obscured the fact that "[m]any features of later European colonialism—as the slaving Mediterranean prepares to move into the Black Atlantic—are clearly forming throughout this earlier period."[36] To pay attention to such a movement is to rethink the connections between emergent notions of race, early English involvement in Mediterranean slavery, and theological debates about blackness, Jewishness, and Islam. Robert Bartlett's important book *The Making of Europe: Conquest, Colonialism and Cultural Change, 950–1350* concludes that "the mental habits and institutions of European racism and colonialism were born out of the medieval world, the conquerors of Mexico knew the problem of the Mudejars: the planters of Virginia had already been planters in Ireland."[37] These mental habits and institutions were deeply rooted in the expansion of European feudalism from the tenth to the thirteenth centuries. Although they do not collapse the distinction between medieval and later periods, these and other scholars indicate the long and often surprising lineages of contemporary identity categories and discriminatory practices, making visible the Mediterranean heralds to transatlantic taxonomies, and showing particularly the foundational importance of religious difference in the development of racial ideologies and practices. While we do not deal in any detail with the medieval period, we believe this collection will make visible some of the most crucial social dynamics addressed in recent medieval scholarship, indicating not only how older ideologies and practices were transformed during the early modern period but also how they shaped the very forms that race and colonialism would take in later times.

MONOGENESIS AND SLAVERY

The writings collected here attest to the fact that neither the theory of monogenesis—the notion that all mankind is derived from Adam—nor the accompanying possibility of non-Christians being converted to Christianity retarded either the growth of the idea of a deep hierarchy between different peoples or the practice of slavery.[38] As Blackburn has shown, the belief that one should not enslave someone of one's own religion entered medieval Christian communities as they confronted the threat of Islam, which had long held such a prohibition; he observes that "[r]eligious adherence and religious imagery usually had the last word in justifications of enslavement, which is why the pagans of Lithuania, the Bogomil heretics of Bosnia, captives from the Caucasus, the Muslims of Andalusia, and the Jews had all been seen as potential slaves in Christian Europe of the later medieval period."[39] Religious difference was a justification for slavery, and hence slavers were in no hurry to convert slaves to Christianity. While ventriloquizing the monologue of a Barbary Moor in his 1555 *The fyrst boke of the introduction of knowledge* (reproduced in this volume), Andrew Boorde suggests that slavers had little compunction regarding the souls of black folk: "Christian men for money oft doth me buy; / If I be unchristened, merchants do not care. / They buy me in markets be I never so bare." Christians also continued to hold and buy previously enslaved Christians. That is why, as Wallace points out, "it was ruled that a person's fitness for enslavement might be determined not by her or his current religion, but rather by culture of origin. So it is that slaves often arrived with their [African and non-Christian] names intact . . . and were given Christian names only when sold and baptized."[40]

Precisely because of the conviction that Christians should not be enslaved, the practice of slavery often retarded the possibility of conversion. In Barbados, when Richard Ligon spoke to a plantation owner in the 1640s concerning the request of a slave to be converted, he was told that "the people of that island were governed by the laws of England, and by those laws we could not make a Christian a slave." Upon Ligon's clarifying that his desire was "to make a slave a Christian," he was told that "being once a Christian, he could no more account him a slave," and thus was "poor *Sambo* kept out of the Church, as ingenious, as honest, and as good natured poor soul as ever wore black or eat green . . ." At the same time, the possibility of conversion could also be invoked as a *justification* for English slavery: "It being a means to better these people, and likewise have influence on these they sell as slaves to the English to persuade them, that by their slavery, their condition will be bettered by their access to knowledge, Arts and Sciences."[41] In a tract reproduced here, Morgan Godwyn reminded his readers that "in regard religion would be apt to create a conscience in their slaves, it might be convenient, in order to make them truer servants."

Eventually, as Cristina Malcolmson points out, there were calls to the English Parliament to proclaim that Africans and indigenous Americans were part of God's plan for salvation and should receive baptism. Not surprisingly, these proposed acts "renounce the traditional view that Christians cannot enslave Christians, affirm the property rights of the slave-owners, and destroy any possibility of freedom achieved through baptism."[42] Attempts to reconcile conversion and slavery also led to colonial laws that reversed earlier assumptions and protocols. Thus, whereas in English law, paternity was considered primary, in Virginia it was proclaimed in 1662 that "children got by any Englishman upon a Negro woman" should follow the slave condition of the mother, a move that would obviously boost the slave population, and eliminate the danger that the children of white men and black women would lay claim to white privilege. What is important is that the English did nothing to hinder the practice of slavery, and instead developed both blunt and ingenious ways to render conversion, monogenesis, and even cross-race sexual contact compatible with the slave trade.[43]

Recent scholarship suggests that English involvement with slavery goes back much earlier than the first slaving voyages of John Hawkins in the 1550s. In the Middle Ages, Bristol had been a center for slavery; while most slaves who passed through the Bristol trade were white, some merchants there kept African servants and traded in with dark-skinned slaves. English merchants in Spain were involved in the African slave trade as early as the 1480s.[44] But in order to understand why European slavery became overwhelmingly connected with blackness, or at least to scrutinize the nexus of color, servitude, and faith that underlies the ideologies of black slavery, it is crucial to turn to older and more complex connections, literal as well as metaphoric, between religion, class, and color.

RELIGION, CLASS, AND COLOR

In England and elsewhere, Saracens and Jews had long been described as metaphorically and often literally black, and many writings collected in this volume attest that during the early modern period the tendency to express religious difference in somatic vocabularies endured and sometimes gained strength. One character in an early modern play asks another: "Doth religion move anything in the shapes of men?" The other replies, "Altogether! What's the reason else that the Turk and the Jew is troubled (for the most part) with gouty legs and fiery nose? To express their heart-burning. Whereas the puritan is a man of upright calf and clean nostril."[45] Sebastian Münster's *The Messias of the Christians and the Jewes* was reprinted in London in 1655, more than a century after its author's death, keeping alive the notion that the "Jews have a peculiar colour of face, different from the form and figure of other men . . . black and uncomely, and not white as other men." Geraldine Heng rightly points out that "[t]o scholarship on race that takes its examples from postmedieval periods, *religion*—which is always understood, in modern fashion, as an exclusively *cultural* system of customs, gestures and practices, and unimplicated in theories of biological essences—is the *a priori* determinant in hierarchical taxonomizations of difference in the *medieval* period, just as *race*—understood in biological and essentialist terms—is concomitantly seen to function as the operative determinant in retrograde hierarchies of power within *postmedieval* periods."[46] The conceptual separation of culture and biology, religion and race, can also be found in the work of many scholars who work on, or consider, medieval and early modern periods. These boundaries are increasingly being questioned by scholarly attention to the discursive overlaps between social categories and biological ones.[47]

The very title of Thomas Calvert's *The blessed Jew of Marocco: or, A Black-moor Made White* . . . (1648) strikingly links skin color and religion via the idea of conversion. Indeed, many of the materials in this volume suggest that the question of religious conversion was a particularly fraught site for the play of anxieties about skin color, and for the development of ideologically charged connections between inner essence and bodily traits with which we are familiar in later racial thought. Medieval writings had widely featured both the possibility and the impossibility of somatic and religious transformations.[48] The thirteenth-century *Cursor Mundi*, with its black and blue Saracens fantastically whitened through literal contact with Christianity, reverberates with a host of writings about Jews and Muslims over the next four centuries. As in the Geneva Bible's (1560) lines, "Can the black Moor change his skin or the leopard his spots? *then* may ye also do good, that are accustomed to do evil," the indelibility of blackness was routinely compared to the unbeliever's stubborn heart. These associations were complicated by commercial, political, and colonial interactions across the globe. Thus, the later, and generally less polemical, Bishop's Bible (1568) uses the words "man of Ind," a term that signifies a range of outsiders in medieval literature, instead of "black Moor," a phrase that reflects the increasing contact with black Africans but also a deepening conflation of blackness with Islam. In the King James Bible (1611) the term used is "the Ethiopian," which connects newer contact with Africa back to an older terminology (the trope of an indelible black skin can be traced to one of Aesop's fables, which features a black Ethiopian servant who cannot be washed white).

A similar conflation of religion and skin color, and also class, turns up in popular emblem books and other discourses that evoke the impossibility of "washing the Ethiope white," as well as in accounts of regions already engaged in slave trading. Thomas Palmer's *Two Hundred Poosees* (1565), England's earliest emblem book, depicted two white men washing a black man in vain, warning that the stubborn "heart of heretics" is black and impossible to wash clean. In Geffrey Whitney's more widely known *A choice of emblemes* (1586), the accompanying verse changes Palmer's "man of Ind" to "blackamore," a shift that we can also trace in stories about Ham's descendants, who were located first in Asia (as in Mandeville's *Travels*) and then, as slave traffic increased, in Africa (see the writings of Best, Pory, Sandys, and Jobson in this volume).[49] In many of these books, blackness is evoked to make a point about the impossibility of religious conversion, and such impossibility in turn fixes dark skin as indelible.

It is no accident that the black figure in Aesop is a servant.[50] Conceptions of class are also crucial to early histories of racial thought. The multiple early modern meanings of the word "race," especially its meaning as "class," "family," and "lineage," are exemplified in Shakespeare's *Antony and Cleopatra*, where Antony laments that in loving a dark-skinned Cleopatra he has "forborne the getting [begetting] of a lawful race" with Octavia (3.13.107). The word "race" indicates, first of all, lineage or a line of descent, as in *Queen Anna's New World of Words* (1611), John Florio's Italian-English dictionary,

which defines "razza" or "race" as "a kind, a brood, a blood, a stock, a pedigree." Likewise, John Foxe's *Acts and Monuments* (1563) speaks of Abraham's
lineage as "the race and stock of Abraham." In Antony's words, we can detect
at least two meanings that would become important to later usage of the term
"race": that of a bloodline or heredity, and that of a moral *hierarchy* between
different bloodlines.[51] Both these meanings were already attached to class. In
advising his son on how to select servants, James VI of Scotland argued in
Basilikon doron (1599) that

> [V]irtue or vice will oftentimes, with the heritage, be transferred from the par-
> ents to the posterity, and run on a blood. . . . Especially choose such minors as
> are come of a true and honest race, and have not had the house whereof they
> are descended, infected with falsehood.

James uses "race" as it was most widely used in this period—as a synonym
for class. At this time, class was seen as an attribute rooted in the blood, or
inherited, rather than a changeable socioeconomic positioning. We might
reflect that in early English literature, crossing class is imagined with less
frequency than crossing gender—a pauper becoming a prince is often a more
fantastic idea than a woman being transformed into a man.[52]

It is therefore not coincidental that, much before it became a rationaliza-
tion of blackness, Noah's curse upon the descendants of his son Ham was
popularly used to explain the servitude of European peasants, as we can
see in the extract from Andrew Horn's *The Mirrour of Justices* (ca. 1290)
in this volume.[53] This is precisely the tradition made available by the biblical account of the story, and it continues well into the seventeenth century
in writings such as William Strachey's *For the colony in Virginea Britannia*
(1612) and Thomas Browne's *Pseudodoxia epidemica* (1646). In the medieval period itself, Wallace writes, "non-white skin" had begun "to be interpreted as a *sign* of slavery," but this fact also reminds us that the notion of
class difference, and of servitude, never quite disappears from later ideas
of race.[54] There continue to develop often contradictory and uneven links
between the consolidation of the African slave trade, and the growing association of Ham with blackness, as also the shifting location of Ham's progeny from Asia to Africa. For in earlier writings such as Mandeville's widely
disseminated *Travels*, Ham is considered the father of the Great Khan and
the ancestor of the Mongols, Shem the progenitor of Africans, and Japhet
of Europeans and "the people of Israel." From the fifteenth century on, this
division of the world was reordered, with Ham being assigned Africa and
Shem Asia, as we can see in the extracts from George Best, George Sandys,
Richard Jobson, Thomas Browne, Robert Boyle, Matthew Hale, Morgan
Godwyn, and John Pory's translation of Leo Africanus in this volume. These
materials suggest the ways in which older associations were debated, discarded, or retained during the early modern period. The Scottish theologian
John Weemes connected the dots in 1627 when he explained, "This curse
to be a servant was first laid upon a disobedient son Cham, and we see to
this day that the Moors, Cham's posterity, are sold like slaves yet."[55] David

Aaron suggests that the biblical passages themselves contain a core association between blackness and servitude; other commentators indicate a long and contentious debate about how blackness entered biblical exegesis.[56] The crucial point is made by Blackburn: "Only in areas where, and times when, black slaves were found were these connections drawn together into a myth justifying black slavery."[57]

Theories about lineage and descent thus dovetailed with questions of both faith and color, and older vocabularies were both discarded and assimilated into newer ones. So for example, when George Best in his *True Discourse of the late voyages of discoverie* (1578) suggests that blackness is not a result of the scorching of the skin by the sun, as was often supposed at the time, but a "curse and infection of blood" that is passed down through "lineal descent," he reverts to the biblical story of Noah's curse upon Ham as an explanation of blackness. Religion, skin color, and lineage are, in Best's discourse, inextricably connected in ways that illuminate the growth and nature of racial ideologies, even though Best himself does not use the word "race." George Sandys argues that it is neither black people's "seed, nor the heat of the climate" that is responsible for their color, because "other races" will not become black in hot climates, and nor will the black "race grow to better complexion [in cold climates];" blackness emanates "rather from the curse of Noe upon Cham in the posterity of Chus."[58] Here, Sandys delinks color from "seed" or climate, but at the same time, he reverts to the story of Ham in order to suggest that blackness originates in sinful behavior that transmits itself over the generations. At the same time, he equates lighter skin with "better complexion," testifying not just to growing color consciousness but also to the semantic reduction of "complexion" to denote simply skin color.

The early modern expression that a Jew is "a slave to the world" demonstrates how other marginalized groups were also described in terms of their fitness for labor.[59] Poor women had long been understood to be hardier in childbirth than their high-born counterparts, and in writings included here, this idea crops up in relation to Native American women, Irish women, and African women.[60] Conversely, we find economically marginalized peoples described in racialized terms. Thus, Michael Drayton compares New World natives to the "meaner sort" of English people, when advising George Sandys in Virginia not to bother writing of American savages since "As savage slaves be in Great Britain here / As any one that you can show me there."[61] The association between class and race is made especially visible in the English statutes banishing gypsies (commonly called "Egyptians" and understood to have come from Egypt). From 1530 on, English authorities proclaimed increasingly harsh punishments for those found within the realm, but also increasingly identified an overlap between gypsies and poor English people identified as "vagabonds" and "rogues," suggesting that both groups were prone to criminality.[62] These views were also expressed in both popular and literary writing, which also drew analogies between different sorts of racialized people. Thus, the playwright Thomas Dekker established

the overlap between gypsies and the English lower classes by turning to the
Irish context:

> Look what difference there is between a civil citizen of Dublin & a wild Irish
> kern, so much difference there is between one of these counterfeit Egyptians
> and a true English beggar. An English rogue is just of the same livery.

These discourses indicate that normative English national identity began to
coalesce via the exclusion of the poor and homeless, as well as of racial or
religious outsiders, and that such exclusions were established by describing
these different groups in interchangeable terms.

RELIGIOUS CONVERSION AND RACE

Shakespeare's Cleopatra draws on Inquisition terminology when she offers
her "blewest veines to kiss: a hand that Kings have lipt." Intended to assert
Cleopatra's nobility, this usage is somewhat ironic because the Egyptian
queen is also described in the play as being "with Phoebus's amorous pinches
black." The phrase "blue blood" is a translation of the Spanish *sangre azul,*
a concept that evolved from the claims of Spanish families who declared
they had never been contaminated by Moorish or Jewish blood (and were
therefore so fair that their blue veins were clearly visible). It is now widely
understood that the possibilities or the fear of mass religious conversions
in Reconquista Spain catalyzed the development of biological notions of
race long before the eighteenth century.[63] As white Christians confronted
the implications of being infiltrated by Jews, Muslims, and blacks, religious
differences were increasingly expressed in somatic terms. Thus, it was the
anxiety about "purity of faith" that gave rise to the idea that one's faith was
also an index of one's "purity of blood."[64]

The documents collected here attest that this shift was hardly exclusive
to the Iberian Peninsula. In 1543 Martin Luther claimed that the blood
of Christian children shed by Jews "still shines forth from their eyes and
their skin." And the 1585 account of Nicolas de Nicolay's visit to Istanbul
anticipates quasi-biological notions of difference by extending Luther's
claim and asserting that the sins of the Jews "hath followed them and their
successors throughout all generations." When the cosmetically whitened
Elizabeth Tudor ordered the deportation of "Negroes and blackamoors"
from England on the grounds that they were depriving her own "Christian
people" of jobs, her terminology also conflated faith and skin color. If her
own white subjects were all Christian, the blacks she sought to expel were
also described as "infidels" who had entered England from Spain "since the
troubles between her highness and the King of Spain." If these were indeed
Spanish Moors, they were not necessarily dark skinned; however, by this
time there was a widespread conflation of "black" and "Moor" in England
so that both dark-skinned non-Muslims and all Muslims could be referred to
as "blackamoors." Elizabeth's edicts also repeatedly describe the people she

expels as a distinct "kind of people." A similar confusion of categories is evident in "An Act against Carnal Copulation between Christian & Heathen," passed in Antigua in 1644, which substitutes "white" for "Christian" and assumes that "heathen" means "black."[65] In 1680 Morgan Godwyn pointed out that, in the same way that "Negro" and "slave" had "by custom grown homogeneous and convertible," so too "Negro and Christian, Englishman and heathen, are by the like corrupt custom and partiality made opposites."

What these examples indicate is that conversion, with all its attendant contradictions, in fact acted as a springboard for the development of quasi-biological vocabularies of difference. While in principle religious conversion was a way of literally overcoming difference by absorbing "the Other" into "the Self," in practice such absorption generated fears about identities on both sides, as can be seen most clearly from the development of the blood laws in Inquisition Spain. Both in England and on the Continent, concerns over interracial sexual contact and mixed-race children increasingly drew together and mystified religious and somatic vocabularies, especially in circumstances with the potential for cultural mixture. Thus, Edward Kellet's 1628 sermon on the occasion of an English renegade's "returne from Argier" denounces Jewish converts to Christianity as "these Christian-Jews or Jewish Christians [who] would join Moses and Christ, forgetting the substance of the precepts given unto them. . . . Thou shalt not let thy cattle gender with diverse kind, thou shalt not sow thy field with a mingled seed." Pronounced in a sermon more generally concerned with Christian conversions to Islam, Kellet's fear of a mingling of Jewish and Christian "seed" anticipates later laws against intergroup marriage by suggesting that the two are physically incompatible. Thus, John Minsheu's 1617 dictionary defines a Mestizo as "a mixture of two kinds, as black-Moore and a Christian, a mongrel dog or beast." Of course, learned writers, including Jean Bodin, George Abbot, and George Sandys, had all roundly dismissed the notion, introduced by Herodotus, that men of certain cultures produce "seed," or semen, manifestly different from others. Kellet's undeterred application of Leviticus 19 therefore points not only toward the relative authority of scripture versus empiricism, but also to the critical role played by religion in ushering in quasi-biological notions of difference.

RACE, GENDER, AND SEXUALITY

In his *Anthropometamorphosis* (1650), John Bulwer observes that "genital parts put a difference between nation and nation, so between one religion and another." A great deal of scholarship has theorized the intersection of race, gender, and sexuality, arguing for the ways in which the alleged departure of non-Europeans and non-Christians from normative gender roles and practices, as well as their sexual exoticism and excesses, has historically erected boundaries, justified conquest, and consolidated normative categories of gender and sexuality at home.[66] The documents in this collection provide ample illustration of the ways in which notions of gender and sexuality are interwoven with questions of race. Virtually every traveler to Asia, Africa, and America, and every commentator on ancient Jews and Muslims, as well as the Irish, has something to say about the gender roles or sexual habits of these peoples. Such observations are knit in a variety of increasingly racialized patterns into the fabric of human difference.

Readers of this volume will note that as European encounters with the non-European world widened, older tropes about particular places were reiterated and recirculated, to new and diverse effects. Thus Herodotus's suggestion that in Egypt men keep house while women go out to work is repeated by Leo Africanus in the sixteenth century as well as by George Sandys in the seventeenth, each of whom also inflects the reversal with newer elements. The idea that Africans are lustful is ubiquitous in a wide variety of writings included here; Africans' aberrant sexuality is increasingly marshaled into a recognizably modern discourse of race, but as this happens, older vocabularies are not always discarded. So Richard Jobson's *The golden trade* (1623) emphasizes, as many contemporary writings began to do, that Africans were bestial and that one of the marks of their bestiality were their enormous penises. But in explaining this in relation to the Mandingo men of Africa, Jobson turns to the ever-pliable tale of Noah's curse; the Mandingo, he writes, are of "the race of Canaan, the son of Ham," and are "furnished with such members as are after a sort burdensome unto them" because Ham gazed upon his father's genitalia. Whereas older versions of the story linked the curse to both blackness and servitude, as Africans began to be enslaved and to be viewed as a self-replenishing commodity, newer writings began to connect Noah's curse with African hypersexuality and fecundity.

Gender reversals as well as "abnormal" sexualities—intemperance, hermaphroditism, lesbianism, and "sodomy" in its various forms—were systematically attributed to people across the globe. In these writings, many of which are included in this volume, Jewish men as well as Brazilian and Egyptian ones have large breasts and give suck; Chinese, Native Americans, Turks, and Negroes are given to sodomy; women in Fez and Turkey have sex with one another, and indeed all over the East there is the tendency toward homosexuality; Irish women, Native American women, and even Portuguese women resident in the colonies have excessive carnal appetites; Guinean, Jewish, and Turkish women all desire white men; non-Western women give birth easily but this is a marker of their "shamelessness." While these and other observations might seem indiscriminate and therefore merely fanciful, the fact is that they fed into so-called scientific discourses about non-Europeans. We have already noted that black skin was associated with sexuality in ways that helped to secure ideologically the practice of enslaving Africans. The idea of men with outsized penises would be invoked to question the humanity of various African peoples. Turkish concubinage or Indian polygamy remained a key trope in later Orientalist discourses. The patriarchy of non-Western, particularly Eastern, societies indicated their inferiority, but so did the *lack* of male control of women, or of Western forms of marriage in various parts of Africa. Early modern writings also begin to posit a difference between men and women of racialized groups that we can recognize in later writings.

Readers of this collection will note that older stories of human copulation with devils and animals in the non-Christian worlds of India and Africa became the basis of pseudo-scientific discourse about human types. Mandeville suggests that Ham's female progeny copulate with "the fiends of hell' to produce "many other diverse shape against kind." Several centuries later, Jean Bodin writes that "promiscuous coition of men and animals took place, wherefore the regions of Africa produce for us so many monsters." Edward Topsell's *The historie of foure-footed beastes*, published in 1607, pictured a baboon, a "Satyre," and an "Aegopithecus" with erect genitals, and located such creatures in Ethiopia and among "Moors" in India. By suggesting that "men that have low and flat nostrils are libidinous as apes that attempt women, and having thick lips the upper hanging over the nether, they are deemed fools, like the lips of asses and apes," Topsell (and later Bulwer) encourages the comparison of apes and black people. By 1634, this connection was made explicit by Thomas Herbert, who had no doubt that Africans "have no better predecessors than monkeys."[67] By the end of the century, Edward Tyson identified the "Orang-outan" as a creature between man and beast; the illustrations accompanying Topsell's and Tyson's writings, which we also reproduce here, graphically underscore the connections of these writings with a quasi-biological discourse about race.

Finally, it is worth noting that women at home and abroad are repeatedly held responsible for threatening "natural" categories of difference in ways that also precipitate a quasi-biological language. Thus, Thomas Tuke's *A discourse against painting and tincturing of women* (1616) compares English women's use of mercury sublimate as a cosmetic whitener to "original sin," not because it seeks to conceal, but because it "goes from generation to generation," rendering "corrupted and rotten" the offspring of a painted mother. The belief that customs might not only transform the body but alter a line of descent leads John Bulwer to conjecture that dark complexions might be the result of cosmetics and fashion. Blackness began, he speculates, with women's "apish desire . . . to change the complexion of their bodies into a new and more fashionable hue," and thus "an artificial device" eventually "impregnated the seed" and rendered "the artificial into a natural impression."

Because women's private desires and intimate practices were at the heart of much unease over the relationship between "nature" and "culture," and because, as Edmund Spenser observed, a child "takes most of his nature from his mother," we often find parallel concerns in narratives of childbirth and childrearing. The classical theory of maternal impression—that women, as Thommaso Buoni writes, "by contemplating and gazing on serpents and Moors in their chambers in the act of generation, have brought forth monstrous births"—also continued to circulate in popular lore. At stake here is the fear of sexual contact between members of different groups, and thus the idea of maternal impression is used to explain away white women's dark-skinned children. Concerns over exogamy similarly inform Spenser's A *Veue of the present state of Irelande* (1633), which worries over the creation of an "evil race" through Anglo-Irish marriages and Irish wet-nurses; Spenser writes that English children "draw into themselves, together with their suck, even the nature and disposition of their [Irish] nurses."[68] At the same time, Spenser also regarded the mixing of peoples as part of God's plan to make "one kindred and blood of all people, and each to have knowledge of him," and other writers, such as Robert Burton, agreed that exogamy was necessary to "avoid hereditary diseases . . . it hath been ordered by God's especial providence, that in all ages there should be (as usually there is) once in 600 years, a transmigration of nations, to amend and purify their blood, as we alter seed upon our land." Women had always been central to dynastic marriages, to controlled and arranged forms of exogamy, but as contact between different groups proliferated in new and often bewildering ways, so did the fear of unregulated sexuality across nations, peoples, and groups, and indeed of unsanctioned forms of carnal contact within groups. Thus, it is not surprising that profound anxieties about forms of coupling and rearing, and about ways in which gender and sexual behaviour indicate the stability or dissolution of recognized social groups, are writ large everywhere in the writings assembled in this collection.

TRAVELING TROPES

"Racisms," as David Theo Goldberg writes, "have a history of traveling and transforming in their circulation."[69] Thus, the potency of cultural forms of difference lies not only in their utility for the enforcement of social and legal norms, but also in their exceptional transferability. Notions of difference might be drawn from one location or people and conceptually assimilated to another to confer value or contempt, and in turn to facilitate political practice. This movement, which can be thought of as a "discursive scrambling," can involve a movement over time, so that older tropes are rehearsed later but with respect to a different set of people or geographies. Thus, as we have already noted, Herodotus's contention that gender roles are reversed among Egyptians is repeated, not just in relation to Egypt, but as a standard way to describe alien cultures. Indeed, comparisons across geographies and cultures were routinely provoked by gender and sexual ideologies, as the previous section has already indicated. Some overlaps were also the result of confusions about "India"—today it is easy to forget that well into the late sixteenth century, Columbus's "mistake" about the New World was not always recognized as an error, so that the "New World" and "Orient" were widely conflated; thus Native Americans were described by Las Casas in terms of innocence and lack of private property, the same terms that had previously been used by Mandeville and Johannes Boemus for the residents of India. These and other overlaps persisted across a wide range of writings.

Discursive transferability is an integral part of attempts to engage with, manage, and control peoples considered exotic, strange, or hostile. Perhaps because the Irish were the earliest people to be colonized by the English, a great many instances of this movement in English writings involved the Irish. Thus the women of Guinea are compared to the women of Ireland—both, according to John Bulwer, "when their children cry to suck . . . cast their dugs backward over their shoulders, and so the child sucketh as it hangs." William Strachey finds Native Americans wearing clothes "after the fashion of the . . . Irish"; Richard Jobson finds "great resemblance" in the livelihoods and weapons of West African Fulbies and the Irish; and Anthony Knyvett describes Brazilian natives who "wear their hair long like wild Irish." A similar process is evident also in relation to the Jews, who had a long and contentious history within England. Mandeville had suggested that Jews come from the Caspian Mountains, and over time Jews were compared to gypsies, to Africans, and to Native Americans—indeed a figure we have reproduced here from Lancelot Addison's *The present state of the Jews* (1675) depicts a Jew as a feathered American.

In each case, the Irish or the Jews are debased by being compared with non-Europeans, and in turn, unfamiliar people are given meaning through comparison to those who are known and already regarded as inferior. Sometimes the same motif circulates back and forth: for example, Barnabe Riche writes that whereas cannibals only devour their enemy's flesh, the Irish are even more bloodthirsty because their cruelty is directed to their own neighbors, an idea that is repeated by Edmund Spenser. But this trope is then transferred by Thomas Herbert to the Anzigues of southwestern Africa, who, he writes, "covet their friends, whom they embowel with a greedy delight." Although Herbert does not mention the Irish at this point, elsewhere he reinforces the comparison by noting that the "apishly sounded" African language is "voiced like the Irish."

Perhaps the most complex kind of movement can be seen in the notion that certain kinds of human beings possess unchangeable qualities, an assumption that was particularly widespread in relation to Jews, but also frequently applied to the Irish, blacks, and Muslims. When the unchangeable traits of different groups were compared, the effect was to connect physical features such as skin color to moral qualities and to establish that both were innate. Thus, on the one hand, various Jewish "traits" (ingratitude, miserliness, stubbornness) were described as unchangeable—hence, Jewish conversion was seen as a superficial process, put on for show, and unable to transform an inner Jewishness that was regarded increasingly as a quality passed down through generations. On the other hand, black skin was also increasingly seen as an "unwashable" taint passed on from parent to child. Not surprisingly, comparisons between Jewish "ingratitude" or "stubbornness" and black skin, that is, between the unchangeable essence of Jewishness and blackness, between one "inner" quality and another "outer" one, proliferated during this period. These comparisons reworked in newly pernicious ways the older correlations of physical characteristics with mental and emotional being.

The crucial ideological work performed by analogies between different marginalized groups has been widely commented on in relation to later histories of race.[70] However, their significance in the early modern period has not been fully explored. The materials collected here will indicate some of the ways in which traveling tropes, comparisons, and analogies helped enforce the terms in which newly encountered groups would be assimilated or excluded; equally, these tropes reinforced existing discriminatory practices, and were used to police behavior and hierarchies, at home.

RACE INTO CULTURE

As we have already discussed, many historians and theorists hold that a discourse of race is dependent upon the advent of modern scientific ways of seeing. Thus, Ivan Hannaford locates the "first stage" of racial thinking after 1684, arguing that in the Renaissance, the "attempts to establish anatomical, physiological, geographical, and astrological relationships between man and man, and man and beast, did not produce a fully developed idea of race, since there was no proper anthropology, natural history, or biology to support it."[71] While we cannot discuss the advent of biological science here, we must ask whether this is not a circular logic—is it particular disciplines that give rise to racial thought, or are various disciplinary formations, and ways of ordering knowledge, themselves shaped by the histories of cross-cultural and colonial encounters? Early ethnography and anthropology developed in the crucible of early colonialism. It was not "anthropology" that engendered racial categories; rather, quasi-ethnographic forms of recording knowledge about marginalized or non-European peoples developed alongside mercantile and colonial encounters across the globe.[72]

We also want to query the analytical separation of culture and biology and the consequence of such a distinction for histories and theories of race. Earlier categories of difference are often considered more malleable than later "pseudobiological" ones because they are regarded as more "cultural." Robert Bartlett, one of the most sophisticated commentators on medieval race relations, has argued that "while the language of race—*gens, natio,* 'blood', 'stock' etc.—is biological, its medieval reality was almost entirely cultural." In practice, races were defined more in social terms of customs, language, and law. Since customs and language, and even religion, could be acquired, he argues that premodern forms of ethnic differentiation were more fluid than their modern counterparts: "When we study race relations in medieval Europe," Bartlett argues, "we are analysing the contact between various linguistic and cultural groups, not between breeding stocks."[73] As we have tried to argue so far, early modern linguistic, geographic, national, religious, class, and cultural groups are often defined precisely in terms of lineage and genealogy. However, as we have also noted, lineage itself is regarded by some critics as a qualitatively different notion from later genealogies of race. For example, one theorist points to the difference between early modern and modern racism by commenting that the blood test in Inquisition Spain was related to the "genealogical context of families" and not to "a belief that Jewishness actually resides in the blood. It reflected the jural dimensions of structured kinship rather than the fact of biological connection, the significance of 'pater' rather than 'genitor.'"[74]

The materials collected here question such divisions on several counts. First, it is not possible to crudely demarcate the family, household, class, nation, and religious groups in the early modern period; key terms used to describe their composition are often interchangeable, and their boundaries are far more fluid than modern commentators have recognized.[75] Second, writings of the period amply demonstrate that the idea of race as bloodline *was* in fact developing at this time, often in complex articulation with other meanings. Thus, when Jewish or Muslim identities are compared to black skin, or when writers such as Best, Sandys, Moryson, Spenser, and Africanus describe black skin and religious difference alike in terms of "infections," the comparisons do not suggest that religion is a more changeable affiliation, but in fact fix both religion and skin color as essential and passed on from parent to child. Third, if earlier vocabularies of race seem less biological than post-Enlightenment ones, it is partly because a full-fledged discourse of biology or genetic transmission is itself missing in the earlier period, and not because "cultural difference" is a necessarily benign idea. As one commentator notes, what we call "race" and what we call "culture" cannot be readily separated, especially during the early modern period, when a "people's inferior culture implied a biologically inferior people."[76] In fact, these early histories of race remind us that even the most "scientific" assertion of race as biology was in fact "cultural"—which is the whole point of calling it *quasi*-biological. Even in the heyday of scientific racism, Jewishness or blackness was never seen to *literally* reside in blood. In searching for the originary moment of a quasi-biological discourse on difference, it is possible to forget that we need to query the terms of racial discourse rather than to take them at face value. Thus, when we say that racial categories are hardened in the wake of the development of science, it is worth recalling that it is not science but society that is responsible for such a hardening.

In her study of eighteenth-century Britain, Kathleen Wilson observes that "the most 'traditional' discourse—of religion, history, community, and descent—could be just as pernicious and essentializing, and create symbolic barriers just as impassable as any scientific or biological ones, in the early modern period and today."[77] When Fynes Moryson describes as "barbarous and most filthy" the Irish customs of eating on the ground, feasting on horse's flesh, and snatching up sharp-tasting shamrocks "like beasts out of the ditches," or how Irish women drink whiskey "till they be drunken, or at least till they void urine in full assemblies of men," he contributes to a body of knowledge figuring the Irish as culturally perverse, subordinate, and even inhuman. This kind of description justifies an English colonial presence in Ireland in the seventeenth century, and is no less potent than the simian "Paddy" of Victorian caricature. Such a caricature is actually anticipated in part by Edmund Spenser's description of young Irish children, who are "like apes, which affect and imitate what they have seen done before them."[78] Barnabe Riche—who served in the army that subdued Ulster—writes that the Irish are "rude, uncleanly, and uncivil" due not "so much to their natural inclination" as to "their education that are trained up . . . in the very puddle of popery." This view of Irish culture was not particularly benevolent, but one that allowed Riche to summon up his violence against the Irish in the mitigating idioms of a civilizing mission. On the other hand, Spenser, who traced a Scythian ancestry for the Irish on account of the similarities in their customs rather than any connection through bloodlines, and who believed that the mingling of nations in Europe would work to spread Christianity and civilization, argued that the Irish could *not* be reformed by introducing English laws in Ireland, for false religion has brought "a great contagion" to Irish souls, and their habits have bred in them a "disease" that will not be easily "cleansed." Here we see categories that we might view as "cultural" generating a vocabulary that is recognizably quasi-biological.

Moreover, the mutability of identity is not always a benign idea, as is underlined by the discourse of degeneracy, which was an essential component of later racial thought. As Ann Laura Stoler shows, eugenics posited that acquired characteristics are as inheritable as skin color.[79] This is very much a medieval and early modern idea that we can trace through myriad writings of the period. Bodin suggested that men mutate like plants if the soil is changed. If Spenser feared that the English in Ireland were degenerating, Matthew Hale was concerned that English planters in Virginia could degenerate there. At the heart of such writings are fears about social mobility, as is evident in writings about the Macrocephali, or people with elongated heads, an image used by Hippocrates that is obsessively revisited during the early modern period. The Spanish humanist Juan Huarte describes the Macrocephali as

> a certain sort of men who, to be different from the vulgar, chose for a token of their nobility to have their head like a sugar-loaf. And to shape this figure by art, when the child was born, the midwives took care to bind their head with swathes, and bands, until they were fashioned to the form. And this artificialness grew to such force as it was converted into nature: for in process of time, all the children that were born of nobility had their head sharp from their mothers' womb. So from thenceforth, the art and diligence of the midwives herein became superfluous.

The idea that cultural practices would result in a natural change—evocative, almost, of Darwin's writings on evolution—is pervasive in early modern writings. Bodin argues that "the influence of custom and training is so great in natural and human affairs that gradually they develop into mores and take on the force of nature." Similarly, John Bulwer's *Anthropometamorphosis* suggests that black skin is a result of artifice and make-up, but this observation does not result in a more benign attitude toward blacks but rather a fear that English men and women are in danger of permanently disfiguring their bodies and corrupting their nature by aping the barbarous customs of Africa, Asia, or America.

Nor does the mutability of identity impede an unequal evaluation of cultures that underwrites acts of violence. In 1562, *An act for the further punishment of vagabonds, calling themselves Egyptians* legislates that individuals "calling themselves *Egyptians,* or counterfeiting, transforming, or disguising themselves by their apparel, speech, or other behavior" into "Egyptians" (or gypsies) "shall therefore suffer pains of death, loss of lands and goods, as in cases of felony by the order of the common laws of this realm. . . ." What is worth noting here is that it is not necessary that the offender *be* a gypsy; he must merely dress, speak, or generally behave like one to mobilize the instruments of judicial enforcement. Thus, even as "Egyptian" or gypsy identity is legally predicated on a porous barrier between "Englishness" and "Egyptian-ness," in practice the category becomes absolute as offenders forfeit the rights of English subjects.

As we have mentioned in the previous section, several early texts draw explicit links between moral qualities and physical traits. A book on the "art of physiognomy" associates thin lips with eloquence and wit, while declaring "great lips" a sign of "dull and foolish people, hard of understanding, unclean, luxurious, inconstant and cruel."[80] Peter Heylyn, in his description of the Tartars in *Microcosmus,* claims, "The men of this country . . . are swarth, not so much by the heat of the sun, as their own sluttishness."[81] Here, it is the behavior of the Tartars that produces their dark complexions, much as diet was sometimes believed to darken the skin of Jews, as in Henry Buttes's argument that that goose "fills the body with superfluous humours," and because "Jews are great Goose-eaters; therefore their complexion is passing melancholious, their colour swart, and their diseases very perilous." Thus too in *Problemes of beautie and all humane affections* (1606), Thommaso Buoni attributes the exceptional fairness of princes and noble women to "their delicate and exquisite diet, both in their meats and drinks, [which] makes their blood more pure, their vital spirits more lively, their complexion more beautiful, and their nature more noble."

Of course, behavior might improve, and diets might change. If the Jew took to eating hare's flesh, would he, as Buttes suggests, become "lean and fair"? Despite this possibility, most of these writings do not visualize changes "up" the social hierarchy, but they often fear the possibility of downward movement, with white people becoming black or immoral by imbibing coffee or chocolate, using foreign cosmetic practices, or adopting foreign religions. Despite a few texts celebrating the conversion of Muslims or Jews, it appears that they, like the Irish and blacks, do not change easily; thus, Francis Bacon's *Apothegems* suggests that "the Moors eat no hare's flesh."[82] Jews are so obdurate that they cannot convert, and even if they do so, they continue to harbor cultural traits that betray the essence of their identity, just as blacks do not become fair when they move into cooler climes. These writings both stage and foreclose the possibility of mobility and change differently from later vocabularies, but they also encode some of the characteristic forms of modern ideologies of race. Rather than argue that they are simply *more* or *less* "benign" than later discourses, it is more useful to locate the multiple axes of power along which their arguments work, and to note how particular human traits are visualized and human groups described.

While we may not find in earlier periods the rigorous attention to classification, order, and method characteristic of Carl Linnaeus's *Systema Naturae* (1735)—one of the foundational texts of "scientific racism"—the division of man into separate varieties is articulated not only by François Bernier's "A New Division of the Earth" (1684), but also by the various sixteenth- and seventeenth-century remediations of both the Ptolemaic and biblical divisions of mankind. To admit that these divisions are not characterized by the rationalism so often considered a marker of scientific racism is merely to recognize, again, that empirical science was not yet as developed a discourse of distinction as religion or climatic humoralism. Nevertheless, the tables in Pierre Charron's *Of Wisdom* (1601) systematically attribute certain qualities to Northerners, Southerners and "Middlers" in ways that are not at an absolute distance from the separation of "Caucasians" from Ethiopians and Mongolians in the work of Johann Friedrich Blumenbach, the German anthropologist sometimes called the father of racial science.[83] Likewise, the well-known image of a primitive man set alongside various ape-like figures in Linnaeus's *Anthropomorpha Quae Praeside* (1760) actually borrows elements from Edward Topsell's *The historie of foure-footed beastes* (1607) and Edward Tyson's *Orang-outang . . . or The anatomy of a pygmie compared with that of a monkey, an ape, and a man* (1699), which features an analogous set of juxtaposed figures. Both here and in Johannes ab Indagine's *Briefe introductions . . . unto the art of chiromancy . . . and physiognomy* (1558), a book published in England seven times before the end of the seventeenth century, the grounds for nineteenth-century comparative anatomy and racial craniometry are prepared with juxtaposed busts and claims such as Indagine's that "the dispositions of most men . . . be judged by nothing sooner or better than by the [shape of the] forehead." The comparison of certain peoples to primates, a practice considered central to nineteenth-century racism, was already common enough in 1680 to disturb the Anglican minister Morgan Godwyn, who noted the way it contributed to the polygenetic argument of Barbadian slaveholders that "Negroes [derive] from a stock different from Adam's," and from thence "justify their reduction of them under bondage [and] disable them from all rights and claims, even to religion itself."

Finally, we must remember that nineteenth-century scientific racism was not itself a unified field. In fact, the range of its concerns and even contradictions is evident in early modern discourses of difference. We have already discussed the overlaps between early modern and twentieth-century writings about degeneracy. At the same time, J. A. Comte de Gobineau's argument for the permanence of human difference on the basis of "affinities and repulsions" among various races of men resonates with Buoni's claim that "every like desireth and loveth his like . . . and therefore the Moor loves the Moor, and so of the rest." Francis Bacon's description, in *The New Atlantis,* of the "inhabitants of America as a young people, younger a thousand years at the least than the rest of the world," lingers in theories postulating the correlation of human differences with evolutionary stages.

But it is not our primary purpose to indicate the possibility of locating the crucial features of scientific racism in earlier works, although we have spent some time indicating this overlap because of the overwhelming scholarly tendency to separate them. It is more important to query, via these earlier histories, the distinction between the politico-cultural and pseudoscientific vocabularies of racial discrimination. We need to rethink the time line of racism that the supposed historical transition of "culture into biology" establishes, and in doing so, query the very boundaries between these categories. Theorists such as Anne Fausto-Sterling, Donna Haraway, and Sandra Harding have been doing precisely this, along with biologists such as Richard Lewontin. Harding points out that it is not enough to challenge the notion that racial categories are natural by reversing the proposition and arguing that they are social. Such a reversal "simply substitutes reification of the social determinants of race for the natural determinants favored in the older view."[84]

We can witness this substitution all across the globe today. Jan Pieterse argues that as its knowledge claims were debunked in the 1960s, scientific racism "gradually changed to the 'new racism' that focuses on cultural difference instead of phenotypical differences."[85] In the United States, the racialization of a group by virtue of its customs, language, religion, and traditions, instead of its physical features, has dovetailed neatly with a neo-conservatism whose politics are more effectively buoyed by an emphasis on aberrant values rather than defective genes.[86] Samuel Huntington's polemic about "the clash of civilizations" is echoed by a host of writers in the United States and Europe who argue that Muslims or Asians can never assimilate into "Western" societies. This view is simply reversed by Islamic fundamentalists, so that the rhetoric of a nonnegotiable cultural boundary is shared by otherwise opposed groups. Pieterse concludes that "cultural difference is the latest boundary of difference."[87] But as we have discussed at some length in this introduction, "culture" is also widely understood to be the *first* boundary of difference! Indeed, in an influential article published more than fifteen years ago, Etienne Balibar drew some provocative connections between this "latest" moment and early modern histories, arguing that the anti-Semitism of Reconquista Spain can teach us something about the dynamics of contemporary neoracism. However, Balibar did not conclude from this that culture is more *benign* than nature, but rather that culture can function "like a nature," which is to say that culture can also function as an uncrossable barrier between "us" and "them."[88]

The documents collected here urge us to go even further in rethinking the nature/culture partition. The centrality of cultural categories to discourses of difference is limited neither to a time "before" the development of scientific racism (protoracism) nor to a period when such racism has given way to a more cultural view of nature (neoracism). In other words, culture is not useful only when analyzing what is now sometimes referred to as "racism without race." Such a conclusion leaves "culture" and "nature" as binary opposites. Instead, early modern writings graphically illustrate how both culture and nature are organically interconnected and historically changing concepts that have *always* been central to the ideologies of human difference. It then becomes clear that culture does not have to function "like nature" in order to be discriminatory; rather, as Harding argues, nature simply cannot be conceptualized as existing outside culture. Speaking in a very different idiom, Albert Memmi writes that

> biology is a metaphor for the destiny imposed on the other. . . . The lessons of history are clear. Racism does not limit itself to biology or economics or psychology or metaphysics; it attacks along many fronts and in many forms, deploying whatever is at hand, and even what is not, inventing when the need arises. To function, it needs a focal point, a central factor, but it doesn't care what that might be—the color of one's skin, facial features, the form of the fingers, one's character, one's cultural tradition. . . .[89]

We have argued here that early modern histories of race are both better viewed through, and themselves lead us to, more flexible conceptual tools. The materials collected in this volume allow us to trace these protean histories of racism, even as they demand that we retheorize the idea of race. Finally, we believe early modern racial histories are increasingly important in understanding contemporary ideologies of difference, where religion has become more, not less, important in defining human collectivities; where national differences have not eroded but have proliferated in the face of increasing international contact; where terminologies of "crusades" or "jihad" are being invoked anew in the context of contemporary geopolitics; and where, despite the so-called flattening of the globe, new battle lines are defined in terms of a "clash of civilizations."[90] In this situation, the documents we present here will illuminate the past as well as the world we live in today, provoking us to rethink the relations between them.

NOTES

1. Although the social effects of race are real and tangible, the term "race" has been increasingly framed within quotation marks in order to signal that it is a socially constructed idea. Because this entire book is devoted to examining the constructions of racial thought, as well as the very real practices engendered by it, we do not use quotation marks except when we focus on the term itself.
2. Stuart Hall, "Minimal Selves," in *Identity Documents; The Real Me: Postmodernism and the Question of Identity,* ed. L. Appignanesi (London: ICA Documents 6, 1988), 45.
3. Benedict Anderson, *Imagined Communities: Reflections on the Origin and Spread of Nationalism* (London and New York: Verso, 1991). Kathleen Wilson, in *The Island Race: Englishness, Empire and Gender in the 18th Century* (London: Routledge, 2003), makes the point that nation in the eighteenth century did the same ideological work that race would in the nineteenth century. See also David Theo Goldberg and John Solomos, eds., *A Companion to Racial and Ethnic Studies* (Malden, MA, and Oxford, UK: Blackwell, 2002), 3.

4. While it is not possible to offer a comprehensive list, see Eldred Jones, *Othello's Countrymen* (London: Oxford University Press, 1965); Elliot H. Tokson, *The Popular Image of the Black Man in English Drama 1550–1688* (Boston: G. K. Hall, 1982); Peter Fryer, *Staying Power: The History of Black People in Britain* (Atlantic Highlands, NJ: Humanities Press, 1984); Peter Hulme, *Colonial Encounters, Europe and the Native Caribbean 1492–1797* (London: Routledge, 1986); Anthony Barthelemy, *Black Face, Maligned Race* (Baton Rouge, LA: Louisiana State University Press, 1987); Ania Loomba, *Gender, Race, Renaissance Drama* (Manchester: Manchester University Press, 1989) and *Shakespeare, Race and Colonialism* (Oxford: Oxford University Press, 2002); Stephen Greenblatt, *Learning to Curse* (New York: Routledge, 1990) and *Marvelous Possessions: The Wonder of the New World* (Chicago: University of Chicago Press, 1991); Jack D'Amico, *The Moor in English Renaissance Drama* (Tampa, FL: University of South Florida Press, 1991); Karen Newman, *Fashioning Femininity and English Renaissance Drama* (Chicago: University of Chicago Press, 1991); Brendan Bradshaw, Andrew Hadfield, and Willy Maley, eds., *Representing Ireland, Literature and Origins of Conflict, 1534–1660* (Cambridge: Cambridge University Press, 1993); Patricia Parker and Margo Hendricks, eds., *Women, "Race" and Writing in the Early Modern Period* (London: Routledge, 1994); John Gillies, *Shakespeare and the Geography of Difference* (Cambridge: Cambridge University Press, 1994); Kim F. Hall, *Things of Darkness: Economies of Race and Gender in Early Modern England* (Ithaca, NY: Cornell University Press, 1995); James Shapiro, *Shakespeare and the Jews* (New York: Columbia University Press, 1996); *William and Mary Quarterly*, 3rd Ser., 54, no. 1 (January 1997), special issue on race; Joyce Green MacDonald, ed., *Race, Ethnicity, and Power in the Renaissance* (Madison, NJ: Fairleigh Dickinson University Press, 1997); Mary Janell Metzger, "'Now by My Hood, a Gentle and no Jew': Jessica, *The Merchant of Venice* and the Discourse of Early Modern English Identity," *PMLA* 113, no. 1 (January 1998): 52–63; Imtiaz Habib, *Shakespeare and Race: Postcolonial Praxis in the Early Modern Period* (Lanham, MD: University Press of America, 1999); Nabil Matar, *Islam in Britain* (Cambridge: Cambridge University Press, 1998) and *Turks, Moors and Englishmen in the Age of Discovery* (New York: Columbia University Press, 1999); Geraldo U. de Sousa, *Shakespeare's Cross-Cultural Encounters* (London: St. Martin's Press, 1999); Peter Erickson and Clark Hulse, eds., *Early Modern Visual Culture: Representation, Race and Empire in Renaissance England* (Philadelphia: University of Pennsylvania Press, 2000); Dympna Callaghan, *Shakespeare Without Women, Representing Gender and Race on the Renaissance Stage* (London: Routledge, 2000); Catherine M. S. Alexander and Stanley Wells, eds., *Shakespeare and Race* (Cambridge: Cambridge University Press, 2000); *Journal of Medieval and Early Modern Studies* 31, no. 1 (2001), special issue on race; Shankar Raman, *Framing "India:" The Colonial Imaginary in Early Modern Culture* (Stanford: Stanford University Press, 2002); Margaret W. Ferguson, *Dido's Daughters, Literacy, Gender and Empire in Early Modern England and France* (Chicago: University of Chicago Press, 2003); Daniel J. Vitkus, *Turning Turk: English Theater and the Multicultural Mediterranean, 1570–1630* (New York: Palgrave Macmillan, 2003); Mary Floyd-Wilson, *English Ethnicity and Race in Early Modern Drama* (Cambridge: Cambridge University Press, 2003); Jennifer Morgan, *Laboring Women: Gender and Reproduction in New World Slavery* (Philadelphia: University of Pennsylvania

Press, 2004); Anu Korhonen, "Washing the Ethiopian White: Conceptualising Black Skin in Renaissance England," in *Black Africans in Renaissance Europe,* ed. T. F. Earle and K. J. P. Lowe (New York: Cambridge University Press, 2005); Sujata Iyengar, *Shades of Difference* (Philadelphia: University of Pennsylvania Press, 2005); Jonathan Burton, *Traffic and Turning: Islam and English Drama, 1579–1624* (Newark, DE: University of Delaware Press, 2005); and Gary Taylor, *Buying Whiteness: Race, Culture and Identity from Columbus to Hip Hop* (New York: Palgrave Macmillan, 2005). Medievalists have also taken up the subject in especially acute ways: see, for example, articles in the two special issues listed above and books mentioned in note 35.

5. See, for example, Kwame Anthony Appiah, "Race," in *Critical Terms for Literary Study,* ed. Frank Lentricchia and Thomas McLaughlin (Chicago: University of Chicago Press, 1990), 274–87; Paul Gilroy, *Against Race: Imagining Political Culture Beyond the Color Line* (Cambridge MA: Harvard University Press, 2000), 31; Roberto Bernasconi and Tommy Lott, *The Idea of Race* (Indianapolis: Hackett Publishing Company, 2000); Brian Niro, *Race* (New York: Palgrave Macmillan, 2003). Ivan Hannaford, in *Race, The History of an Idea in the West* (Baltimore: Johns Hopkins University Press, 1996), does go back to the classical period but also concludes that racism was the product of Enlightenment categories. Joyce Chaplin contends that racism was not engendered in English thought until the development of Atlantic slavery; see Chaplin, "Race," in *The British Atlantic World, 1500–1800,* ed. David Armitage and Michael J. Braddick (New York: Palgrave, 2002), 154–72. Roxann Wheeler, in *The Complexion of Race: Categories of Difference in Eighteenth-Century British Culture* (Philadelphia: University of Pennsylvania Press, 2000), rightly takes issue with those histories of race that begin in the nineteenth century and privilege skin color or disregard earlier intellectual categories, but curiously concludes that those who trace racism back to the sixteenth century are guilty of making anti-black racism a "constant feature of white people's psyche" and of disregarding historical change (300).

6. This is the logic followed by many theorists; see, for example, Niro, *Race,* 16, 48–52.

7. See Thomas Hahn, "The Difference the Middle Ages Makes: Color and Race before the Modern World," *Journal of Medieval and Early Modern Studies* 31, no.1 (2001): 1–37, 9. Concerning the use of the terms "race" and "ethnicity" see Robert Bartlett, "Medieval and Modern Concepts of Race and Ethnicity," *Journal of Medieval and Early Modern Studies* 31, no. 1 (2001): 39–56; and Werner Sollors, "Ethnicity and Race," in Goldberg and Solomos, *Companion to Racial and Ethnic Studies,* 97–104.

8. In this regard our approach to the early modern period resembles that of recent theorists such as Stuart Hall (see Dave Morley and K. H. Chen, eds., *Stuart Hall: Critical Dialogues in Cultural Studies* [London: Routledge, 1996]), Goldberg and Solomos (see "General Introduction," *A Companion to Racial and Ethnic Studies,* 1–12) and Michael Omi and Howard Winant (see *Racial Formation in the United States: From the 1960s to the 1990s* [New York: Routledge, 1994]). However, most theorists do not challenge conventional periodizations of race. Thus, while for Omi and Winant, racial formations comprise the various and sundry "historically situated projects in which human bodies and social structures are represented and organized" to the principal end of redistributing resources (55–56), their history of race begins, like so many, with the arrival of Europeans in the Americas.

9. An extract from Bodin is reproduced in this collection. In this introduction, when we quote from writings included in this volume, we do not provide further citations.

10. See Sujata Iyengar, *Shades of Difference* (Chapter 1) for a discussion of early modern writers' engagement with Heliodorus. For additional examples of maternal impression in this volume, see Hippocrates, Topsell, and Münster. Heliodorus's *Aithiopika* was translated into English by Thomas Underdown in 1569.

11. Sujata Iyengar has located over twenty commentaries on the Song of Songs produced between 1549 and 1662 (*Shades of Difference*, 46).

12. These "manners" include cosmetic practices as well as clothing, about which there has been a rich discussion in relation to the construction of Renaissance identity; see Ann Rosalind Jones and Peter Stallybrass, *Renaissance Clothing and the Materials of Memory* (Cambridge: Cambridge University Press, 2000).

13. David Theo Goldberg, "Racial Americanization" in *Racialization: Studies in Theory and Practice*, ed. Karim Murji and John Solomos (New York: Oxford University Press, 2005), 87.

14. See Benjamin Braude, "The Sons of Noah and the Construction of Ethnic and Geographic Identities in the Medieval and Early Modern Periods," *William and Mary Quarterly* 3rd Ser., 54, no. 1 (January 1997): 103–42, 109; Denys Hay, *Europe, the Emergence of an Idea* (Edinburgh: Edinburgh University Press, 1957).

15. See William Dalrymple, "Foreword," in *Re-Orienting the Renaissance: Cultural Exchanges with the East,* ed. Gerald MacLean (New York: Palgrave Macmillan, 2005).

16. See Robin Blackburn, "The Old World Background to European Colonial Slavery," *William and Mary Quarterly* 3rd Ser., 54, no. 1 (January 1997): 65–102, 91–92.

17. Al-Dimashqî (Dm), in *Corpus of Early Arabic Sources for West African History,* edited and annotated by N. Levitzion and J. F. P. Hopkins (Princeton, NJ: Markus Wiener Publishers, 2000), 212. See also James Sweet, "The Iberian Roots of American Racist Thought," *William and Mary Quarterly* 3rd Ser., 54, no. 1 (January 1997): 143–66, esp. 148–49.

18. Sweet, "Iberian Roots" (150), suggests that Christians learned to disparage blackness from Iberian Muslims, but we think more complex interconnections need to be traced. Blackburn, "Old World Background," offers a more nuanced account of these intersections.

19. In selecting our copy texts, however we do not always use the earliest edition available.

20. See Martin Japtok and Winfried Schleiner. "Genetics and 'Race' in *The Merchant of Venice,*" *Literature and Medicine* 18, no. 2 (Fall 1999): 155–72.

21. Thus, for example, Mandeville is published in the first edition of Hakluyt's *Principall Navigations* but, along with Pliny, dropped in the second edition. Thanks to David Wallace for pointing this out; see also David Wallace, *Premodern Places: Calais to Surinam, Chaucer to Aphra Behn* (Malden, MA: Blackwell, 2004), 120.

22. See, for example, Dipesh Chakrabarty, "History as Critique and Critique of History," *Economic and Political Weekly,* September 14, 1991, 2262–8; Wallace, *Premodern Places.* Medievalists have been particularly sensitive to this question.

23. See, for example, Chaplin, "'Race.'"
24. Edward Said, *Orientalism* (London: Routledge, 1978), 43, 57.
25. See Geoffrey Parker, "Europe and the Wider World, 1500–1750," in *The Political Economy of Merchant Empires*, ed. James D. Tracy (Cambridge: Cambridge University Press, 1991), 161–195; Ania Loomba, "Shakespeare and Cultural Difference," in *Alternative Shakespeares*, Vol. 2, ed. Terence Hawkes (New York: Routledge, 1996), 164–91; Bartels, "*Othello* and Africa"; Gerald MacLean, *The Rise of Oriental Travel* (New York: Palgrave, 2004); Matar, *Turks, Moors and Englishmen* and *Islam in Britain;* Vitkus, *Turning Turk;* Lisa Jardine and Jerry Brotton, *Global Interests* (Ithaca, NY: Cornell University Press, 2000); and Robert Markley, *The Far East and the English Imagination, 1600–1730* (New York: Cambridge University Press, 2006).
26. See Wallace, *Premodern Places;* Hall, *Things of Darkness.*
27. Walter Mignolo, *The Darker Side of the Renaissance: Literacy, Territoriality & Colonization* (Ann Arbor: University of Michigan Press, 1995).
28. For a survey of the debate in American history over the causal relationship of racism and slavery, see Alden T. Vaughan, *The Roots of American Racism* (New York: Oxford University Press, 1995), 136–74. We are mindful of the need to distinguish between prejudice and racism; however, even if racism is characterized by systematic discrimination it does not follow that the early modern world was free of it.
29. Several essays in Goldberg and Solomos suggest this: Jan Nederveen Pieterse, "Europe and Its Others" (17–25); Peter Fitzpatrick, "Doctrine of Discovery" (25–31); and especially Sollors, "Ethnicity and Race."
30. Hannaford, *Race,* 9, 147.
31. Blackburn, "Old World Background," 87.
32. Aristotle, *Politics,* trans. Benjamin Jowett (New York: Random House, 1941), 7.7, 1286; Machiavelli is quoted by Hannaford, *Race,* 154. Also see Bartlett's discussion of this passage in "Medieval and Modern Concepts," 46.
33. An extract from Strachey is reproduced here.
34. See Stuart Hall, "Gramsci's Relevance for the Study of Race and Ethnicity," in Morley and Chen, *Stuart Hall,* 411–40, 431.
35. See essays in *Journal of Medieval and Early Modern Studies* 31, no. 1 (2001) (special issue on race); Jeffrey Jerome Cohen, ed., *The Postcolonial Middle Ages* (New York: Palgrave Macmillan, 2001); Dorothee Metlitzki, *The Matter of Araby in Medieval England* (New Haven and London: Yale University Press, 1977); Sharon Kinoshita, "'Pagans are wrong and Christians are right': Alterity, Gender, and Nation in the *Chanson de Roland,*" *Journal of Medieval and Early Modern Studies* 31, no.1 (2001): 79–111, 86–7; David Nirenberg, *Communities of Violence, Persecution of Minorities in the Middle Ages* (Princeton, NJ: Princeton University Press, 1996); Lisa Lampert, *Gender and Jewish Difference from Paul to Shakespeare* (Philadelphia: University of Pennsylvania Press, 2004); Geraldine Heng, *Empire of Magic, Medieval Romance and the Politics of Cultural Fantasy* (New York: Columbia University Press, 2003). See also Julia Reinhard Lupton, "*Othello* Circumcised: Shakespeare and the Pauline Discourse of Nations," *Representations* 57 (Winter 1997): 73–89, as well as the work by Burton, Matar, Shapiro, and Vitkus mentioned in note 4, which traces the early modern contexts of this legacy.
36. Wallace, *Premodern Places,* 189.

37. Robert Bartlett, *The Making of Europe, Conquest, Colonization and Cultural Change 950–1350* (Princeton, NJ: Princeton University Press, 1993), 313.
38. It is widely suggested that the idea of monogenesis—the notion that all mankind is derived from Adam—is incompatible with the racist division of humans into different kinds, or even species. See for example, Hannaford, *Race*, 257–58, 268–69. Colin Kidd, *British Identities before Nationalism, Ethnicity and Nationhood in the Atlantic World 1600–1800* (Cambridge: Cambridge University Press, 1999), explicitly argues that the idea of monogenesis retarded the development of racism (22–23) and even nationalism (33).
39. Hannaford, *Race*, 87.
40. Wallace, *Premodern Places*, 190.
41. This anonymous document in the papers of the scientist Robert Boyle is quoted by Cristina Malcolmson, "Biblical Monogenesis: Race and Gender in the Early Royal Society," forthcoming in her book *Race, Religion, and Science in the Works of Robert Boyle and Margaret Cavendish*. We are grateful to her for sharing her work with us.
42. Ibid.
43. For examples of attempts to reconcile conversion and slavery, see the 1662 Virginia statute in this volume, and Morgan Godwyn's reminder that "in regard religion would be apt to create a conscience in their slaves, it might be convenient, in order to make them truer servants."
44. Gustav Ungerer, "Portia and the Prince of Morocco," *Shakespeare Studies* 31 (2003): 89–126, 91; also his 'The Forerunners of the English Slave Trade in Early Modern Spain, 1480–1532," unpublished paper. We are grateful to Ungerer for sharing this work with us.
45. Robert Daborne, *A Christian turn'd Turk* (6, 9–13), in *Three Turk Plays From Early Modern England*, ed. Daniel J. Vitkus (New York: Columbia University Press, 2000), 174.
46. Heng, *Empire of Magic*, 231.
47. See for example, Heng, *Empire of Magic*, 229–37 especially, 420–21, n74; Loomba, *Shakespeare, Race and Colonialism*, 22–74; Steven F. Kruger, "Conversion and Medieval Sexual, Religious and Racial Categories," in *Constructing Medieval Sexuality*, ed. Karma Lochrie, Peggy McCracken, and James A. Schultz (London and Minneapolis: University of Minnesota Press, 1997), 158–79; Bruce Holsinger, "The Color of Salvation," in *The Tongue of the Fathers: Gender and Ideology in Twelfth-Century Latin*, ed. David Townsend and Andrew Taylor (Philadelphia: University of Pennsylvania Press, 1998), 156–86; Sweet, "Iberian Roots"; as discussed in the next section, scholarship on early modern Spain has been especially important in challenging these binaries.
48. See Heng, *Empire of Magic*, chapter 5.
49. Imagining an even further migration, William Strachey's *For the colony in Virginea Britannia. Lawes divine, morall and martiall* (1612) condones enslaving American Indians, who, as Ham's scattered progeny, in "what country soever [they] happened to possess, there began both the ignorance of true godliness and a kind of bondage and slavery to be taxed one upon another."
50. Indeed, the Latin word *servus* indicates both a male servant and a slave. We thank David Wallace for pointing this out to us.
51. These multiple meanings are often invoked to suggest a distance between ideologies of difference in this period and later racial discourses; see Lynda E.

Boose, "'The Getting of a Lawful Race': Racial Discourse in Early Modern England and the Unrepresentable Black Woman," in Hendricks and Parker, *Women, "Race" and Writing*, 35–54.

52. Galenic science posited that women were simply incomplete men, thus the two genders were regarded as part of the same continuum. See Thomas Laqueur, *Making Sex: Body and Gender from Greeks to Freud* (Cambridge, MA: Harvard University Press, 1990); Valerie Traub, *The Renaissance of Lesbianism in Early Modern England* (Cambridge: Cambridge University Press, 2002), esp. 191–97.

53. Paul Freedman, *Images of the Medieval Peasant* (Stanford: Stanford University Press, 1994), 94.

54. Wallace, *Premodern Places*, 200n48.

55. John Weemes, *The Portraiture of the Image of God in Man* (London: M. Flesher and G. Wood, 1627), 279.

56. David H. Aaron, "Early Rabbinical Exegesis on Noah's Son Ham and the So-Called 'Hamitic Myth,'" *Journal of the American Academy of Religion* 63 (1995): 752, is cited by Blackburn, "Old World Background," 91–92, n61. The debate is discussed extensively by Braude, "Sons of Noah."

57. Blackburn, "Old World Background," 92n61.

58. George Sandys, "Relations of Africa," in Samuel Purchas, *Hakluytus Posthumus or Purchas His Pilgrimes* (Glasgow: James MacLehose and Sons, 1905), 6: 213.

59. "The Travels and Most Miserable Captivity of William Davies," (1614), in Thomas Osborne, *A Collection of Voyages and Travels* (London, 1745), 1: 484.

60. Jennifer L. Morgan, "'Some Could Suckle over Their Shoulder': Male Travelers, Female Bodies, and the Gendering of Racial Ideology, 1500–1770," *William and Mary Quarterly*, 3rd Series, 54, no. 1 (January 1997): 167–91.

61. Michael Drayton, "To Master George Sandys, Treasurer for the English Colonie in Virginia" (1622), in *The Works of Michael Drayton*, ed. J. William Hebel (Oxford: B. Blackwell, 1931–41), 3: 206–8.

62. See Linda Woodbridge, *Vagrancy, Homelessness and English Renaissance Literature* (Urbana: University of Illinois Press, 2001), 1–37. Sujata Iyengar argues that as more gypsies were born within England, their existence within a realm that began to define itself in increasingly nationalistic ways became more, not less, difficult (*Shades of Difference*, 177–80). See also Bryan Reynolds, *Becoming Criminal: Transversal Performance and Cultural Dissidence in Early Modern England* (Baltimore: Johns Hopkins UP, 2002).

63. For this centrality see George Mariscal, "The Role of Spain in Contemporary Race Theory," *Arizona Journal of Hispanic Cultural Studies* 2 (1998): 7–23; Deborah Root, "Speaking Christian: Orthodoxy and Difference in Sixteenth-Century Spain," *Representations* 23 (Summer 1998): 118–34; Jerome Friedman, "Jewish Conversion, the Spanish Pure Blood Laws and Reformation: A Revisionist View of Racial and Religious Anti-Semitism," *Sixteenth Century Journal* 18 (1987): 3–29; Andrew C. Hess, *The Forgotten Frontier, A History of the Sixteenth-Century Ibero-African Frontier* (Chicago and London: University of Chicago Press, 1978); David Nirenberg, *Communities of Violence: Persecution of Minorities in the Middle Ages* (Princeton, NJ: Princeton University Press, 1996), 52–99.

64. For a fuller development of this argument, see Loomba, *Shakespeare, Race and Colonialism*, 24–27, 67–70.

65. *An Act against Carnal Copulation between Christian & Heathen, Antigua, 20 November 1644,* "Lawes, Regulations and Orders in force at the Leeward Islands From 1668 to 1672," pp. 49–50, Colonial Papers CO 154/1, Public Record Office, Kew. We are very grateful to Carla Pestana for alerting us to this manuscript and providing us notes for it.

66. We can only cite some representative examples here. Hall, *Things of Darkness;* Traub, *Renaissance of Lesbianism;* Loomba, *Gender, Race, Renaissance Drama;* Hendricks and Parker, *Women, "Race" and Writing;* Hulme, *Colonial Encounters;* Dympna Callaghan, *Shakespeare Without Women;* Iyengar, *Shades of Difference;* Kathleen Brown, "Native Americans and Early Modern Concepts of Race," in *Empire and Others: British Encounters with Indigenous Peoples, 1600–1850,* ed. Martin Daunton and Rick Halpern (Philadelphia: University of Pennsylvania Press, 1999), 79–100, 198–202; Jonathan Goldberg, "Sodomy in the New World: Anthropologies Old and New," *Social Text* 9, no. 4 (1991): 46–56; Ferguson, *Dido's Daughters.* More generally, Anne McClintock, *Imperial Leather: Race, Gender and Sexuality in the Colonial Contest* (New York: Routledge, 1995); Sander Gilman, *Difference and Pathology, Stereotypes of Sexuality, Race and Madness* (Ithaca and London: Cornell University Press, 1985); Nancy Leys Stepan, "Race and Gender, the Role of Analogy in Science," in *The Anatomy of Racism,* ed. David Theo Goldberg (Minneapolis and London, University of Minnesota Press, 1982); Jenny Sharpe, *Allegories of Empire, The Figure of Woman in the Colonial Text* (London and Minneapolis, University of Minnesota Press, 1993); and essays in Andrew Parker, Mary Russo, Doris Sommer, and Patricia Yaegar, eds., *Nationalism and Sexualities* (London: Routledge, 1992).

67. Sir Thomas Herbert, *A relation of some yeares travaile, begunne anno 1626* (London, 1634), 17.

68. Likewise, Jerome Friedman, "Jewish Conversion," indicates that in Reconquista Spain it was feared that the milk of Jewish wet nurses, "being of infected persons," would "engender perverse inclinations" in any Old Christian children they suckled (17).

69. Goldberg, "Racial Americanization," 87.

70. See Gilman, *Difference and Pathology;* Stepan, "Role of Analogy."

71. Hannaford, *Race,* 183.

72. The literature on this subject is by now vast. Talal Asad's introduction to *Anthropology and the Colonial Encounter* (London: Ithaca Press, 1973) is the classic statement of the linkage between colonialism and anthropology; Margaret Hodgen, *Early Anthropology in the Sixteenth and Seventeenth Centuries* (Philadelphia: University of Pennsylvania Press, 1998) details the early modern foundations of the discipline.

73. Bartlett, *Making of Europe,* 197–99. However, Bartlett sees continuities between medieval and modern colonizations as well as between ethnicity and race, and we are indebted throughout to his work. His essay "Medieval and Modern Concepts of Race and Ethnicity" revises his earlier position somewhat, but still argues that the theory of environmental influence on groups and "the social and cultural component of ethnic identity" makes medieval race-thinking qualitatively distinct from psuedo-biological racism.

74. Audrey Smedley, *Race in North America,* quoted by Vijay Prashad, *Everybody Was Kung Fu Fighting* (Boston: Beacon Press, 2001), 15.
75. See Loomba, *Shakespeare, Race and Colonialism,* Chapter 1, for a development of this argument.
76. Sweet, "Iberian Roots," 144.
77. Kathleen Wilson, *The Island Race,* 12. For similar points, see Loomba, *Shakespeare, Race and Colonialism,* 38; Vaughan, *Roots of American Racism,* 163–64; Mariscal, "Role of Spain," 17–18; and Heng, *Empire of Magic,* "Introduction."
78. For nineteenth-century caricatures of the Irish, see L. Perry Curtis, *Apes and Angels: The Irishman in Victorian Caricature* (Washington: Smithsonian Institution Press, 1971).
79. Ann Laura Stoler, "Carnal Knowledge and Imperial Power: Gender, Race, and Morality in Colonial Asia," in *Gender at the Crossroads of Knowledge: Feminist Anthropology in the Postmodern Era,* ed. Micaela di Leonardo (Berkeley: University of California Press, 1991), 51–101. See also Gilman, *Difference and Pathology.*
80. Johannes ab Indagine, *Briefe introductions . . . unto the art of chiromancy . . . and physiognomy* (London: John Daye, 1558), H4^{r-v}.
81. Peter Heylyn, *Microcosmus* (Oxford: John Lichfield and James Short, 1621), 343.
82. James Spedding, Robert Leslie Ellis, and Douglas Denon Heath, eds., *The Works of Francis Bacon* (Boston: H. O. Houghton and Company, 1878), 13: 374.
83. Blumenbach's work *On the Natural Variety of Mankind,* was revised throughout his life, but the most influential version was the third edition of 1795, in which he named the varieties and introduced the term "Caucasian."
84. Sandra Harding, "Science, Race, Culture, Empire," in Goldberg and Solomos, *A Companion to Racial and Ethnic Studies,* 217–28, 220. See also Harding, *Science and Social Inequality, Feminist and Postcolonial issues* (Urbana and Chicago: University of Illinois Press, 2006), 7–8, 73.
85. Pieterse, "Europe and Its Others," 22. See also Martin Barker, *The New Racism* (New York: Greenwood, 1981); and Michel Wieviorka, "The Development of Racism in Europe," in Goldberg and Solomos, *A Companion to Racial and Ethnic Studies,* 462.
86. Stephen Steinberg, "America Again at the Crossroads," in *Theories of Race and Racism: A Reader,* ed. Les Back and John Solomos (London and New York: Routledge, 2000), 568.
87. Pieterse, "Europe and Its Others," 22.
88. Etienne Balibar, "Is There a Neo-racism?" in Etienne Balibar and Immanuel Wallerstein, *Race, Nation, Class: Ambiguous Identities* (New York: Verso, 1991), 22.
89. Albert Memmi, *Racism* (Minneapolis and London: University of Minnesota Press, 2000), 55, 78.
90. Not surprisingly, it is medievalists who have made such arguments most compellingly; see Lisa Lampert, 'Race, Periodicity, and the (Neo-) Middle Ages', *Modern Language Quarterly* 65, no. 3 (2004): 391–421; Kathleen Davis, "Time Behind the Veil: the Media, the Middle Ages and Orientalism Now," in Cohen, *Postcolonial Middle Ages,* 105–22; Heng, *Empire of Magic,* 10–15.

SECTION I

CLASSICAL TEXTS

Aesop (6th Century bce)

Fables

Source: *Mythologia ethica, or, Three centuries of Aesopian fables* (London: Printed for Thomas Hawkins, 1689), 251–52.

Herodotus identifies Aesop as a slave on the Greek island of Samos in the sixth century BCE. Plutarch identifies him as a fabulist at the court of Croesus in Lydia. Some traditions hold him to have been an African and indeed suggest that his name, "Aisopos," is the ancient Greek word for "The Ethiop." Aesop's fable of the Moor or Aethiopian appears in various forms in Bibles (Jeremiah 13), sermons (Dove), and emblem books (Palmer, Whitney) throughout the early modern period, becoming an emblem for both wasted labor and the fixity of color and identity.

Keywords: Washing the Ethiope—Moors—Blackness—Fixity of Color

Fable 34. The *Moor* or Aethiopian.

Strangely was a man mistaken, who having bought an Aethiopian, or Black-a-moor, imagined that that swarthy colour came by the fellow's slothfulness, in neglecting to keep himself clean; and with great labour and industry would fain have washed him white, but it was impossible; for all the many changes of water, and all the pains taken in rubbing and scrubbing him, could not make the Aethiopian change his hue.

This shows the impossibility of changing that which nature has fixed in man; and exposes their folly, who would attempt things which are impossible to be done.

HERODOTUS (484–425? BCE)

The Histories (440 BCE)

Source: *The famous hystory of Herodotus* (London: Printed by Thomas Marshe, 1584), 78ʳ–79ʳ.

Author of the first secular narrative history known to the Western world, Herodotus gathered his material through travels in North Africa and the Near East. Although *The Histories* became a source for later writers on monstrosity and barbarism, it is equally important as an example of comparative ethnography, focusing more on social practices than on physiological traits.

Keywords: Egypt—Inversion of Gender Roles—Diet—Circumcision—
Cannibalism—Black Sperm—Indians

Let us yet proceed to speak further of Egypt, both for that the country itself hath more strange wonders than any nation in the world, and also because the people themselves have wrought sundry things more worthy [of] memory than any other nation under the sun. . . . [A]s in the temperature of the air, and nature of the river, [the Egyptians dissent] from all other: even so in their laws and customs they are unlike and disagreeing from all men.

In this country the women follow the trade of merchandise in buying and selling, also victualing and all kind of sale and chapmandry, whereas contrariwise the men remain at home and play the good housewives in spinning and weaving such like duties.[1] In like manner, the men carry their burdens on their heads, the women on their shoulders. Women make water standing, and men crouching down and cowering to the ground. They discharge and unburden their bellies of that which nature voideth at home, and eat their meat openly in the streets and highways, yielding this reason why they do it, for that . . . such things as be unseemly and yet necessary ought to be done in the eyes and view of all men. No woman is permitted to do service or minister to the gods or goddesses, that duty being proper and peculiar to men. The son refusing to nourish and sustain his parents hath no law to force and constrain him to it, but the daughter be she never so unwilling, is perforce drawn and compelled thereto. The priests and ministers of the gods in other countries wear long hair, and in Egypt are all razed and shaven. Likewise with other people it is an usual custom in sorrowing for the dead to pull their locks, and especially such as are nearest touched with grief, but contrariwise the Egyptians at the decease of their friends suffer their hair to grow, being at other times accustomed to pull and cut it to the stumps. Moreover, the people of all lands use to make difference between their own diet and the food of beasts, saving in Egypt where in barbarous and swinish manner men and beasts feed jointly together. Besides this the

---

[1] Chapmandry = Mercantile business.

people elsewhere have their greatest sustenance by wheat, rye, and barley, which the Egyptians may not taste of without great reproach and contumely, using nevertheless a kind of wheat whereof they make very white and fine bread, which of some is thought to be darnel or bearbarley. This at the first having mingled it with liquor, they work and mold with their feet, kneading the same afterwards with their hands.

In this country also the manner is to circumcise and cut round about the skin from their privy parts, which none other use except those that have taken letter and learned the custom from the Egyptians. The men go in two garments and the women in one, stitching to the inside of the vesture a tape of caddis to gird their apparel close to them, which the people of other regions are wont to wear outwardly. The Graecians in writing and casting account frame their letters and lay their counters from the left hand to the right, the Egyptians contrariwise proceed from the right to the left. . . .

Source for the following extract: Herodotus, *The Histories*, ed. A. D. Godley (1921–24). Free online edition via http://www.perseus. tufts.edu, Section 3, lines 98–101.

. . . There are many Indian nations, none speaking the same language; some of them are nomads, some not; some dwell in the river marshes and live on raw fish, which they catch from reed boats. . . .

Other Indians, to the east of these, are nomads and eat raw flesh; they are called Padaei. It is said to be their custom that when anyone of their fellows, whether man or woman, is sick, a man's closest friends kill him, saying that if wasted by disease he will be lost to them as meat; though he denies that he is sick, they will not believe him, but kill and eat him. . . .

These Indians whom I have described have intercourse openly like cattle; they are all black-skinned, like the Ethiopians. Their semen too, which they ejaculate into the women, is not white like other men's, but black like their skin, and resembles in this respect that of the Ethiopians.[2] These Indians dwell far away from the Persians southwards, and were not subjects of King Darius.

HIPPOCRATES (460–377? BCE)

On Airs, Waters, Places (ca. 400 BCE)

Latin translation published in Scotland: *Hippocrates Contractus* (Edinburgh: J. Reid, 1685).

Source: *On Airs, Waters, Places,* translated by Francis Adams (1849). Free online edition via http://classics.mit.edu/Hippocrates/ airwatpl.html, Sections 14, 16, 17, 23, 24.

[2] The idea that Ethiopian sperm is black appears again in Boemus and Lopes. It would be refuted in later discussions of blackness by Bodin, Abbot, Sandys, Browne, and Bernier.

Referred to as the "Father of Medicine," Hippocrates attributed physical characteristics as well as ailments to an imbalance of the four humors. He held that the humors were glandular secretions and the imbalances resulted from external forces such as food or weather. His theories about the relationship between environment and body appear in *Airs, Waters, Places*, a text that would be cited throughout the early modern period by figures including Jean Bodin, Juan Huarte, Robert Burton, and Thomas Browne.

Keywords: Macrocephali—Asiatic Feebleness—Scythian Amazons— Culture and Nature—Environmental Influence

There is no other race of men which have heads in the least resembling [the Macrocephali]. At first, usage was the principal cause of the length of their head, but now nature cooperates with usage. They think those the most noble who have the longest heads. It is thus with regard to the usage: immediately after the child is born, and while its head is still tender, they fashion it with their hands, and constrain it to assume a lengthened shape by applying bandages and other suitable contrivances whereby the spherical form of the head is destroyed, and it is made to increase in length. Thus, at first, usage operated, so that this constitution was the result of force: but, in the course of time, it was formed naturally; so that usage had nothing to do with it; for the semen comes from all parts of the body, sound from the sound parts, and unhealthy from the unhealthy parts. If, then, children with bald heads are born to parents with bald heads; and children with blue eyes to parents who have blue eyes . . . and if the same may be said of other forms of the body, what is to prevent it from happening that a child with a long head should be produced by a parent having a long head? But now these things do not happen as they did formerly, for the custom no longer prevails owing to their intercourse with other men. . . .

And with regard to the pusillanimity and cowardice of the inhabitants, the principal reason the Asiatics are more unwarlike and of gentler disposition than the Europeans is, the nature of the seasons, which do not undergo any great changes either to heat or cold, or the like; for there is neither excitement of the understanding nor any strong change of the body whereby the temper might be ruffled and they be roused to inconsiderate emotion and passion. . . . It is changes of all kinds which arouse understanding of mankind, and do not allow them to get into a torpid condition. For these reasons, it appears to me, the Asiatic race is feeble, and further, owing to their laws; for monarchy prevails in the greater part of Asia, and where men are not their own masters nor independent, but are the slaves of others, it is not a matter of consideration with them how they may acquire military discipline. . . . Thus, then, if any one be naturally warlike and courageous, his disposition will be changed by the institutions. . . .

In Europe there is a Scythian race, called Sauromatae, which inhabits the confines of the Palus Maeotis, and is different from all other races.[3] Their women mount on horseback, use the bow, and throw the javelin from their horses, and fight with their enemies as long as they are virgins; and they do not lay aside their virginity until they kill three of their enemies, nor have any connection with men until they perform the sacrifices according to law. Whoever takes to herself a husband, gives up riding on horseback unless the necessity of a general expedition obliges her. They have no right breast; for while still of a tender age their mothers heat strongly a copper instrument constructed for this very purpose, and apply it to the right breast, which is burnt up, and its development being arrested, all the strength and fullness are determined to the right shoulder and arm.

The other races in Europe differ from one another, both as to stature and shape, owing to the changes of the seasons. . . . These changes are likely to have an effect upon generation in the coagulation of the semen, as this process cannot be the same in summer as in winter, nor in rainy as in dry weather; wherefore, I think, that the figures of Europeans differ more than those of Asiatics. . . . And the same may be said of their dispositions, for the wild, and unsociable, and the passionate occur in such a constitution; for frequent excitement of the mind induces wildness, and extinguishes sociableness and mildness of disposition, and therefore I think the inhabitants of Europe more courageous than those of Asia; for a climate which is always the same induces indolence, but a changeable climate, laborious exertions both of body and mind. . . .

. . . Such as inhabit a country which is mountainous, rugged, elevated, and well watered, and where the changes of the seasons are very great, are likely to have great variety of shapes among them, and to be naturally of an enterprising and warlike disposition; and such persons are apt to have no little of the savage and ferocious in their nature; but such as dwell in places which are low-lying, abounding in meadows and ill ventilated, and who have a larger proportion of hot than of cold winds, and who make use of warm waters—these are not likely to be of large stature nor well proportioned, but are of a broad make, fleshy, and have black hair; and they are rather of a dark than of a light complexion, and are less likely to be phlegmatic than bilious; courage and laborious enterprise are not naturally in them, but may be engendered in them by means of their institutions. . . . [S]uch as inhabit a high country, and one that is level, windy, and well-watered, will be large of stature, and like to one another; but their minds will be rather unmanly and gentle. Those who live on thin, ill-watered, and bare soils, and not well attempered in the changes of the seasons, in such a country they are likely to be in their persons rather hard and well braced, rather of a blond than a dark complexion, and in disposition and passions haughty and self-willed. . . . [I]n general, you will find the forms and dispositions of mankind to correspond with the nature of the country. . . .

[3] Palus Maeotis = The Sea of Azov.

ARISTOTLE (384–322 BCE)

The Politics (350 BCE)

First English translation by I.D., *Aristotle's politiques, or Discourses of government* (London: Adam Islip, 1598).

Source: Translation by Benjamin Jowett (1905), free online edition via http://www.constitution.org/ari/polit_01.htm, Section V.

Aristotle was a student of Plato and later became tutor to Alexander the Great. In addition to his best-known works such as the *Organum, Physics, Metaphysics, De Anima, Nichomachean Ethics, Eudemian Ethics,* and *Poetics,* Aristotle produced various works of natural science that demonstrate a desire to understand the anatomy and physiology of animals. Although Aristotle saw men as a single and unique genus, his argument in *The Politics* that certain men were naturally subordinate to others would be instrumental to early modern debates on slavery and the conversion of non-European subjects (see John Mair, extracted in this volume).

Keywords: Natural Slavery—Soul and Body—Men and Animals

But is there any one thus intended by nature to be a slave, and for whom such a condition is expedient and right, or rather is not all slavery a violation of nature?

There is no difficulty in answering this question, on grounds both of reason and of fact. For that some should rule and others be ruled is a thing not only necessary, but expedient; from the hour of their birth, some are marked out for subjection, others for rule.

And there are many kinds both of rulers and subjects . . . for in all things which form a composite whole and which are made up of parts, whether continuous or discrete, a distinction between the ruling and the subject element comes to light. Such a duality exists in living creatures, but not in them only; it originates in the constitution of the universe; even in things which have no life there is a ruling principle, as in a musical mode. . . . The same holds good of animals in relation to men; for tame animals have a better nature than wild, and all tame animals are better off when they are ruled by man; for then they are preserved. Again, the male is by nature superior, and the female inferior; and the one rules, and the other is ruled; this principle, of necessity, extends to all mankind.

Where then there is such a difference as that between soul and body, or between men and animals (as in the case of those whose business is to use their body, and who can do nothing better), the lower sort are by nature slaves, and it is better for them as for all inferiors that they should be under the rule of a master. For he who can be, and therefore is, another's and he who participates in rational principle enough to apprehend, but not to have, such a principle, is a slave by nature. . . . Nature would like to distinguish between the bodies of freemen and slaves, making the one strong for servile labor, the other upright, and although useless for such services, useful for political life in the arts both of war and peace. But the opposite often happens—that some have the souls and others have the bodies of freemen. And doubtless if men differed from one another in the mere forms of their bodies as much as the statues of the gods do from men, all would acknowledge that the inferior class should be slaves of the superior. And if this is true of the body, how much more just that a similar distinction should exist in the soul? But the beauty of the body is seen, whereas the beauty of the soul is not seen. It is clear, then, that some men are by nature free, and others slaves, and that for these latter slavery is both expedient and right.

PLINY, THE ELDER (23–79 CE)

The Historie of the World (ca. 77 CE)

Source: *A summarie of the antiquities, and wonders of the worlde, abstracted out of the sixtene first books of the excellent historiographer Plinie . . . , translated out of French into English by I.A.* (London: Henry Denham, 1566), B3ᵛ–B8ᵛ.

The only complete surviving work by the Roman naturalist Gaius Plinius Secundus is the *Historia Naturalis*, a thirty-seven-volume encyclopedia of natural history featuring accounts of monstrous, hybrid races that remained influential well into the seventeenth century. Although Philemon Holland's 1601 translation is the most often cited English edition, an English version of Pierre de Chingy's abstract of Pliny was published in London forty-five years earlier. De Chingy's text does not, however, contain Pliny's influential account of maternal impression, the idea that a child's appearance might be affected by the mother's imagination at the moment of conception.[4]

Keywords: Monstrous Races—Cannibals—Pygmies—Maternal Impression—Childbirth—Libyans—Ethiopians

[4] Another important foundational source for the notion of maternal impression is Helidorus's third-century Greek romance, *Aithiopika*, in which an Ethiopian royal couple gives birth to a white child because the mother has gazed upon the picture of a white woman during conception. The *Aithiopika* was widely translated in the sixteenth century and freely adapted to different locales. It influenced Tasso's *Jerusalem Delivered* and is cited by Thomas Browne in this volume. First printed at Basel in 1534, the *Aithiopika* was translated into English in 1569 by Thomas Underdowne as his *Aethiopian Historie*. Ten years later, Thomas Lupton's *A Thousand Notable Things of Sundrie Sorts*, featured a "noble matron" of Spain who produced a black child, and was accused of having "lain with some one of the slaves of the Saracens" but ultimately freed because it was proved that she had merely looked upon the picture of a Ethiopian.

Of the Ethiopians there are diverse forms and kinds of men. Some there are towards the East, that have neither nose nor nostrils, but the face all full. Others that have no upper lip, they are without tongues, and they speak by signs, and they have but a little hole to take their breath at, by which they drink with an oaten straw. . . . In a part of Africa be people called Ptoemphane, for their king they have a dog, at whose fancy they are governed, to whom they do prognosticate their doings, and their conduct in war. Towards the west there is a people called Arimaspi, that hath but one eye in their foreheads, they are in the desert and wild country. The people called Agriphagi, live with the flesh of panthers and lions; and the people called Anthropophagi, which we call Cannibals, live with human flesh. The Cinamolgi, their heads are almost like to the heads of dogs. . . .

In Libya which is at the end of the Ethiopes, there are people, differing from the common order of others, they have among them no names, and they curse the sun for his great heat, by the which they are all black saving their teeth, and a little the palm of their hands, and they never dream. The others called Troglodites, have caves and holes in the ground, and have no other houses. Others called Gramantes, they make no marriages, but all women are common. Gamphasantes they go all naked. Blemmy is a people so called; they have no heads, but have their mouth and their eyes in their breasts. And others there are that go more by training of their hands than with their feet. . . .

In India there are high men, and also marvelous high beasts, as for a witness there are dogs as great as asses, trees as high as any archer can scarce shoot to the top, and under the shadow of one fig tree may a hundred horses stand, because of the fertility of the land, the temperance of the air, and the abundance of waters, there are men five cubits in height, the which never use to spit, nor are troubled with pain of the head, eyes, or teeth, and are seldom sick. Others there are in the mountains, with heads like dogs. In a part of India the women never bear children but once, whose children wax straightaway old. And others called Sciopedae that have their feet so broad that when they are laid, they cover them therewith from the heat of the sun, and they be very swift in running. Some toward the East have no heads but have eyes in their shoulders, and others called Epithami Pigmei that are of one yard high. In the farther part of India towards the East near to the River of Ganges, there is a people clad with leaves, that live by smelling, they never eat nor drink in their journeys, they bear flowers and roots to smell at, and they are easily killed by filthy smells and savours. There are little men called Pigmei, among which the highest passeth not the height of two cubits, having a wholesome air and pleasant country where they dwell, the which men are molested with cranes, as writeth Homer. . . .

Some there are in the valleys called Pandore that live two hundred years, in their youth having white hair, in age their hairs become black. There is a people that have long hairy tails growing. These things and others hath nature made monstrous, for our examples. Among the women there are diverse childings, some have had six children, some eight, and some nine, and sometimes children of diverse kinds, which are called hermaphrodites, which are both man and woman. There hath been that have had in their lifetime thirty children, and among the marvels of the world, a child being new born did enter again into his mother's womb, in the city of Saguntra. And it is no fable nor tale, to have seen women and maids transformed into men. . . .

From *The Historie of the world. Commonly called, the naturall historie of C. Plinius Secundus, translated into English by Philemon Holland* (London: Adam Islip, 1601), Book VII, Chap. XII, p. 161.

Examples of many that have been very like and resembled one another

. . . Some women there be that bring all their children like themselves; and others again, as like to their husbands; and some like neither the one nor the other. Ye shall have women bring all their daughters like to their fathers, and contrariwise, their sons like the mothers. The example is notable, and yet undoubted true, of one Nicæus, a famous wrestler of Constantinople, who having to his mother a woman begotten in adultery by an Ethiopian, and yet with white skin, nothing different from other women of that country, was himself black, and resembled his grandsire, the Ethiopian abovesaid. Certes, the cogitations and discourses of the mind make much for these similitudes and resemblances whereof we speak; and so likewise many other accidents and occurrent objects, are thought to be very strong and effectual therein, whether they come by sight, hearing, and calling to remembrance; or imaginations only conceived, and deeply apprehended in the very act of generation, or the instant of conception. The wandering cogitation also and quick spirit either of father or mother, flying to and fro all on a sudden, from one thing to another, at the same time, is supposed to be one cause of this impression, that maketh either the foresaid uniform likeness, or confusion and variety.

CLAUDIUS PTOLEMAEUS (ca. 90 CE–ca. 168 CE)

Tetrabiblos (2ND CENTURY CE)

Source: http://penelope.uchicago.edu/Thayer/E/Roman/Texts/ Ptolemy/Tetrabiblos/2A*.html#2.

Ptolemy, as he is known in English, was a geographer, astronomer, and astrologer who lived in the Hellenistic culture of Roman Egypt. The *Tetrabiblos*, his four-book treatise on the influence of the planets on man, circulated in Arabic, Greek, and Latin manuscripts before its initial publication in Latin in Nürnberg in 1535. No English edition appeared before 1701, but Latin editions circulated widely. Ptolemy's designation of national characteristics according to latitudinal position was enormously influential throughout the classical and medieval periods and was engaged with by many of the early modern texts in this volume (Mair, Lopes, D'Anghiera, Gainsh).

Keywords: Climatic Theory—Lines of Latitude—Ethiopians—Scythians

Book 2, Section 2: Of the Characteristics of the Inhabitants of the General Climes.

The demarcation of national characteristics is established in part . . . through [people's] position relative to the ecliptic and the sun. For while the region which we inhabit is in one of the northern quarters, the people who live under the more southern parallels, that is, those from the equator to the summer tropic, since they have the sun over their heads and are burned by it, have black skins and thick, woolly hair, are contracted in form and shrunken in stature, are sanguine of nature, and in habits are for the most part savage because their homes are continually oppressed by the heat; we call them by the general name Ethiopians. . . .

Those who live under the more northern parallels, . . . since they are far removed from the zodiac and the heat of the sun, are therefore cooled; but because they have a richer share of moisture . . . they are white in complexion, straight-haired, tall and well-nourished, and somewhat cold by nature; these too are savage in their habits because their dwelling-places are continually cold. . . . We call these men, too, by a general name, Scythians.

The inhabitants of the region between the summer tropic and the Bears, however, since the sun is neither directly over their heads nor far distant at its noon-day transits, share in the equable temperature of the air, which varies, to be sure, but has no violent changes from heat to cold. They are therefore medium in colouring, of moderate stature, in nature equable, live close together, and are civilized in their habits. The southernmost of them are in general more shrewd and inventive, and better versed in the knowledge of things divine because their zenith is close to the zodiac and to the planets revolving about it. Through this affinity the men themselves are characterized by an activity of the soul which is sagacious, investigative, and fitted for pursuing the sciences specifically called mathematical. . . .

SECTION II

THE BIBLE

The Bible

Source: *The Holy Bible conteyning the Olde Testament, and the Newe* (London: Robert Barker, 1611).

In 1604 James I convened forty-seven scholars to produce an "authorized" translation of the Bible. Seven years later the assembled churchmen produced a text that was accessible, familiar, and devoid of the inflammatory anti-Catholicism that marked the very popular Geneva Bible (1560). In time, the "King James Version" would become the most printed book in history. It was generally accepted as the standard English Bible for more than three centuries and was the first English-language Bible printed in America. The biblical passages excerpted here were central to arguments about cultural difference, skin color, crossbreeding, slavery, conversion, and polygenesis throughout the medieval and early modern periods, and are cited in dozens of works in this volume.

Keywords: Sons of Noah—Slavery—Babel—Jacob and Laban—
Maternal Impression—Crossbreeding—Blackness—Washing
the Ethiope White—Blood

Genesis 9:18–27

And the sons of Noah that went forth of the ark were Shem, and Ham, and Japheth: and Ham is the father of Canaan. These are the three sons of Noah: and of them was the whole earth overspread. And Noah began to be an husbandman, and he planted a vineyard: And he drank of the wine, and was drunken; and he was uncovered within his tent. And Ham, the father of Canaan, saw the nakedness of his father, and told his two brethren without. And Shem and Japheth took a garment, and laid it upon both their shoulders, and went backward, and covered the nakedness of their father; and their faces were backward, and they saw not their father's nakedness. And Noah awoke from his wine, and knew what his younger son had done unto him. And he said, Cursed be Canaan; a servant of servants shall he be unto his brethren. And he said, Blessed be the Lord God of Shem; and Canaan shall be his servant. God shall enlarge Japheth, and he shall dwell in the tents of Shem; and Canaan shall be his servant.

Genesis 11:1–9

And the whole earth was of one language, and of one speech. . . . And they said, Go to, let us build us a city and a tower, whose top may reach unto heaven; and let us make us a name, lest we be scattered abroad upon the face of the whole earth. And the Lord came down to see the city and the tower, which the children of men builded. And the Lord said, Behold, the people is one, and they have all one language; and this they begin to do: and now nothing will be restrained from them, which they have imagined to do. Go to, let us go down, and there confound their language, that they may not understand one another's speech. So the Lord scattered them abroad from thence upon the face of all the earth: and they left off to build the city. Therefore is the name of it called Babel; because the Lord did there confound the language of all the earth: and from thence did the Lord scatter them abroad upon the face of all the earth.

Genesis 30:25–43

And it came to pass, when Rachel had born Joseph, that Jacob said unto Laban, Send me away, that I may go unto mine own place, and to my country. Give me my wives and my children, for whom I have served thee, and let me go: for thou knowest my service which I have done thee. And Laban said unto him, I pray thee, if I have found favour in thine eyes, tarry: for I have learned by experience that the Lord hath blessed me for thy sake. And he said . . . Thou knowest how I have served thee, and how thy cattle was with me. For it was little which thou hadst before I came, and it is now increased unto a multitude; and the Lord hath blessed thee since my coming: and now when shall I provide for mine own house also? And he said, What shall I give thee? And Jacob said, Thou shalt not give me any thing: if thou wilt do this thing for me, I will again feed and keep thy flock. I will pass through all thy flock today, removing from thence all the speckled and spotted cattle, and all the brown cattle among the sheep, and the spotted and speckled among the goats: and of such shall be my hire. . . . And Laban said, Behold, I would it might be according to thy word. And he removed that day the he goats that were ringstraked and spotted, and all the she goats that were speckled and spotted, and every one that had some white in it, and all the brown among the sheep, and gave them into the hand of his sons. And he set three days' journey betwixt himself and Jacob: and Jacob fed the rest of Laban's flocks. And Jacob took him rods of green poplar, and of the hazel and chestnut tree; and pilled white strakes in them, and made the white appear which was in the rods.[1] And he set the rods which he had pilled before the flocks in the gutters in the watering troughs when the flocks came to drink, that they should conceive when they came to drink. And the flocks conceived before the rods, and brought forth cattle ringstraked, speckled, and spotted. And Jacob did separate the lambs, and set the faces of the flocks toward the ringstraked, and all the brown in the flock of Laban; and he put his own flocks by themselves, and put them not unto Laban's cattle. And it came to pass, whensoever the stronger cattle did conceive, that Jacob laid the rods before the eyes of the cattle in the gutters, that they might conceive among the rods. . . . And the man increased exceedingly, and had much cattle, and maidservants, and menservants, and camels, and asses.

Leviticus 19:19–20

. . . Ye shall keep my statutes. Thou shalt not let thy cattle gender with a diverse kind: thou shalt not sow thy field with mingled seed: neither shall a garment mingled of linen and woollen come upon thee. And whosoever lieth carnally with a woman that is a bondmaid, betrothed to an husband, and not at all redeemed, nor freedom given her; she shall be scourged; they shall not be put to death, because she was not free.

Leviticus 25:38–46

I am the Lord your God, which brought you forth out of the land of Egypt, to give you the land of Canaan, and to be your God. And if thy brother that dwelleth by thee be waxen poor, and be sold unto thee; thou shalt not compel him to serve as a bondservant: But as an hired servant, and as a sojourner, he shall be with thee, and shall serve thee unto the year of Jubilee: And then shall he depart from thee, both he and his children with him, and shall return unto his own family, and unto the possession of his fathers shall he return. For they are my servants, which I brought forth out of the land of Egypt: they shall not be sold as bondmen. Thou shalt not rule over him with rigour; but shalt fear thy God. Both thy bondmen, and thy bondmaids, which thou shalt have, shall be of the heathen that are round about you; of them shall ye buy bondmen and bondmaids. Moreover of the children of the strangers that do sojourn among you, of them shall ye buy, and of their families that are with you, which they begat in your land: and they shall be your possession. And ye shall take them as an inheritance for your children after you, to inherit them for a possession; they shall be your bondmen for ever: but over your brethren the children of Israel, ye shall not rule one over another with rigor.

Song of Solomon 1:1–15

The Song of Songs, which is Solomon's. Let him kiss me with the kisses of his mouth: for thy love is better than wine. . . . Draw me, we will run after thee: the

---

[1] Pilled strakes = Pealed streaks.

king hath brought me into his chambers: we will be glad and rejoice in thee, we will remember thy love more than wine: the upright love thee. . . . I am black, but comely, O ye daughters of Jerusalem, as the tents of Kedar, as the curtains of Solomon. Look not upon me, because I am black, because the sun hath looked upon me: my mother's children were angry with me; they made me the keeper of the vineyards; but mine own vineyard have I not kept.

Song of Solomon 5:8–14

I charge you, O daughters of Jerusalem, if ye find my beloved, that ye tell him, that I am sick of love. What is thy beloved more than another beloved, O thou fairest among women? What is thy beloved more than another beloved, that thou dost so charge us? My beloved is white and ruddy, the chiefest among ten thousand. His head is as the most fine gold, his locks are bushy, and black as a raven. His eyes are as the eyes of doves by the rivers of waters, washed with milk, and fitly set. His cheeks are as a bed of spices, as sweet flowers: his lips like lilies, dropping sweet smelling myrrh. His hands are as gold rings set with the beryl: his belly is as bright ivory overlaid with sapphires. . . . His mouth is most sweet: yea, he is altogether lovely. This is my beloved, and this is my friend, O daughters of Jerusalem.

Acts 17:24–27

God that made the world and all things therein, seeing that he is Lord of heaven and earth, dwelleth not in temples made with hands. Neither is worshipped with men's hands, as though he needed any thing, seeing he giveth to all life, and breath, and all things. And hath made of one blood all nations of men for to dwell on all the face of the earth, and hath determined the times before appointed, and the bounds of their habitation. That they should seek the Lord, if haply they might feel after him, and find him, though he be not far from every one of us.

Galatians 4:22–31

For it is written, that Abraham had two sons, the one by a bondmaid, the other by a freewoman. But he who was of the bondwoman was born after the flesh; but he of the freewoman was by promise. Which things are an allegory: for these are the two covenants; the one from the Mount Sinai, which gendereth to bondage, which is Agar. For this Agar is Mount Sinai in Arabia, and answereth to Jerusalem which now is, and is in bondage with her children. But Jerusalem which is above is free, which is the mother of us all. . . . Now we, brethren, as Isaac was, are the children of promise. But as then he that was born after the flesh persecuted him that was born after the Spirit, even so it is now. Nevertheless what sayeth the scripture? Cast out the bondwoman and her son: for the son of the bondwoman shall not be heir with the son of the freewoman. So then, brethren, we are not children of the bondwoman, but of the free.

Jeremiah 13:23–25

And if thou say in thine heart, Wherefore come these things upon me? For the greatness of thine iniquity are thy skirts discovered, and thy heels made bare. Can the Ethiopian change his skin, or the leopard his spots? Then may ye also do good, that are accustomed to do evil. Therefore will I scatter them as the stubble that passeth away by the wind of the wilderness. This is thy lot, the portion of thy measures from me, sayeth the Lord; because thou hast forgotten me, and trusted in falsehood.

From The Geneva Bible (1560)

Can the black Moor change his skin? Or the leopard his spots? Then may ye also do good that are accustomed to do evil.

From The Bishop's Bible (1568)

May a man of Inde change his skin, and the cat of the mountain her spots? So may ye that be exercised in evil do good?

SECTION III

MEDIEVAL TEXTS

St. Augustine, Bishop of Hippo (354–430 CE)

The City of God (ca. 413–426 CE)

Source: *Of the citie of God with the Learned Comments of Io. Lod. [Juan Luis] Vives,* translated by John Healey (London: George Eld, 1610), 580–82.

Augustine was born in the Roman province of Numidia (now Algeria). In 391 CE, during a visit to Hippo (now Annaba in Algeria), he was chosen against his will to be a Christian priest, and later became a bishop. Augustine's discussion of monstrous races would be influential in early modern debates over the theory of polygenesis (see Paracelsus, Bruno, Whitaker, Boyle, and Hale), which held that all men might not be derived from the same biblical patriarch.

Keywords: Monstrosity—Monogenesis

Whether Adam's or Noah's sons begot any monstrous kinds of men

It is further demanded whether Noah's sons, or rather Adam's (of whom all mankind came), begot any of those monstrous men that are mentioned in profane histories, as some that have but one eye in their mid fore-head; some with their heels where their toes should be; some with both sexes in one, & their right pap a man's & the left a woman's, & both begetting and bearing children in one body; some without mouths, living only by air and smelling; some but a cubit high, called Pigmies, of the Greek word; some, where the women bear children at the fifth year of their age; some that have but one leg . . . being called Sciopodæ, because they sleep under the shade of this their foot; some neck-less, with the face of a man in their breasts. . . . What shall I speak of the Cynocephali that had dogs' heads and barked like dogs? Indeed we need not believe all the monstrous reports that run concerning this point. But whatsoever he be that is man, that is, a mortal reasonable creature, be his form, voice, or what ever never so different from an ordinary man's, no faithful person ought to doubt that he is of Adam's progeny.[1] . . . For God made all, and when or how he would form this or that, he knows best, having the perfect skill how to beautify this universe by opposition and diversity of parts. But he that cannot contemplate the beauty of their whole stumbles at the deformity of the part, not knowing the congruence that it hath with the whole. . . . In our time (some few years ago) was one born that was two from the middle up-wards, and but one down-ward. This was in the East. He had two heads, two breasts, four hands, one belly and two feet, and lived so long that a multitude of men were eyewitness of this shape of his.

But who can reckon all the births extraordinary? Wherefore as we may not say but those are really descended from the first man, so what nations soever have shapes different from that which is in most men and seem to be exorbitant from the common form, if they be definable to be reasonable creatures and mortal, they must be acknowledged for Adam's issue. . . . Wherefore to close this question up with a sure lock, either the stories of such monsters are plain lies, or if there be such, they are either no men, or if they be men they are the progeny of Adam.

PETER ABELARD (1079–1142)

Letter 4 to Héloïse (ca. 1130–36)

Source: *The Letters of Abelard and Héloïse,* translation and introduction by Betty Radice (New York: Penguin, 1974), 138–40.

Abelard's discussion of the bride of the Canticles in a letter sent to his cloistered lover, Héloïse, anticipates later exegeses that insist that the bride's blackness can be nothing more than a metaphor for her tribulations. At the same time, it compares her to Ethiopian women in terms that are not simply metaphorical. For his controversial theological stances, Abelard was subsequently persecuted by Bernard of Clairvaux, whose commentary on the bride follows.

Keywords: Song of Songs—Blackness—Skin Color—Skin Texture— Ethiopian Women—Sexuality

The bride in the Canticles, an Ethiopian (such as the one Moses took as a wife) rejoices in the glory of her special position and says: "I am black but lovely, daughters of Jerusalem; therefore the king has loved me and brought

---

[1] Augustine's term here is "protoplastos."

me into his chamber."² And again, "Take no notice of my darkness, because the sun has discoloured me." In general it is the contemplative soul which is described in these words and especially called the bride of Christ. . . .

The Ethiopian woman is black in the outer part of her flesh and as regards exterior appearance looks less lovely than other women; yet she is not unlike them within, but in several respects she is whiter and lovelier, in her bones, for instance, or her teeth. Indeed, whiteness of teeth is also praised in her spouse, in reference to "his teeth whiter than milk." And so she is black without but lovely within; for she is blackened outside in the flesh because in this life she suffers bodily affliction through the repeated tribulations of adversity, according to the saying of the Apostle: "Persecution will come to all who want to live a godly life as Christians."³ As prosperity is marked by white, so adversity may properly be indicated by black. . . .

She is black too in outward things because while she is still an exile on life's pilgrimage, she keeps herself humble and abject in this life so that she may be exalted in the next, which is hidden with Christ in God, once she has come into her own country. So indeed the true sun changes her colour because the heavenly love of the bridegroom humbles her in this way, or torments her with tribulations lest prosperity lifts her up. He changes her colour, that is, he makes her different from other women who thirst for earthly things and seek worldly glory. . . .

. . . Indeed, the disfigurement of her blackness makes her choose what is hidden rather than open, what is secret and not known to all, and any such wife desires private, not public delights with her husband, and would rather be known in bed than seen at table. Moreover it often happens that the flesh of black women is all the softer to touch though it is less attractive to look at, and for this reason the pleasure they give is greater and more suitable for private than for public enjoyment, and their husbands take them into a bedroom to enjoy them rather than parade them before the world.

BERNARD OF CLAIRVAUX (1091–1153)

On the Song of Songs (ca. 1136–53)

Source: Bernard of Clairvaux, *Cantica Canticorum: Eighty-Six Sermons on the Song of Solomon,* edited by Samuel J. Eales (London: Elliot Stock, 1895), 150–54.

A key figure in the spread of the Cistercian order in France, Bernard exercised enormous influence on both political and ecclesiastical affairs. He led an eight-year (1130–38) struggle to elect Innocent II; persuaded Lombardy to accept Emperor Lothair II; held great influence with popes, particularly his former pupil, Eugene III; preached the Second Crusade; and was instrumental

² Numbers 12:1.
³ 2 Timothy 3:12.

in the condemnation of Abelard and Arnold of Brescia. Among
his most influential writings, Bernard's eighty-six sermons on
the Canticles offer the possibility that Jesus himself was black,
although that blackness is never explicitly ascribed to his skin.

Keywords: Song of Songs—Blackness—Blackness of Christ

Sermon 25: That the Bride, namely, the Church, is Black, yet Comely.

Let us examine now that which is said: *I am black, but comely.* Is this not
a contradiction in terms? By no means. I speak for the unlearned, who are
unable to distinguish between colour and form—form is inherent in the
composition of the thing spoken of; colour is but the quality of it. Not everything, then, which is black, is necessarily on that account ill-favoured. . . . She
is black, perhaps on account of the life that she led formerly in the shadow,
under the control of the prince of this world, in which she still bore the image
of the earthly; while she is beautiful with the image of the heavenly, with
which, when afterwards she walked in the newness of life, she was thenceforth
invested. . . . If we consider the exterior of those who are holy, how humble
and abject it is, how vile and neglected in outward appearance; and yet, at the
very same time they are inwardly contemplating with unveiled face the glory
of the Lord, they are being transformed into the same image from glory to
glory, as by the Spirit of the Lord. . . . does it not seem to you that each of
these souls will be able to reply to those who reproach him with his blackness:
I am black, but comely? . . . This being so, the bride has good ground for
counting that as a glory to herself which by her envious rivals is blamed as a
deformity, and to boast not only of her beauty, but also of her blackness. She
does not blush for her blackness, which she knows that her spouse in former
days likewise bore. . . . It is, so to speak, a blackness, but a blackness that is
the form and likeness of the Lord Jesus. . . . He was truly black, who had no
form nor comeliness; black, because He was a worm and no man, a reproach
of men, and despised of the people. . . . Behold him! Covered with rags, livid
with stripes, defiled with spitting, pale with the pallor of death; can you even
then hesitate to confess he is black?

BARTHOLOMAEUS ANGLICUS (ca. 1201–72)
De Proprietatibus Rerum (ca. 1230–40)

Source: Robert Steele, *Mediaeval Lore from Bartholomew Anglicus.* Free
online edition via http://www.gutenberg.org/dirs/etext04/
mdvll10.txt; Section IV, Medieval Geography.

In addition to glossing places and things mentioned in the Bible, the
Franciscan Bartholomaeus's encyclopedia, *De Proprietatibus Rerum
(Encyclopedia on the Properties of Things),* collected for the first time
Greek, Jewish, and Arabic scholarly views on medical and scientific

MEDIEVAL TEXTS 63

subjects and surveyed different regions of the world. As a result, his commentary exemplifies the way in which competing modes of differentiating groups might coexist in early works. Intended as an aid to study and preaching, it was translated into English by John Trevisa in 1398, and printed by Wynkyn de Worde in 1495.

Keywords: Amazons—Marriage—Englishness—Ethiopia—India—Monstrosity—Childbirth—Ireland—Scotland—Body Painting—Scarification

Amazonia, women's land, is a country part in Asia and part in Europe, and is nigh to Albania, and hath that name of Amazonia, of women that were the wives of the men that were called Goths, the which men went out of the nether Scythia, and were cruelly slain, and then their wives took their husbands' armor and weapons, and reised on the enemies with manly hearts, and took wreck of the death of their husbands.[4] For with dint of sword they slew all the young males, and old men, and children, and saved the females, and departed prey, and purposed to live ever after without company of males. . . . And they were made so fierce warriors in short time, that they had a great part of Asia under their lordship nigh a hundred years: among them they suffered no male to live nor abide, in no manner of wise. But of nations that were nigh to them, they chose husbands because of children, and went to them in times that were ordained, and when the time was done, then they would compel their lovers to go from them, and get other places to abide in, and would slay their sons, or send them to their fathers in certain times. And they saved their daughters, and taught them to shoot and to hunt. And for the shooting of arrows should not be let with great breasts, in the 7th year (as it is said), they burnt off their breasts, and therefore they were called Amazons. . . .[5]

England . . . is beclipped all about by the sea, and departed from the roundness of the world, and hight sometimes Albion: and had that name of white rocks, which were seen on the sea cliffs. And by continuance of time, lords and noble men of Troy, after that Troy was destroyed, went from thence, and were accompanied with a great navy, and fortuned to the cliffs of the foresaid island, and . . . as it is said . . . fought with giants long time that dwelled therein, and overcame the giants, both with craft and with strength, and conquered the island, and called the land Britain, by the name of Brute that was prince of that host. . . . And long time after, the Saxons won the island with many and diverse hard battles and strong, and their offspring had

[4] To reise = To go on a military expedition; To take wreck = Revenge.
[5] Versions of this account appear in William Painter's *The palace of pleasure beautified* . . . (1566) and in *The history of Diodolus Siculus . . . done into English by H.C., Gent.* Other accounts of Amazons in this volume include those by Mandeville and Raleigh. In his essay "Of Cripples," Montaigne writes that in the Amazon Republic, "to evade the dominion of the males, they lamed them in their infancy—arms, legs, and other members that gave them advantage over them, and only made use of them in that wherein we, in these parts of the world, make use of them."

possession after them of the island, and the Britons were slain or exiled. . . . Isidore sayeth, that this land hight Anglia, and hath that name of Angulus, a corner, as it were land set in the end, or a corner of the world. But Saint Gregory, seeing English children to sell at Rome, when they were not christened, and hearing that they were called English: according with the name of the country, he answered and said: Truly they be English, for they shine in face right as angels: it is need to send them message, with word of salvation. For as Beda sayeth, the noble kind of the land shone in their faces. . . .

Ethiopia, blue men's land, had first that name of colour of men.[6] For the sun is nigh, and roasteth and toasteth them. And so the colour of men showeth the strength of the star, for there is continual heat. . . . In this land be many nations with diverse faces wonderly and horribly shapen: Also therein be many wild beasts and serpents. . . . There be two Ethiopias, one is in the east, and the other is in Mauritania in the west, and that is more near Spain. . . . The men of Ethiopia have their name of a black river, and that river is of the same kind as Nilus. . . . In the wilderness there be many men wonderly shapen. Some oft curse the sun bitterly in his rising and down going, and they behold the sun and curse him always: for his heat grieveth them full sore. And other as Troglodytes dig them dens and caves, and dwell in them instead of houses; and they eat serpents, and all that may be got; their noise is more fearful in sounding than the voice of other. Others there be which like beasts live without wedding, and dwell with women without law, and such be called Garamantes. Others go naked, and be not occupied with travail, and they be called Graphasantes.[7] There be other that be called Bennii, and it is said, they have no heads, but they have eyes fixed in their breasts. And there be Satyrs, and they have only shape of men, and have no manners of mankind. . . .

. . . And as among all countries and lands India is the greatest and most rich: so among all lands India is most wonderful. . . . In India be many huge beasts bred, and more greater hounds than in other lands. . . . Also there be men of great stature, passing five cubits in height, and they never spit, nor have never headache nor toothache, nor sore eyes, nor they be not grieved with passing heat of the sun, but rather made more hard and sad therewith. . . . Also there, in some mountains be men with soles of the feet turned backwards, and the foot also with 8 toes on one foot. Also there be some with hounds' heads, and be clothed in skins of wild beasts, and they bark as hounds, and speak none otherwise. . . . Also among some nations of India be women that bear never child but once, and the children wax whitehaired anon as they be born. There be satyrs and other men wondrously shapen. Also in the end of East India, about the rising of Ganges, be men without mouths, and they be clothed in moss and in rough hairy things, which they gather off trees, and live commonly by odor and smell at the nostrils. And they neither eat nor

---

[6] See the black and blue Ethiopians in *Cursor Mundi* in this volume.

[7] The Garamantes and their alleged promiscuity were first described at length by the third-century CE Roman geographer Solinus. The name Graphasantes was far less common, but English authors commonly applied their characteristic idleness to a range of ethnographic subjects in the early modern period, including Irish, African, Native American, and Javanese people.

drink, but only smell odor of flowers and of wood apples, and live so, and they die anon in evil odor and smell. And other there be that live full long, and age never, but die as it were in middle age. Also some be hoar in youth, and black in age. . . .

Solinus speaketh of Ireland, and sayeth the inhabitants thereof be fierce, and lead an unhuman life. The people there use to harbor no guests, they be warriors, and drink men's blood that they slay, and wash first their faces therewith: right and unright they take for one. Men of Ireland be singularly clothed and unseemly arrayed and scarcely fed, they be cruel of heart, fierce of cheer, angry of speech, and sharp. Nevertheless they be free hearted, and fair of speech and goodly to their own nation, and namely those men that dwell in woods, marshes, and mountains. These men . . . give them more to plays and to hunting, than to work and travail.

The land Scotia hath the name of Scots that dwell therein, and the same nation that was sometime first in Ireland, and all according thereto in tongue, in manners, and in kind. The men are light of heart, fierce, and courageous on their enemies . . . and though the men be seemly enough of figure and of shape, and fair of face generally by kind, yet their own Scottish clothing disfigures them full much. And Scots be said in their own tongue of bodies painted, as it were cut and slit. For in old time they were marked with diverse figures and shapes on their flesh and skin, made with iron pricks. And by cause of meddling with Englishmen, many of them have changed the old manners of Scots into better manners for the more part, but the wild Scots and Irish account great worship to follow their forefathers in clothing, in tongue, and in living, and in other manner doing . . .

ANONYMOUS

Cursor Mundi (13TH CENTURY CE)

Cursor Mundi is a 30,000-line Christian history of the world. It was probably composed in the thirteenth century, in the north or northeast Midlands. The most complete manuscript, dating from the late fourteenth century, is Cotton MS. Vesp. Aiii, held in the British Library. Lines 8071–8128 reproduced here have been translated from the Middle English by Kellie Robertson. The representation of supernatural black conversion excerpted here is in keeping with the popular notion that to alter blackness was an impossibility.

Keywords: Saracens—Skin Color—Deformity—Conversion—Noble Blood

> They proceeded down the high street,
> Four Saracens going to meet the king;
> They were black and blue as lead.

They carried with them great treasure,
The likes of which no man had ever seen before that hour.
Such ill-shaped creatures!
Their blackness was truly a wonder;
Their mouths were set in their chests;
Their brows were long and wide
And hung down around their ears.
Their mouths were wide, their eyes broad;
Unhappily were those faces made!
Their eyes were set in their foreheads,
But they could not glance upwards.
Their arms, covered in matted hair,
Were joined to their trunks at the elbows.
Their knees were crooked and their backs hunched.
The king wondered at them and spoke;
When they drew near to the king,
None could hold back their laughter.[8]
The Saracens kneeled down,
And greeted the king courteously,
Saying to him in this manner,
"Sir, be you safe now and always,
That thing that you have, let us see;
For, God willing, we would find it.
Show us the saving tree, Sir King,
For we know well, without lying,
On that tree he will suffer torture,
The king of bliss and all his people.
Show us the tree that all will stand in wonder of,
For that is why we have come.
You have stared at us enough,
Seen our ill-favored shape.
For we are loathely, and the wicked man
Is deformed in both soul and body.
The three rods there within their root,
They contain the remedy against all evils.
Right before your eyes, they will restore to us
All our fairness, through the grace of the Lord.
From them redemption will still come,
And they will pledge their pardon to all
Those who ask mercy for their sins
From Jesus of David's kin;
Let us prove the strength of them."
At this the king took off his glove;

---

[8] Because this line seems to be corrupt in the Cotton manuscript, the translator has substituted the sense of the other three versions.

The branches of such great bliss,
He held them out for the Saracens to kiss.
They kneeled down and kissed them quickly;
Their skin became white as milk,
Taking its colour from noble blood,
And all their bodies were transformed.
No limb had been left out,
Since in their place the same were set.
The Saracens fell to their knees before the king
And made their prayer to him.
All those who had seen this marvel,
They cried for joy and gave thanks to the Lord.

ANDREW HORN (d.1328)

The mirrour of justices (ca. 1290)

First published in French in London in 1642; First English translation by
W.H. [William Hughes] (London: Matthew Walbancke, 1646).

Source: Andrew Horne, *The Mirrour of Justices,* ed. William C. Robinson
(Washington D.C.: John Byrne & Co., 1903), 122–24.

Originally written in Old French, Andrew Horn's *Mirrour* is a
handbook of legal rules derived from various sources. Of especial
interest here is Horn's justification of serfdom with reference to
Noah's curse of Canaan, a biblical citation that would later be
central to discussions of skin color and blackness in particular. The
first printed edition was 1642. It was then translated in 1646.

Keywords: Slavery—Sons of Noah

Chapter 2. Section 28: Of villeinage and niefty[9]

The villeinage of man is a subjection of such great antiquity, that by the
memory of man no free stock can be found thereof; which slavery according to some is the curse which Noah gave to Caanan the son of Cham his
son, and to his issue, and according to others of the Philistines, who became
slaves at the battle which was betwixt David and the children of Israel of the
one party, and Goliath the Philistine on the other part.

And as other creatures are kept in inclosures, so are villains kept to guard
the possessions of their lords, and from thence are said regardants; and so men
are villains by the law of God, by the law of man, and by the canon law.[10]

---

[9] Villeinage and niefty are interchangeable terms signifying the tenure by which a villain, or
serf, held or occupied his land while subject to a lord or superior.
[10] Regardants = Serfs attached to a manor.

From Shem and Japhet come the gentile Christians, and from Cham, the villains which the Christians may give away, or sell as they do other chattels, but not devise by will, because they are astriers, who are annexed to the frank-tenement, and of them there are many others.[11]

MARCO POLO (1254–1324)

Description of the World (1298)

First English version: *The most noble and famous travels of Marcus Paulus,* trans. John Frampton (London, Ralph Newberry, 1579).

Source: "The first Booke of Marcus Paulus Venetus, or of Master Marco Polo, a Gentleman of venice, his Voyages" in Samuel Purchas, *Hakluytus Posthumus, or Purchas his Pilgrimes* (Glasgow: James MacLehose and Sons, 1905–07), Volume XI: 233, 236–37, 247–48, 295, 298, 299, 300, 301.

In his own writings, the Venetian Marco Polo claims to have traveled through Palestine, Persia, and Afghanistan, to arrive in 1275 at Kublai Khan's capital at Cambaluc (Peking). More than twenty years later, while in a Genoese prison, he dictated his account of the East (*Divisament dou monde*) to Rusticiano of Pisa. While some scholars doubt whether Polo made the trip at all, none deny that fifteenth-century Latin editions of his report of Eastern wealth and sophistication encouraged the establishment of trade routes to China, Japan, and the East Indies throughout the early modern period.

Keywords: China—Kublai Khan—Wealth—Money—Polygamy— Java—Pygmies

In this book I purpose to write of all the great and marvelous acts of the present Can called Cublai Can, which is in our tongue Lord of Lords, the greatest prince in peoples, cities and treasures that ever was in the world. He . . . is the sixth emperor of that country, beginning to reign in the year of our Lord 1256, being twenty seven years old and ruling the people with great wisdom and gravity. . . .

Cublai is a comely and fair man of mean stature, of a red and white face, black and goodly eyes, well fashioned nose, and all the lineaments of his body consisting of a due proportion. He hath four wives which he accounteth lawful, and the first-born of them succeedeth him in the kingdom. And every one of these is called empress, and holdeth a peculiar court, and that princely in a proper palace, having about three hundred chosen hand-maids, and

[11] Astriers = Residents at a particular hearth or house. Frank-tenement = Freehold.

maid-servants, and many eunuch servants, and at least ten thousand persons in their family. The king also hath many concubines.

There is a certain nation of fair people, Tartars, called Ungut, whither every second year he sendeth ambassadors to purvey the fairest lasses for him of greatest esteem for beauty, which bring him four or five hundred more or less as they see cause. . . .

Three months of the year, to wit, December, January and February, Cublai remaineth ordinarily in Cambalu . . . and there on the south part by the new city is seated a great palace . . . the greatest that hath been seen. . . . It has no ceiling, but a very high roof: the foundation of the pavement ten palms high, with a wall of marble round about it, two paces wide, as it were a walk. In the end of the wall without, is a fair turret with pillars. In the walls of the halls and chambers are carved dragons, soldiers, birds, beasts of diverse kinds, histories of wars, gilded. The roof is so made, that nothing is seen but gold and imagery. In every square of the palace is a great hall of marble, capable of great multitudes. The chambers are disposed the best that may be devised: the roof is red, green, azure, and of all colours. Behind the palace are great rooms, and private store-houses for his treasures and jewels, for his women, and other secret employments. . . .

It is incredible what multitudes of people, merchants and merchandises of all sorts are seen in Cambalu. The money of the Great Can is not made of gold or silver, or other metal, but they take the middle bark from the mulberry tree, and this they make firm, and cut it into diverse and round pieces, great and little, and imprint the King's mark thereon. Of this matter therefore, the Emperor causeth an huge mass of money to be made in the city of Cambalu, which sufficeth for the whole empire: and no man under pain of death may lawfully coin any other, or spend any other money, or refuse it in all his kingdoms and countries. Nor any coming from any other kingdom dare spend any other money in the empire of the great Can. Whereby it cometh to pass that Merchants often coming from far remote countries and regions unto the city of Cambalu bring with them gold, silver, pearl, and precious stones, and receive the King's money for them. And because this money is not received in their countries, they change it again in the Empire of the great Can for merchandise, which they carry away with them. . . . Wherefore, there is not a king to be found in this world, who exceedeth him in treasure, not expended on the mint as elsewhere. . . .

[In Felech, one of the islands near Java] the idolators by frequent trade of the Saracens are converted to the law of Mahomet, in the cities, the mountainers being beastly, eating man's flesh and all impure food; and worship all day what they first see in the morning. Next to that is Basma, which hath a language by it self; they live without law, like beasts and sometimes send hawks to the Can . . . for presents. . . . They have apes, and of diverse fashions. . . . There are certain small apes faced like men, which they put in boxes, and preserve with spices, and sell them to merchants, who carry them through the world for pygmies or little men. . . .

JOHN MANDEVILLE

The voyages and travailes of Sir John Mandevile knight (ca. 1366)

Source: *The Travels of Sir John Mandeville*, ed. David Price (Macmillan and Co., 1900). Free online edition via http://www.gutenberg. org/dirs/etext97/tosjm10h.htm.

First produced anonymously in France, *The Voyages de Jehan de Mandeville Chevalier* details the alleged adventures of an English knight who traveled for many years throughout Egypt, Jerusalem, China, and other non-Christian lands. It was first published in English in 1496, and by 1500 it circulated in German, Italian, Dutch, Spanish, Irish, Danish, Czech, and Latin. Cobbled together from earlier travel narratives, encyclopedias, and the alleged *Letter of Prester John,* it was the most widely read travel narrative of the medieval and early modern world, used by other writers to embellish their own tales, and supposedly relied upon by Christopher Columbus and Martin Frobisher for practical geographical information. Mandeville's descriptions of monstrous races were both repeated and challenged in the early modern period (see Sir Walter Raleigh and George Abbot in this volume).

Keywords: Saracens—Muhammad—Amazons—Ethiopians—Skin Color—Marriage Practices—Cannibalism—Monstrous Races—China—the Great Khan—Sons of Noah—Jews

Chapter 15

Now, because that I have spoken of Saracens and of their country—now, if ye will know a part of their law and of their belief, I shall tell you after that their book that is clept Alkaron telleth . . . that the good shall go to paradise, and the evil to hell; and that believe all Saracens. And if a man ask them what paradise they mean, they say, to paradise that is a place of delights where men shall find all manner of fruits in all seasons, and rivers running of milk and honey, and of wine and of sweet water; and that they shall have fair houses and noble, every man after his desert, made of precious stones and of gold and of silver; and that every man shall have four score wives all maidens, and he shall have ado every day with them, and yet he shall find them always maidens. . . .

And ye shall understand that Mahomet was born in Arabia, that was first a poor knave that kept camels, that went with merchants for merchandise. And so befell, that he went with the merchants into Egypt; and they were then Christian in those parts. . . . After began he . . . to wax wise and rich. . . . And . . . he took the lady to wife that hight Gadrige. And Mahomet fell often in the great sickness that men call the falling evil; wherefore the lady was full sorry that ever she took him to husband. But Mahomet made her to believe, that all times, when he fell so, Gabriel the angel came for to speak with him, and for the great light and brightness of the angel he might not sustain him from falling. . . .

Chapter 17

Beside the land of Chaldea is the land of Amazonia, that is the land of Feminye. And in that realm is all women and no man; not, as some men say, that men may not live there, but for because that the women will not suffer no men amongst them to be their sovereigns.

For sometime there was a king in that country. And men married, as in other countries. And so befell that the king had war with them of Scythia, the which king hight Colopeus, that was slain in battle, and all the good blood of his realm. And when the queen and all the other noble ladies saw that they were all widows, and that all the royal blood was lost, they armed them and, as creatures out of wit, they slew all the men of the country that were left; for they would that all the women were widows as the queen and they were. . . . And when they will have any company of man then they draw them towards the lands marching next to them. And then they have loves that use them; and they dwell with them an eight days or ten, and then go home again. And if they have any knave child they keep it a certain time, and then send it to the father when he can go alone and eat by himself; or else they slay it. And if it be a female they do away that one pap with an hot iron. And if it be a woman of great lineage they do away the left pap that they may the better bear a shield. And if it be a woman on foot they do away the right pap, for to shoot with bow turkeys: for they shoot well with bows. . . .[12]

And from that other coast of Chaldea, toward the south, is Ethiopia, a great country that stretcheth to the end of Egypt. Ethiopia is departed in two parts principal, and that is in the east part and in the meridional part; the which part meridional is clept Mauritania; and the folk of that country be black enough and more black than in the other part, and they be clept Moors. . . . In Ethiopia, when the children be young and little, they be all yellow; and, when that they wax of age, that yellowness turneth to be all black. In Ethiopia is the city of Saba, and the land of the which one of the three kings that presented our Lord in Bethlehem, was the king of. . . .

Chapter 20

. . . And a fifty-two days' journey from this land that I have spoken of, there is another land that is full great, that men clepe Lamary. In that land is full great heat. And the custom there is such, that men and women go all naked. And they scorn when they see any strange folk going clothed. . . . And they say, that they that be clothed be folk of another world, or they be folk that trow not in God. And they say, that they believe in God that formed the world,

---

[12] This discussion of Amazons later appears in a digested form in John Bulwer's *Anthropometamorphosis*.

and that made Adam and Eve and all other things. And they wed there no wives, for all the women there be common and they forsake no man. And they say they sin if they refuse any man; and so God commanded to Adam and Eve and to all that come of him, when he said, *Crescite et multiplicamini et replete terram.*[13] . . . And when they have children, they may give them to what man they will that hath companied with them. And also all the land is common. . . . And also all the goods of the land be common . . . and every man there taketh what he will without any contradiction, and as rich is one man there as is another.

But in that country there is a cursed custom, for they eat more gladly man's flesh than any other flesh; and yet is that country abundant of flesh, of fish, of corns, of gold and silver, and of all other goods. Thither go merchants and bring with them children to sell to them of the country, and they buy them. And if they be fat they eat them anon. And if they be lean they feed them till they be fat, and then they eat them. And they say that it is the best flesh and the sweetest of all the world.

Chapter 22

In one of these [South Asian?] isles be folk of great stature, as giants. And they be hideous for to look upon. And they have but one eye, and that is in the middle of the front. And they eat nothing but raw flesh and raw fish. . . . And in another isle toward the south dwell folk of foul stature and of cursed kind that have no heads. And their eyes be in their shoulders. . . . And in another isle be folk that have the face all flat, all plain, without nose and without mouth. But they have two small holes, all round, instead of their eyes, and their mouth is . . . also without lips. . . . And in another isle be folk of foul fashion and shape that have the lip above the mouth so great, that when they sleep in the sun they cover all the face with that lip. . . . And in another isle there be little folk, as dwarfs. . . . And they have no mouth; but instead of their mouth they have a little round hole, and when they shall eat or drink, they take through a pipe or a pen or such a thing, and suck it in, for they have no tongue; and therefore they speak not, but they make a manner of hissing as an adder doth, and they make signs one to another as monks do, by the which every of them understandeth other. . . . And in another isle be folk that have great ears and long, that hang down to their knees. . . . And in another isle be folk that have horses's feet. And they be strong and mighty, and swift runners; for they take wild beasts with running, and eat them. . . . And in another isle be folk that go upon their hands and their feet as beasts. And they be all skinned and feathered, and they will leap as lightly into trees, and from tree to tree, as it were squirrels or apes. . . . And in another isle be folk that be both man and woman, and they have kind; of that one and of that other. And they have but one pap on the one side, and on that other none. And they have members of generation of man and woman, and they use both when they list, once that one, and another time that other. And they get children,

[13] "Be fruitful, and multiply, and replenish the earth" (Genesis 1:28).

when they use the member of man; and they bear children, when they use the member of woman. . . .

Chapter 23

Cathay is a great country and a fair, noble and rich, and full of merchants. Thither go merchants all years for to seek spices and all manner of merchandises, more commonly than in any other part. And ye shall understand, that merchants that come from Genoa or from Venice or from Romania or other parts of Lombardy, they go by sea and by land eleven months or twelve, or more some-time, ere they may come to the isle of Cathay that is the principal region of all parts beyond. . . .

And [at] great solemn feasts before the [Great Chan's] table men bring great tables of gold, and thereon be peacocks of gold and many other manner of diverse fowls, all of gold and richly wrought and enameled. And men make them dance and sing, clapping their wings together, and make great noise. And whether it be by craft or by necromancy I wot never. . . . But I have the less marvel, because that they be the most subtle men in all sciences and in all crafts that be in the world: for of subtlety and of malice and of farcasting they pass all men under heaven.[14] And therefore they say themselves, that they see with two eyes and the Christian men see but with one, because that they be more subtle than they. For all other nations, they say, be but blind in cunning and working in comparison to them. . . .

Chapter 24

Ye shall understand that all the world was destroyed by Noah's flood, save only Noah and his wife and his children. Noah had three sons, Shem, Cham, and Japhet. This Cham was he that saw his father's privy members naked when he slept, and scorned them, and showed them with his finger to his brethren in scorning wise. And therefore he was cursed of God. And Japhet turned his face away and covered them. . . .

These three brethren had seisin in all the land.[15] And this Cham, for his cruelty, took the greater and the best part, toward the east, that is clept Asia, and Shem took Africa, and Japhet took Europe. And therefore is all the earth parted in these three parts by these three brethren. Cham was the greatest and the most mighty, and of him came more generations than of the other. And of his son Chus was engendered Nimrod the giant, that was the first king that ever was in the world; and he began the foundation of the tower of Babylon. And that time, the fiends of hell came many times and lay with the women of his generation and engendered on them diverse folk, as monsters and folk disfigured, some without heads, some with great ears, some with one eye, some giants, some with horses' feet, and many other diverse shape against kind. And of that generation of Cham be come the Paynims and

[14] Farcasting = Forethought, shrewdness, cunning.
[15] Seisin = Possession.

diverse folk that be in isles of the sea by all Ind. And forasmuch as he was the most mighty, and no man might withstand him, he cleped himself the son of God and sovereign of all the world. And for this Cham, this emperor clepeth him Cham, and sovereign of all the world. . . .

And of the generation of Shem be come the Saracens. And of the generation of Japhet is come the people of Israel. And though that we dwell in Europe, this is the opinion, that the Syrians and the Samaritans have amongst them. . . . Natheles, the sooth is this; that Tartars and they that dwell in the great Asia, they came of Cham; but the Emperor of Cathay clepeth him not Cham, but Can, and I shall tell you how.[16]

Chapter 29

In that same region be the mountains of Caspian that men clepe Uber in the country. Between those mountains the Jews of ten lineages be enclosed, that men clepe Gog and Magog and they may not go out on no side. . . .

And also ye shall understand, that the Jews have no proper land of their own for to dwell in, in all the world, but only that land between the mountains. And yet they yield tribute for that land to the Queen of Amazonia, the which that maketh them to be kept in close full diligently, that they shall not go out on no side but by the coast of their land; for their land marcheth to those mountains. . . .

And yet, natheles, men say they shall go out in the time of anti-Christ, and that they shall make great slaughter of Christian men. And therefore all the Jews that dwell in all lands learn always to speak Hebrew, in hope, that when the other Jews shall go out, that they may understand their speech, and to lead them into Christendom for to destroy the Christian people. . . .

---

[16] Thus in this widely disseminated work, Ham is considered the father of the Great Khan and the ancestor of the Mongols, Shem the progenitor of Africans, and Japhet of Europeans and "the people of Israel." From the fifteenth century on, this division of the world was reordered, with Ham being assigned Africa, and Shem Asia (see, for example, the extract from George Best in this volume).

SECTION IV

EARLY MODERN TEXTS

JOHN MAIR (ca. 1469–1547)

In Secundum Librum Sententiarum (Paris, 1519)

Source: Anthony Pagden, *The Fall of Natural Man: The American Indian and the Origins of Comparative Ethnology* (New York: Cambridge University Press, 1982), 38.

The Scottish theologian John Mair achieved celebrity as a writer and teacher at the Collège de Sorbonne in Paris. In 1510, he wrote *In Secundum Sententiarum,* a work that considers the legitimacy of Christian rule over pagans. Here, in his commentary on the second of Peter Lombard's *Sentences,* Mair draws on Aristotle's *Politics* (a text that was little known at the time) to locate Native Americans within a moral and theological framework.

Keywords: Natural Slavery—New World—Aristotle

These people [the inhabitants of the Antilles] live like beasts on either side of the equator; and beneath the poles there are wild men as Ptolemy says in his *Tetrabiblos.* And this has now been demonstrated by experience, wherefore the first person to conquer them, justly rules over them because they are by nature slaves. As the philosopher [Aristotle] says in the third and fourth chapters of the first book of the *Politics,* it is clear that some men are by nature slaves, others by nature free; and in some men it is determined that there is such a thing [i.e., a disposition to slavery] and that they should benefit from it. And it is just that one man should be a slave and another free, and it is fitting that one man should rule and another obey, for the quality of leadership is also inherent in the natural master. On this account the philosopher says in the first chapter of the aforementioned book that this is the reason why the Greeks should be masters over the barbarians, because, by nature, the barbarians and slaves are the same.

PARACELSUS (1493–1541)

Das Buch von der Gebärung (1520) and *Astronomia Magna* (1537–38)

Source: J.S. Slotkin, *Readings in Early Anthropology* (Chicago: Aldine Publishing Company, 1965), 42. *Das Buch von der Gebärung* first appeared in Latin in *Operum Medico-Chimicorum Sive Paradoxorum . . .* (Frankfurt, 1603).

Born Theophrastus Bombastus von Hohenheim, Paracelsus was dissatisfied with traditional approaches to healing, and traveled throughout Europe and possibly the Levant, looking for alternative medical treatments. His rejection of traditional theories, particularly the humoral theory developed by Galen, and his belief that disease derived from external factors, earned him the contempt of his contemporaries. He is of interest here primarily for his contributions to ongoing debates over the theory of polygenesis.

Keywords: Monstrosity—Polygenesis—New World

Das Buch von der Gebärung

The same god, who gives and has given everything, and who is known by philosophy, did not allow such forms and so many kinds of people to come from one father but from many, and neither did he order anything unnatural or monstrous, but given all an equal soul, though not similar forms, for quite manifold forms have been born through the father. It might also seem proper to tell who was the first father of the bipeds, if we could calculate back; however, this is not philosophical, but would be an amusing joke. In order to know the first father from whom all children are born, we must have been there; therefore, what philosophy will tell us how he was born?

Astronomia Magna

However this may be, we are all descended from Adam, and we are all those that ought to be called men, and our first father was made by God with his hands. . . . That is the creation of man. But still another thing has to be considered, namely, that the children of Adam did not inhabit the whole world. That is why some hidden countries have not been populated by Adam's children, but through another creature, created like men outside of Adam's creation. For God did not intend to leave them empty, but has populated the miraculously hidden countries with other men. . . . [T]hat is why it is not necessary to prove that the people in the hidden countries are descended from Adam.

. . . And I cannot refrain from making a brief mention of those who have been found in hidden islands and are still little known. To believe that they have descended from Adam is difficult to conceive—that Adam's children have gone to the hidden islands. But one should well consider, that these people are from a different Adam. It will be difficult to maintain that they are related on the basis of flesh and blood.

ANDREA VESALIUS (1514–64)

De Humani Corporis Fabrica (Basel: Joannis Oporini, Mense Junio, 1543)

Source: J.S. Slotkin, *Readings in Early Anthropology* (Chicago: Aldine Publishing Company, 1965), 40.

While lecturing on surgery and carrying out anatomical experiments on the bodies of executed Paduan criminals, the Belgian physician Andreas van Wesele produced the work for which he is best remembered, *De Humani Corporis Fabrica* (*On the Fabric of the Human Body*). This work countered the prevailing understanding of physiology established by Galen, the second-century anatomist whose knowledge of the human body derived from the physiology of animals. The discussion here of the influence of customs on the body draws on Hippocrates and is in dialogue with later writers such as Bodin and Huarte.

Keywords: Shapes of Heads—Midwives—Artifice

It seems that certain nations have something peculiar in the shape of their head. The heads of Genoese, and more particularly of Greeks and Turks, almost exhibit a round shape. To this also (which not a few of them think elegant and consider to be well adapted to the turbans which they use in various ways) the midwives sometimes contribute at the urgent request of the mother. The Germans, indeed, have a very flattened occiput and a broad head, because the boys always lie on their backs in their cradles.[1] . . . More oblong heads are reserved to the Belgians . . . because their mothers permit their little boys to sleep turned over in their beds, and as much as possible on their sides.

MARTIN LUTHER (1483–1546)

"Of the Jews and their Lies" (1543)

Source: *Luther's Works, The Christian in Society IV*, Vol. 47, Ed. Franklin Sherman, Trans. Martin H. Bertram (Philadelphia: Fortress Press, 1971), 268–78.

This principal figure of the German Reformation preached that salvation derived from God's grace, received through the

---

[1] Occiput = The posterior of the head.

individual's faith, and not through his or her deeds. His ver-
nacular translation of the New Testament (1522) was intended
to provide laypersons access to the word of God. Luther is often
remembered as the charismatic figure behind the 95 Theses,
which questioned, among other things, the pope's right to grant
indulgences. In the 1530s he moved from advocating the civic
emancipation of Jews to justifying the destruction of their property and their banishment.

Keywords: Jews—Blood Libel—Poisoners—Indolence—Expulsion
        of Jews

[The Jews] have been bloodthirsty bloodhounds and murderers of all Christendom for more than fourteen hundred years in their intentions, and would
undoubtedly prefer to be such with their deeds. Thus they have been accused
of poisoning water and wells, of kidnapping children, of piercing them
through with an awl, of hacking them in pieces, and in that way secretly
cooling their wrath with the blood of Christians, for all of which they have
often been condemned to death by fire. . . .

What shall we Christians do with this rejected and condemned people, the
Jews? . . . I shall give you my sincere advice:

First, to set fire to their synagogues or schools and to bury and cover
with dirt whatever will not burn, so that no man will ever again see a stone
or cinder of them. . . . Second, I advise that their houses also be razed and
destroyed. . . . Third, I advise that all their prayer books and Talmudic
writings, in which such idolatry, lies, cursing, and blasphemy are taught,
be taken from them. . . . Fourth, I advise that their rabbis be forbidden to
teach henceforth on pain of loss of life and limb. . . . Fifth, I advise that safe-
conduct on the highways be abolished completely for the Jews. . . . Sixth,
I advise that usury be prohibited to them, and that all cash and treasure of
silver and gold be taken from them. . . . Seventh, I recommend putting a
flail, an ax, a hoe, a spade, a distaff, or a spindle into the hands of young,
strong Jews and Jewesses and letting them earn their bread in the sweat of
their brow, as was imposed on the children of Adam (Gen. 3: 19). For it is
not fitting that they should let us accursed *Goyim* toil in the sweat of our
faces while they, the holy people, idle away their time behind the stove, feasting and farting, and on top of all, boasting blasphemously of their lordship
over the Christians by means of our sweat.[2] No, one should toss out these
lazy rogues by the seat of their pants. . . .

I have read and heard many stories about the Jews which agree with this
judgment of Christ, namely, how they have poisoned wells, made assassina-
tions, kidnapped children, as related before. I have heard that one Jew sent
another Jew, and this by means of a Christian, a pot of blood, together with a
barrel of wine, in which when drunk empty, a dead Jew was found. There are

---

[2] Goyim = Jewish designation of a non-Jew, a Gentile.

many other similar stories. For their kidnapping of children they have often been burned at the stake or banished. . . . I am well aware that they deny all of this. However, it all coincides with the judgment of Christ which declares that they are venomous, bitter, vindictive, tricky serpents, assassins, and children of the devil who sting and work harm stealthily wherever they cannot do it openly. For this reason I should like to see them where there are no Christians. The Turks and other heathen do not tolerate what we Christians endure from these venomous serpents and young devils. Nor do the Jews treat any others as they do us Christians. That is what I had in mind when I said earlier that, next to the devil, a Christian has no more bitter and galling foe than a Jew. There is no other to whom we accord as many benefactions and from whom we suffer as much as we do from these base children of the devil, this brood of vipers.

QUEEN MARY I (1516–58) AND KING PHILIP (1527–98)

An act against certain persons calling themselves Egyptians (1554)

Source: Danby Pickering (ed.), *The Statutes at Large* (Cambridge: J. Bentham, 1763), 27.

In early modern England, gypsies were referred to as Egyptians and were widely supposed to have originally come from Egypt. Such confusion became part of English legal vocabulary (see Cowell's dictionary of legal terms, *The Interpreter,* extracted in this volume). From 1530 onward, English authorities repeatedly banished gypsies from the realm and forbade their alleged use of sorcery and other tricks. The following Act was passed in the reign of Mary Tudor (1553–58) and her consort, Philip, heir to the throne of Spain. It differs from later legislation enforced under Elizabeth I in its linking of gypsy status to non-participation in the legal economy.

Keywords: Gypsies—Egyptians—Falsehood—Englishness—Expulsion of Gypsies

Whereas in a parliament holden at Westminster in the twenty-second year of the reign of our late sovereign lord King Henry the Eighth, for the avoiding and banishing out of this realm of certain outlandish people calling themselves Egyptians, using no craft nor feat of merchandises for to live by, but going from place to place in great companies, using great, subtle and crafty means to deceive the king's subjects, bearing them in hand, that they by palmistry could tell men's and women's fortunes, and so many times by craft and subtlety deceive the people of their money, and committed diverse great and heinous felonies and robberies, to the great hurt and deceit of the people; it was amongst other things then enacted, that from the time of the making of the said act no such persons should be suffered to come within the king's realm, upon pain of forfeiture to the King of all their goods and chattels, and then to be commanded to avoid the realm, within fifteen days next after the commandment upon pain of imprisonment; and such persons calling themselves Egyptians, as were then within this realm, should depart within sixteen days next after proclamation of the said act, upon pain of imprisonment, and forfeiture of all their goods and chattels . . . forasmuch as diverse of the said company, and such other like persons, not fearing the penalty of the said statute, have enterprised to come over again into this realm . . . to the perilous and evil example of our sovereign lord and lady the King and Queen's Majesties most living subjects, and to the utter and extreme undoing of diverse and many of them. . . .

II. For the reformation whereof, be it ordained and enacted . . . that if any person or persons . . . do willingly transport, bring or convey into this realm of England or Wales, any such persons calling themselves, or commonly called, Egyptians, then he or they . . . shall forfeit and lose for every time so offending, forty pounds of lawful money of England.

III. And be it further enacted . . . that if any of the said persons called Egyptians, which shall be transported and conveyed into this realm of England or Wales as is aforesaid, do continue and remain within the same by the space of one month, that then he or they so offending shall by virtue of this act be deemed and judged a felon and felons . . . and shall therefore suffer pains of death, loss of lands and goods, as in cases of felony. . . .

VII. . . . [T]his present act . . . shall not extend to any of the said persons commonly calling themselves Egyptians, which within the said time of twenty days next after the said proclamation is made as is aforesaid, shall leave that naughty, idle and ungodly life and company, and be placed in the service of some honest and able inhabitant or inhabitants within this realm, or that shall honestly exercise himself in some lawful work or occupation. . . .

JOHANNES BOEMUS (ca. 1485–1535)

The fardle of facions conteining the anciente maners, customes, and lawes, of the peoples enhabiting the two parts of the earth, called Affrike and Asie (London: John Kingstone and Henry Sutton, 1555), L1ʳ⁻ᵛ.

Johannes Boemus's popular Latin work on the manners, laws, and customs of peoples ancient and modern, *Omnium Gentium Mores,* was first published in Augsburg in 1520. By the early seventeenth century it had appeared in twenty-three editions and five languages, including the English, *The fardle of facions.* Although he has been called the "first anthropologist," Boemus draws primarily on older sources such as Herodotus rather than incorporating recent eyewitness accounts of the New World. His account of Indian "blackness" draws on Aristotle's "one-seed" theory of conception, whereby the child's appearance is determined by the father alone.

Keywords: India—Blackness—Blackness of Seed—Simplicity of Indians

Chapter 8: Of Inde, and the uncouth trades and manners of life of the people therein.

All the Indians generally wear long hair: dyed either after a bright ash colour, or else an orange tawny. Their chief jewels, are of pearl and precious stones. Their apparel is very diverse: and in few, one like another. Some go in mantles of woollen, some of linen, some naked, some only breeched to cover the privities, and some wrapped about with pilles, and lithe barks of trees. They are all by nature black of hue: even so dyed in their mother's womb according to the disposition of the father's nature, whose seed also is black: as likewise in the Aethiopians, tall men and strongly made. They are very spare feeders, namely when they are in camp. Neither delight they in much praise. . . . They live by law, but not written. They have no knowledge of letters, but administer altogether without book. And for which they are void of guile, and of very sober diet: all things prospereth well with them. They drink no wine, but when they sacrifice to their gods. . . .

. . . They have no laws concerning pledges or things committed to another man's keeping. No witnessings, no handwritings, no sealings, no such like tokens of treachery and untrust: but without all these, they trust and be trusted, they believe and are believed, yea, they oftentimes leave their houses wide open without keeper. Which truly are all great signs of a just and upright dealing among them.

PIETRO MARTIRE D'ANGHIERA (1457–1526)

The decades of the newe worlde or West India . . ., translated by Richard Eden, (London: Guilhelmi Powell, 1555), aii^r–aiv^v, 208–9, 310–11.

Peter Martyr, as he was known to the English, was a Milanese scholar who, as a member of Charles V's Council of the Indies, was charged with the task of collecting the writings of European travelers to the New World. His masterwork, *The decades,* includes letters describing the exploits of Columbus, Balboa, Cortes, Magellan, Davila, and others. It was published in installments from 1516 to 1530, and translated into English in 1555 by Richard Eden. In addition to adding more recent Spanish accounts, Eden censured the English for their failure to emulate Spain in its two-pronged mission of civilizing the Americas while exorcising Europe of Muslims and Jews.

Keywords: Spanish Colonialism—Spanish Expulsions—Conversion—
          Native Americans—Marriage Practices—Interracial Sex—
          Nakedness—Childbirth—Skin Color

Richard Eden to the Reader

It is . . . apparent that the heroic facts of the Spaniards of these days deserve
so great praise that the author of this book (being no Spaniard) doth wor-
thily extol their doing above the famous acts of Hercules and Saturnus and
such other, which for their glorious and virtuous enterprises were accounted
as gods among men. . . . But some will say, they possess and inhabit [the
Indians'] regions and use them as bondmen and tributaries, where before they
were free. They inhabit their regions indeed: yet so, that by their diligence and
better manuring the same, they may now better sustain both, than one before.
Their bondage is such as is much rather to be desired than their former liberty,
which was to the cruel cannibals rather a horrible licentiousness than a liberty,
and to the innocent so terrible a bondage that in the midst of their fearful
idleness they were ever in danger to be a prey to those manhunting wolves.
But now . . . the Spaniards, as the ministers of grace and liberty, brought unto
these new gentiles the victory of Christ's death, whereby they being subdued
with the worldly sword are now made free from the bondage of Satan's
tyranny. . . . [A]ll good wits and honest natures (I doubt not) will not only
rejoice to see the kingdom of God to be so far enlarged upon the face of the
earth, to the confusion of the devil and the Turkish Antichrist, but also do the
uttermost of their power to further the same. . . . Is it not well known to all
the world what a defense and brazen wall [the King of Spain] hath been to all
Christendom in that he hath quite driven out of Spain the Moors or Saracens
and Jews, which so many hundred years possessed a great part of Spain to no
small danger of the whole Christian Empire, and yet could never before be
clean vanquished until the days of this noble and Catholic prince? . . . The
which thing doubtless may seem so much the greater and more difficult,
forasmuch as in the midst of the chief heat of his chargeable wars against the
Moors of Granada he even then and at the same time sent forth ships for the
conquesting of the Indies, as though he and the nation of the Spaniards had
been appointed by God either to subdue the enemies of the faith or to bring
them to Christ's religion. . . . [A]lthough some will object that the desire of
gold was the chief cause that moved the Spaniards and Portugals to search the
new-found lands, . . . yet doth it not follow that it was the only cause, forasmuch as nothing letteth but that a man may be a warrior or a merchant, and
also a Christian. . . . Even so may these barbarians by the only conversation
with the Christians (although they were enforced thereto) be brought to such
familiarity with civility and virtue that not only we may take great commodity
thereby, but they may also herewith imbibe true religion as a thing accidental, although neither they nor we should seek the same. For like as they that
go much in the sun are coloured therewith although they go not for that

purpose, so may the conversation of the Christians with the gentiles induce them to our religion, where there is no greater cause of contrary to resist as is in the Jews and Turks, who are already drowned in their confirmed error. But these simple gentiles, living only after the law of nature, may well be likened to a smooth and bare table unpainted or a white paper unwritten, upon the which you may at the first paint or write what you list, as you cannot upon tables already painted, unless you raze or blot out the first forms. . . .

Of the manners and customs of the Indians of the firm land, and of their women[3]

The manners and customs of these Indians are diverse in diverse provinces. Some of them take as many wives as they list, and others live with one wife, whom they forsake not without consent of both parties, which chanceth especially when they have no children. The nobility, as well men as women, repute it infamous to join with any of base parentage or strangers, except Christians, whom they count noble men by reason of their valiantness, although they put a difference between the common sort and the other to whom they show obedience, counting it for a great matter and an honorable thing if they be beloved of any of them. In so much that if they know any Christian man carnally, they keep their faith to him, so that he be not long absent far from them. . . . Many of them have this custom, that when they perceive that they are with child, they take an herb wherewith they destroy that is conceived. For they say that only well-aged women should bear children, and that they will not forbear their pleasures and deform their bodies with bearing of children, whereby their teats become loose and hanging, which thing they greatly dispraise. When they are delivered of their children they go to the river and wash them. Which done, their blood and purgation ceaseth immediately. And when after this they have a few days abstained from the company of men, they become so straight, as they say which have had carnal familiarity with them, that such as use them cannot without much difficulty satisfy their appetite. They also which never had children are ever as virgins. In some parts they wear certain little [aprons] round about them before and behind, as low as to their knees and hams, wherewith they cover their privy parts, and are naked all their body beside. The principal men bear their privities in a hollow pipe of gold: but the common sort have them enclosed in the shells of certain great whelks, and are beside utterly naked. For they think it no more shame to have their cod seen than any other part of their bodies. And in many provinces both the men and women go utterly naked without any such coverture at all. . . .

[A] thing which I have often times noted in these Indians . . . is, that they have the bones of the skulls of their heads four times thick and much

---

[3] Eden's source is Gonzalo Fernandes de Oviedo, *Historia general y natural de las Indias Occidentales* (Seville, 1535).

stronger than ours. So that in coming to hand strokes with them, it shall be requisite not to strike them on the heads with swords. For so have many swords been broken on their heads with little hurt done. . . .

Of the colour of the Indians[4]

One of the marvelous things that God useth in the composition of man is colour, which doubtless cannot be considered without great admiration in beholding one to be white and another black, being colours utterly contrary. Some likewise to be yellow which is between black and white, and other of other colours, as it were of diverse liveries. And as these colours are to be marveled at, even so is it to be considered how they differ one from another as it were by degrees, forasmuch as some men are white after diverse sorts of whiteness, yellow after diverse manners of yellow, and black after diverse sorts of blackness; and how from white they go to yellow after discolouring to brown and red, and to black by ash colour, and murrey somewhat lighter than black, and tawny like unto the west Indians which are all together in general either purple, or tawny like unto sod quinces, or of the colour of chestnuts or olives, which colour is to them natural and not by their going naked as many have thought, albeit their nakedness have somewhat helped thereunto.[5] Therefore in like manner and with such diversity as men are commonly white in Europe and black in Africa, even with like variety are they tawny in these Indies, with diverse degrees diversely inclining more or less to black or white. No less marvel is it to consider that men are white in Seville and black at the cape of Buena Speranza, and of chestnut colour at the river of Plata, being all in equal degrees from the equinoctial line. Likewise that the men of Africa and Asia that live under the burnt line (called Zona Torrida) are black, and not they that live beneath or on this side the same line as in Mexico, Yucatan, Quauhtema, Lian, Nicaragua, Panama, Santo Domingo, Paria, Cape, Saint Augustine, Lima, Quito, and other lands of Peru which touch in the same equinoctial. . . . By reason whereof it may seem that such variety of colours proceedeth of man, and not of the earth, which may well be although we be all born of Adam and Eve, and know not the cause why God hath so ordained it, otherwise than to consider that his divine majesty hath done this as infinite other to declare his omnipotency and wisdom in such diversities of colours as appear not only in the nature of man, but the like also in beasts, birds, and flowers. . . . Another thing is also greatly to be noted as touching these Indians. And this is that their hair is not curled as is the Moors' and Ethiopians' that inhabit the same clime, neither are they bald except very seldom, and that by little. All which things may give further occasion to philosophers to search the secrets of nature and complexions of men with the novelties of the New World.

---

[4] Eden's source is Francisco Lopez de Gomara, *La historia general de las Indias con la conquista de Mejico y de la Nueva Espana* (Medina, 1553; Antwerp, 1554).

[5] Murrey = Reddish purple or blood red.

ANDREW BOORDE (1490?–1549)

The fyrst boke of the introduction of knowledge. The which doth teach a man to know . . . the usage and fashion of all maner of countreys. (London: W. Middleton, 1555), I1ᵛ–I2ᵛ, M3ᵛ–N2ᵛ.

The physician Andrew Boorde traveled extensively through France, Spain, and Portugal, as described in his *Itinerary of Europe*, a manuscript apparently lost by his patron, Thomas Cromwell. Intended as a medical treatise, *The fyrst boke of the introduction of knowledge* was illustrated with woodcuts and records Boorde's observations made on a lengthy tour of Europe. Featuring rhymed verse and snippets of dialect, Boorde relies upon details concerning diet, fashion, business, and weather to distinguish between various groups of people.

Keywords: Venetians—Turks—Moors—Slavery—Egyptians—Jews—Barbary

The twenty-fourth chapter treateth of Venice, and of the natural disposition of the people of the country, of their money and of their speech

> I am a Venetian both sober and sage;
> In all mine acts and doings I do not outrage;
> Gravity shall be found ever in me,
> Specially if I be out of my country.
> My apparel is rich, very good and fine.
> All my possession is not fully mine,
> For part of my possession, I am come tributor to the Turk.
> To live in rest and peace, in my city I do lurk.
> Some men do say I do smell of the smoke;
> I pass not for that, I have money in my poke⁶
> To pacify the Pope, the Turk, and the Jew:
> I say no more, good fellow, now adieu!

Whosoever hath not seen the noble city of Venice, he hath not seen the beauty & riches of this world . . . for to Venice is a great confluence of merchants, as well Christians, as all sorts of infidels. . . . The merchants of Venice goeth in long gowns like priests, with close sleeves. The Venetians will not have no lords or knights amongst them, but only the Duke. The Duke of Venice is chosen for term of his life; he shall not marry, because his son shall claim no inheritance of his dukedomship, the Duke may have lemons & concubines as many as he will. . . .⁷

---

⁶ Poke = A bag or small sack.
⁷ Lemon = A paramour or lover.

The thirty-sixth chapter treateth of the Mores which do dwell in Barbary

> I am a black More born in Barbary;
> Christian men for money oft doth me buy;
> If I be unchristened, merchants do not care,
> They buy me in markets be I never so bare.
> Yet will I be a good diligent slave,
> Although I do stand instead of a knave;
> I do gather figs and with some I wipe my tail:
> To be angry with me what shall it avail?

Barbary is a great country and plentiful of fruit, wine, and corn. The inhabitants be called the Mores, there be white Mores and black Moors, they be infidels and unchristened. There be many Moores brought into Christendom, in to great cities and towns, to be sold, and do all manner of service, but they be set most commonly to vile things, they be called slaves. They do gather grapes and figs, and with some of the figs they surely will wipe their tail and put them in the frail.[8] They have great lips, and knotted hair black and curled. Their skin is soft, and there is nothing white but their teeth and the white of the eye. When a merchant or any other man do buy them they be not all of one price, for some be better cheap than some. They be sold after as they can work and do business. When they do die they be cast into the water or on a dung hill, that dogs and [mag]pies and crows may eat them, except some of them that be christened. They be buried. They do keep much of Macomites law as the Turks do. They have now a great captain called Barbarossa, which is a great warrior. They doth harm diverse times to the . . . . other countries that do border on them . . . for they will come over the straits & steal pigs and geese and other things. . . .

The thirty-seventh chapter treateth of the natural disposition of the Turks and of Turkey, and of their money and their speech

> I am a Turk and Machamytes law do keep;
> I do prowl for my prey when others be asleep;
> My law willeth me no swine's flesh to eat;
> It shall not greatly force for I have other meat.
> In using my raiment I am not variable,
> Nor of promise I not mutable. . . .

The thirty-eighth chapter treateth of Egypt, and of their money and of their speech

Egypt is a country joined to Jewry. The country is plentiful of wine, corn, and honey. There be many great wildernesses, in which be many great wild beasts. In the which wilderness lived many holy fathers, as it appeareth in

[8] Frail = Basket.

Vitas Patrum. The people of the country be swart, and doth go disguised in their apparel, contrary to other nations, they be light fingered and use picking.[9] They have little manners and evil lodging. And yet they be pleasant dancers. There be few or none of the Egyptians that doth dwell in Egypt, for Egypt is repleted now with infidel aliens. . . .

The thirty-ninth chapter treateth of the natural disposition of the Jews, and of Jewry, & of their money and of their speech

> I am an Hebrycyon, some call me a Jew;
> To Jesu Christ I was never true.
> I should keep Moses old law;
> I fear at length I shall prove a daw;[10]
> Many things of Moses laws do I not keep;
> I believe not the prophets, I lie too long asleep.

JOANNES AB INDAGINE (d. 1537)

Briefe introductions . . . unto the art of chiromancy, or manuel divination, and physiognomy with circumstances upon the faces of the signes (London: John Daye, 1558), pp. G7ᵛ, H2ᴿ–H4ᵛ, H8ᵛ–I1ᴿ.

Joannes ab Indagine was a German priest whose work on physiognomy was first published in Germany in 1523. Indagine's introduction to physiognomy offers a guide to using a person's outer appearance, primarily the face, to deduce the nature of his character or personality. Published in England seven times before the end of the seventeenth century, Indagine's work provides some of the language for Edward Topsell's comparison of men and primates, as well as preparing the ground for nineteenth-century comparative anatomy and racial craniometry.

Keywords: Physiognomy—Noses—Lips—Foreheads—Skin Color—Humors

It is not to be let pass, the sure judgment that is to be taken by the forehead of man, the which doth alter & change at every sudden passion of the mind. For it is well perceived and known that the dispositions of most men to be judged by nothing sooner or better than by the forehead. . . .

This is the judgment of such as have crooked noses like unto a goshawk or an eagle. Such as with the same crookedness have a certain rising upward, the crookedness somewhat abated . . . are to be judged liberal, stout, eloquent, and proud . . . the grossness and largeness of the nostrils, betoken dullness, foolishnesses, and madness, derision, deceit, and immoderate venerious

---

[9] Swart = Dark in color; black or blackish; dusky, swarthy.
[10] Daw = A jackdaw, or simpleton.

appetite. The nose broad and flat in the midst and elevate and rising in the end showeth a lying, stubborn, cruel, babbling, and a wanton person. . . .

. . . [A] narrow close mouth signifieth a keeper of secrets, also a modest, sober, chaste, fearful, and liberal person . . . . But this is found by experience, thin lips do betoken great talkers, eloquent, witty, prudent, and ingenious men. Great lips with the nether lip hanging down that the teeth do appear do declare dull and foolish people, hard of understanding, unclean, luxurious, inconstant and cruel. . . .

. . . [I]f a man be so curious, he may have the colour & proportion whereby to judge, for as the uttermost colour in a picture doth show temperance thereof, even so in the face it doth argue good or evil. Red colour is always suspect, declaring a hot complexion, a swarth & leaden colour is never commendable for besides a saturnine disposition and black choler doth also show the evil affections of the mind, as envy, anger, rancor, machinations & privy hatreds, a white feminine colour, soft & cold, declareth a cold, soft and tender person, except when a certain sanguine redness be mixed with it, as we may behold in sanguine complexion, this colour is only most commendable, for it causeth also a man to be inclined and disposed to all good & honest things, & apt to all things. . . .

GIROLAMO RUSCELLI, PSEUD. ALLESIO PIEMONTESE (1500–65)

The secretes of the reverende Mayster Alexis of Piemount. . . . with the manner to make distillations, parfumes, confitures, dyinges, colours, fusions, and meltynges, translated by William Warde (London: Henry Sutton, 1559), 69, 72.

Girolamo Ruscelli was a Tuscan physician, alchemist, and cartographer. His book of secrets, including roughly 350 recipes for medicinal compounds, cosmetics, pigments, and metallurgy, was enormously popular, going through 104 editions between 1555 and 1699. In addition to the recipes for whitening the skin reproduced here, Ruscelli is interesting for his notion of science as a great hunt after the unknown secrets of nature, an idea that resonates with the numerous authors who sought to unravel the mystery of blackness.

Keywords: Cosmetics—Skin Color

A water to make the skin white, and to take away the sun burning

Take half a pot full of rainwater and fill it up with verjuice, then seeth it until it be half consumed.[11] And in the meantime that it yet boileth, fill it with the

---

[11] Verjuice = The acid juice of green or unripe grapes, crab-apples, or other sour fruit, expressed and formed into a liquor; formerly much used in cooking, as a condiment, or for medicinal purposes.

juice of lemons. When it hath sodden take it from the fire, and put to it the white of four eggs new laid, and well beaten, but the foresaid substances must be cold before you put in the said white of the eggs. And then is it made.

To make a water for to make the face white[12]

Take litharge [of] silver sublimed the value of a groat, and put it into some vessel with strong white vinegar, then boil it until it be diminished the height of two fingers. Let it stand and rest, then strain it and keep it.[13] Also milk and the juice of oranges mixed with the oil of wine lees is very good.[14]

QUEEN ELIZABETH I OF ENGLAND (1533–1603)

An act for the further punishment of vagabonds, calling themselves Egyptians (1562)

Source: Danby Pickering (ed.), *The Statutes at Large* (Cambridge, J. Bentham, 1763), 211–12.

This Act, passed under the reign of Elizabeth I, refers to the earlier proclamation by Philip and Mary, and established strictures against English people who associate with and impersonate gypsies.

Keywords: Gypsies—Egyptians—Clothing and Identity—Vagabonds—Englishness

Whereas sithence the act made in the first and second years of the late King and Queen, King Philip and Queen Mary, for the punishment of that false and subtle company of vagabonds calling themselves Egyptians, there is a scruple and doubt arisen, whether such persons as being born within this realm of England, or other the Queen's highness's dominions, and are or shall become of the fellowship or company of the said vagabonds, by transforming or disguising themselves in their apparel, or in a certain counterfeit speech or behaviour, are punishable by the said act in like manner as others of that sort are, being strangers born and transported into this realm of England. . . .

III. . . . [B]e it enacted by the authority aforesaid, that all and every person and persons, which from and after the first day of May now next ensuing shall be seen or found within this realm of England or Wales, in any company or fellowship of vagabonds, commonly calling themselves Egyptians,

---

[12] In John Wecker's *Cosmeticks. Or, The beautifying part of physick* (1660), a recipe appears instructing women in the use of "waters . . . with which if you wet the face or hands, they grow black by degrees, like to an Aethiopian" (35).

[13] Litharge of silver = A name given to a protoxide of lead produced as a by-product in the separation of silver from lead.

[14] Lees = Sediment.

or counterfeiting, transforming, or disguising themselves by their apparel, speech, or other behaviour, like unto such vagabonds, commonly called or calling themselves Egyptians, and so shall do or continue and remain in the same, either at one time or several times, by the space of one month: that then the said person or persons, shall by virtue of this act be deemed and judged a felon and felons; (2) and shall therefore suffer pains of death, loss of lands and goods, as in cases of felony by the order of the common laws of this realm. . . .[15]

GIROLAMO BENZONI (1519–?)

History of the New World (*La historia del Mondo Nuovo;* Venice: Francesco Rampazetto, 1565)

Source: Girolamo Benzoni, *History of the New World*, trans. W. H. Smyth (London: Hakluyt Society, 1857), 3–4, 8, 52–53.

The Milanese Benzoni journeyed to the New World in 1541, visiting the Antilles, Central America, the west coast of South America, and Guatemala. His *Historia del Mundo Nuovo* (translated into Latin 1578) offers a history of Spanish brutality in the New World, and records impressions of the regions visited and indigenous people he saw during his travels between 1541 and 1556. Theodor De Bry printed an illustrated translation of Benzoni in his compendium *Grands Voyages; America* (1613). This reprinting helped promote the anti-Spanish "Black Legend." The initial passages describe events that took place in Venezuela.

Keywords: Venezuela—Indians—Nakedness—Monstrosity—Spanish Justification of Slavery—Cannibalism

Whilst we remained at Cumaná there came an Indian woman, wife of one of the principal chiefs of the province, with a basket-full of fruit, such a woman as I have never before nor since seen the like of; so that my eyes could not be satisfied with looking at her for wonder. . . . [H]er appearance was like the following:

She was quite naked, except where modesty forbids, such being the custom throughout all this country; she was old, and painted black, with long hair down to her waist; and her earrings had so weighed her ears down, as to make them reach her shoulders, a thing wonderful to see; she had them split down the middle and filled with rings of a certain carved wood, very light. . . . Her nails were immoderately long, her teeth were black, her mouth large, and she

---

[15] English authorities continually attempted to rid England of Irish immigrants as well as gypsies; gypsies were widely supposed to have come into England via Ireland and the two groups are explicitly connected in Charles I's 1633 *A proclamation for the speedy sending away of Irish beggers . . . and for the suppression of English rogues and vagabonds.*

had a ring in her nostrils, called by them caricori; so she appeared like a monster to us, rather than a human being. . . .

. . . Before I go on to speak of other things, I must here relate why the Indians from the mainland were given as slaves. In the beginning, when the admiral Columbus discovered the main land of India, many Spaniards crowded there from the abundance of riches they found, going and coming, some in one province and some in another. But the Indians began to dislike and even to hate these strangers, because they were made to labor excessively, and were very ill-treated by them, their tongues never tiring of asking for gold, silver, pearls, emeralds. Wherefore, unable to put up with such labor and misery, they determined to kill and extirpate them from the country, cursing themselves for not having killed them all at first. Now the Spaniards seeing, both laity and clergy, that, from the habits of these people, they would not accept of the friendship of the Christians, nor receive the faith of Christ; that, on the contrary, they ridiculed it, saying that those things might do for men of Castile but not for them, some monks of the order of Saint Dominic went back to Spain and reported to the king, Don Ferdinand, the way of living of these brutish races, persuading him that they deserved to be sold as slaves, rather than to be allowed to live at liberty, alleging the following reasons: that the Indians of the mainland were idolaters, pathics, liars, dirty, ugly, void of judgment or perception, lovers of novelty, fierce, inhuman, and cruel.[16] They use poisoned darts, so that when a man is wounded by them he goes mad and dies. They go naked and are devoid of shame. They wear no beard, and if a few hairs appear, with certain little pincers they pull them out. They eat human flesh, and also the flesh of some extremely dirty animals . . . such as spiders, lice, and horrid worms. All their delight is drunkenness; and in matrimony they observe no faith or loyalty, so that it is impossible to make them alter their habits. They are devoid of pity towards the infirm, and let them be ever so closely related they abandon them to the woods or the mountains to die, like wild animals. Finally, to include all in one sentence that might be said in many words, they affirmed that no nation more wicked or wretched can be found under heaven.

JEAN BODIN (1530–96)

Method for the Easy Comprehension of History
(Paris: Martin Le Jeune, 1566)

Source: Jean Bodin, *Method for the Easy Comprehension of History*, translated by Beatrice Reynolds (New York: Columbia University Press, 1945), 85–146, 359–64.

French jurist, political philosopher, economist, and cosmologist, Jean Bodin studied and taught civil law before entering the

---

[16] Pathic = the passive partner in homosexual anal intercourse.

service of François, duc d'Alençon, brother to King Henri III.
His *Method for the Easy Comprehension of History* (published in
Latin) is regarded by some scholars to offer the first articulation
of modern categories of race, although he draws often on older
thinkers. He offers a way of substantiating Aristotle's claim,
which he cites, that nature makes certain people slaves.

Keywords: Climatic and Environmental Influence—Degeneracy—
    Sons of Noah—Northerners—Southerners—Humors—
    Fixity of Color—Classification of Humans—Influence of
    Religion—Interracial Sex—Migration—Jews

Chapter 5: The Correct Evaluation of Histories

[A]bout the various laws, religions, sacrifices, public banquets, and institutions of peoples . . . no generalizations can be made, because they vary infi-
nitely and change within a brief period through natural growth or at the will
of a prince. Since that is so, let us seek characteristics drawn, not from the
institutions of men, but from nature, which are stable and are never changed
unless by great force or long training, and even if they have been altered,
nevertheless eventually they return to their pristine character. . . .

To topographical diversity we must relate the opinion which Plato
expresses in Book V of the *Laws*, where he says that some people are made
better than others and some worse from the very difference of site; on
account of this it is necessary to restrain these peoples by laws often contradictory and varying from one district to another. This difference proceeds
also from the waters and the air and even from the variety of foods. . . .

. . . I can hardly be persuaded that men are made black from the curse of
Chus, as a certain learned man reports.[17] For a long time they have ridiculed
the opinion of Herodotus, who thought that the seed of the Ethiopians was
black. He argued that the Ethiopians would be born black in Scythia and the
Scythians white in Ethiopia, although all peoples for a long time have been
fused in repeated waves of migration. . . .

. . . Yet we see men as well as plants degenerate little by little when the
soil has been changed, and it is for the same reason that fire and sun color
men black, as Aristotle reported. . . . Since the maximum of cold or heat is
under the Tropics and each pole, there will be under the equator the same
moderation of climate as in those areas situated under the thirtieth parallel.
Indeed the Leuko-Ethiopians are reported to be in both places. Under the
Tropics they are unusually black; under the pole, for the opposite reason,
they are tawny in colour. After that, down to the sixtieth parallel, they
become ruddy; thence to the forty-fifth they are white; after that to the thirtieth they become yellow, and when the yellow bile is mingled with the black

[17] Guillaume Postel, *Cosmographicae disciplinae compendium* (Basle, 1561).

[melancholy], they grow greenish, until they become swarthy and deeply black under the Tropics. . . .

Let us therefore adopt this theory, that all who inhabit the area from the forty-fifth parallel to the seventy-fifth toward the north, grow increasingly warmer within, while the southerners, since they have more warmth from the sun, have less from themselves. . . . [T]he strength of inward heat brings it about that those who live in northerly lands are more active and robust than the southerners. Even in the opposite area, beyond Capricorn's circle, the same thing happens: the further men move from the equator, the larger they grow, as in the land of the Patagonians, who are called giants, in the very same latitude as the Germans. This, then, is the reason why Scythians have always made violent attacks southward; and what seems incredible, but is nevertheless true, the greatest empires have always spread southward—rarely from the south toward the north. . . .[18]

Those who occupy the middle region are impatient of both cold and heat, since the mean contends with each extreme; both, however, they endure equally well. . . . The southerners nearer to us, then, are the Spanish, Sicilians, Peloponnesians, Cretans, Syrians, Arabs, Persians, Susians, Gedrosians, Indians, Egyptians, Cyrenaeians, Phoenicians, Numidians, Libyans, Moors, and the Americans who inhabit Florida, but they are such that those who dwell in the same latitude further west are of a colder temperament. The northerners, in turn, are those who inhabit the land from the fiftieth parallel to the sixtieth. They are, however, more temperate than their neighbors who have their homes near the seventieth. In the former tract are Britain, Ireland, Denmark, part of Gothland, Lower Germany from the Main and the Bug River even to farthest Scythia and Tartary, which cover a good part of Europe and Greater Asia.

. . . Since the body and the mind are swayed in opposite directions, the more strength the latter has, the less has the former; and the more effective a man is intellectually, the less strength of body he has, provided the senses are functioning. It is plain, therefore, that the southerners excel in intellect, the Scythians in body. . . . Africans . . . have more than enough wisdom, but not enough strength.

But if from want of reasoning and wisdom the northerners cannot control their appetites and furthermore are regarded as intemperate, suspicious, perfidious, and cruel why are the southerners much more cruel and perfidious even than these? . . .

The cruelty of the southerners and of the Scythians is . . . very different, because the latter are driven to wrath by impulse alone and to revenge by a certain magnanimous valor of the soul; after they have been irritated, they can easily be mollified. The southerners are not easily angered, but when once angry they can with difficulty be softened: they attack the enemy with a

---

[18] This discussion is repeated by Fynes Moryson in his 1617 An *itinerary . . . containing his ten yeeres travel . . . .*

foxlike cunning, not with open violence, and they inflict horribly painful torture upon the conquered. This savagery comes partly from that despotism
which a vicious system of training and undisciplined appetites have created in
a man, but much more from a lack of proportion in the mixing of humors. . . .
So it happens that those who are in the furthest regions are more inclined to
vices. As black bile is removed from the blood [with difficulty], in the same
way as dregs from wine, so disturbances of the intellect which proceed from
black bile are difficult to eradicate.

Now the southerners abound in black bile, which subsides like lees to the
bottom when the humors have been drawn out by the heat of the sun and
increases more and more through emotions, so that those who are mentally
constituted in this manner are plainly implacable.

. . . [I]t is evident that the southerners are seized by frenzy more easily
than are the northerners, since men become mad more easily than animals.
Leo the African wrote that there was a great multitude of raving men in Africa
and that everywhere public buildings were set apart for the unbalanced.

. . . [T]he southerners, who have more wisdom and reasoning power,
have through their special gift brought it to pass that they might sin more
freely for the sake of pleasure. Because self-control was difficult, particularly
when plunging into lust, they gave themselves over to horrible excesses. Promiscuous coition of men and animals took place, wherefore the regions of
Africa produce for us so many monsters. Hence is derived that unbelievable
jealousy of the southerners and of the Carthaginians referred to in Leo, from
which the Germans are entirely free.

Out of this difficulty remains the question, what judgment must be
formed of the historians who attack the superstition, impiety, magic, infamous lusts, and cruelties of the Greeks, Egyptians, Arabs, and Chaldeans, yet
omit the qualities which are praiseworthy? From these people letters, useful
arts, virtues, training, philosophy, religion, and lastly *humanitas* itself flowed
upon earth as from a fountain. The Scythians, however, do not lack industry,
nor do those who hold the middle region, but the southerners attained the
most outstanding gifts from immortal God. . . .

Again, this division of peoples into three groups can be referred to the
threefold universe: that is, the intellectual, consisting of the minds; the
celestial, the stars; the elemental, where the origin and destruction of things
occurs. . . . Since these things are so, the race of man in its three varieties,
Scythians, I say, southerners, and men of the middle regions, can be related
to the triple activities of the soul, wisdom, prudence and creative ability,
which abide in contemplation, action, and production . . . and they can be
applied to the most certain judgment of all history. . . .

The southerners, however, Asiatics and Africans, unless indeed by miracles
from heaven or by force of arms, do not abandon the religion they once
adopted. . . . Certainly that race [the Jews] could never by any reward or
punishment be enticed from its doctrines and, dispersed over the whole
world, alone it has vigorously maintained its religion, received three thousand years ago. When Mohammed himself could not impose his doctrine

either by miracles or speeches, he finally turned to arms, and having offered liberty to the slaves he accomplished by violence what he could not do by reasoning. . . .

In Ethiopia, where, we have said, the race of men is very keen and lustful, no one varies markedly from the uniform type.[19] They are all small, curly-haired, black, flat-nosed, blubber-lipped, and bald, with white teeth and black eyes. Among the Scythians there are no differences. . . . We have discovered, in reality, that the farther one moves from the middle region, the more the faces resemble each other, while within that zone we see an infinite divergence among men. . . . This state of affairs ought, then, to be attributed to the blending of peoples, who are wont to move from the extremes to the middle region, as though to the region of most equable climate. . . .

Therefore as we see diverse forms develop from the diverse kinds of living beings and plants . . . so we must make a similar judgment about variations in human beings. . . . Thus if the Scythians were crossed with the Ethiopians, there is no doubt but that a varied and different kind of man would be produced. . . . In this way, then, it came about, I think, that Danes, Saxons, and English mingled with Britons, making them more ferocious, while they themselves became more kindly.[20] Indeed, when the Britons, driven from their homes, entered Gaul, they renounced with difficulty their wild courage and redeemed themselves gradually from servitude to the Gauls. . . . Then, unlike plants, which when transplanted elsewhere quickly lose their identity and adapt themselves to the nature of the soil whence they take their nourishment, men do not change the innate characteristics of their own nature easily, but after a long period of time.

Then it remains to consider how much training can accomplish in changing the nature of men. Now training is two-fold, divine and human; the latter may be wrong or right. Each, of course, has power sufficient to overcome nature fairly often. . . . Was there ever a race so huge and savage which, when it had sound leaders, was not carried forward upon the path of civilization? What race once instructed in the most refined arts, but ceasing to cultivate the humanities, did not sink sometime into barbarity and savagery? Although innumerable examples of this exist, yet none is more illustrious than that of the Germans, who as they themselves confess were once not very far from the level of wild beasts. . . . Nevertheless, they have now so far advanced that in the humanities they seem superior to the Asiatics; in military matters, to the Romans; in religion, to the Hebrews; in philosophy, to the Greeks, in geometry, to the Egyptians; in arithmetic, to the Phoenicians; in astrology, to the Chaldeans; and in various crafts they seem to be superior to all peoples. . . .

[19] In *The New Atlantis* (1627), Francis Bacon imagines the Spirit of Fornication as "a little foul ugly Æthiope" and the Spirit of Chastity as a "fair beautiful cherubin."

[20] In *A restitution of decayed intelligence: in antiquities* (London, 1605), Richard Verstegan argues intead that, "whereas some do call us a mixed nation by reason of these Danes and Normans coming in among us, I answer . . . that the Danes and the Normans were once one same people with the Germans, as were also the Saxons; and we not to be accompted mixed by having only some such joined unto us again, as sometime had one same language, and one same original with us . . ." (187).

. . . Since our forefathers thought long faces more beautiful, the midwives gradually arranged that they should seem very long indeed. These may be seen in old statues and pictures. In western India the forehead is very wide and the nose of immense size; we read that this is due to obstetricians. . . . But if the influence of custom and training is so great in natural and human affairs that gradually they develop into mores and take on the force of nature, how much more true is this in divine matters? We see that the power and influence of religions is such as to change profoundly the habits and corrupt the character of men, although it can hardly happen that the traces of our earlier dispositions can be altogether obliterated. . . .

Chapter 9: Tests for the Origins of People

[The] migration of the human race is constant; daily they lay foundations of new cities, new names of new races arise from earlier ones, extinct or altered. . . . The fecundity of nature is such that in a short time we observe countless numbers are procreated from the stock of one man. . . . Why do I commemorate what will seem incredible to posterity, the fusion of Circassians with Egyptians, of Spanish with Americans, of Portuguese with Indians, or the relationship of Goths and Vandals with Spanish and Africans? From these illustrations . . . it is understood that all men for a long time have been so fused in migrations and also in the teeming colonial populations, as well as in wars and captivity, that none can boast about the antiquity of their origin and the great age of their race except the Jews.

THOMAS PALMER (1540–1626)

Two Hundred Poosees (London, 1566)

Source: John Manning ed., *The Emblems of Thomas Palmer: Two Hundred Poosees* (New York: AMS Press, 1988), 56.

Thomas Palmer's *Two Hundred Poosees* is England's earliest extant manuscript of emblems, although modern scholars often neglect it in favor of Geffrey Whitney's *A Choice of Emblemes*, which it preceded by twenty years. The emblem "Impossible Things" first appeared in an unauthorized 1531 edition of Andrea Alciato's *Book of Emblems*, where the figure being washed was white. In editions from 1534 on, the man was rendered black. Whereas Alciato, like Aesop, features an Ethiopian, Palmer changes him into a "man of Inde," and he is further transformed into a "blackamoor" by Whitney.

Keywords: Washing the Ethiope—Skin Color—Obduracy of Heretics—
        Fixity of Color

> Why washest thou the man of Inde?
> Why takest thou such pain?
> Black night thou mayest as soon make bright

Figure 1 "Impossible Things," from Thomas Palmer, *Two Hundred Poosees* (1566). Reproduced by permission of the British Library.

> Thou labourest all in vain.
> A fool he is that doth attempt,
> That he cannot attain:
> The foaming flood against the stream
> To cut, is little gain.
> Indurate heart of heretics
> Much blacker than the mole;
> With word or writ who seeks to purge,
> Stark dead he blows the coal.

PIERRE BOAISTUAU (ca. 1517–66)

Certaine secrete wonders of nature, containing a description of sundy strange things, seming monstrous in our eyes and judgement . . . , translated by Edward Fenton (London: Henry Bynneman, 1569), 12–16, 26–27.

Pierre Boaistuau adapted into French six Bandello novellas that would become, in William Painter's translation, a source for

Shakespeare's *Romeo and Juliet*. As the first English edition of Boaistuau's very popular *Histoires Prodigeuses* (1560), *Certaine Secrete Wonders* compiles marvels of nature, history, and mythology. In its tales of freak births, monstrous deeds, and demonic beasts, the work regularly attributes non-normative physical conditions to the ire of God and associates both black skin and Jews with monstrousness.

Keywords: Monstrosity—Jacob and Laban—Maternal Impression—Jews—Blood Libel—Body Odor

Of the bringing forth of monsters, and the cause of their generations

. . . It is most certain that these monstrous creatures, for the most part do proceed of the judgment, justice, chastisement, and curse of God, which suffereth that the fathers and mothers bring forth these abominations as a horror of their sin, suffering themselves to run headlong, as do brute beasts without guide to the puddle or stink of their filthy appetites, having no respect or regard to the age, place, time, or other laws ordained of nature.[21] . . . The ancient philosophers amongst others, which have searched the secrets of nature, have declared other great causes of this wonderful and monstrous childbearing, which Aristotle, Hippocrates, Empedocles, and Pliny have referred to an ardent and obstinate imagination, which the woman hath, whilst she conceives the child, which hath such power over the fruit that the beams and characters continue upon the rock of the infant, whereupon they find an infinite number of examples to prove the same, worthy of memory, the which albeit may seem but jests or fables, if the authority and truth of those which write them were not their sufficient warrant. And for a further certainty thereof, Damascenus, a grave author, doth assure this to be true, that being present with Charles IV, Emperor and King of Boeme, there was brought to him a maid, rough and covered with hair like a bear, the which the mother had brought forth in so hideous and deformed a shape, by having too much regard to the picture of St. John clothed with a beast's skin, the which was tied or made fast continually during her conception at her bed's feet. By the like means Hippocrates saved a princess accused of adultery, for that she was delivered of a child black like an Ethiopian, her husband being of a fair and white complexion, which by the persuasion of Hippocrates, was absolved and pardoned, for that the child was like unto a Moor accustomably tied at her bed. Read of this in Genesis . . . how Jacob deceived Laban his father-in-law, and

---

[21] A warning to the same effect and linking sinful English to Africans appeared in the same year in *The true description of two monstrous children* by John Mellys. In doggerel verse about conjoined twins born in Buckinghamshire, Mellys writes: "I read how Afric land was fraught / for their most filthy life, / With monstrous shapes, confusedly / that therein were full rife. / But England now pursues their vile / and detestable path, / Embracing eke all mischiefs great / that moves God's mighty wrath. / As these unnatural shapes and forms, / thus brought forth in our days, / Are tokens true and manifest, / how God by diverse ways / Doth steer us to amendment of/our vile and cankered life, / Which too too much abused is, / in man, in child, in wife."

thereby enriched himself with his cattle, having pilled a rod and put the beasts to drink, to the end the goats and sheep beholding the diversity of the colours of this rod might bring forth little ones marked with sundry several marks.[22] Besides these causes spoken of before of the generation of monsters, the best learned in the secrets of nature have yet assigned us others. For Empedocles and Dephilus do attribute the same to come of the superabundance or default and corruption of the seed and womb. . . . The Astrologians (as Alcabitius) have referred these monsters to the influence of the stars, judging that if the moon be in certain degrees in conjunctions when the woman conceiveth, her fruit shall be monstrous. Even so Julius Maternus writeth . . . that sometimes these monsters be engendered of the corruption and filthy unsavory meats, as burning coals, man's flesh, and other like things that women desire after they have conceived, the which is very contagious and hurtful to their fruit. . . .[23]

Wonderful Histories of the Jews

This wicked sect of the Jews hath from time to time so much disquieted and molested our Christian public weal . . . that whosoever shall read their cruel blasphemies and abominable execrations which they continually publish and set forth against Jesus Christ the savior of all the world in a certain book . . . which they call *Talmud*, will judge the same a cause sufficient to exile and abandon them out of all the provinces and places where Christ is to be honored. For like as these people blinded and led in the mists of error have not only gone about to defame the name of our savior by their writings, but also that which is worse, they have most shamefully travailed to extirp[ate] and blot out the remembrance of him forever. Even so in the year a thousand, a hundred and four score and in the reign of King Philip, these wicked people in the despite of the passion of Jesus Christ, upon Good Friday, when they judged the Christians were most occupied in celebrating that day, they enclosed themselves yearly in a cave, where having stolen a young child, they whipt him, crowning him with thorns, making him to drink gall, and in the end crucified him upon a cross, continuing in this sort of cruel doings till the Lord grudging greatly with the death of so many poor innocents suffered them as thieves to be taken with the deed, and after he had caused them to be examined and tormented for the same, they confessed that they had used this many years before, murdering a great number of infants in this sort. Whereof King Philip being ascertained,

---

[22] This biblical tale was widely cited by medical and other writers in the early modern period to affirm that "what is strongly conceived in the mind, imprints the force into the infant conceived in the womb," as the French surgeon Ambrose Paré wrote in his popular book on natural deformities, *The works of that famous chirurgeon Ambrose Parey.* Paré uses the story to account for the birth of "monsters," which include children who are a different color from their parents (see Figure 7). In this respect, Heliodorus's Greek romance, *Aithiopika* (see note 5 above), was another foundational text.

[23] Montaigne, in "Of a Monstrous Child," writes, "Those that we call monsters are not so to God, who sees in the immensity of his work the infinite forms that he has comprehended therein; and it is to be believed that this figure which astonishes us has relation to some other figure of the same kind unknown to man."

caused them not only to be chased from his realm, but also broiled of them, to the number of eighty in a hot burning cauldron. After that King Philip seeing himself oppressed with wars, and wanting money to maintain the same, for a better supply of his necessity, he (for a sum of money paid to him in hand by the said Jews for their outrageous living) licensed them to return and travail into France. But even as vices be chained together, drawing one another, so these wicked people yet smelling of this first injury which they had received, determined and fully resolved amongst themselves, to extirp[ate] at one instant the name of Christians, destroying them all by poison. And for a further help in these wicked practices, they allied themselves in consort with diverse lepers, by whose succors and means they made an ointment, with a confection of the blood of man's brine composed with certain venomous herbs, wrapped in a little linen cloth, tying a stone to the same to make it sink to the bottom: they nightly cast in the said infection into all the fountains and wells of the

Figure 2   Jewish poisoner, from Pierre Boaistuau, *Certaine secrete wonders of nature* (1569). Reproduced by permission of the Folger Shakespeare Library.

Christians. Whereupon this corruption engendered such contagious diseases in all Europe, that there died well nigh the third person throughout the same. . . . And like as in time diverse of those wells and fountains became dry, by which means the empoisoned bags were found in the bottom of the water. Even so by conjecture and suspicion, diverse of these malefactors were apprehended, and being grievously tormented, confessed the fact, whereupon grew such sharp and severe punishment, as well to all the Jews, as lepers, throughout all the province of Europe, being found culpable thereof, that their posterities smell thereof till this day: for they having proved so many kinds of torments and martyrdoms, that upon their imprisonments they had greater desire to kill and broil one another, than become subject to the mercy of the Christians.

WILLIAM HARRISON (1534–93)

"The Description of Britain," in Raphael Holinshed, *The firste volume of the chronicles of Englande, Scotlande, and Irelande . . .* (London: John Hunne, 1577)

Source: *The first and second volumes of Chronicles . . . first collected and published by Raphael Holinshed . . .* (London: Henry Denham, 1587), 114–15.

The Anglican clergyman William Harrison dedicated much time to writing his *Chronology*, an unfinished work in which Satan's plots against England are seen to take the form of Roman Catholicism, Spain, and courtly conspiracies. His "Description of Britain" appeared in Holinshed's *Chronicles*, a major source for Shakespeare's and other history plays. Harrison's discussion of the British "constitution" attempts to reinterpret "northern" traits earlier denigrated by Bodin, rendering northern simplicity a virtue tantamount to upright honesty.

Keywords: Englishness—Complexion—Northern Hardiness— Degeneracy—Female Beauty

Chapter 20: Of the general constitution of the bodies of the Britons

Such as are bred in this island are men for the most part of a good com-plexion, tall of stature, strong in body, white of colour, and thereto of great boldness and courage in the wars. As for their general comeliness of person, the testimony of Gregory the Great, at such time as he saw English captives sold at Rome, shall easily confirm what it is. . . .[24]

Leland noting somewhat of the constitution of our bodies sayeth these words (grounding I think upon Aristotle, who writeth that such as dwell near the north are of more courage and strength of body than skillfulness or

---

[24] For Gregory's assessment of English whiteness, see Bartholomaeus Anglicus in this volume.

wisdom): The Britons are white in colour, strong of body, and full of blood, as people inhabiting near the north, and far from the equinoctial line, where the soil is not so fruitful, and therefore the people are less of stature, weaker of body, more nice, delicate, fearful by nature, blacker in colour, and some so black in deed as any crow or raven. . . . Howbeit, as those which are bred in sundry places of the main do come behind us in constitution of body, so I grant, that in pregnancy of wit, nimbleness of limbs, and politic inventions, they generally exceed us. Notwithstanding that otherwise these gifts of theirs do often degenerate into mere subtlety, instability, unfaithfulness, and cruelty. . . . And for that we dwell northward, we are commonly taken by the foreign historiographers to be men of great strength and little policy, much courage and small shift, because of the weak abode of the sun with us, whereby our brains are not made hot and warmed. . . . And thus also doth Comineus burden us after a sort in his history, and after him Bodinus. But thanked be God, that all the wit of his countrymen, if it may be called wit, could never compass to do so much in Britain, as the strength and courage of our Englishmen (not without great wisdom and forecast) have brought to pass in France. . . . Certes in accusing our wisdom in this sort, he doth (in mine opinion) increase our commendation. For if it be a virtue to deal uprightly with singleness of mind, sincerely and plainly, without any such suspicious fetches in all our dealings, as they commonly practice in their affairs, then are our countrymen to be accounted wise and virtuous. But if it be a vice to colour craftiness, subtle practices, doubleness, and hollow behavior with a cloak of policy, amity, and wisdom, then are Comineus and his countrymen to be reputed vicious. . . .

. . . And albeit that our women through bearing of children do after forty begin to wrinkle apace, yet are they not commonly wretched and hard favored to look upon in their age, as the French women, and diverse of other countries with whom their men also do much participate; and thereto be so often wayward and peevish, that nothing in manner may content them.

I might here add somewhat also of the mean stature generally of our women, whose beauty commonly exceedeth the fairest of those of the main, their comeliness of person and good proportion of limbs, most of theirs that come over unto us from beyond the seas. . . .

RICHARD WILLES (1546–79)

The history of travayle in the West and East Indies
(London: Richard Jugge, 1577)

Source: Richard Hakluyt, *The Principal Navigations, Voyages, Traffiques, and Discoveries of the English Nation* (London: George Bishop, Ralph Newberie, and Robert Barker, 1599–1600), Vol. 2:68–78, 80–83, 87.

The history of travayle offered a substantial revision of Richard Eden's edition of *The decades of the newe worlde*. Willes added new material on Asia, most of which was derived from continental sources, and translated accounts of China and Japan that were previously unpublished in English. Richard Hakluyt used this and other material in the *Principal Navigations*. Willes balances admiration for the civility and industriousness of Asian cultures with a condemnation of Eastern religious practices.

Keywords: China—Cities—Diet—Idolatry—Japan—Civility—
          Superstitiousness—Moors

Certain Reports of the province of China learned through the Portugals there imprisoned and chiefly by the relation of Galeotto Perera. . . . Done out of Italian into English by Richard Willes (1599–1600)

This land of China is parted into 13 shires, the which sometimes were each one a kingdom by itself, but these many years they have been all subject unto one king. . . . [T]his country is so well inhabited near the sea side, that you cannot go one mile but you shall see some town, borough or hostry, the which are so abundantly provided of all things, that in the cities and towns they live civilly. Nevertheless such as dwell abroad are very poor, for the multitude of them every where is so great, that out of a tree you shall see many times swarm a number of children, where a man would not have thought to have found any one at all.

From these places in number infinite, you shall come unto two cities very populous, and, being compared with Cinceo, not possibly to be discerned which is the greater of them. These cities are as well walled as any cities in all the world. As you come in to either of them, there standeth so great and mighty a bridge, that the like thereof I have never seen in Portugal nor else where. I heard one of my fellows say, that he told in one bridge 40 arches. . . . This causeth us to think, that in all the world there be no better workmen for buildings, than the inhabitants of China. The country is so well inhabited, that no one foot of ground is left untilled: . . . it so falling out, that the Chineans are the greatest eaters in all the world, they do feed upon all things, specially on pork, which, the fatter it is, is unto them the less loathsome. . . . Frogs are sold at the same price that is made of hens, and are good meat amongst them, as also dogs, cats, rats, snakes, and all other unclean meats. . . .

. . . [A]ll the people of China, are wont to eat their meat sitting on stools at high tables as we do, and that very cleanly, although they use neither table-cloths nor napkins. . . they feed with two sticks, refraining from touching their meat with their hands, even as we do with forks: for the which respect they less do need any table-cloths.[25] Nor is the nation only civil at meat, but

---

[25] In a text included by Richard Eden in his edition of *The decades of the newe worlde or West India. . . .*, Antonio Pigafetta notes, "Those people of China are white men as we are, and eat their meat on tables as we do" (fol. 231). Whereas southern China extends below the Tropic of Cancer, the whiteness of the Chinese contributed to the deterioration of the Ptolemeian model of the world.

also in conversation, and in courtesy they seem to exceed all other. Likewise in their dealings after their manner they are so ready, that they far pass all other gentiles and Moores: the greater states are so vain, that they line their clothes with the best silk that may be found. . . . The inhabitants of China be very great idolaters, all generally do worship the heavens. . . . Some do worship the Sun and some the Moon. . . . In their temples, the which they do call Meani, they have a great altar in the same place as we have. . . . At the right hand standeth the devil much more ugly painted than we do use to set him out, whereunto great homage is done by such as come into the temple to ask counsel, or to draw lots: this opinion they have of him, that he is malicious and able to do evil. If you ask them what they do think of the souls departed, they will answer that they be immortal, and that as soon as any one departeth out of this life, he becometh a devil if he have lived well in this world, if otherwise, that the same devil changeth him into a buffalo, ox, or dog. Wherefore to this devil they do much honour, to him do they sacrifice, praying him that he will make them like unto himself, and not like other beasts. . . .

. . . If at any time this country might be joined in league with the kingdom of Portugal, in such wise that free access were had to deal with the people there, they might all be soon converted. The greatest fault we do find in them is sodomy, a vice very common in the meaner sort, and nothing strange amongst the best. This sin were it left of them, in all other things so well disposed they be, that a good interpreter in a short space might do there great good: If, as I said, the country were joined in league with us. . . . .

When we lay at Fuquien, we did see certain Moores, who knew so little of their sect, that they could say nothing else but that Mahomet was a Moore, my father was a Moore, and I am a Moore, with some other words of their Alcoran, wherewithal, in abstinence from swine's flesh, they live until the devil take them all. . . . I asked them whether they converted any of the Chinish nation unto their sect: they answered me, that with much ado they converted the women with whom they do marry, yielding me no other cause thereof, but the difficulty they find in them to be brought from eating swine's flesh and drinking of wine. I am persuaded therefore, that if this country were in league with us, forbidding them neither of both, it would be an easy matter to draw them to our religion, from their superstition, whereat they themselves do laugh when they do their idolatry.

Of the Island Japan, and other little Isles in the East Ocean

The extreme part of the known world unto us is the noble island . . . Japan. . . . The people are tractable, civil, witty, courteous, without deceit, in virtue and honest conversation exceeding all other nations lately discovered, but so much standing upon their reputation, that their chief idol may be thought honour. . . . If at any time they do swear, for that seldom they are wont to do, they swear by the Sun: many of them are taught good letters, wherefore they may so much the sooner be brought unto Christianity. Each one is contented with one wife: they be all desirous to learn, and naturally inclined unto honesty and courtesy: godly talk they listen unto willingly, especially when they understand it thoroughly.

. . . [T]he curious readers may peruse . . . four volumes of Indian matters written long ago in Italian, and of late compendiously made Latin, by Petrus Matteius my old acquainted friend, entitling the same, *De Rebus Japonicis*.[26] One whole letter out of the fifth book thereof, specially entreating of that country, I have done into English word for word in such wise as followeth:

Aloisius Froes to his companions in Jesus Christ that remain in China and India

. . . [I] will discharge in this epistle, that you consider how artificially, how cunningly, under the pretext of religion, that crafty adversary of mankind leadeth and draweth unto perdition the Japanish minds, blinded with many superstitions and ceremonies, may the more pity this nation.

The inhabiters of Japan, as men that never had greatly to do with other nations, in their geography divided the whole world into three parts, Japan, Siam, and China. And albeit the Japans received out of Siam and China their superstitions and ceremonies, yet do they nevertheless condemn all other nations in comparison of themselves, and standing in their own conceit do far prefer themselves before all other sorts of people in wisdom and policy.

. . . The country is full of silver mines otherwise barren, not so much by fault of nature, as through the slothfulness of the inhabitants: howbeit oxen they keep and that for tillage sake only. The air is wholesome, the waters good, the people very fair and well bodied: bare-headed commonly they go, procuring baldness with sorrow and tears, eftsoon rooting up with pincers all the hair of their heads as it groweth, except it be a little behind, the which they knot and keep with all diligence. . . . They delight most in warlike affairs, and their greatest study is arms. Men's apparel diversely coloured is worn down half the legs and to the elbows: women's attire made handsomely like unto a veil, is somewhat longer. . . . The merchant, although he be wealthy, is not accounted of. Gentlemen, be they never so poor, retain their place: most precisely they stand upon their honour and worthiness, ceremoniously striving among themselves in courtesies and fair speeches. . . . Want, though it trouble most of them, so much they do detest, that poor men cruelly taking pity of their infants newly home, especially girls, do many times with their own feet strangle them. Noble men, and other likewise of meaner calling generally have but one wife a piece, by whom although they have issue, yet for a trifle they divorce themselves from their wives, and the wives also sometimes from their husbands, to marry with others. . . . In great towns most men and women can write and read. . . .

I come now to other superstitions and ceremonies, that you may see, dear brethren, that which I said in the beginning, how subtly the devil hath

---

[26] Petrus Maffeius (1536?–1603), a Jesuit who compiled a history of the Indies entitled *Historiarum Indicarum* (1588), containing letters from Jesuit missionaries in Japan.

deceived the Japonish nation, and how diligent and ready they be to obey & worship him. And first, all remembrance and knowledge not only of Christ our redeemer, but also of that one God the maker of all things is clean extinguished and utterly abolished out of the Japans' hearts. Moreover their superstitious sects are many, whereas it is lawful for each one to follow that which liketh him best. . . .

. . . At the hour of sermon each sect of the Japans resorteth to their own doctors in diverse temples. . . . These preachers be for the most part eloquent, and apt to draw with their speech the minds of their hearers. Wherefore to this end chiefly (such is their greediness) tendeth all their talk, that the people be brought under the colour of godliness to enrich their monasteries, promising to each one so much the more happiness in the life to come, how much the greater costs and charges they be at in church matters and obsequies. . . . Thus then, dear brethren, may you think how greatly they need the help of God. . . . So much the more it standeth you upon that so earnestly long for the health of souls, to commend specially these Japanish flocks unto our Lord. . . .

GEORGE BEST (d. 1584)

A True Discourse of the late voyages of discoverie, for the finding of a passage to Cathaya by the Northweast . . . (London: Henry Bynnyman, 1578), 24–26.

George Best was second in command to Martin Frobisher on voyages in search of a northwest passage to China. In recent years Best has drawn interest for his appraisal of several early modern theories concerning skin color, and particularly for the terms of his biblical explanations that anticipate a pseudo-scientific discourse.

Keywords: Interracial Sex—Skin Color—Climatic Influence—Sons of Noah—Hereditary Infection—Blackness of Moors

Therefore to return again to the black Moores, I myself have seen an Ethiopian as black as a coal brought into England, who taking a fair English woman to wife, begat a son in all respects as black as the father was, although England were his native country, and an English woman his mother: whereby it seemeth this blackness proceedeth rather of some natural infection of that man, which was so strong, that neither the nature of the clime, neither the good complexion of the mother concurring, could any thing alter, and therefore we cannot impute it to the nature of the clime.[27] And for a more fresh example,

[27] This rapidly became the prevalent notion about blackness—see also Reginald Scot's views in this volume.

our people of *Meta Incognita* (of whom and for whom this discourse is taken in hand) that were brought this last year into England, were all generally of the same colour, that many nations be, lying in the midst of the middle zone.[28] And this their colour was not only in the face which was subject to sun and air, but also in their bodies, which were still covered with garments, as ours are, yea, the very sucking child, of twelve months age, had his skin of the very same colour that most have under the equinoctial, which thing can not proceed by reason of the clime, for that they are at least ten degrees more towards the north, than we in England are . . . whereby it followeth, that there is some other cause than the climate, or the sun's perpendicular reflection, that should cause the Ethiopians great blackness. And the most probable cause to my judgment is, that this blackness proceedeth of some natural infection of the first inhabitants of that country, and so all the whole progeny of them descended, are still polluted with the same blot of infection. Therefore it shall not be far from our purpose, to examine the first original of these black men, and how by lineal descent they have hitherto continued thus black.

It manifestly and plainly appeareth by holy scripture, that after the general inundation and overflowing of the earth, there remained no more men alive, but Noe and his three sons, Sem, Cham, and Japhet, who only were left to possess and inhabit the whole face of the earth: therefore all the land that until this day hath been inhabited by sundry descents, must needs come of the offspring either of Sem, Cham, or Japhet, as the only sons of Noe, who all three being white, and their wives also, by course of nature, should have begotten and brought forth white children. . . . When Noe at the commandment of God had made and entered the ark . . . he straightly commanded his sons and their wives, that they should with reverence and fear behold the justice and mighty power of God, and that during the time of the flood, while they remained in the Ark, they should use continency, and abstain from carnal copulation with their wives. . . . Which good instructions and exhortations notwithstanding, his wicked son Cham disobeyed, and being persuaded that the first child born after the flood (by right and law of nature) should inherit and possess all the dominion of the earth, he, contrary to his father's commandment, while they were yet in the ark, used company with his wife, and craftily went about, thereby to disinherit the offspring of his other two brethren, for the which wicked and detestable fact, as an example for contempt of Almighty God, and disobedience of parents, God would a son should be born, whose name was Chus, who not only itself, but all his posterity after him, should be so black and loathsome, that it might remain a spectacle of disobedience to all the world. And of this black and cursed Chus came all these black Moores which are in Africa, for after the water was vanished from off the face of the earth, and that the land was dry, Sem chose that part of the land to inhabit in which now is called Asia, and Japhet had that which now is called Europa wherein we dwell, and Africa remained

---

[28] Frobisher brought five Inuit captives back to England who did not survive long.

for Cham, and his black son Chus. . . . being perhaps a cursed, dry, sandy, and unfruitful ground, fit for such a generation to inhabit in.[29] Thus you see, the cause of the Ethiopians's blackness, is the curse and infection of blood, and not the distemperature of the climate, which also may be proved by this example, that these black men are found in all parts of Africa, as well without the Tropics, as within, even unto Capo d'Buona Speranza southward, where, by reason of the sphere, should be the same temperature as is in Spain, Laddigna, and Sicilia, where all be of very good complexions.

STEPHEN BATMAN (1542–84)

Batman uponn Bartholome, his booke De proprietatibus rerum
(London: Thomas East, 1582), 390–91.

Church of England clergyman, author, limner, and antiquarian, Stephen Batman comments upon Bartholomaeus Anglicus's thirteenth-century encyclopedia, *De Proprietatibus Rerum* (extracted earlier in this volume) in his *Batman upon Bartholomew*. Notable here is the connection between bodily humors and skin color, which is a staple feature of early humoral medicine

Keywords: Skin Color—Humors—Passion—Climate—Blackness of
          Moors

De Colorum mutatione, Chapter 10

. . . [The] colour of the skin is . . . gendered and cometh sometime of humours inward, and sometime of passions of the soul. Also changing of colour in the skin cometh of inner things: sometime by hot humours, and sometime by cold, for it happeneth that hot humours, both compound and simple, cooleth and be cold, and also cold humours or cooled heateth, and according thereunto the colour in the skin is wont to vary, for when the cold humours were hot, white colour turneth into citrine or into red. And when hot humours doth cool, then red colour doth change to white or pale, and so of other it is to be understood. Also changing in the skin cometh of passions of the soul. The red waxeth pale for anguish or for dread, for in dread the heart closeth, and heat that is in the outer parts draweth inward, and therefore the outer parts wax pale. Also the pale waxeth red for wrath, for in wrath the heart openeth and desireth wreak, and the heat passeth suddenly from the inner parts to the outer parts, and so the blood heateth, and is

[29] In earlier accounts, such as those of Mandeville (see extract in this volume), Cham (or Ham) was understood to have inherited Asia, and Shem Africa. Also, in earlier writings, servitude rather than blackness was seen to be the curse that attached to Ham's progeny, as in Andrew Horn's *The mirrour of justices* (1290), extracted in this volume. This tradition survives in later writings, as can be seen in the extracts from King James's Bible (1611), William Strachey's *For the colony in Virginea Britannia* (1612) and Thomas Browne's *Pseudodoxia epidemica* (1646). The nature of Ham's crime also shifts in all these different accounts.

between the skin and the flesh, and so red colour is suddenly gendered. Also in men of the nation of Moors, the black colour cometh of the inner parts, and whitish colour in Almains and Dutchmen. For the country Mauritania is the most hottest country in Ethiopia, in the which country for great heat the blood is burnt between the skin and the flesh, and maketh all the members black. And so he that first dwelled in Ethiopia was made black. But afterward by continual heat of the sun such blackness sprang into all his offspring. And of black father and black mother cometh black children. But in that place only the father and mother be continually burnt with the heat of the sun, and therefore in temperate countries and land that be somewhat cold, swart coloured men getteth children temperate in colour, as Macrobius, Aristotle, and Avicenna mean.[30] And contrariwise, the Almaynes and Scots that dwell in cold countries, for in them cold stoppeth the holes and pores without and the heat is drawn inward, and therefore the skin is white without.

BARTOLOMÉ DE LAS CASAS (1474–1566)

The Spanish colonie, or Briefe chronicle of the acts and gestes of the Spaniardes in the West Indies, called the newe world, trans. by M.M.S (London, William Brome, 1583), A1r–A3v, C3v–C4v.

Bartolomé de las Casas traveled to Hispaniola in the West Indies, where he sought to reform the conditions of the indigenous population, focusing particularly on conversion, the abolition of slavery, and forced Indian labor in the *encomienda* system, a type of modified feudalism under which the Indians supposedly retained their rights to the land. In practice, the system produced cheap labor for the Spanish. As Bishop of Chiapa, Las Casas was charged with enforcing new laws declaring the *encomienda* non-hereditary (and requiring owners to free their workers after one generation). His indictment of Spanish cruelty circulated widely in England and Europe, creating what came to be known as "the Black Legend." Protestants used this critique to argue for their own supposedly more humanitarian form of colonialism.

Keywords: Spanish Colonialism—Simplicity—Cannibalism—
Conversion—Native Americans—Colonial Violence

. . . God created all these innumerable multitudes [of Indians] in every sort, very simple, without subtlety, or craft, without malice, very obedient, and very faithful to their natural liege lords, and to the Spaniards, whom they serve very humble, very patient, very desirous of peace making, and peaceful, without brawls and strugglings, without quarrels, without strife, without rancour or hatred, by no means desirous of revengement.

[30] Batman's statement indicates that the attribution of skin color to climate could also accommodate the association of skin color with moral qualities.

They are also people very gentle and very tender and of an easy complexion, and which can sustain no travail, and do die very soon of any disease whatsoever, in such force as the very children of princes and noblemen brought up amongst us, in all commodities ease, and delicateness, are not more soft than those of that country, yea although they be the children of labourers.[31] They are also very poor folk, which possess little, neither yet do so much as desire to have much worldly goods, and therefore neither are they proud, ambitious, nor covetous. Their diet is such as it seemeth the holy fathers in the desert hath not been more scarce. Their appareling is commonly to go naked, all save their shamefast parts alone covered. . . . They have their understanding very pure and quick, being teachable and capable of all good learning, very apt to receive our holy Catholic faith, and to be instructed in good and virtuous manners, having less encumbrances and disturbances to the attaining thereunto than all the folk of the world besides, and are so enflamed, ardent, and importune to know and understand the matters of the faith after they have but begun once to taste them, as likewise the exercise of the sacraments of the church, and the divine serves, that in truth, the religion men have need to a singular patience to support them. . . .

Upon these lambs so meek, so qualified and endowed of their maker and creator, as hath been said, entered the Spanish incontinent as they knew them, as wolves, as lions, and as tigers most cruel of long time famished, and have not done in those quarters these 40 years be past neither yet do at this present, ought else save tear them in pieces, kill them, martyr them, afflict them, torment them, and destroy them by strange sorts of cruelties. . . .

We are able to yield a good and certain account that there is within the space of the said 40 years, by those said tyrannies and devilish doings of the Spaniards, done to death unjustly and tyrannously more than twelve millions of souls, men, women, and children. And I verily do believe and think not to mistake therein, that there are dead more than fifteen millions of souls. . . .

The cause why the Spanish have destroyed such an infinite [number] of souls hath been only that they had held it for their last scope and mark to get gold, and to enrich themselves in a short time, and to mount at one leap to very high estates, in no wise agreeable to their persons, or for to say in a word, the cause hereof hath been their avarice and ambition, which hath seized them the exceedingest in the world in consideration of those lands so happy and rich, and the people so humble, so patient, and so easy to be subdued. . . .

---

[31] The idea that Native Americans were childlike could also be used to justify their necessary subjugation, as Francisco de Vitoria argued: "It would seem that for these barbarians the same applies as to the feebleminded, for they cannot govern themselves better than simple-minded idiots. They are not even better than beasts and wild animals, because they take neither more dainty nor better food than these. Their stupidity is much greater than that of the children or feebleminded of other peoples" (cited in Tzvetan Todorov, *The Conquest of America: The Question of the Other*, translated by Richard Howard [New York: Harper & Row, 1984], 181).

In the Isle of Hispaniola, which was the first (as we have said) where the Spaniards arrived, began the great slaughters and spoils of the people, the Spaniards having begun to take their wives and children of the Indians, for to serve their turn and to use them ill, and having begun to eat their victuals, gotten by their sweat and travail, not contenting them with that which the Indians gave them of their own goodwill. . . .

. . . The Spaniards with their horses, their spears and lances, began to commit murders and strange cruelties. They entered into towns, boroughs, and villages, sparing neither children, nor old men, neither women with child, neither them that lay in, but that they ripped their bellies and cut them in pieces, as if they had been opening of lambs shut up in their fold. They laid wagers such as [who] with one thrust of a sword would paunch or bowel a man in the midst, or with one blow of a sword would most readily and deliverly cut off his head, or that would best pierce his entrails at one stroke.[32] They took the little souls by the heels, ramping them from the mother's dugs, and crushed their heads against the cliffs. Others they cast into the rivers, laughing and mocking, and when they tumbled into the water, they said, "Now shift for thy self such-a-one's corpse." They put others together with their mothers and all that they met to the edge of the sword. They made certain gibbets long and low, in such sort that the feet of the hanged, touched in a manner the ground, every one enough for thirteen, in the honour and worship of our saviour and his twelve apostles (as they used to speak) and setting to fire, burned them all quick that were fastened. . . .

Of the province of Nicaragua

. . . [W]hen they wanted bread, the Spaniards took away from the Indians their maize, which they had in store for provision, to nourish them and their children. Whereby there died of famine more than twenty or thirty thousand souls. And it came to pass that a woman fallen mad with the famine slew her son to eat him. . . .

This tyrant [Governor Pedrarias Davila] had a custom, when as he went to make war upon any city or province, to carry thither of the Indians already under yoke, as many as he could, to make war upon the other Indians. And as he gave unto [the] ten or twenty thousand men which he led along no sustenance, he allowed them to eat the Indians which they took. And so by this means he had in his camp an ordinary shambles of man's flesh, where, in his presence, they killed and roasted children. . . .

The Kingdom of Spain is in so great danger to be lost, robbed, oppressed and made desolate by foreign nations, namely by the Turks and Moors, because that God who is the most just, true, and sovereign king over all the world, is wrath for the great sins and offenses that the Spaniards have committed throughout the Indies, by afflicting, oppressing, tyrannous dealings, robbing and slaying such and so many people without law or equity. . . .

[32] Deliverly = Nimbly, quickly, deftly.

REGINALD SCOT (1537/38?–99)

*The discoverie of witchcraft, wherein the lewde dealing
of witches and witchmongers is notablie detected . . .*
(London: Henry Denham, 1584), 152–53, 311–12.

The discoverie of witchcraft challenged contemporary writings on
witchcraft, arguing that all the women persecuted for witchcraft
were innocent, either deluded or the victims of torture. Scott
widened his attack to include many other kinds of superstition, in
which he included Catholicism and astrology. He dismissed the idea
of maternal impression, like alchemy, as a type of confidence trick.

Keywords: Skin Color—Monstrosity—Jacob and Laban—Maternal
Impression—Blackness of Moors

Book 7, chapter 15: Of vain apparitions, how people have been brought
to fear bugs, which is partly reformed by preaching of the gospel, the true
effect of Christ's miracles[33]

But certainly, some one knave in a white sheet hath cozened and abused
many thousands that way. . . . The Scythians, being a stout and warlike
nation (as diverse writers report) never see any vain sights or spirits. It is a
common saying, "A lion feareth no bugs." But in our childhood our mothers's maids have so terrified us with an ugly devil having horns on his head,
fire in his mouth, and a tail in his breech, eyes like a basin, fangs like a dog,
claws like a bear, a skin like a Niger, and a voice roaring like a lion, whereby
we start and are afraid when we hear one cry "boo."[34]

Book 13, chapter 16: How some are abused with natural magic, and
sundry examples thereof when illusion is added thereunto, of Jacob's pied
sheep, and of a black Moor

. . . [I]f we shall yield that to be divine, supernatural, and miraculous, which
we cannot comprehend; a witch, a papist, a conjuror, a cozener, and a juggler may make us believe they are gods. Or else with more impiety we shall
ascribe such power and omnipotence unto them, or unto the devil, as only
and properly appertaineth to God. . . . And at the discovery of these miraculous toys, we shall have leave to wonder at them, and begin to wonder at our
selves, that could be so abused with baubles. Howbeit, such things as God
hath laid up secretly in nature are to be weighed with great admiration, and
to be searched out with such industry as may become a Christian man. . . .
We find in the Scriptures diverse natural and secret experiments practiced,

[33] Bug = An object of terror, usually an imaginary one; a bugbear or hobgoblin.
[34] In Book 15, Chapters 34 and 36, Scot debunks the story of St. Margaret doing combat
with a devil who is compared to a "Niger" (455–59).

as namely that of Jacob, for pied sheep: which are confirmed by profane authors, and not only verified in lambs and sheep, but in horses, peacocks, conies, etc. We read also of a woman that brought forth a young black Moor, by means of an old black Moor who was in her house at the time of her conception, whom she beheld in fantasy, as is supposed. Howbeit a jealous husband will not be satisfied with such fantastical imaginations. For in truth a black Moor never faileth to beget black children, of what colour soever the other be. . . . .[35]

NICOLAS DE NICOLAY (1517–83)

The navigations, peregrinations and voyages, made into Turkie . . . , translated by T. Washington (London: Thomas Dawson, 1585), 8, 10, 11, 53, 58–60, 69, 71, 73–74, 117, 119, 125, 130–31.

Nicolas de Nicolay went to Constantinople in 1551 as part of an embassy from the French king to Suleiman the Magnificent. His account, describing the cities, customs, and institutions of the Turks, features fifty-eight illustrations detailing the dress of Ottoman subjects from the Grand Vizier in Constantinople to Moorish slaves in Algiers. For many English readers, Nicolay's numerous reports of Christians "turned Turk" would have been as disturbing as his account of Ottoman diversity was stunningly foreign.

Keywords: Conversions—Renegades—Turks—Veiling—Baths—
        Women's Desire for Women—Slavery—Concubinage—
        Persian Women's Beauty—Jews

The most part of the Turks of Algier, whether they be of the king's house-hold or the gallies, are Christians renied,[36] or Mahumetised, of all nations, but most of them, Spaniards, Italians, and of Provence, of the islands and coasts of the Sea Mediterranean, given all to whoredome, sodometry, theft, and all other most detestable vices, living only of rovings, spoils, and pill[ag]ing at the seas, and the island, being about them: and with their prac-tical art bring daily to Algiers a number of poor Christians, which they sell unto the Moores, and other merchants of Barbary for slaves, who afterward transport them and sell them where they think good, or else beating them miserably with staves, do employ and constrain them to work in the fields, and in all other vile and abject occupations and servitude almost intolerable: And therefore it is not to be marveled at though these poor Christian slaves

---

[35] Scot's skepticism in regard to the notion of maternal impression stands in contrast to sev-eral authors in this volume, including Hippocrates, Boaistuau, Best, Buoni, and Topsell. See also the story of Jacob and Laban, extracted here from Genesis 30 of the King James Bible, and its redactions in Browne and Munster.

[36] Renied (also renyed) = The past participle of renegade.

Figure 3 "Maiden Moriscoe Slave" from Nicolas de Nicolay, *The navigations, peregrinations and voyages, made into Turkie* (1585). Reproduced by permission of the Folger Shakespeare Library.

made of it no scruple at all in putting of us in danger, to set themselves at liberty. . . . [A]ll along the river and the shore the Moorish women and maiden slaves of Alger do go to wash their linen, being commonly whole naked, saving that they wear a piece of cotton cloth of some strange colour to cover their secret parts, (which notwithstanding for a little piece of money they will willingly uncover). . . . But as for the wives of the Turks or Moores, they are not seen [to] go uncovered, for they wear a great bernuche made of a blanket of white, black, or violet colour, which covereth their whole body and the head. . . .

There is moreover within the midst of [Constantinople], the old Sarail, which first was builded and inhabited by Mehmet the Second . . . within which do dwell the wives and concubines of the great Turk, which in number are above 200 being the most part daughters of Christians, some being taken by courses on the seas or by land . . . some of the other are bought of merchants, and afterwards . . . presented unto the great Turk, who keepeth them within this Sarail, well apparelled, nourished and entertained under straight keeping of . . . an eunuch of the late Barbarousse. . . .

The Turks's wives . . . do delight at all times to haunt the baths, as well for the continuance of their health, as beautifying of their persons. . . . [T]he other and principalest reason is, to have good occasion and honest excuse to go abroad out of their houses, within the which they are continually closed up for the great jealousy of their husbands . . . and oftentimes under colour of going to baths, they resort to other places where they think good to accomplish their pleasures. . . . [They] do familiarly wash one another, whereby it cometh to pass . . . sometimes [they] become so fervently in love the one of the other as if it were with men, in such sort that perceiving some maiden, or woman of excellent beauty, they will not cease until they have found means to bathe with them, and to handle and grope them everywhere at their pleasures, so full they are of luxuriousness and feminine wantonness. . . .

Azamoglans are children which the Turk sendeth for to be levied in form of tribute . . . throughout all Grecia, Albania, Valaquia, Serbia, Bosnia, Trebisond, Mingrelia and all other provinces of his dominion of the Christians dwelling within the same, taking away by tyranny more than barbarous, of every three male children one . . . which ought to be a great consideration and compassion unto all true Christian princes for to stir and provoke them unto a good peace and Christian unity, and to apply their forces jointly, to deliver the children of their Christian brethren . . . amongst which the most fairest are chosen to be put into the sarail of the great Turk, where they are nourished and brought up in the law of Mahomet, and by diverse masters being eunuchs, are instructed well to ride horses, shooting, and all other exercises of arms and agility, to the intent in process of time to make them the more obeisant. . . .

. . . Of these azamoglans, Christian children Mahometised, the venomous nature is so great, mischievous and pernicious, that incontinent after they are taken from the laps of their parents and instructed in the laws of the Turks, they do declare themselves, as well by words as deeds mortal enemies unto the Christians, so as they practice nothing else than to do unto them all injuries and wrongs possible, and how great or aged soever they become, they will never acknowledge their fathers, mothers, nor other friends: . . . so as nowadays the renyed Christians, are a great deal worse unto their Christian brethren, yea unto those of their own blood, than the natural Turks are, so doth this unhappy bringing up of them deprive them of their first nature, and inclination. . . .

. . . [The] janissaries . . . are likewise of the number of those which have been taken away from the hands of their fathers and mothers, brought to leave the true faith and light of Jesus Christ, and to follow the dark and blind sect of the false prophet Mahumet. . . . [T]he number of them now is 1200 in their order, which is the principal strength and most puissant force of the army of the great Turk. . . . [S]ince that these janissaries have perceived their company to . . . become so great in number, force and authority, they have usurped and maintained such a bold advantage, that so soon as their emperor is dead, incontinently are given unto them for a prey and pillage all the money, clothes, merchandises, and movables of the Jews and Christians. . . . Being a custom certainly very barbarous and cruel and more than tyrannical, which reasonably to consider as well the time past, present, and to come, is a true and manifest token of the ruins threatened of this Oriental empire; which by the same forces whereby now it is maintained, shall one day be clean overthrown: for even as the Roman Empire (without comparison both greater and better ordered than that of the Turks) was overthrown, and in the end brought into decay from the time that the Caesars and Antonys failed, and the Pretorian legions (which nowadays representeth the estate of these janissaries) began to become rulers over their masters, under pretext of such a military gift: even so by these means shall it happen unto the Turks. . . .

. . . Persians nowadays, contrary to their ancient customs, are much given to all pleasure and voluptuousness, appareling themselves very sumptuously . . . using singular perfumes, and taking pleasure and delight in all jewels and precious stones. By their law it is permitted unto them to have many wives which because they are very jealous of them, they keep shut up under the keeping of the eunuchs, and nevertheless like unto the Turks and other nations of the East parts, they are so given unto the detestable sin against nature, that they take it for no shame, but have places appointed and ordained for the same. . . . [B]ut to say truth, I do find them without comparison, more noble, more civil, more liberal, and of better spirit and judgment than the Turks are, unto whom (what countenance soever they do show) they are mortal enemies. . . .

If amongst the women of the East parts, the Persians have of all ancestry obtained the laud and praise to be the most gentle, and proper in their apparel and clothing, so are they likewise no lessfull made in proportion of their bodies and natural beauty: namely, and above all other, those of the ancient and royal city of Sciras, which are so praised in their beauty, whiteness, pleasant civility and shamefast grace, that the Moors of an old and common proverb will say, that their Prophet Mahomet would not go to Scyras, for fear that he having once tasted of the pleasures of those women, his soul after his death could never have entered into paradise. We have moreover sufficient testimony of the singular beauty of these Persian women by Alexander the Great, who, keeping the daughters of the King Darius as his prisoners, would never salute them but with his eyes looking downwards, and besides so seldom as he could, for the fear which he had of being overcome with their beauty. . . .

The number of the Jews dwelling throughout all the cities of Turkey and Grecia, and principally at Constantinople is so great, that it is a thing marvelous and incredible, for the number of these, using trade and traffic of merchandise, like of money at usury, doth there multiply so from day to day . . . that it may be said with good reason that at this present day they have in their hands the most and greatest traffic of merchandise and ready money, that is in all Levant. And likewise their shops and warehouses the best furnished of all rich sorts of merchandises, which are in Constantinople are those of the Jews. Likewise they have amongst them workmen of all arts and handicrafts most excellent; and specially of the Maranes of late banished and driven out of Spain and Portugal, who to the great detriment and damage of Christianity, have taught the Turks diverse inventions, crafts and engines of war, as to make artillery, harquebuses, gunpowder, shot and other munitions. . . . [T]hey have also the commodity and usage to speak and understand all other sorts of languages used in Levant, which serveth them greatly for the communication and traffic, which they have with other strange nations, to whom oftentimes they serve for dragomans, or interpreters. Besides, this detestable nation of the Jews, are men full of all malice, fraud, deceit, and subtle dealing, exercising execrable usuries amongst the Christians and other nations without any consciences or reprehension. . . . [S]ince their extermination and the vengeance upon Jerusalem unto this present day, they had at no time any certain dwelling place upon the face of the earth, but have always gone straying dispersed and driven away from country to country. And yet even at this day in what region soever they are permitted to dwell under tribute, they are abhorred of God and men, and more persecuted of the Turks . . . than of any other nation, who have them in such disdain and hatred, that by no means they will eat in their company, and much less marry any of their wives or daughters, notwithstanding that oftentimes they do marry with Christians, whom they permit to live according to their law, and have a pleasure to eat and be conversant with Christians: and that which is worse, if a Jew would become a Muselman, he should not be received, except first leaving his Judaical sect he became a Christian. The Jews which dwell in Constantinople, Adrianople, Bursia, Salonica, Gallipoli, and other places of the dominion of the great Turk, are all appareled with long garments, like unto the Grecians, and other nations of Levant, but for their mark and token to be known from others, they wear a yellow turban. . . .

GEFFREY WHITNEY (1548–1600/1601)

A choice of emblemes, and other devises, for the most part gatherd out of sundrie writers, Englished and moralized . . .
(Leyden: Francis Raphelengius, 1586), 57.

Whitney's *A choice of emblemes* was the earliest published and best-known English emblem book, although preceded by others in manuscript form, notably Thomas Palmer's *Two Hundred Poosees* (also extracted in this volume). *A choice of embleme* contains 248 emblems, consisting of illustrations, mottos, and explicating verses generally drawing a moral lesson. "Aethiopem Lavare," the emblem reproduced here, echoes an old idea, found as early as Aesop (see entry in this volume). It is significant that Aesop's Ethiopian becomes a 'Man of Inde' in Palmer and a 'blackamoor' in Whitney.

Keywords: Washing the Ethiope—Skin Color—Fixity of Color

Figure 4 "Aethiopem Lavare," from Geffrey Whitney, *A choice of emblemes, and other devises* (Leyden, 1586). From the collections of The Rare Book & Manuscript Library, University of Illinois at Urbana-Champaign.

Leave off with pain the blackamoor to scour
With washing oft and wiping more than due:
For thou shalt find that nature is of power,
Do what thou canst to keep his former hue:
Though with a fork we nature thrust away.
She turns again if we withdraw our hand:
And though we oft to conquer her assay,
Yet all in vain she turns if still we stand.
    Then evermore, in what thou dost assay,
    Let reason rule, and do the things thou may.

THÉODORE DE BÈZE (1519–1605)

Master Bezaes sermons upon the three chapters of the canticle of canticles (Oxford: Joseph Barnes, 1587), 76, 84–85.

As Calvin's successor, the French theologian Théodore de Bèze was a key figure in securing the establishment of Calvinism in

Europe. His numerous sermons and commentaries were influential in the development of Reformed theology; his Greek editions and Latin translations of the New Testament were basic sources for the Geneva Bible and the King James Version (1611). In his exegesis of the Song of Songs, Bèze takes pains to point out that the bride is not actually black or Ethiopian.

Keywords: Song of Songs—Skin Color—Moorishness—Sun-burn—Female Beauty

The spouse therefore speaking unto [the Daughters of Jerusalem] . . . upbraideth them. . . : "I see what the matter is. You think me not fair because my hue is sun-burned and black in comparison of you who have so fresh & fair a hue. Now I confess that I am indeed black, but yet notwithstanding, I have a fair and pleasant beauty which you see not. For as, if you behold me outwardly, I am as black & as tanned as if I had been brought up under the skins and cabins of these Moors and Arabians: so if you consider of my beauty through this blackness, there is no pavilion or tent of Solomon, that rich & mighty king, so fair, and so glittering as my self." Afterward she addeth, that this tanned hue of hers is not natural, but that it hath happened unto her, as unto a young maiden driven by her naughty and wicked brethren out of her father's house . . . and made to endure abroad the parching of the sun and other injuries of the weather. . . .
     . . . [T]his spouse although such persecutions do darken, and as I may so say, do utterly take away her native and ingenious beauty, yea make her to look more like a Moor or Arabian . . . so is it notwithstanding that through this blackness of hers remain certain traces of beauty. Nay farther, as white showeth more white being laid near unto black, so afflictions, which are meant by this blackness, cause her to show more beautiful and fair. . . .

WILLIAM RANKINS (fl. 1587–1601)

The English ape, the Italian imitation, the footesteppes of Fraunce
(London: Robert Robinson, 1588), 3.

William Rankins is best known for his strident denunciation of the theater in *A Mirrour of Monsters* (1587). His career as a pamphleteer was marked by moralistic tirades. Like *A Mirrour of Monsters's* concern with theater-goers transformed by the spectacle of a play, *The English ape* worries over the transformation of Englishmen who adopt foreign fashions or manners.

Keywords: Fashion—Imitation—Climate—Englishness—Infidels—Barbarity

Hence cometh to pass that our Englishmen blinded (with an Italian disguise) and disfiguring themselves (with every French fashion) corrupt their natural manners (by their climate created perfect) with the peevish pelf of every peacock's plume, (and like as Aesop's daw) bedeck themselves with others' deformity.[37] Thus continual strife to frame a uniformity of inward condition to external habit breedeth such intolerable inconvenience: that we seem rather the mean which nature hath marked for a prodigious spectacle of her contrary opinions than a people where politic proceedings and peaceable government swayeth with law and equity. Look we awhile into the manners of heathen men: into the disposition of infidels, whose rudeness might privilege such barbarous besottedness, and whose wit (grossly composed) yieldeth not the perseverance of every ill, and whose sensual appetite dulleth the conceit of discerning of every secret mischief. Where we shall find such a hatred of incest, such a love of temperance, such a despising of delicacies and such a contending of moderation in manners that they may rather seem the chief cherishers of virtue. . . .

ROBERT FABYAN (d. 1513)

"Of three savages which Cabot brought home and presented unto the kyng . . . mentioned by Robert Fabyan," in Richard Hakluyt, *The principall navigations, voiages and discoveries of the English nation* (London: George Bishop and Ralph Newberie, 1589), 515.

Robert Fabyan, a London merchant, wrote *The Concordaunce of Hystoryes*, which chronicled the history of England and France from the alleged founding of Albion (Britain) by Brutus in the first century to the reign of King Henry VII. This book was published four times under various titles including *The new chronicles of England and of France* (1516) and *Fabyans cronycle* (1533). None of these editions contain the passage reproduced here, which was found in a manuscript authored by Fabyan and first published by Hakluyt. It indicates that fashion could be as powerful a marker of difference as skin color or language.

Keywords: Native Americans—Captivity—Diet—Clothing and Identity—Englishness

Of three savages which Cabot brought home and presented unto the king in the fourteenth year of his reign, mentioned by the foresaid Robert Fabyan

This year also were brought unto the king three men taken in Newfound Island that before I spake of, in William Purchas time being mayor. These were clothed in beasts skins, and did eat raw flesh, and spake such speech that no man could understand them, and in their demeanor like to brute beasts,

---

[37] Pelf = Junk, trash; frippery. Thomas Nashe expresses a similar concern in *Christs tears over Jerusalem* when he refers to England as "the players' stage of gorgeous attire, the ape of all nations' superfluities" (73).

whom the king kept a time after. Of the which upon two years after, I saw two appareled after the manner of Englishmen in Westminster Palace, which that time I could not discern from Englishmen, til I was learned what they were, but as for speech, I heard none of them utter one word.

RICHARD HAKLUYT (1552–1616)

"The worthy and famous voyage of the Master Thomas Candish made round about the globe of the earth . . . begun in the yeare 1586," in Richard Hakluyt, *The principall navigations, voiages and discoveries of the English nation* (London: George Bishop and Ralph Newberie, 1589), 809, and Richard Hakluyt, *The Principal Navigations, Voyages, Traffiques, and Discoveries of the English Nation* (London: George Bishop, Ralph Newberie, and Robert Barker, 1599–1600), Vol. 3, 819–22.

Richard Hakluyt published accounts of Thomas Cavendish's (also known as Candish) 1586–88 circumnavigation of the globe in both editions of his *Principal Navigations*, the most important English collection of narratives of exploration, discovery, and travel. Ascribed in the second edition to Francis Petty, the narrative was more likely to have been compiled by Hakluyt from several briefer accounts. Hakluyt's roles as both churchman and editor were combined in his ardent advocacy of English overseas trade and colonization. The first extract (from the first edition) describes the English violence against Africans, which was expunged from the second edition. The second extract (from the second edition) describes the natives of what are now the Marianas Islands in terms of their sexual excesses and the natives of Java in terms of despotic government, attributes not remarked upon in the first edition, but which became central to later justifications of imperialism.

Keywords: Java—Guinea—Nakedness—Sodomy—Tyranny—Skin Color

From the first edition:

The fifth day of August we fell with the Island of Forteventura, and sailed thence to Cape Blank and so to the coast of Guinea unto a harbour called Sierra Leone, where having conference with the Negroes we fell at variance, so that threescore of our men went on shore, and drove them from their town, and sacked their houses, and burnt their dwellings. . . .

The first of September we burned there some one-hundred-and-fifty houses because of their bad dealing with us and all the Christians in this place we redeemed a Portingal whom by treason they had caught and held in very miserable captivity. . . .

Thus sailing through the straits, the twentieth day of January in the midway we espied savages of a reasonable stature, and went to them, and conferred with them: but such was their brutishness and their treachery, that they would have betrayed us under show of amity: but we espying their treason gave the first onset, and every one of us chose his man, and by that means slew some, and hurt more, the rest escaped. . . .

From the second edition:

We rode for the space of nine days about this island of Capul, where we had diverse kinds of fresh victuals, with excellent fresh water in every bay, and great store of wood. The people of this island go almost all naked, and are tawny of colour. The men wear only a strap about their waists of some kind of linen of their own weaving, which is made of plantain-leaves, and another strap coming from their back under their twists, which covereth their privy parts, and is made fast to their girdles at the navels. . . . Every man and man-child among them hath a nail of tin thrust quite through the head of his privy part, being split in the lower end, and riveted, and on the head of the nail is as it were a crown which is driven through their privities when they be young, and the place growth up again, without any great pain to the child. And they take this nail out and in as occasion serveth. And for the truth thereof, we ourselves have taken one of these nails from a son of one of the kings, which was of the age of ten years, who did wear the same in his privy member. This custom was granted at the request of the women of the country, who finding their men to be given to the foul sin of sodomy, desired some remedy against that mischief, and obtained this before named of the magistrates. Moreover, all the males are circumcised, having the foreskin of their flesh cut away. These people wholly worship the devil, and oftentimes have conference with him, which appeareth unto them in most ugly and monstrous shape. . . .

There came two Portugals to us, which enquired of Don Antonio their king, then in England, and told us of the Javanese as followeth. The name of the king of that part of the Island was Raja Bolamboam, who was a man had in great majesty and fear among them. . . . The king himself is a man of great years and hath an hundred wives; his son hath fifty. The custom of the country is that whensoever the king doth die, they take the body so dead, and burn it, and preserve the ashes of him, and within five days next after, the wives of the said king so dead, according to the custom and use of their country, every one of them go together to a place appointed . . . and every one with a dagger in their hand . . . stab themselves to the heart, and with their hands all to be-bath themselves in their own blood, and falling groveling on their faces, so end their days. This thing is as true as it seemeth to any hearer to be strange. The men of themselves be very politic and subtle, and singularly valiant, being naked men, in any action they undertake, and wonderfully at commandment and fear of their king. For example: If their king command them to undertake any exploit, be it never so dangerous or desperate, they dare not refuse it, though they die every man in the execution of the same. For he will cut off the heads of every one of them which return alive without bringing of their purpose to pass, which . . . maketh them the most valiant people in all the southeast parts of the world, for they never fear any death. . . . Moreover, although the men be tawny of colour and go continually naked, yet their women be fair of complexion and go more appareled

JOHN HAWKINS (1532–95)

"The first voyage of the right worshipful and valiant knight, Sir John Hawkins, now treasurer of Her Majesty's navie Royall, made to the West Indies, 1562," in Richard Hakluyt, *The principall navigations, voiages and discoveries of the English nation* (London: George Bishop and Ralph Newberie, 1589), 521–522.

John Hawkins led the first English slave-trading voyage to the Guinea coast and the Spanish West Indies. In further voyages in 1564 and 1567, investors included Queen Elizabeth, William Cecil, and the Earls of Leicester and Pembroke. As a reward for his profitable ventures, Hawkins was knighted and assigned a coat of arms featuring an African slave. Hawkins's privateering

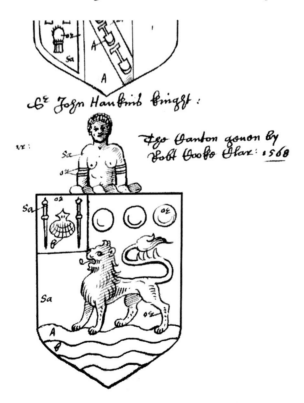

Figure 5   Arms of Sir John Hawkins. Reproduced by permission of the College of Arms, London.

was at the center of an undeclared naval war with Spain that was to continue until 1604. This brief account of his landmark first voyage indicates the exchange value of African slaves.

Keywords: Atlantic Slavery—Commodification of African Slaves

Master John Hawkins having made diverse voyages to the Isles of the Canaries, and there by his good and upright dealing being grown in love and favour with the people, informed himself amongst them by diligent inquisition, of the state of the West India. . . . And being amongst other particulars assured that Negroes were very good merchandise in Hispaniola, and that store of Negroes might easily be had upon the coast of Guinea, resolved with himself to make trial thereof, and communicated that device with his worshipful friends of London. . . .

With this company he put off and departed from the coast of England in the month of October 1562, and in his course touched first at Teneriffe, where he received friendly entertainment. From thence he passed to Sierra Leona, upon the coast of Guinea . . . where he stayed some good time, and got into his possession, partly by the sword, and partly by other means, to the number of 300 Negroes at the least, besides other merchandises which that country yieldeth. With this prey he sailed over the ocean sea unto the island of Hispaniola, and arrived first at the port of Isabella: and there he had reasonable utterance of his English commodities, as also of some part of his Negroes, trusting the Spaniards no further than by his own strength he was able to master them. From the port of Isabella he went to Puerto de Plata, where he made like sales, standing always upon his guard. From thence also he sailed to Monte Christi, another port on the north side of Hispaniola, where he had peaceable traffic, and made vent of the whole number of his Negroes, for which he received in those three places by way of exchange such quantity of merchandise that he did not only lade his own three ships with hides, ginger, sugars, and some quantity of pearls, but he freighted also two other hulks with hides and other like commodities, which he sent into Spain. And thus leaving the island, he returned and disembarked, passing out by the islands of the Caicos, without further entering into the Bay of Mexico, in this his first voyage to the West India. And so with prosperous success and much gain to himself and the aforesaid adventurers, he came home, and arrived in the month of September 1563.[38]

---

[38] In a deposition to the High Court Admiralty on Saturday 23 April 1569, Hawkins testified that in November 1567 he bought "a good quantity of Negroes" in Guinea and took them to the West Indies where he did brisk business to the tune of "29, 743 pesos of gold." At Vera Cruz, some of his human cargo was captured by the Spanish. Hawkins estimated that each slave might have been sold "for four Pesos of gold every Negro (the peso of gold being worth fifteen reals of plate as aforesaid). . . . And by that experience knoweth that such choice Negroes had been commonly sold there for one hundred and fifty pesos of gold. And sayeth that this last year there was one choice Negro sold at Rio de Hacho for one hundred and fifty pesos of gold. . . ." See *Documents Illustrative of the History of the Slave Trade to America, Vol. 1: 1441–1700*, Elizabeth Donnan, Washington D.C.: Carnegie Institution of Washington, 1930), 70–71.

ROBERT GAINSH (1533–1615)

"The Second Voyage to Guinea," in Richard Hakluyt, *The principall navigations, voiages and discoveries of the English nation* (London: George Bishop and Ralph Newberie, 1589), 94–97.

The likely author of this unattributed report on the 1564 voyage to Guinea printed by Hakluyt, Robert Gainsh is identified in a marginal note as the master of the ship *John Evangelist*. Notably, the report is among the first published accounts of England's involvement in the African slave trade, and Gainsh is blamed in a later account for turning the Guinea natives against the English when he abducted, among others, the son of a chief. Perhaps in defense of the slave trade, Gainsh's account draws on an unusually wide range of classical, biblical, and climatic notions of difference.

Keywords: Africans—Moors—Blackness—Brutishness—Monstrous Races—Cannibalism—Nakedness—Slavery—Climate— Skin Color—Scarification

. . . It is to be understood, that the people which now inhabit the regions of the coast of Guinea, and the middle parts of Africa, as Libya the inner, and Nubia, with diverse other great & large regions about the same, were in old time called Ethiopes and Nigritae, which we now call Moores, Moorens, or Negroes, a people of beastly living, without a God, law, religion, or common wealth, and so scorched and vexed with the heat of the sun, that in many places they curse it when it riseth. Of the regions and people about the inner Libya (called Libya interior) Gemma Phrysius writeth thus.

Libya interior is very large and desolate, in the which are many horrible wildernesses & mountains, replenished with diverse kinds of wild and monstrous beasts and serpents. First from Mauritania or Barbary toward the South is Getulia, a rough and savage region, whose inhabitants are wild and wandering people. . . . The Ethiopians called Nigritae occupy a great part of Africa, and are extended to the West Ocean. Southward also they reach to the river Nigritis . . . on the one side thereof, the inhabitants are of high stature and black, and on the other side, of brown or tawny colour, and low stature. . . .[39]

There are also other people of Libya called Garamantes, whose women are common: for they contract no matrimony, neither have respect to chastity. . . . But to speak somewhat more of Ethiopia, although there are many nations of people so named, yet is Ethiopia chiefly divided into two parts, whereof the one is called Ethiopia under Egypt, a great & rich region. To this pertaineth the island Meroe, embraced round about with the streams of the

[39] Gainsh appears to borrow the idea of a river that forms a natural boundary between peoples of varying skin colors from the stories of the River Senaga circulated by Pory and later Browne, Ross, and Boyle.

river Nilus. In this island women reigned in old time. Josephus writeth, that it was sometime called Saba: and that the Queen of Saba came from thence to Jerusalem, to hear the wisdom of Solomon. From hence toward the east reigneth the said Christian Emperor Prester John, whom some call Papa Johannes, & other say that he is called Pean Juan (that is) Great John, whose empire reacheth far beyond Nilus, and is extended to the coasts of the Red Sea & Indian Sea. . . . After these is the region called Troglodytica, whose inhabitants dwell in caves and dens: for these are their houses, & the flesh of serpents their meat, as writeth Pliny, and Diodorus Siculus. They have no speech but rather a grinning and chattering. There are also people without heads, called Blemines, having their eyes and mouth in their breast. Likewise Strucophagi, and naked Ganphasantes: Satyrs also, which have nothing of men but only shape. . . .

The other Ethiope, called Ethiopia interior (that is) the inner Ethiope, is not yet known for the greatness thereof, but only by the sea coasts: yet is it described in this manner: First from the equinoctial toward the south, is a great region of Ethiopians, which bringeth forth white elephants, tigers, and the beasts called rhinoceroses. . . . Also the kingdom of Habech or Habasia, a region of Christian men, lying both on this side and beyond Nilus. Here are also the Ethiopians, called Ichthiophagi (that is) such as live only by fish, and were sometimes subdued by the wars of great Alexander. Furthermore the Aethiopians called Rhapsii, & Anthropophagi, which are accustomed to eat man's flesh, inhabit the regions near unto the mountains called *Montes Lunae* (that is) the Mountains of the Moon. . . .

[A]lthough in the stead of winter they have a cloudy and tempestuous season, yet is it not cold, but rather smothering hot, with hot showers of rain also, and somewhere such scorching winds, that what by one means and other, they seem at certain times to live as it were in furnaces, and in manner already half way in Purgatory or Hell. . . .

. . . Among other things therefore, touching the manners and nature of the people, this may seem strange, that their princes and noble men use to pounce and rase their skins with pretty knots in diverse forms, as it were branched damask, thinking that to be a decent ornament. And albeit they go in manner all naked, yet are many of them, and especially their women, in manner laden with collars, bracelets, hoops, and chains, either of gold, copper, or ivory. I myself have one of their bracelets of ivory, weighing . . . eight and thirty ounces: this one of their women did wear upon her arm. . . . Some have on every arm one, and as many on their legs, wherewith some of them are so galled, that although they are in manner made lame thereby, yet will they by no means leave them off. . . .

They are very wary people in their bargaining, and will not lose one spark of gold of any value. They use weights and measures, and are very circumspect in occupying the same. They that shall have to do with them, must use them gently: for they will not traffic or bring in any wares if they be evil used. . . .

. . . There died of our men at this last voyage about twenty and four, whereof many died at their return into the clime of the cold regions, as

between the islands of Azores and England. They brought with them certain
black slaves, whereof some were tall and strong men, and could well agree
with our meats and drinks. The cold and moist air doth somewhat offend
them. Yet doubtless men that are born in hot regions may better abide
cold, than men that are born in cold regions may abide heat, forasmuch as
vehement heat resolveth the radical moisture of men's bodies, as cold con-
straineth and preserveth the same.

This is also to be considered as a secret work of nature, that throughout
all Africke, under the equinoctial line, and near about the same on both
sides, the regions are extreme hot, and the people very black. Whereas contrarily such regions of the West Indies as are under the same line are very
temperate, and the people neither black, nor with curled and short wool on
their heads, as they of Africke have, but of the colour of an olive, with long
and black hair on their heads: the cause of which variety is declared in diverse
places in the *Decades*. . . .[40]

GIORDANO BRUNO (1548–1600)

De Immenso et Innumerabilibus and *De Monade Numero et Figura*
(both Frankfurt: Johann Wechel & Peter Fishcer, 1591)

Source: J.S. Slotkin, *Readings in Early Anthropology* (Chicago: Aldine
Publishing Company, 1965), 43.

Ordained in 1572, Bruno was deemed a heretic and excommu-
nicated in quick succession by the Roman Catholic Church (that
ultimately burned him at the stake) and the Reformed Church.
Visiting England in the 1580s, Bruno published half a dozen
books and his contacts included John Florio, Philip Sidney,
Fulke Greville, and Walter Raleigh. Although Bruno's theories
and his promotion of Copernicanism are seen today as precur-
sors to liberal philosophy and modern science, he was also an
early exponent of polygenetic theory as evidenced in the passages
included here.

Keywords: Polygenesis—Ethiopians—Pygmies—Monstrous Races

De Immenso et Innumerabilibus

> For of many colours
> Are the species of men, and the black race
> Of the Ethiopians, and the yellow offspring of America,
> And that which lies hidden in the caves of Neptune,
> And the Pygmies always shut up in the hills,
> Inhabitants of the veins of the earth, and custodians

---

[40] Peter Martyr, *The decades of the newe worlde.*

Of the mines, and the gigantic monsters of the South,
Cannot be traced to the same descent, nor are they sprung
From the generative force of a single progenitor.
Every island everywhere can give a beginning to things,
Although the same form is not preserved everywhere the same,
For one species flourishes in one place, another in another.

It is said in the prophets, and is well known among the same people [i.e., the Jews], that all races of men are to be traced to one first father, or to three, as we learn and firmly believe from the Hebrew remains, of which some trace the only superior race, that is, the Jews, to one protoplast, and the other races to the two first, which were created two days before. The religion of the recently discovered Chinese enumerate three differently named protoplasts, twenty thousand years ago. No one of sound judgment can refer the Ethiopian race to that protoplast.

De Monade Numero et Figura

The regions of the heavens are three; three of air; the water
Is divided into three; the earth is divided into three parts.
And the three races had three patriarchs,
When mother Earth produced animals, first
Enoch, Leviathan, and the third of which is Adam;
According to the belief of the Jews,
From whom alone was descended the sacred race.

GILES FLETCHER (1546–1611)

Of the Russe common wealth. Or Maner of government by the Russe emperour . . . (London: Thomas Dawson, 1591), 155, 172–73, 268–71.

Giles Fletcher was sent to Russia with instructions to conclude an alliance between England and Russia. Following his return to England in 1589 he wrote *Of the Russe common wealth*, a comprehensive account of Russian geography, government, law, methods of warfare, religion, and manners. Initially suppressed at the request of the Muscovy Company, it was reprinted in a less provocative version by Hakluyt and Purchas before being restored to its full form in 1643. Much of Fletcher's account of the Russian people draws on climatic humoralism, which characterized the people of cold, northern lands as barbaric, dull, and intellectually sluggish.

Keywords: Russians—Tartars—Complexion—Diet—Climate—
Cosmetics

Of the Tartars, and other borderers to the country of Russia

For person and complexion they have broad and flat visages, of a tanned colour into yellow and black, fierce and cruel looks, thin haired upon the upper lip and pit of the chin, light and nimble bodied, with short legs, as if they were made naturally for horsemen: whereto they practice themselves from their childhood, seldom going afoot about any business.[41] Their speech is very sudden and loud, speaking as it were out of a deep hollow throat. When they sing you would think a cow lowed, or some great bandog howled.[42] . . . They are the very same that sometimes were called Scythæ Nomades, or the Scythian shepherds, by the Greeks and Latins. Some think that the Turks took their beginning from the nation of the Crim Tartars. . . .

Of the private behaviour, or quality of the Russe people

The private behaviour and quality of the Russe people may partly be understood by that which hath been said concerning the public state and usage of the country. As touching the natural habit of their bodies, they are for the most part of a large size, and of very fleshly bodies: accounting it a grace to be somewhat gross and burly, and therefore they nourish and spread their beards, to have them long and broad. But for the most part, they are very unwieldy and inactive withal. Which may be thought to come partly of the climate and the numbness which they get by the cold in winter, and partly of their diet that standeth most of roots, onions, garlic, cabbage, and such like things that breed gross humors, which they use to eat alone, and with their other meats.

Their diet is rather much than curious. At their meals they begin commonly with a chark or small cup of aqua vitae (which they call Russe wine), and then drink not till towards the end of their meals, taking it in largely, and all together, with kissing one another at every pledge. And therefore after dinner there is no talking with them, but every man goeth to his bench to take his afternoon's sleep, which is as ordinary with them as their night's rest. When they exceed, and have variety of dishes, the first are their baked meats (for roast meats they use little) and then their broths or pottage. Their common drink is mead, the poorer sort use water and a third drink called

---

[41] In his *Microcosmus* (1621), Peter Heylyn says of the Tartars, "The men of this country . . . are swarth, not so much by the heat of the sun, as their own sluttishness; ill-favoured, thick-lipp'd, flat-nosed, broad shouldered, swift of foot, laborious, and vigilant, barbarous everywhere in behaviour" (343). A similar comment is found in Thomas Gainsford's *The glory of England, or A true description of many excellent prerogatives . . . whereby she triumpheth over all the nations of the world* (1618), which attributes the appearance of the Tartars to "the air and their sluttish customs [that] corrupts both their blood and bodies . . ." (B3v–B4r).

[42] Bandog = A dog tied or chained up, either to guard a house, or on account of its ferocity.

quasse, which is nothing else (as we say) but water turned out of his wits, with a little bran meshed with it.[43]

. . . These two extremities, especially in the winter of heat within their houses, and of extreme cold without, together with their diet, make them of a dark and sallow complexion, their skins being tanned and parched both with cold and with heat: especially the women that for the greater part are of far worse complexions than the men. Whereof the cause I take to be their keeping within the hot houses, and busying themselves about the heating, and using of their bath stoves. . . .

The women, to mend the bad hue of their skins, use to paint their faces with white and red colours, so visibly that every man may perceive it. Which is made no matter because it is common and liked well by their husbands who . . . delight themselves much to see them of foul women to become such fair images. This parcheth the skin, and helpeth to deform them when their painting is off.

THOMAS NASHE (1567–1601)

Christs teares over Jerusalem. Whereunto is annexed, a comparative admonition to London (London: James Roberts, 1593), 71–78.

Thomas Nashe, a pamphleteer, also authored *The Unfortunate Traveler* (1594), sometimes described as the first English adventure novel. *Christs teares over Jerusalem* is a plea to London to forsake its evil ways, which are said to rival those of the Turks and Moors. In the passage excerpted here, Nashe worries over cosmetics intended to whiten the skin ultimately blackening the soul.

Keywords: Women—Cosmetics—Skin Color—Beauty—Judgment Day

Ever since Evah was tempted and the serpent prevailed with her, women have took upon them both the person of the tempted and the tempter. . . . If not to tempt, and be thought worthy to be tempted, why die they and diet they their faces with so many drugs as they do, as it were to correct God's workmanship and reprove him as a bungler, and one that is not his craft's master?

Even as angels are painted in church windows, with glorious golden fronts beset with sun beams, so beset they their foreheads on either side with glorious borrowed gleamy bushes, which rightly interpreted, should signify beauty to sell, since a bush is not else hanged forth, but to invite men to buy. . . .

. . . Only this humble caveat let me give you by the way, that you looketh a devil come not to you, in the likeness of a tailor or painter; that however

---

[43] Quasse = Possibly a variant of the word "kvass," a fermented beverage made from rye in general use in Russia.

you disguise your bodies, you lay not your colours so thick that they sink into your souls. That your skins being too white without, your souls be not all black within. . . .

In skins of beasts Adam and Eve were clothed, in nought but thine own skin, at the Day of Judgment shalt thou be clothed. If thou beest more deformed, than the age wherein thou died should make thee, the devil shall stand up and certify that with painting and physicking thy visage thou so deformedst it. Whereto God shall reply, What have I to do with thee, thou painted sepulcher? Thus hast so differenced and divorced thy self from my creation, that I know thee not for my creature.

The print of my finger thou hast defaced, and with art's vanishing varnishment made thy self a changeling from the form I first cast thee in; Satan take her to thee, with black boiling pitch, rough cast over her counterfeit and white. And whereas she was wont in ass's milk to bathe her, to engrain her skin more gentle, pliant, delicate, and supple, in bubbling scalding lead and fatty flame-feeding brimstone see thou uncessantly bathe her. With glowing hot irons, singe and suck up that adulterized sinful beauty wherewith she hath branded herself to infelicity. . . .

. . . We hate and cry out against them that like Turks and Moors sell their Christian brethren as slaves; how much more ought we to hate & cry out against them that sell themselves and their souls unto sin as slaves? Those skin-plastering painters . . . do not so much alter God's image (by artificial over-beautifying their bodies) as these do, by debasing themselves to everyone that brings coin. Ere they come to forty, you shall see them worn to the bare bone. At twenty their lively colour is lost, their faces are sodden & parboiled with French surfeits. That colour on their cheeks you behold superficialized is but Sir John White's or Sir John Redcap's livery.

JUAN HUARTE (1529?–88)

Examen de ingenios. The examination of mens wits. . . . Translated out of the Spanish tongue by M. Camillo Camilli. Englished out of his Italian, by R. C. Esquire (London: Adam Islip, 1594), A2ᵛ–A3ʳ, 194–95, 199–200, 316–17.

Regarded as a forerunner of physiognomy and phrenology, the Spanish physician Juan Huarte argued that intellectual talents were apparent in a man's physique, which in turn derived from his temperament. His *Examination* draws on climatic and humoral theory to account for differences in human intelligence and to advocate a system of assigning vocations according to the temperament.

Keywords: Class—Artificial Transformation—Macrocephali—
Theories of Human Generation—Interracial Sex

To the Majesty of Don Philip, our Sovereign, . . . [A] law should be enacted, that no carpenter should exercise himself in any work which appertained to the occupation of an husbandman, nor a tailor to that of an architect, and that the advocate should not minister physic, nor the physician play the advocate, but each one exercise only that art to which he beareth a natural inclination, and let pass the residue. . . . [N]ow to the end he may not err in choosing that which fitteth best his own nature, there should be deputed in the commonwealth men of great wisdom who might discover each one's wit in his tender age, and cause him perforce to study that science which is agreeable to him, not permitting him to make his own choice. . . .

Hippocrates recounteth of a certain sort of men who, to be different from the vulgar, chose for a token of their nobility to have their head like a sugar-loaf. And to shape this figure by art, when the child was born, the midwives took care to bind their head with swathes, and bands, until they were fashioned to the form. And this artificialness grew to such force as it was converted into nature: for in process of time, all the children that were born of nobility had their head sharp from their mothers's womb. So from thenceforth, the art and diligence of the midwives herein became superfluous. But so soon as they left nature to her liberty, and her own ordering, without oppressing her any longer with art, she turned by little and little to recover again the figure which she had before.

In like sort it might befall the children of Israel, who, notwithstanding the region of Egypt, the manna, the delicate waters, and their sorrowfulness, wrought those dispositions of wit in that seed: yet those reasons and respects surceasing, and other contrary growing on, it is certain that by little and little the qualities of the manna would have worn away, and other far different therefrom have grown on, conformable to the country where they inhabited, to the meats they fed upon, to the waters which they drank, and to the air which they breathed. . . .

. . . And if any man will not herewith rest satisfied, let us say, that as God brought out of Egypt the 12 tribes of Israel, so he had taken then 12 male and 12 female moors of Aethiopia, and had placed them in our country, in how many years think we, would these moors and their posterity linger to leave their native colour, not mixing themselves the while with white persons: to me it seemeth a long space of years would be requisite. For though 200 years have passed over our heads, sithence the first Egyptians came out of Egypt into Spain, yet their posterity have not forlorn [that] their delicacy of wit and promptness, not yet that roasted colour which their ancestors brought with them from Egypt. Such is the force of man's seed when it receiveth thereinto any well rooted quality. And as in Spain, the moors communicate the colour of their elders by means of their seed, though they be out of Aethiopia, so also the people of Israel coming from thence may communicate to their descendants their sharpness of wit without remaining in Egypt or eating manna: for to be ignorant or wise is as well an accident in man as to be black or white. True it is, that they are not now so quick and prompt, as they were a thousand years since: for from the time that they left to eat manna, their posterity have ever lessened hitherto, because they used contrary meats, and inhabited countries different from Egypt: neither drank waters of such delicacy as in the wilderness. As also by mingling with those who descended from the gentiles, who wanted this difference of wit: but that which cannot be denied them is that as yet they have not lost it altogether. . . .

. . . Therefore nature provided that in the engendering of a creature two seeds should concur; which being mingled, the mightier should make the forming and the other serve for nourishment. And this is seen evidently so to be: for if a blackamoor beget a white woman with child, and a white man a Negro woman, of both these unions will be born a creature partaking of either quality.[44] Out of this doctrine I gather that to be true, which many authentic histories affirm, that a dog carnally companying with a woman made her to conceive; and the like did a bear with another woman, whom he found alone in the fields. And likewise, an ape had two young ones by another. . . . The matter herein of most difficulty for the vulgar to conceive is how it may be that these women should bring forth perfect men, and partakers of the use of reason, seeing the parents who engendered them were brute beasts. To this I answer that the seed of every of these women was the agent and former of the creature, as the greater in force, whence it figured the same, with his accidents of man's shape. The seed of the brute beast (as not equal in strength) served for aliment and for nothing else . . . but a thing which these histories specify is that children born of such copulations give token in their manners and conditions that their engendering was not natural.

QUEEN ELIZABETH I OF ENGLAND (1533–1603)

"An Open letter to the Lord Maiour of London and th'Aldermen his brethren" (1596)

Source: *Acts of the Privy Council*, New Series, 1596–97 (London: Mackie and Co., 1902), 16–17.

By the later 1590s the English were suffering from war-weariness, high taxation, inflation, a succession of bad harvests, and recurrent plague. Real wages were at their lowest point in centuries, and there was a corresponding rise in crime and vagrancy. Concerned that the presence of African servants caused her own subjects economic hardships and could even produce the vagrancy outlawed by past proclamations, Elizabeth, who earlier invested in the slaving voyages of Sir John Hawkins, arranged for the deportation of Africans who would be exchanged for Englishmen imprisoned by the Spanish.

[44] In this Huarte differs from George Best, who affirms that blackness will always be dominant (see his *True Discourse* . . . in this volume).

Keywords: Blackamoors—Servants—Englishness—Expulsion of
        Blackamoors

An open letter to the Lord Mayor of London and the Aldermen his brethren, and to all other mayors, sheriffs, etc. Her Majesty understanding that there are of late diverse blackamoors brought into this realm, of which kind of people there are already here too many, considering how God hath blessed this land with great increase of people of our own nation as any country in the world, whereof many for want of service and means to set them on work fall on idleness and to great extremity. Her Majesty's pleasure therefore is that those kind of people should be sent forth of the land, and for that purpose there is direction given to this bearer Edward Baines to take of those blackamoors that in this last voyage under Sir Thomas Baskerville were brought into this realm the number of ten, to be transported by him out of the realm. Wherein we require you to be aiding and assisting unto him as he shall have occasion, and thereof not to fail.

"An open warrant to the Lord Maiour of London" (1596)

Source: *Acts of the Privy Council*, New Series, 1596–97 (London: Mackie and Co., 1902), 20–21.

An open warrant to the Lord Mayor of London and to all vice-admirals, mayors and other public officers whatsoever to whom it may appertain. Whereas Caspar van Senden, a merchant of Lubeck, did by his labour and travel procure 89 of her Majesty's subjects that were detained prisoners in Spain and Portugal to be released, and brought them into this realm at his own cost and charges, for the which his expenses and declaration of his honest mind towards those prisoners he only desireth to have license to take up so much blackamoors here in this realm and to transport them into Spain and Portugal. Her Majesty in regard of the charitable affection the suppliant hath showed, being a stranger, to work the delivery of our countrymen that were there in great misery and thralldom and to bring them home to their native country, and that the same could not be done without great expense, and also considering the reasonableness of his requests to transport so many blakamoors from hence, doth think it a very good exchange and that those kind of people may be well spared in this realm, being so populous and numbers of able persons the subjects of the land and Christian people that perish for want of service, whereby through their labour might be maintained. They are therefore in their Lordships's name required to aide and assist him to take up such blackamoors as he shall find within this realm with the consent of their masters, who we doubt not, considering her Majesty's good pleasure to have those kind of people sent out of the land and the good deserving of the stranger towards her Majesty's subjects, and that they shall do charitably and like Christians rather to be served by their own countrymen then with those kind of people, will yield those in their possession to him.

SIR WALTER RALEIGH (1554–1618)

The Discoverie of the large, rich and bewtiful empire of Guiana . . .
(London: Robert Robinson, 1596)

Source: Sir Walter Raleigh, *The Discovery of Guiana*. Free online edition
via http://www.gutenberg.org/dirs/etext00/guian10.txt.

Sir Walter Raleigh rose to prominence fighting against the Irish
in Munster in the 1580s and quickly became one of Elizabeth I's
favorite courtiers. After falling out of the Queen's favor, Raleigh
led an expedition to South America in 1595, the record of which
can be found in his *The Discoverie of the large, rich and bewtiful
empire of Guiana* . . . . Although the expedition failed to fulfill
its promise of a golden bounty, *The Discoverie* gained popular
acclaim, perhaps due to its fantastic tales of privateering, gold,
and Plinian hybrids.

Keywords: Amazons—Monstrous Races—Indian and English Women
Compared—Cannibalism

The nations of these [warlike] women are on the south side of the river
in the provinces of Topago, and their chiefest strengths and retracts are
in the islands situated on the south side of the entrance, some 60 leagues
within the mouth of the said river. The memories of the like women are
very ancient as well in Africa as in Asia. In Africa those that had Medusa for
queen; others in Scythia, near the rivers of Tanais and Thermodon. We find,
also, that Lampedo and Marthesia were queens of the Amazons. In many
histories they are verified to have been, and in diverse ages and provinces;
but they which are not far from Guiana do accompany with men but once
in a year, and for the time of one month, which I gather by their relation,
to be in April; and that time all kings of the borders assemble, and queens
of the Amazons; and after the queens have chosen, the rest cast lots for their
valentines. This one month they feast, dance, and drink of their wines in
abundance; and the moon being done they all depart to their own provinces.
They are said to be very cruel and bloodthirsty, especially to such as offer to
invade their territories. . . .

The master of my ship, John Douglas, took one of the canoes which came
laden from thence with people to be sold, and the most of them escaped;
yet of those he brought, there was one as well favoured and as well shaped
as ever I saw any in England; and afterwards I saw many of them, which but
for their tawny colour may be compared to any in Europe. . . .

Of these people those that dwell upon the branches of Orenoque, called
Capuri, and Macureo, are for the most part carpenters of canoes; . . . And
notwithstanding the moistness of the air in which they live, the hardness
of their diet, and the great labors they suffer to hunt, fish, and fowl for their

living, in all my life, either in the Indies or in Europe, did I never behold a more goodly or better-favoured people or a more manly. They were wont to make war upon all nations, and especially on the cannibals, so as none durst without a good strength trade by those rivers; but of late they are at peace with their neighbors, all holding the Spaniards for a common enemy. . . . Those nations which are called Arwacas, which dwell on the south of Orenoque, of which place and nation our Indian pilot was, are dispersed in many other places, and do use to beat the bones of their lords into powder, and their wives and friends drink it all in their several sorts of drinks. . . .

That cacique [of the town of Toparimaca] that was a stranger had his wife staying at the port where we anchored, and in all my life I have seldom seen a better favored woman.[45] She was of good stature, with black eyes, fat of body, of an excellent countenance, her hair almost as long as herself, tied up again in pretty knots; and it seemed she stood not in that awe of her husband as the rest, for she spake and discoursed, and drank among the gentlemen and captains, and was very pleasant, knowing her own comeliness, and taking great pride therein. I have seen a lady in England so like to her, as but for the difference of colour, I would have sworn might have been the same. . . .

. . . Next unto Arui there are two rivers Atoica and Caura, and on that branch which is called Caura are a nation of people whose heads appear not above their shoulders; which though it may be thought a mere fable, yet for mine own part I am resolved it is true, because every child in the provinces of Aromaia and Canuri affirm the same. They are called Ewaipanoma; they are reported to have their eyes in their shoulders, and their mouths in the middle of their breasts, and that a long train of hair groweth backward between their shoulders. . . . Such a nation was written of by Mandeville, whose reports were holden for fables many years; and yet since the East Indies were discovered, we find his relations true of such things as heretofore were held incredible. . . .

. . . Guiana is a country that hath yet her maidenhead, never sacked, turned, nor wrought; the face of the earth hath not been torn, nor the virtue and salt of the soil spent by manurance. The graves have not been opened for gold, the mines not broken with sledges, nor their images pulled down out of their temples. It hath never been entered by any army of strength, and never conquered or possessed by any Christian prince. . . .

The West Indies were first offered her Majesty's grandfather by Columbus, a stranger, in whom there might be doubt of deceit; and besides it was then thought incredible that there were such and so many lands and regions never written of before. This empire is made known to her Majesty by her own vassal, and by him that oweth to her more duty than an ordinary subject. . . .

. . . And I hope, as we with these few hands have displanted the first garrison, and driven them out of the said country, so her Majesty will give order for the rest, and either defend it, and hold it as tributary, or conquer and keep it as empress of the same. For whatsoever prince shall possess it, shall

---

[45] Cacique = Chief.

be greatest; and if the king of Spain enjoy it, he will become unresistible. Her Majesty hereby shall confirm and strengthen the opinions of all nations as touching her great and princely actions. And where the south border of Guiana reacheth to the dominion and empire of the Amazons, those women shall hereby hear the name of a virgin, which is not only able to defend her own territories and her neighbours, but also to invade and conquer so great empires and so far removed. . . .

DUARTE LOPES (fl. 1578–89)

A report of the kingdome of Congo, a region of Africa. And of countries that border rounde about the same . . ., translated by Abraham Hartwell (London: John Wolfe, 1597), 13–14, 18–19.

The Portuguese merchant Duarte Lopes provided one of the earliest European descriptions of Central Africa. In 1578, he became the ambassador of Congo's King Alvaro II to the pope and to Philip II of Spain. He argued for the Congo's need for missionaries and for the advantages of free trade. His papers were published by Fillipo Pigafetta (1533–1604) in 1591, and remained one of the chief sources for information concerning central Africa up to the middle of the nineteenth century.

Keywords: Skin Color—Seed—Interracial Sex—White Moors

The men are black & so are the women, and some of them also somewhat inclining to the colour of the wild olive. Their hair is black & curled, and some also red. The stature of the men is of an indifferent bigness, and excepting their blackness they are very like to the Portingalles. The apples of their eyes are of diverse colours, black and of the colour of the sea. Their lips are not thick, as the Nubians and other Negroes are: and so likewise their countenances are some fat, some lean, and some between both, as in our countries there are, and not as the Negroes of Nubia and Guinea, which are very deformed. . . .

All the ancient writers have certainly believed, that the cause of black colour in men is from the heat of the sun. For by experience it is found, that the nearer we approach to the countries of the South, the browner & blacker are the inhabitants therein. And contrariwise, the farther you go towards the north, the whiter shall you find the men, as the French, & the Dutch, & the English, and others. Notwithstanding it is as certain a thing as may be, that under the equinoctial, there are people which are born almost all white, as in the kingdom of Melinde & Mombaza situate under the equinoctial, & in the isle of San Thomas which lieth also under the same climate, and was at the first inhabited by the Portingalles, though afterwards it was disinhabited, and for the space of a hundred years and upwards their children were continually white, yea and every day still become whiter and whiter. And so likewise the children of the Portingals, which are born of the women of Congo, do incline somewhat towards white. So that Signor Odoardo was of opinion, that the black colour did not spring from the heat of the sun, but from the nature of the seed, being induced thereunto by the reasons above mentioned. And surely this his opinion is confirmed by the testimony of Ptolemy, who in his description of the innermost parts of Libya maketh mention of white Ethiopians which he calleth in his language . . . white Moores. . . .

JAN HUIGHEN VAN LINSCHOTEN (1563–1611)

John Huighen van Linschoten. His discours of voyages into ye Easte & West Indies (London : [John Windet for] John Wolfe, 1598)

Source: "John Huighen van Linschoten his Voyage to Goa, and observations of the East Indies, abbreviated," in *Purchas his Pilgrimes* (London: William Stansby, 1625), Vol. 2, 1752, 1753, 1756–57, 1760, 1762–67.

The Dutch traveler Jan Huighen van Linschoten served for six years (1583–89) as bookkeeper to the archbishop of Portuguese Goa. His account of India was published in his *Itinerario* (1595–96), which was translated into German (1598), English (1598), Latin (1599), and French (1610). The *Itinerario* describes sea routes to the Indies and descriptions of the lands and peoples of Africa and India, including an early discussion of caste. Of particular interest is the discussion of women in the colonies, which conflates Indian and Portuguese women resident in India, providing an early representation of the European abroad as a hybrid or "mestizo."

Keywords: Portuguese Colonialism—Castiços/Mestiços—India— Women's Lust—Widow Burning—Castes—Indian and European Men Compared—Mozambique—Slavery— Nakedness—Skin Color—Inquisition—Scarification

Touching the Portugals's justice and ordinances, as well in worldly as spiritual causes, they are all one as they are in Portugal. They dwell in the town among all sorts of nations, as Indians, Heathens, Moors, Jews, Armenians, Gujeratis, Benianes, Brahmins, and of all Indian nations and people, which do all dwell and traffic therein, every man holding his own religion, without constraining any man to do against his conscience, only touching their ceremonies of burning the dead, and the living, of marrying and other superstitions, and devilish inventions, they are forbidden by the Archbishop to use them openly, or in the island, but they may freely use them upon the firm land, and secretly in their houses, thereby to shun and avoid all occasions of dislike that might be given to Christians, which are but newly baptised: but . . . he that is once christened, and is after found to use any heathenish superstitions, is subject to the Inquisition, whatsoever he be, or for any point of religion whatsoever. . . .

The Portugals in India are many of them married with the natural born women of the country, and the children proceeding of them are called mestiços, that is, half-countrymen. These mestiços are commonly of yellowish colour, notwithstanding there are many women among them that are fair and well formed. The children of the Portugals, both boys and girls, which are born in India, are called castiços, and are in all things like unto the Portugals, only somewhat differing in colour, for they draw toward a yellow colour: the children of those castiços are yellow, and altogether like the mestiços, and the children of mestiços are of colour and fashion like the natural born countrymen or Decaniins of the country, so that the posterity of the Portugals, both men and women being in the third degree, do seem to be natural Indians, both in colour and fashion. . . . [I]n Goa there is held a daily assembly or meeting together . . . which is like the meeting upon the bourse in Antwerp . . . and there are all kinds of Indian commodities to sell, so that in a manner it is like a fair. . . . [T]hey have running about them, many sorts of captives and slaves, both men and women, young and old, which are daily sold there, as beasts are sold with us, where every one may choose which liketh him best, every one at a certain price. . . .

The Portugals, mestiços, and Indian-Christian women in India, are little seen abroad, but for the most part sit still within the house, and go but seldom forth, unless it be to church, or to visit their friends . . . and when they go abroad, they are well provided not to be seen, for they are carried in a palanquin covered with a mat or other cloth, so that they cannot be seen.

When they go to church, or to visit any friend, they put on very costly apparel, with bracelets of gold, and rings upon their arms. . . . Within the house they go bare headed, with a waistcoat called *baju*, that from their shoulders covereth their navels, and is so fine that you may see all their body through it, and downwards they have nothing but a painted cloth wrapped three or four times about their bodies. . . . The women eat no bread or very little, nor yet the slaves . . . [because] they are so used to eat rice, that they desire no other . . . and so eat it with their hands: for there they eat nothing with spoons, and if they should see any man do so, they would laugh at him. . . . The men are very jealous of their wives, for they will never bring any man into their houses, how special a friend soever he be, that shall see their wives or their daughters. . . . The women are very luxurious and unchaste, for there are very few among them, although they be married, but they have besides their husbands one or two of those that are called soldiers, with whom they take their pleasures: which to effect, they use all the slights and practises they can devise, by sending out their slaves and bawds by night, and at extraordinary times, over walls, hedges, and ditches, how narrowly soever they are kept and looked unto. They have likewise an herb called deutroa, which . . . they . . . give . . . to their husbands, either in meat or drink, and presently therewith, the man is as though he were half out of his wits, and without feeling, or else drunk, doing nothing but laugh, and sometime it taketh him sleeping, whereby he lieth like a dead man, so that in his presence they may do what they will, and take their pleasure with their friends, and the husband never know of it. . . .[46]

The countrymen in the villages round about Goa, and such as labour and till the land are most Christians: but there is not much difference among them from the other heathens, for that they can hardly leave their heathenish superstitions, which in part are permitted them, and is done to draw the other heathens to be christened, as also that otherwise they would hardly be persuaded to continue in the Christian faith. There is in every place of the street exchangers of money . . . which are all Christian Jews. . . . The Indian heathens have a custom, that no man may change nor alter trade or occupation, but must use his father's trade, and marry men's daughters of the same occupation, trade, or dealing, which is so nearly looked unto, that they are divided and set apart, each occupation by itself, as countries and nations are, and so they call one another: for if they speak to a man, they ask him of what trade he is. . . .

The Brahmins are the honestest and most esteemed nation among all the Indian heathens: for they do always serve in the chiefest places about the king, as receivers, stewards, ambassadors, and such like offices. They are likewise the priests and ministers of the *pagods*, or devilish idols. . . .

. . . When the Brahmins die, all their friends assemble together, and make a hole in the ground, wherein they throw much wood and other things: and if the man be of any account, they cast in sweet sanders and other spices, with rice, corn, and such like, and much oil because the fire should burn the stronger.[47] Which done, they lay the dead Brahmins in it: then cometh his wife with music and many of her nearest friends all singing certain praises in commendation of her husband's life, putting her in comfort, and encouraging her to follow her husband, and go with him into the other world. Then she taketh all her jewels, and parteth them among her friends, and so with a cheerful countenance, she leapeth into the fire, and is presently covered with wood and oil: so she is quickly dead, and with her husband's body burned to ashes: and if it chance, as not very often it doth, that any woman refuseth to be burnt with her husband, then they cut the hair clean off from her head: and while she liveth she must never after wear any jewels more, and from that time she is despised, and accounted for a dishonest woman. . . .

The Gujeratis and Banianes, are of the country of Cambaia; many of them dwell in Goa, Diu, Chaul, Cochin, and other places of India, because of their trade and traffic in merchandise. . . . They are most subtle and expert in casting of accounts and writing, so that they do not only surpass and go beyond all Jews and other nations thereabouts, but also the Portugals: and

---

[46] Deutroa = Variant of "dewtry." The thorn-apple, *datura stramonium,* and other Indian species of the genus; a drug or drink prepared from this, employed to produce stupefaction.
[47] Sanders = Sandalwood.

in this respect they have no advantage, for that they are very perfect in the trade of merchandise, and very ready to deceive men.

. . . [T]hey had rather die for hunger and thirst than once to touch the Christians's meat. . . . They are of a yellow colour like the Brahmins, and somewhat whiter, and there are women among them which are much whiter and clearer of complexion than the Portugal women. They are formed and made both in face, limbs, and in all other things like men of Europe, colour only excepted. . . .

The Canariins and Corumbiins are the countrymen, and such as deal with tilling the land, fishing and such like labours. These are the most contemptible, and the miserablest people of all India, and live very poorly, maintaining themselves with little meat. . . . They are in a manner black, or of a dark brown colour, many of them are Christians, because their chief habitation and dwelling places are on the sea-side, in the countries border-ing upon Goa. . . . When the women are ready to travail with child, they are commonly delivered when they are all alone, and their husbands in the fields. . . . They are so miserable, that for a penny they would endure to be whipped, and they eat so little, that it seemeth they live by the air they are likewise most of them lean, and weak of limbs, of little strength and very cowards, whereby the Portugals do them great outrage and villainy, using them like dogs and beasts. . . .

The black people or Caffares of the land of Mozambique, and all the coast of Ethiopia, and within the land to the *Cape de Bona Speranza*, go all naked, although those of Mozambique, (that is the women) do a little cover them-selves.[48] . . . Some have all their bodies rased and seared with irons, and all figured like rased satin and damask, wherein they take great pride, thinking there are no fairer people then they in all the world, so that when they see any white people, that wear apparel on their bodies, they laugh and mock at them, thinking us to be monsters and ugly people: and when they will make any devilish form and picture, then they invent one after the form of a white man in his apparel. There are among them that file their teeth as sharp as needles, which they likewise esteem for a great ornament.[49]

There are some of them that are become Christians since the Portugals came thither, but there is no great pains taken about it in those countries, because there is no profit to be had, as also that it is an infectious and unwholesome country: And therefore the Jesuits are wary enough not to make any houses or habitations therein, for they see no great profit to be reaped there for them, as they do in India and the islands of Japan, and in

---

[48] Caffares = Although by the eighteenth century this term was used to disparage the Bantu people of Southern Africa, as well as those black Africans and whites who might associate with them, Linschoten's usage seems to derive from *kafir*, the Arabic term for infidel, or unbeliever.

[49] The association of white people with devils is also to be found in several other writings of the period, such as Joao Dos Sanctos's *Aethiopia Orientalis* (1597). In that text, however, whites who are taken to be devils are the offspring of black parents, both in Africa and in India (Samuel Purchas, *Hakluytus Posthumus* [Glasgow: James MacLehose and Sons, 1905–7], Vol. IX, 216–17).

other places, where they find great quantities of riches, with the sap whereof they increase much and fill their beehives, therewith to satisfy their thirsty and insatiable desires. . . .

From Mozambique great numbers of these Caffares are carried into India, and many times they sell a man or woman that is grown to their full strength, for two or three ducats. . . .

The Malabares are those that dwell on the sea-coast between Goa, and the Cape de Comoriin southward from Goa, where the pepper groweth. They have a speech by themselves, and . . . they go all naked only their privy members covered, the women likewise have but a cloth from their navel down to their knees, all the rest is naked, they are strong of limbs, and very arrogant and proud, of colour altogether black, yet very smooth both of hair and skin, which commonly they anoint with oil, to make it shine; they wear their hair as long as it will grow, tied on the top or crown of their heads with a lace, both men and women: the lobes of their ear are open, and are so long that they hang down to their shoulders, and the longer and wider they are, the more they are esteemed among them, and it is thought to be a beauty in them. Of face, body and limbs; they are altogether like men of Europe, without any difference, but only in colour, the men are commonly very hairy, and rough upon the breast, and on their bodies, and are the most lecherous and unchaste nation in all the Orient, so that there are very few women children among them, of seven or eight years old, that have their maidenheads: They are very ready to catch one from another, though it be but for a small penny. . . .

Of these Malabares there are two manner of people, the one is noblemen or gentlemen, called Nayros, which are soldiers, that do only wear and handle arms, the other is the common people, called Polyas, and they may wear no weapons, nor bear any arms. . . . Not any of them are married, nor may not marry during their lives, but they may freely lie with the Nayros daughters, or with any other that liketh them, what women soever they be, yea though they be married women. . . . As these Nayros go in the streets, they use to cry *Po, Po,* which is to say, Take heed, look to your selves, or I come, stand out of the way, for that the other sort of people called Polyas, that are no Nayros, may not once touch or trouble one of them; for if any of the Polyas should stand still, and not give them place, whereby he should chance to touch their bodies, he may freely thrust him through, and no man ask him why he did it. . . . Likewise they must not be touched by any Christian, or any other man. And when the Portugals came first into India, at Cochin it was concluded . . . that two men should be chosen, one for the Nayros, and the other for the Portugals, that should fight body to body, and he that should be overthrown, that nation should give place unto the other, this was done in the presence of both nations, and the Portugal overcame the Nayro, whom he slew; whereupon it was agreed, that the Nayros should give place unto the Portugal, and stand aside until he be past wheresoever they meet.

GEORGE ABBOT (1562–1633)

A briefe description of the whole worlde (London: T. Judson, 1599)

Source: The fifth edition (London, 1664), 26–27, 38–39, 61–64, 91–93,
96, 97 101, 105–6, 144–49, 162–63, 175–77, 181–86, 188–90,
248–71, 298–99, 305–23.

Before becoming Bishop of Lichfield, Coventry, and Canterbury,
George Abbot published *A briefe description of the whole worlde,*
a work surveying peoples and regions with regard to geography,
politics, and trade. Abbot's frequently reprinted and expanded
work indicates not only the range of discourses used to differenti-
ate the peoples of the seventeenth-century world, but also the lack
of a standardized system to describe cultural difference.

Keywords: Interracial Sex—Muhammad—Gypsies—Monstrous
Races—Prester John—Skin Color—Sodomy—Artificial
Transformations

Of Germany

This is to be noted of the Germans; that they may boast this above other
more westernly nations of Europe, that they are an unmixed nation: for
whereas the Lombards and Goths at several times, have set down in Italy, and
mixed themselves with the people thereof, the Goths, Vandals, and Saracens
in Spain, the Franks in Gaul or France, and the Normans also; the Saxons,
Angles, Danes and Normans, in Great Britain; they have been free from
such inundation and mixture; yea, many of the people that have afflicted
and inhabited these other nations, have come from thence, so that therein
Germany hath an advantage of these other nations that have been subject
hereunto.

Of Russia, or Moscovia

The people of this country are rude and unlearned, so that there is very little
or no knowledge amongst them of any liberal or ingenious art: yea, their
very priests & monks (whereof they have many) are almost unlettered so
that they can hardly do anything more than read their ordinary service: And
the rest of the people are, by reason of their ignorant education, dull and
incapable of any high understanding; but very superstitious, having many
ceremonies, and idolatrous solemnities; as the consecrating of their rivers
by their patriarch at one time of the year, when they think themselves much
sanctified by the receiving of those hallowed waters; yea, and they bathe their
horses and cattle in them. . . .

Of Asia, and first of Tartary

On the South side of Asia, [even] unto the dominion of the Emperor of Russia, is Tartary, in ancient time Scythia. . . . The Tartarians which now inhabit it, are men of great stature, rude of behaviour, no Christians but gentiles; neither do they acknowledge Mahomet. They have few or no cities among them, but after the manner of the old Scythians, do live in wildernesses, lying under their carts, and following their droves of cattle, by the milk whereof they do nourish themselves. . . .

They have great wars with the countries adjoining, but especially with the Muscovite, and sometimes with the Turk: from hence came Tamberlaine, who brought 700,000 of the Tartarians at once into the field, wherein he distressed and took prisoner Bajazet the great Turk, whom he afterward forced to feed as a dog under his table. . . .

Of Cathay and China

The people of China are learned almost in all arts, very skilful workmen in curious fine works of all sorts, so that no country yieldeth more precious merchandise than the workmanship of them. They are great soldiers, very politic and crafty, and in respect thereof, contemning the wits of others using a proverb, that all other nations do see but with one eye; but they themselves have two. . . .

Of the East Indies

This is that country so famous in ancient time, for the great riches thereof, for the multitude of people, for the conquest of Bacchus over it, for the passage thither for Alexander the Great, throughout all the length of Asia. . . . And certainly thither it was that Solomon did send once in three years for his gold and other rich merchandise . . .

The men of the south part of India are black, and therefore are called men of Inde. . . . The people of the country when the Portugals came first thither, were for the most part gentiles, believing in no one god: yea, at this day there are diverse of them who do adore the Sun as their God, and every morning at the rising thereof, do use very superstitious ceremonies, which our merchants, who do trade to Aleppo do oftentimes see. . . . but in one town called Granganor, they found certain Christians dissenting in many things from the Church of Rome, and rather agreeing with the Protestants, which Christians had received (by succession) their religion from the time of Thomas the Apostle; by whom . . . part of India was converted.

Of Persia

The Persians are all at this day Sarazens in religion, believing in Mahomet: but as Papists and Protestants do differ in opinion, concerning the same Christ, so do the Turks and Persians about their Mahomet: the one pursuing the other, as heretics, with most deadly hatred, insomuch that there is, in this respect, almost continual war between the Turk and the Persians.

Of Arabia

This is that country wherein Mahomet was born, who being of mean parent-age, was brought up in his youth in the trade of merchandise; but afterward joining himself with thieves and robbers, his life was to rob such merchants as passed through Arabia; and to this purpose having gotten together many of his own country-men, he had afterward a whole legion or more of the Roman soldiers, who being offended with Heraclius the Roman emperor, for want of their pay, joined themselves to him; so that at length he had a great army, wherewith he spoiled the countries adjoining: And this was about the year of Christ 600.

To maintain his credit and authority with his own men, he feigned that he had conference with the Holy Ghost, at such times as he was troubled with the falling sickness: and accordingly he ordained a new religion, consisting partly of Jewish ceremonies, and partly of Christian doctrine, and some other things of his own invention, that he might inveigle both Jews and Christians, and yet by his own fancy distinguish his own followers from both.

The book of his religion is called the *Alcaron*. The people which are secta-ries (whereas indeed they came of Hagar, the hand-maid of Sarah, Abraham's wife, and therefore should of her be called Ishmaelites or Hagarens) because they would not seem to come of a bond-woman, and from him whom they suppose a bastard; they term themselves Saracens, as coming from Sarah; they are called by some writers, Arabians instead of Saracens, their name being drawn from their first country. . . .[50]

Their own books do mention that Mahomet . . . was much given to lascivi-ousness, and all uncleanness of body, even with very beasts; and his followers are so senseless, that in imitation of him, they think no such wickedness to be unlawful: For they are utterly unlearned, and most receive whatsoever is deliv-ered unto them out of the *Alcaron*, Mahomet having made it a matter of death to dispute, sift, or call in question any thing which is written in his law.

Of Africke and Egypt

Although this country of Egypt doth stand in the self-same climate that Mauritania doth, yet the inhabitants there are not black, but rather dun, or tawny, of which colour Cleopatra was observed to be; who by enticement, so won the love of Julius Caesar and Antony. And of that colour do those run-nagates (by devices make themselves to be) who go up and down the world under the name of Egyptians, being indeed but counterfeits and the refuse of rascality of many nations.

---

[50] The Arabist William Bedwell offers an alternative etymology in "The Arabian Trudg-man," an appendix to *Mohammedis Imposturae* (1615): "Sarraceni, *Sarazins,* Sarrasins, are those people which otherwise of the ancients were called Arabs, or Arabians. Neither were they so named of Sara, Abraham's wife, as some men do think, but of 'saraka,' which signifi-eth 'furari,' to rob or steal. And indeed the Arabians have been and are to this day accounted great sharkers and robbers."

Of the other countries of Africke, lying near the sea

From beyond the hill Atlas Major, unto the south of Africke, is nothing almost (in antiquity) worthy the reading: and those things which are written for the most part, are fables: For towards the south part of Africke, as well as towards the north part of Europe and Asia, be supposed to be men of strange shapes, as some with dogs's heads, some without heads, and some with one foot alone, which was very huge, and such like. . . .

In the new writers there are some few things to be observed: as first, that all the people in general to the south, lying with the *Zona Torrida*, are not only blackish like the Moor, but are exceeding black. And therefore as in old time by an excellency, some of them are called *Nigritae*, so at this day they are named Negros, as them whom no men are blacker.

Secondly, the inhabitants of all these parts which border on the sea coast, even unto *Caput Bonae Spei* [The Cape of Good Hope], have been gentiles, adoring images and foolish shapes for their gods, neither hearing of Christ, nor believing on Mahomet, till such time as the Portugals coming among them, having professed Christ for themselves, but have won few of the people to embrace their religion.

Of Abissines, and the Empire of Prester John

In the inland of Africke, lyeth a very large country, extending itself on the east, to some part of the Red Sea, on the south to the Kingdom of Molinda, and a great way farther, on the north to Egypt; on the west to Manicongo. The people whereof are called Abissini, and itself the dominion of him whom we commonly call in English Prester John. . . . This is a very mighty prince, and reputed to be one of the greatest emperors in the world.

. . . The people therefore are Christians, as is also the prince, but differing in many things from the west Church; and in no sort acknowledging any supreme prerogative of the Bishop of Rome. It is thought that they have retained Christianity even from the time of our saviour. . . .

There be other countries in Africke . . . but this may be said of Africke in general, that it bringeth forth store of all sorts of wild beasts, as elephants, lions, panthers, tigers, and the like. . . . Oftentimes, new and strange shapes of wild beasts are brought forth there; the reason whereof is, that the country being very hot, and full of wildernesses, which have in them little water, the beasts of all sorts being enforced to meet at those few watering places that be, where oftentimes contrary kinds have conjunction the one with the other: so that there ariseth a new kind of species which taketh part of both. . . .[51]

[51] Abbot's notion of interspecies generation may derive from Bodin's speculation (reproduced in this volume) that because of the lust of Southerners, "Promiscuous coition of men and animals took place, wherefore the regions of Africa produce for us so many monsters." For nineteenth-century race theory, hybrid unions such as these would become the subject of intense debates that were meant to determine whether blacks and whites were of the same species.

Of America, or the New World

. . . [A]t the first arriving of the Spaniards there they found in those places, nothing showing traffic, or knowledge of any other nation; but the people naked, uncivil, some of them devourers of men's flesh ignorant of shipping, without all kind of learning, having no remembrance of history or writing, among them; never having heard of any such religion as in other places of the world is known, but being utterly ignorant of scripture, or Christ, or Moses, or any God. . . .

But that in all ages it hath appeared, that Satan hath used ignorance as one of the chiefest means whereby to increase idolatry, and consequently to enlarge his kingdom it were other wise incredible, that any who have in them reason, and the shape of men, should be so brutishly ignorant of all kind of true religion, devotion, and understanding. . . .

It may seem a kind of miracle, unto him who looketh no higher than the ordinary rules of nature, and doth not expect the extraordinary and unlimited power of God, that whereas a great part of America doth lie in the *Zona Torrida*, in the self same climate with Ethiopia, and the hottest parts of the East Indies, where the inhabitants are not only tawny, as all be in Egypt, and in Mauritania, but also coal black and very Negroes; here there should be no man whose colour is black, except it be those which are brought out of Africa, but that the people should be of a reasonable fair complexion; which is to be ascribed only unto God's peculiar will, and not to that which some foolishly have imagined, that the generative seed of those people should be white, and that other of the Ethiopians black; for that is untrue in as much as the Ethiopians case doth not differ from the quality of other men. . . .

It is certain, that by the very light of nature, and by the ordinary course of human shape, there were among this people very many good things, as affability in their kind, hospitality towards strangers, which had not offended them, according to their ability, and open and plain behaviour. . . . But withal, as it could not choose but be so, there were many other grievous sins amongst them: as adoration of devils, sodomy, incest, and all kind of adultery; ambition in very high measure; a deadly hatred each of other: which proceeded all from the fountain of ignorance wherewith Satan had blinded their eyes: yet there were among them some which, by a kind of blind witchcraft, had to evil purpose acquaintance and intercourse with foul spirits. . . .

Of Peru and Brazil

. . . In many parts both of Hispania Nova, and Peru, as also in the islands near adjoining, they have an herb whereof they make great use; of which some is brought into diverse parts of Europe, under the name of tobacco, paetum, or nicosiana. . . . [T]he inhabitants there do use it most as a remedy against that which is called *lues venerea*, whereunto many of them are subject, being unclean in their conversation; and that not only in fornication and adultery with women, but also their detestable and execrable sin of sodomy. . . .

Our men that traveled to Guiana . . . did report . . . that near unto Guiana . . . there were men without heads; which seemed to maintain the opinion to be true which in old time was conceived by the historians and philosophers, that there were Acephali, whose eyes were in their breasts, and the rest of their face there also situated: and this our English travelers have reported to be so ordinarily . . . mentioned unto them in those parts where they were, that no sober man should any way doubt of the truth thereof.

Now because it may appear that the matter is but fabulous, in respect of the truth of God's creating of them, and that the opinion of such strange shapes and monsters as were said to be in old time, that is, men with heads like dogs, some with ears down to their ankles, others with one huge foot alone, whereupon they did hop from place to place, was not worthy to be credited although Sir John Mandeville of late age fondly hath seemed to give credit and authority thereunto. . . . It is fit that the certainty of the matter concerning these in Peru should be known: & that is that in Quinbaia, and some other parts of Peru, the men are born as in other places, & yet by devises which they have, after the birth of children, when their bones and gristles, and other parts are yet tender, and fit to be fashioned, they do crush down the heads of the children unto the breasts and shoulders, and do with frames of wood, & other such devices keep them there, that in time they grew continuate to the upper part of the trunk of the body, and so seem to have no necks or heads. And again, some other of them thinking that the shape of the head is very decent, if it be long and erect after the fashion of a sugarloaf, do frame some other to that form by such wooden instruments, as they have for that purpose, and by binding and swathing them to keep them so afterwards.[52]

HENRY BUTTS (d. 1632)

Dyets dry dinner: consisting of eight sevrall courses . . .
(London: Thomas Creede, 1599), I8ᵛ–K2ᵛ, K7ᵛ–K8ʳ.

Butts was Master of Corpus Christi College and Vice-Chancellor of the University of Cambridge. His dietary, organized by types of meat, grains, fruits, vegetables, and herbs, details the influence of diet on the body's humoral complexion, which, in turn, is seen as capable of affecting outward appearances.[53]

Keywords: Diet—Humors—Jews—Skin Color

[52] Abbot's discussion of Peruvian "sugarloaf" heads derives from Hippocrates, whose "Macrocephali" are also discussed by Bodin, Huarte, and Bulwer in this volume.
[53] John Archer argues in *Every man his own doctor* (1673) that "if I know by the fore-written signs, that I am a choleric person, I will resolvedly beware the evils of that temperament, both of body and mind . . . I will bridle Nature." See also Thomas Twyne, *The schoolmaster, or teacher of table philosophie* (London: Richard Jones, 1576) and William Vaughan, *Approved directions for health* (London: T. Snodham, 1612).

Gosling

Choice	Young, fat, bred in the champian and free air.[54]
Use	Yields very good nourishment, fatteth the macilent.[55]
Hurt	Fills the body with superfluous humors, is slowly concocted (the flesh of one old goose causeth a fever)
Correction	Stifled with borage-smoke let in at the throat, then sauced with sweet herbs, and spices, and for roast.[56]
Degrees	Not in the first, moist in the second
Season	
Age	
Constitution	In cold weather, for hot stomachs, and great exercises

Story for Table-talk

The Jews are great goose-eaters. Therefore their complexion is passing melancholious, their colour swart, and their diseases very perilous. The liver and wings are best, especially of fat geese. . . . A goose is the emblem of mere modesty.

Hare

Choice	Young, well coursed
Use	It maketh slender, causeth good fresh colour in the face
Hurt	Slowly digested, engenders melancholic blood; much eaten, makes sleepy and drowsy
Preparation	Sauced with suet, or gobbets of lard, and spices
Degree	Hot and dry in the second
Season	In winter, for youth & sanguine
Age	Not for melancholists or students
Constitution	

Story for Table-talk

Hare's flesh is good for those that would be lean and fair. It is a received opinion, that use of hare's flesh procureth beauty, fresh colour, and cheerful countenance, for a seven-night space, in so much as the Italians have a by-word, which speaketh thus of a fair man, "He hath eaten an hare."

KING JAMES VI OF SCOTLAND (1566–1625)

Basilikon doron (Edinburgh: Robert Waldegrave, 1599)

Source: *The Political Works of James I.*, Ed. Charles Howard McIlwain (Cambridge: Harvard University Press, 1918), 22, 30–31, 33, 36.

---

[54] Champian = An expanse of level open country.
[55] Macilent = Thin.
[56] Borage = A genus of plants formerly esteemed as a cordial, and is still used in making cool tankard, claret cup, etc.

James became king of Scotland before the age of two, and thirty-three years later, following the death of Elizabeth I in 1603, king of England (as James I). Among his best-known writings are *Basilikon doron* (1599) on the art of government, *King James his counterblast to tobacco* (1604), theological works, and poetry in Scots, Latin, and English. In *Basilikon doron*, James's advice to his son Prince Henry counsels close attention to "race," which here seems to combine an older sense of the term as lineage with one denoting a hierarchy of bloodlines.

Keywords: Civility—Lineage—Class—Blood—Servants—Marriage

As for the highlands, I shortly comprehend them all in two sorts of people: the one, that dwelleth in our main land, that are barbarous for the most part, and yet mixed with some show of civility: the other, that dwelleth in the isles, and are all utterly barbarous, without any sort or show of civility. For the first sort, put straightly to execution the laws made already by me against their over-lords, and the chiefs of their clans, and it will be no difficulty to danton them.[57] As for the other sort, follow forth the course that I have intended, in planting colonies among them of answerable in-lands subjects, that within short time may reform and civilize the best inclined among them; rooting out or transporting the barbarous and stubborn sort, and planting civility in their rooms. . . .

All your servants and court must be composed partly of minors such as young lords, to be brought up in your company, or pages and such like; and partly of men of perfect age, for serving you in such rooms, as ought to be filled with men of wisdom and discretion. For the first sort, ye can do no more, but choose them within age, that are come of a good and virtuous kind, *in fide parentum* [in the faith of their parents], as baptism is used: For though *anima non venit ex traduce* [the soul is not inherited], but is immediately created by God, and infused from above; yet it is most certain, that virtue or vice will oftentimes, with the heritage, be transferred from the parents to the posterity, and run on a blood (as the proverb is) the sickness of the mind becoming as kindly to some races, as these sicknesses of the body, that infect in the seed. Especially choose such minors as are come of a true and honest race, and have not had the house whereof they are descended, infected with falsehood. . . .

And for conclusion of my advice anent [regarding] the choice of your servants, delight to be served with men of the noblest blood that may be had: for besides that their service shall breed you great good-will and least envy, contrary to that of startups ye shall oft find virtue follow noble races, as I have said before speaking of the nobility. . . .

And lastly, remember to choose your wife as I advised you to choose your servants: that she be of a whole and clean race, not subject to the hereditary sicknesses, either of the soul or the body: For if a man will be careful to breed

---

[57] Danton = To daunt, subdue, or tame.

horses and dogs of good kinds, how much more careful should he be, for the breed of his own loins?

JOANNES LEO AFRICANUS (ca. 1492–ca. 1550)

A geographical historie of Africa, written in Arabicke and Italian by John Leo a More, born in Granada and brought up in Barbarie. . ., translated and collected by John Pory (London: George Bishop, 1600), 3, 6, 27–29, 39–42, 71, 88, 130–31, 146–49, 163, 251, 306, 313–15, 396–97.

Joannes Leo Africanus was the Christian name of the Granadan-born Moroccan Hassan ibn Muhammad al-Wazzan. While returning to Fez from a trip to Egypt, al-Wazzan was captured by Sicilian pirates and subsequently presented as a gift to Pope Leo X, who baptized him a Christian. In Italy, Africanus wrote *A geographical historie*, a work that challenged European orthodoxies concerning African barbarism and monstrosity and informed almost every European text on Africa published until the end of the eighteenth century. First published in Giambattista Ramusio's *Primo volume delle navigationi et viaggi* (Venice, 1550), *A geographical historie* was translated into English in 1600 by John Pory, who encrusted the text with his own commentaries and fabulous accounts of African monstrosity.

Keywords: Skin Color—Sons of Noah—Lawlessness—Arabs and Arab Civility—Lust—Women's Desire for Women—Negro Bestiality—Arts in Fez—Female Witches—Sheba and Solomon—Gender Inversion—Ethiopian Christians

[Pory's Introduction] "To the Reader"

. . . [T]his part of the world is inhabited especially by five principal nations, to wit, by the people called Cafri or Cafates, that is to say outlaws, or lawless, by the Abassins, the Egyptians, the Arabians, and the Africans or Moors, properly so called; which last are of two kinds, namely white or tawny Moors, and Negros or black Moors. Of all which nations some are gentiles which worship idols; others of the sect of Mahumet; some others Christians; and some Jewish in religion; the greatest part of which people are thought to be descended from Cham the cursed son of Noah; except some Arabians of the lineage of Sem, which afterward passed into Africa. Now the Arabians inhabiting Africa are divided into many several kinds, possessing diverse and sundry habitations and regions; for some dwell near the sea shore, which retain the name of Arabians; but others inhabiting the inland, are called Baduini. There be likewise infinite swarms of Arabians, which with their wives and children, lead a vagrant and roguish life in the deserts, using tents in stead of houses: these are notable thieves, and very troublesome both to their neighbour-inhabitants, and also to merchants. . . .

Africanus, Book One

. . . The inhabitants of Barbary continued for many years idolaters; but before the coming of Mahomet above 250, years, they are said to have embraced the Christian faith: . . . When the Arabians therefore came to conquer that part of Africa they found Christians to be lords over the regions adjacent; of whom, after sundry hot conflicts, the said Arabians got the victory. Whereupon the [Christians] being deprived of all their dominions and goods went part of them into Italy and part into Spain. And so about two hundred years after the death of Mahumet, almost all Barbary was infected with his law. . . .

. . . Those Arabians which inhabit in Barbary or upon the coast of the Mediterranean Sea, are greatly addicted unto the study of good arts and sciences: and those things which concern their law and religion are esteemed by them in the first place. Moreover they have been heretofore most studious of the mathematics, of philosophy, and of astrology: but these arts (as it is aforesaid) were four hundred years ago, utterly destroyed and taken away by the chief professors of their law. The inhabitants of cities do most religiously observe and reverence those things which appertain unto their religion: yea they honour those doctors and priests, of whom they learn their law, as if they were petty-gods. Their churches they frequent very diligently, to the end they may repeat certain prescript and formal prayers. . . . Moreover those which inhabit Barbary are of great cunning and dexterity for building and for mathematical inventions, which a man may easily conjecture by their artificial works. Most honest people they are, and destitute of all fraud and guile; not only embracing all simplicity and truth, but also practising the same throughout the whole course of their lives: albeit certain Latin authors, which have written of the same regions, are far otherwise of opinion. Likewise they are most strong and valiant people, especially those which dwell upon the mountains. They keep their covenant most faithfully; insomuch that they had rather die than break promise. No nation in the world is so subject unto jealousy; for they will rather lose their lives, than put up any disgrace in the behalf of their women. So desirous they are of riches and honour, that therein no other people can go beyond them. They travel in a manner over the whole world to exercise traffic. For they are continually to be seen in Egypt, in Ethiopia, in Arabia, Persia, India, and Turkey: and whithersoever they go, they are most honorably esteemed of: for none of them will profess any art, unless he hath attained unto great exactness and perfection therein. They have always been much delighted with all kind of civility and modest behaviour: and it is accounted heinous among them for any man to utter in company, any bawdy or unseemly word. . . .

. . . Never was there any people or nation so perfectly endowed with virtue, but that they had their contrary faults and blemishes: now therefore let us consider, whether the vices of the Africans do surpass their virtues and good parts. Those which we named the inhabitants of the cities of Barbary are somewhat needy and covetous, being also very proud and high-minded, and wonderfully addicted unto wrath. . . . So rustical they are and void of good manners, that scarcely can any stranger obtain their familiarity and friendship. Their wits are but mean; and they are so credulous, that they will believe matters impossible, which are told them. So ignorant are they of natural philosophy that they imagine all the effects and operations of nature to be extraordinary and divine. They observe no certain order of living nor of laws. Abounding exceedingly with choler, they speak always with an angry and loud voice. . . . By nature they are a vile and base people, being no better accounted of by their governors than if they were dogs. . . . No people under heaven are more addicted unto covetise than this nation: neither is there (I think) to be found among them one of an hundred, who for courtesy, humanity, or devotion's sake, will vouchsafe any entertainment upon a stranger. . . . Concerning their religion, the greater part of these people are neither Mahumetans, Jews, nor Christians; and hardly shall you find so much as a spark of piety in any of them. They have no churches at all, nor any kind of prayers, but being utterly estranged from all godly devotion, they lead a savage and beastly life. . . . Likewise the inhabitants of Libya live a brutish kind of life; who neglecting all kinds of good arts and sciences, do wholly apply their minds unto theft and violence. . . . There cannot any treachery or villainy be invented so damnable, which for lucre's sake they dare not attempt. They spend all their days either in most lewd practises, or in hunting, or else in warfare; neither wear they any shoes nor garments. The Negros likewise lead a beastly kind of life, being utterly destitute of the use of reason, of dexterity of wit, and of all arts. Yea they so behave themselves, as if they had continually lived in a forest among wild beasts. They have great swarms of harlots among them; whereupon a man may easily conjecture their manner of living; except their conversation perhaps be somewhat more tolerable, who dwell in the principal towns and cities: for it is like that they are somewhat more addicted to civility.

Book Two

[The] castle [in Morocco] containeth a most noble college, which hath thirty halls belonging thereunto. In the midst whereof is one hall of a marvelous greatness, wherein public lectures were most solemnly read, while the study of learning flourished among them. . . . I have heard that in old time here was great abundance of students, but at my being there I found but five in all: and they have now a most senseless professor, and one that is quite void of all humanity. . . .
    . . . [T]he King of Portugal, being allured for gain, hath often sent most warlike fleets to surprise this town [of Azamur]. . . . The inhabitants were presently dispersed hither and thither; some fleeing on horseback and others on foot. . . . Neither do I think that God for any other cause brought this calamity upon them, but only for the horrible vice of sodomy, whereunto the greatest part of the citizens were so notoriously addicted, that they could scarce see any young stripling, who escaped their lust.

Book Three

The innkeepers of Fez . . . go apparelled like women, and shave their beards, and are so delighted to imitate women, that they will not only counterfeit their speech, but will sometimes also sit down and spin. Each one of these hath his concubine, whom he accompanieth as if she were his own lawful wife; albeit the said concubines are not only ill-favoured in countenance, but notorious for their bad life and behaviour. They buy and sell wine so freely that no man controls them for it. None resort hither but most lewd and wicked people, to the end that they may more boldly commit villainy. . . . [T]he very company of these innkeepers is so odious and detestable in the sight of all honest men, all learned men, and merchants, that they will in no wise vouchsafe to speak unto them. And they are firmly enjoined not to enter into the temple, the bourse, nor into any bath. Neither yet are they permitted to resort unto those inns which are next unto the great temple, and wherein merchants are usually entertained. All men in a manner are in utter detestation of these wretches. . . .

In Fez there are diverse most excellent poets, which make verses in their own mother tongue. Most of their poems and songs entreat of love. Every year they pen certain verses in the commendation of Mahumet, especially upon his birthday: for then betimes in the morning they resort unto the palace of the chief judge or governour, ascending his tribunal-seat, and from thence reading their verses to a great audience of people: and he whose verses are most elegant and pithy, is that year proclaimed prince of the poets. . . . .

. . . The third kind of diviners are women-witches, which are affirmed to have familiarity with devils . . . and when they will tell any man's fortune, they perfume themselves with certain odours, saying, that then they possess themselves with that devil which they called for: afterward changing their voice, they feign the devil to speak within them. . . . But the wiser and honester sort of people call these women *sahoat*, which in Latin signifieth fricatrices, because they have a damnable custom to commit unlawful venery among themselves, which I cannot express in any modester terms.[58] If fair women come unto them at any time, these abominable witches will burn in lust towards them no otherwise than lusty yoonkers do towards young maids, and will in the devil's behalf demand for a reward that they may lie with them: and so by this means it often falleth out, that thinking thereby to fulfill the devil's command they lie with the witches.[59] Yea some there are, which being allured with the delight of this abominable vice, will desire the company of these witches, and feigning themselves to be sick, will either call one of the witches home to them, or will send their husbands for the same purpose . . . . With these words her silly husband being persuaded, doth not only permit her so to do, but makes also a sumptuous banquet unto the damned crew of witches: which being done, they use to dance very strangely

[58] Fricatrice = A lewd woman.
[59] Yoonker = A young and fashionable nobleman or gentleman; also, a boy or junior seaman on board ship.

at the noise of drums: and so the poor man commits his false wife to their filthy disposition. Howbeit some there are that will soon conjure the devil with a good cudgel out of their wives: others feigning themselves to be possessed with a devil, will deceive the said witches, as their wives have been deceived by them. . . .

. . . All the maidservants in the king's family are Negro-slaves, which are partly chamberlains, and partly waiting-maids. And yet his queen is always of a white skin. Likewise in the king of Fez his court are certain Christian captives, being partly Spanish, and partly Portugal women, who are most circumspectly kept by certain eunuchs that are Negro-slaves.

Book Eight

Cairo is commonly reputed to be one of the greatest and most famous cities in all the whole world. . . . Cairo is an Arabian word, corruptly pronounced by the people of Europe: for the true Arabian word is *El Chahira*, which signifieth an enforcing or imperious mistress. . . .

. . . The women [of Cairo] go costly attired, adorning their foreheads and necks with frontlets and chains of pearl, and on their heads they wear a sharp and slender bonnet of a span high, being very precious and rich. . . . These women are so ambitious and proud, that all of them disdain either to spin or to play the cooks: wherefore their husbands are constrained to buy victuals ready dressed at the cooks shops: for very few, except such as have a great family, use to prepare and dress their victuals in their own houses. Also they vouchsafe great liberty unto their wives: for the good man being gone to the tavern or victualling-house, his wife tricking up her self in costly apparel, and being perfumed with sweet and precious odours, walketh about the city to solace herself, and parley with her kinsfolk and friends.[60]

Appendix: A relation touching the state of Christian Religion in the dominions of Prete Janni, taken out of an oration of Matthew Dresserus, Professor of the Greek and Latin tongues, and of histories, in the University of Lipsia

In times past Ethiopia was governed by queens only. Whereupon we read in the history of the old testament, that the Queen of the South came to King Salomon from Saba, to hear his admirable wisdom, about the year of the world 2954. The name of this queen (as the Ethiopians report) was Maqueda, who from the head-city of Ethiopia called Saba (which like an isle, is environed on all sides by the river Nilus) traveled by Egypt and the Red Sea to Jerusalem. And she brought unto Salomon an hundred and twenty talents of gold, which amount to 720,000 golden ducats of Hungary, that is, seven tons of gold, and 20,000 Hungarian ducats besides. This mighty sum of gold, with other things of great value, she presented unto Salomon, who

---

[60] Africanus's discussion of Egyptian women recalls the gender inversion previously identified with Egypt in *The Histories* of Herodotus, also in this volume.

likewise requited her with most princely gifts. She contended with him also in propounding of sage questions, and obscure riddles. . . .

The Ethiopian kings suppose, that they are descended from the lineage of David, and from the family of Solomon. . . . For Queen Maqueda (say they) had a son by Salomon, whom they named Meilech. But afterward he was called David. This Meilech (as they report) being grown to twenty years of age, was sent back by his mother unto his father and instructor Solomon, that he might learn of him, wisdom and understanding. Which so soon as the said Meilech or David had attained: by the permission of Salomon, taking with him many priests and nobles, out of all the twelve tribes, he returned to his kingdom of Ethiopia, and took upon him the government thereof. As likewise he carried home with him the law of God, and the rite of circumcision.

These were the beginnings of the Jewish religion in Ethiopia. And it is reported, that even till this present none are admitted into any ministry or canonship in the court, but such as are descended of their race that came first out of Jewry . . . [w]hich manifestly appeareth out of the history of the Ethiopian eunuch, whose name was Indich, which was a principal governor under Queen Candaces, properly called Judith. . . . [T]his eunuch baptized the Queen, and a great part of her family and people. From which time the Ethiopians began to be Christians, who since that have continually professed the Christian faith. . . .

QUEEN ELIZABETH I OF ENGLAND (1533–1603)

"Licensing Caspar van Senden to Deport Negroes" [draft] (1601)

Source: Paul L. Hughes and James F. Larkin, eds., *Tudor Royal Proclamations*, Vol. 3 (New Haven and London: Yale University Press, 1969), 221.

In 1601 Elizabeth renewed Caspar Van Senden's 1596 license (included earlier in this volume) to remove "negroes and blackamoors" from the realm, evidencing an African presence that remained visible in London despite efforts to legislate the expulsion of blacks. In the updated license, Elizabeth expands the economic and nationalistic terms of her earlier complaint to emphasize her subjects' religious obligation to give up their African servants.

Keywords: Blackamoors—Infidels—Englishness—Expulsion of
          Blackamoors

Whereas the Queen's Majesty, tending the good and welfare of her own natural subjects, greatly distressed in these hard times of dearth, is highly discontented to understand the great number of Negroes and blackamoors, which (as she is informed) are carried into this realm since the troubles between her highness and the King of Spain, who are fostered and powered here, to the great annoyance of her own liege people that which co[vet?] the relief which these people consume, as also for that the most of them are infidels having no understanding of Christ or his Gospel: hath given a special commandment that the said kind of people shall be with all speed avoided and discharged out of Her Majesty's realms; and to that end and purpose hath appointed Caspar van Senden, merchant of Lubeck, for their speedy transportation, a man that hath somewhat deserved of this realm in respect that by his own labour and charge he hath relieved and brought from Spain diverse of our English nation who otherwise would have perished there.

These shall therefore be to will and require you and every [one] of you to aid and assist the said Caspar van Senden or his assignees to taking such Negroes and blackamoors to be transported as aforesaid as he shall find within the realm of England; and if there shall be any person or persons which be possessed of any such blackamoors that refuse to deliver them in sort aforesaid, then we require you to call them before you and to advise and persuade them by all good means to satisfy her Majesty's pleasure therein; which if they shall eftsoons willfully and obstinately refuse, we pray you to certify their names to us, to the end her Majesty may take such further course therein as it shall seem best in her princely wisdom.

ABRAHAM ORTELIUS (1527–98)

Abraham Ortelius his epitome of the Theater of the worlde (Antwerp and London: James Shaw, 1603), 14, 16, 19, 96, 112, 113, 114, 120.

Abraham Ortelius's *Theatrum Orbis Terrarum* (1570) became the most popular atlas of the sixteenth century and was translated into various European languages. It spawned the pocket atlas, or *Epitome*, in which the maps were accompanied by text that offered pithy descriptions of different regions, rather like George Abbot's survey of world cultures (also in this volume). Also instantly popular, the *Epitome* continued to be published until 1724. Its stereotypical decriptions are often inconsistent, hence black color is seen to be the result of the sun in one description and has nothing to do with the sun in another.

Keywords: Skin Color—New World Brutishness—Conversion to Christianity

Description of Africa

The strangest is that in Africa near unto Guinea and in the country of the Negroes between the equinoctial and the tropic, the people are all black moors, and yet in Prester John's land right under th'equinoctial they are but tawny moors, which is strange against the general opinion which seems of reason to yield that the whiteness or blackness of the people proceedeth from the nearness of the sun. Moreover, near to the Cape of Good Hope the people are very black, and yet near the Strait of Magellan they are most white, yet are they both almost of equal distance from the equinoctial to the southward. Therefore we esteem the sun doth not make the people black. For both in Spain and Italy where they are white, they are also within 30 and 40 degrees of the equinoctial northward, as those of the Cape of Good Hope are southward. . . . Africa surpasseth Europe in largeness . . . [and] produceth moreover innumerable quantity of wild and monstrous beasts, which Pliny attributeth unto other great huge deserts therein and great want of water, for continually new forms and strange manners of beasts are seen, whence rose the proverb, *Africa semper aliquid novi apportat* [Africa always presents something new]. . . .

The Description of America

The people were not only idolators, but almost brute beasts without sense, having only the human shape. But sithence the Spaniards have governed the same, they are most reduced to the Christian faith, and live more politically and more civilly. So that in very short space it is hoped that they will be wholly converted. . . .

Ireland

This country generally belongeth unto the crown of England, and kept in great subjection, unless it be some part thereof, the which is inhabited by a sort of wild brutish people, subject unto none. Their habits are commonly very slight of black wool . . . almost of a barbarous fashion, and are most commonly covered with a hair black rug. . . . They go to the wars in a manner naked. In fine they are utterly brute, esteeming no manner of delights to idleness, nor no riches to liberty. . . .

The East Indies with the Isles

The inhabitants [of islands in the Indian Ocean] are very ingenious, much inclined unto all sciences, and in their religion and customs they much resemble the Christian, adoring one sole God, whom they paint with three heads, howbeit they can not yield the reason thereof. They baptize their children, they fast, and use diverse other signs, which are greatly conformable unto the Christian religions. . . .

Persia, or the Empire of the Sophy

The Persians are valiant, courteous, lovers of sciences and arts, they honour and love true nobility, a thing most contrary unto the Turks, with the which they have continual wars, because they do not agree about the exposition of their *Alcoran*. . . .

The Empire of the Turk

The Turks are of nature great observators of their false laws, slaves unto their lords, good soldiers, both on foot and on horseback, patient in labour, sparing in their food, and for the rest very inconstant. . . .

Barbary and Biledugerid

The people are generally all tawny, moors, very sturdy and strong of body. The citizens are skillful in architecture and the mathematics, and other sciences, as by their buildings may be judged. They are good of nature (so they were Christians) without dissimulation, loving the truth, and observing their promises with all faith. They are very jealous of their wives, ambitious, greedy, and covetous of wealth, and therefore are great merchants.

MICHEL DE MONTAIGNE (1533–92)

The essays or morall, politike and millitarie discourses, translated by John Florio (London: Val. Sims, 1603)

Source: Free online edition via http://www.uoregon.edu/~rbear/ montaigne/

Michel de Montaigne is best known for his *Essays*, first published in 1580, which engage with traditional humanist concerns (education, morality, war, law), but are particularly interesting for their tolerance and relativism. Montaigne's denunciation of the burning of witches and the maltreatment of American Indians attempts to counter the dogmatism of his age, though his relativism sometimes worked by circulating stereotypes such as those about the simplicity and unworldiness of Native Americans.

Keywords: Cannibalism—Widow Burning—New World Cities—New World Innocence—Barbarism

Of the Cannibals

Now to return to my purpose I find . . . there is nothing in [Brazil] that is either barbarous or savage, unless men call that barbarism which is not common to them. . . . Those nations seem therefore so barbarous unto me, because they have received very little fashion from human wit, and are yet near their original naturality. The laws of nature do yet command them which are but little bastardized by ours, and that with such purity, as I am sometimes grieved the knowledge of it came no sooner to light, at what time there were men that better than we could have judged of it. . . . It is a nation, would I answer *Plato*, that hath no kind of traffic, no knowledge of letters, no intelligence of numbers, no name of magistrate, nor of politic superiority; no use of service, of riches or of poverty; no contracts, no successions, no partitions, no occupation but idle; no respect of kindred, but common, no apparel but natural, no manuring of lands, no use of wine, corn, or metal. The very words that import lying, falsehood, treason, dissimulation, covetousness, envy, detraction, and pardon, were never heard of amongst them. How dissonant would he find his imaginary common-wealth from this perfection? . . .

They war against the nations that lie beyond their mountains, to which they go naked, having no other weapons than bows or wooden swords. . . . Every victor brings home the head of the enemy he hath slain as a trophy of his victory, and fasteneth the same at the entrance of his dwelling place. After they have long time used and entreated their prisoners well, and with all commodities they can devise, he that is the master of them, summoning a great assembly of his acquaintance, tieth a cord to one of the prisoners arms, by the end whereof he holds him fast, with some distance from him, for fear he might offend him, and giveth the other arm, bound in like manner, to the dearest friend he hath, and both in the presence of all the assembly kill him with swords: which done, they roast and then eat him in common, and send some slices of him to such of their friends as are absent. It is not, as some imagine, to nourish themselves with it (as anciently the Scythians wont to do), but to represent an extreme and inexpiable revenge. Which we prove thus: some of them perceiving the Portugales, who had confederated themselves with their adversaries, to use another kind of death when they took them prisoners, which was, to bury them up to the middle, and against the upper part of the body to shoot arrows, and then being almost dead, to hang them up, they supposed, that the people of the other world (as they who had sowed the knowledge of many vices amongst their neighbors, and were much more cunning in all kinds of evils and mischief than they) undertook not this manner of revenge without cause, and that consequently it was more smartful and cruel than theirs, and thereupon began to leave their old fashion to follow this. I am not sorry we note the barbarous horror of such an action, but grieved, that prying so narrowly into their faults we are so blinded in ours. I think there is more barbarism in eating men alive, than to feed upon them being dead; to mangle by tortures and torments a body full of lively sense, to roast him in pieces, and to make dogs and swine to gnaw and tear him in mammocks (as we have not only read, but seen very lately . . . not amongst ancient enemies, but our neighbors and fellow-citizens; and which is worse, under pretence of piety and religion) than to roast and eat him after he is dead.

Of Virtue

A late writer affirrmeth that himself hath seen this custom highly reputed in the new discovered East Indies, where not only the wives are buried with their husbands, but also such slaves as he hath enjoyed, which is done after this manner. The husband being deceased, the widow may, if she will (but few do it), request two or three months's space to dispose of her business. The day come, adorned as a sumptuous bride, she mounteth on horseback, and with a cheerful countenance telleth everybody she is going to lie with her bridegroom, holding in her left hand a looking-glass, and an arrow in the right. Thus . . . she is brought into a public place, purposely appointed for such spectacles; which is a large open place, in the midst whereof is a pit or grave full of wood, and near unto it an upraised scaffold, with four or five steps to ascend, upon which she is brought, and served with a stately and sumptuous banquet, which ended, she beginneth to dance and sing, and when she thinks good, commandeth the fire to be kindled. That done, she cometh down again, and taking the nearest of her husband's kindred by the hand, they go together to the next river, where she strips herself all naked and distributeth her jewels and clothes among her friends, then plungeth herself in the water, as if she meant to wash away her sins; then coming . . . they return unto the mount, where she speaks unto the people, to whom (if she have any) she recommendeth her children. . . . Her speech ended, a woman presenteth her with a vessel full of oil, therewith to anoint her head and body, which done, she casteth the rest into the fire, and therewithal suddenly flings herself into it: which is no sooner done but the people cast great stores of faggots and billets upon her, lest she should languish over-long: and all their joy is converted into grief and sorrow. If they be persons of mean quality, the dead man's body is carried to the place where they intend to bury him, and there he is placed sitting; his widow kneeling before him with her arms close about his middle, and so keepeth herself whilst a wall is erected up about them both, which raised to the height of her shoulders, some of her kindred taking her by the head behind, wrings her neck about, and having given the last gasp, the wall is immediately made up close over their heads, wherein they remain buried.

THOMMASO BUONI (fl. 1605)

Problemes of beautie and all humane affections, translated by Samson Lennard (London: G. Eld, 1606), 14–15, 23–28, 54–55, 67–68.

First published in Venice, Thomasso Buoni's book of inquiries into beauty, speculates about the influence of climate, diet, the heavens, and the imagination on outward appearances. His claim that "every like desireth and loveth his like" anticipates arguments made two centuries later by Joseph Arthur, Comte de Gobineau, for the permanence of racial types on the basis of affinities and repulsions.[61]

Keywords: Beauty and Skin Color—Attraction—Human Generation— Climate—Diet—Maternal Impression—Class and Lineage

[61] Joseph Arthur, Comte de Gobineau, *Essai sur l'inégalité des Races Humaines* (Paris: Firmin-Didot, 1853–55).

Problem 13: Why are there born in some provinces, cities, castles, and villages, beautiful women, in others beautiful men, in some countries men of tall stature, fat, and white, in others lean of body and of a sallow complexion?

. . . [W]hether it be by reason of the strong imagination, or the operation of the seed, or the concurrence of the blood, or any other cause that worketh in the act of generation, we must conclude howsoever that the first women of those provinces, cities, castles, villages, having been of a right excellent complexion, and due proportion of members . . . were the first original causes of the beauty of the women in those places, unto which we may likewise add, the influences of the heavens upon those territories, the fitness and temperature of the climates, with the concurrence of meats, and drinks, befitting those celestial operations. . . . The like may be said of those men who in the beginning by reason of their tall stature, big bones, [and] pleasant aspect, accompanied with a kind of lord-like majesty, by virtue of their active seed, and the climate disposed to the like temperature, have made their progeny admirable and beautiful. But as touching fatness and leanness, accompanied with a certain kind of whiteness, or blackness, perhaps the one is caused by the coldness of the climate, which being far distant from the force of the sun, makes the digestion more strong, whereby much of the nutriment is converted to the benefit of nature, and consequently the party made more fat and more fair, as doth plainly appear in our women, of high, and low Germany, whereas the contrary cause works the contrary effect, that is, makes women lean, and of a sallow complexion, which we may easily see in the women of Spain and for as much as the Italian is neither so near the North as the German, nor the South as the Spaniard, he participates of both their natures and flies both their extremes.

Problem 14: Why doth the beauty of women consist sometimes in one colour, sometimes in the variety of colours?

Perhaps because corporal beauty is not only placed in due proportion or site, or quantity, or quality of the members, but much more in the appetites which by reason of the diversity of complexion where it resideth, willeth and desireth diversely. And therefore to the eye of the Moor, the black, or tawny countenance of his Moorish damsel pleaseth best, to the eye of another, a colour as white as the lily, or the driven snow, to another the colour neither simply white, nor black, but that well meddled beauty betwixt them both. . . . Or perhaps because every like desireth and loveth his like, whereby even for the public good, there remaineth nothing despised, because there is nothing but hath his like . . . and therefore the Moor loves the Moor, and so of the rest. Or perhaps because beauty consisteth not so much in the colour as in the illumination, or illustration of those colours, which giveth grace, and luster to every countenance, and without which all beauties are languishing . . . which we may plainly see in the faces of those Moors which though they are black do many times betray a strange kind of beauty in them, and therefore no marvel though many praise the beauty of one only colour. . . .

Problem 29: Why do princes and women of honorable birth prove for the most part fairer both in body and mind than women of baser condition?

Perhaps because their delicate and exquisite diet, both in their meats and drinks, makes their blood more pure, their vital spirits more lively, their complexion more beautiful, and their nature more noble, so that passing their time without interruption of any troublesome, or disorderly molestations, they become by their high thoughts, and honorable imaginations, both beautiful and gentle in aspect, about other women of inferior condition, who by reason of their base estate, taking a contrary course in whatsoever belongeth unto their life, they participate in contrary effects. . . . Or perhaps because their education being even from their infancy under a discipline more noble and excellent (to omit the generous blood of their parents from whom they descend, and the pure milk which they draw from the dugs of women of a most temperate constitution) they cannot in common judgment but prove admirable in the world.

Problem 35: Why is it the custom to hang beautiful pictures in the chambers of those women that are with child?

Perhaps because those strange occurrences that in former times have fallen out are an instruction to men in these days to prevent the like events. For great women, by contemplating and gazing on serpents and Moors in their chambers in the act of generation, have brought forth monstrous births, in some figure and proportion like unto them. By which strange events men being terrified, to the end they may prevent the like dangerous issues, they hang their chambers with beautiful images and pictures. Or perhaps the desire of parents to have beautiful children is so great . . . that knowing the great force of the imagination and conceit in the act of generation they are careful to furnish their chambers with fair and beautiful pictures to the end that their children may come into the light in some sort answerable to their desires. . . .

EDWARD TOPSELL (1572–1625?)

The historie of foure-footed beastes (London: William Jaggard, 1607), 2–15, 295–96.

A curate, Edward Topsell wrote largely on religious themes, but his masterwork is *The historie of foure-footed beastes*, which depicts both common animals and fantastic creatures such as gorgons, sphinxes, and unicorns. The collection draws on diverse sources including poetry and the scriptures as well as natural history.

Topsell's comparisons of the physical and libidinal features of African primates and black people anticipate later writings.

Keywords: Primates—Pygmies—Men Resembling Primates—Animal and Human Lust—Crossbreeding—Maternal Impression

Of the Ape

The countries where apes are found are Libya, and all that desert woods betwixt Egypt, Ethiopia and Libya, and that part of Caucasus which reacheth to the Red Sea. In India they are most abundant, both red, black, green, dust-colour, and white ones, which they use to bring into cities (except red ones, who are so venerous that they will ravish their women) and present to their kings, which grow so tame that they go up and down the trees so boldly and civilly as if they were children, frequenting the market places without any offence. . . .

. . . In the region of Basman, subject to the great Cham of Tartaria, are many and diverse sorts of apes, very like mankind, which, when the hunters take, they pull off their hairs, all but the beard and the hole behind, and afterward dry them with hot spices, and powdering them, sell them to merchants, who carry them about the world, persuading simple people that there are men in islands of no greater stature. . . . As for a chymara, which Albertus maketh an ape, it is but a figment of the poets. The same man maketh pigmies a kind of apes, and not men, but Niphus proveth that they are not men because they have no perfect use of reason, no modesty, no honesty, nor justice of government, and although they speak, yet is their language imperfect; and above all they cannot be men because they have no religion, which (Plato sayeth truly) is proper to every man. Besides, their stature being not past three, four, or five spans long, their life not above eight years, and their imitation of man do plainly prove them rather to be apes than men, and also the flatness of their noses, their combats with cranes and partridges for their eggs, and other circumstances I will not stand upon, but follow the description of apes in general. . . .

. . . The genital or privy part of the female is like a woman's, but the male's is like a dog's. Their nourishment goeth more forward than backward, like the best horses, and the Arabian seraph, which are higher before than behind, and that ape whose meat goeth forward by reason of the heat of heart and liver is most like to a man in standing upright. Their eyes are hollow, and that thing in men is accounted for a sign of a malicious mind, as little eyes are a token of a base and abject spirit. Men that have low and flat nostrils are libidinous as apes that attempt women, and having thick lips, the upper hanging over the nether, they are deemed fools, like the lips of asses and apes. . . .

Of the Prasian Apes

. . . There is another kind of monkey, for stature, bigness and shape like a man, for by his knees, secret parts, and face, you would judge him a wild man, such as inhabit Numidia and the Lapones, for he is altogether overgrown with hair. No creature except a man can stand so long as he; he loveth women and children dearly, like other of his own kind, and is so venerous that he will attempt to ravish women. . . .

Of the Cynocephale or Baboon

Cynocephales are a kind of apes whose heads are like dogs and their other part like a man's. . . .

The west region of Libya and Ethiopia have great store of cynocephals, baboons, and acephals, beasts without a head, whose eyes and mouth are in their breasts. In like sort, in Arabia, from Dira southward in a promontory, there are many baboons . . . and those which Apollonius saw betwixt the rivers Ganges and Hyphasis seem to be of this sort, in that he describeth them to be black-haired, dog-faced, and like little men; wherewithal Aelianus seemeth to be deceived in saying that there are men cynoprosopoi, dog-faced, whereas it is the error of vulgar people to think that baboons are men, differing only in the face or visage.

. . . It hath a grim and fearful face, and the female hath naturally her womb cast out of her body, and so she beareth it about all her life long. Their voice is a shrill wheezing, for they cannot speak, and yet they understand the Indian language. . . .

. . . They will imitate all human actions, loving wonderfully to wear garments, and of their own accord they clothe themselves in the skins of wild beasts they have killed. They are as lustful and venerous as goats, attempting to defile all sorts of women, and yet they love little children, and their females will suffer them to suck their breasts if they be held to them, and some say they will suck women's breasts like little children. There was such a beast brought to the French king, his head being like a dog's and his other parts like a man's, having legs, hands, and arms naked like a man's, and a white neck, he did eat food flesh so mannerly and modestly, taking his meat in his hands, and putting it to his mouth, that any man would think he had understood human conditions. He stood upright like a man, and sat down like a man. He discerned men and women asunder, and above all loved the company of women and young maidens. His genital member was greater than might match the quantity of his other parts. . . .

The Satyr

As the cynocephall or baboon-apes have given occasion to some to imagine (though falsely) there were such men, so the satyr, a most rare and seldom seen beast, hath occasioned others to think it was a devil . . . for there are many things common to the satyr-apes and devilish satyrs, as their human shape, their abode in solitary places, their rough hair, and lust to women, wherewith all other apes are naturally infected, but especially satyrs. Wherefore the ancient Graecians conjecture their name to be derived as it were of stathes, signifying the yard or virile member. . . .

The satyrs are in the islands Satyrida, which are three in number, standing right over against India on the farther side of Ganges, of which Euphemus Car rehearseth this history: that when he sailed into Italy, by the rage of wind and evil weather they . . . brought us to the Satyrian Islands, where we saw the inhabitants red, and had tails joined to their back, not much less than horses. These, being perceived by the mariners to run to the ships and lay hold on the women that were in them, the ship-men, for fear, took one of the barbarian women and set her on the land among them, whom in most odious and filthy manner they abused, not only in that part that nature hath ordained, but over the whole body most libidinously, whereby they found them to be very brute beasts. . . .

. . . It is certain that devils do many ways delude men in the likeness of satyrs. . . . Yet is it likely that there are men also like satyrs inhabiting in some desert places, for St. Jerome, in the life of Paul the Eremite, reporteth there appeared to Saint Anthony . . . a little man having crooked nostrils, horns growing out of his forehead, and the nether part of his body had goats' feet. The holy man not dismayed . . . asked him who he was, and received this answer: I am a mortal creature, one of the inhabitants of this desert, whom the Gentiles (deceived with error) do worship and call fauni, satyrs, and incubi; I am come in ambassage from our flock, entreating that thou wouldst pray for us unto the common God, who came to save the world. . . .

Figure 6   "Satyr," from Edward Topsell, *The historie of foure-footed beastes* (1607). From the collections of The Rare Book & Manuscript Library, University of Illinois at Urbana-Champaign.

Of the choice of Stallions and breeding Mares

. . . Horse-keepers have devised to make their mares conceive strange colours, for when the mares would go to the horse, they paint a stallion with diverse colours, and so bring him into the sight and preference of the mare, where they suffer him to stand a good while until she perfectly conceive in her imagination the true idea and full impression of those pictures, and then they suffer him to cover her; which being performed she conceiveth a foal of those colours. . . .

THOMAS DEKKER (1572–1632)

Lanthorne and candle-light. Or, The bell-mans second nights walke
(London: Edward Allde, 1609), D1^r–D2^v.

The author of the enormously popular play, *The Shoemaker's Holiday*, Dekker turned more frequently in the seventeenth century to writing pamphlets, focusing on contemporary events such as Elizabeth I's death, the plagues, and the Catholic Gunpowder Plot. *Lanthorne and candle-light* follows a devil in a tour of his followers in London—usurers, extortionists, gamblers, and the gypsies described here exclusively in terms of their cultural difference from law-abiding Englishmen.

Keywords: Gypsies—Egyptians—Vagabonds—Complexion—Artificial
Coloring—Clothing and Identity—Gypsy Lust

Chapter 8: Moon men

A discovery of a strange wild people, very dangerous to towns and country villages.
A moon-man signifies in English, a mad-man, because the Moon hath greatest domination (above any other planet) over the bodies of frantic persons. But these moon-men . . . are neither absolutely mad, nor yet perfectly in their wits. Their name they borrow from the moon, because as the moon is never in one shape two nights together, but wanders up & down heaven, like an antic, so these changeable-stuff-companions never tarry one day in a place, but are the only . . . base runagates upon earth. And as in the moon there is a man that never stirs without a bush of thorns at his back, so these moon-men lie under bushes, & are indeed no better than hedge creepers.
They are a people more scattered than Jews, and more hated: beggarly in apparel, barbarous in condition, beastly in behavior, and bloody if they meet advantage. A man that sees them would swear they had all the yellow jaundice, or that they were tawny Moors' bastards, for no red-ochre man carries a face of a more filthy complexion, yet are they not born so, neither has the sun burnt them so, but they are painted so, yet they are not good painters neither: for

they do not make faces, but mar faces.[62] By a byname they are called gypsies; they call themselves Egyptians; others in mockery call them moon-men.

If they be Egyptians, sure I am they never descended from the tribes of any of those people that came out of the land of Egypt: Ptolemy (king of the Egyptians) I warrant never called them his subjects: no nor Pharaoh before him. Look what difference there is between a civil citizen of Dublin & a wild Irish kern, so much difference there is between one of these counterfeit Egyptians and a true English beggar. An English rogue is just of the same livery.

They are commonly an army about four-score strong, yet they never march with all their bags and baggage together, but (like boot-halers) they forage up and down countries, four, five, or six in a company.[63] As the Switzer has his wench and his cock with him when he goes to the wars, so these vagabonds have their harlots with a number of little children following at their heels. . . . But if they can straddle once, then as well the she-rogues as the he-rogues are horsed, seven or eight upon one jade, strongly pinioned, and strangely tied together.

One shire alone & no more is sure still at one time, to have these Egyptian lice swarming within it, for like flocks of wild-geese, they will evermore fly one after another: let them be scattered worse than the quarters of a traitor are after he's hanged, drawn and quartered, yet they have a trick (like water cut with a sword) to come together instantly and easily again. . . .

Their apparel is odd, and fantastic, though it be never so full of rents: the men wear scarves of calico, or any other base stuff, hanging their bodies like morris dancers, with bells, & other toys, to entice the country people to flock about them, and to wonder at their fooleries or rather rank knaveries. The women as ridiculously attire themselves, and (like one that plays the rogue on a stage) wear rags, and patched filthy mantles uppermost, when the under garments are handsome and in fashion. . . .

The cabins where these land-pirates lodge in the night are the outbarns of farmers & husbandmen, (in some poor village or other) who dare not deny them, for fear they should ere morning have their thatched houses burning about their ears. . . . These barns are the beds of incests, whoredoms, adulteries, & of all other black and deadly-damned impieties; here grows the cursed tree of bastardy, that is so fruitful: here are written the books of all blasphemies, swearings, & curses that are so dreadful to be read. . . .

WILLIAM BIDDULPH (fl. 1600–12)

The travels of foure English men and a preacher into Africa, Asia, Troy, Bythnia, Thracia. . . . and to sundry other places
(London: Th. Haveland, 1609)

Source: Samuel Purchas, *Purchas his Pilgrimes. In five books.* Vol. 2 (London: Printed by William Stansby for Henrie Fetherstone, 1625), 1339–1343.

---

[62] Red-ochre man = a man who works or deals in ochre, any of various natural earthy materials or clays; a colorman.

[63] Boot-haler = A marauder, a marauding or foraging soldier; a highwayman, or brigand.

William Biddulph was one of the earliest chaplains appointed by the Levant Company to Aleppo and was the first English clergyman to write about the Ottoman Empire. An account of his overland journey in 1600 from Aleppo to Jerusalem, framed as letters sent back to England, was published as *The travels of foure English men and a preacher . . .* (1609). In this account, Biddulph encourages English readers to compare their own lives with those of Turkish men and women.

Keywords: Turks—Sons of Noah—Arabs—Saracens—Jews in Turkey—
        Interracial Sex—Religious Conversions

. . . These Turcomanny are kind, and simple people . . . the men following their flocks of sheep and herds of cattle, the women keep their tents, and spend their time in spinning, or carding, or knitting, or some household housewifery, not spending their time in gossiping and gadding abroad from place to place, and from house to house, from ale-house to wine-tavern, as many idle housewives in England do. . . .

Aleppo is inhabited by Turks, Moors, Arabians, Jews, Greeks, Armenians, Chelfalines, Nostranes, and people of sundry other nations. The Turks come of Magog the son of Japheth. . . .

The Moors are more ancient dwellers in Aleppo than Turks, and more forward and zealous in Muhammedanism than Turks: yea all the churchmen amongst the Turks are Moors (whom the Turks count a base people in regard of themselves, and call them Tots). Yet their churchmen they have in great reverence; and not only theirs, but they reverence churchmen of all nations, and call them holy men, saints, and men of God. . . . [In] all my ten years's travels, I never received, neither was offered wrong by any nation but mine own countrymen, and by them chiefly whom it chiefly concerned to protect me from wrongs. . . .

[Among the Turks] the witness of a dervish or of a churchman, will pass better than any man's witness besides, yea, better than Shereffes whom they account of Mahomet's kindred, and they are known from others by their green sashes, which no man else may wear: for green they account Mahomet's colour, and if they see any Christian wearing a garment of that colour, they will cut it from his back, and beat him, and ask him how he dare presume to wear Mahomet's colour, and whether he be kin to God or not? This I have known put in practice upon Christians (not acquainted with the customs of the country) since my coming: one for having but green shoestrings had his shoes taken away. Another wearing green breeches under his gown (being espied) had his breeches cut off, and he reviled and beaten. . . .[64]

There are also many Arabians in Aleppo, called vulgarly Arabs or Bedweens [Bedouins]. They call themselves Saracens, of Sara; but they are rather Ishmaelites, of Ishmael, Abraham's son by Hagar. . . . They are a base, beggarly, and roguish people, wandering up and down, and living by spoil,

---

[64] This idea is repeated by George Sandys and William Lithgow.

which they account no sin because they are Mahomet's countrymen, and he allowed them liberty to live by theft. . . . [F]or the most part their lodgings are on some dunghill or other, or odd corner of the city, with some silly tent over their heads. Their wives wear rings in their noses, either of silver or brass, fastened to the middle gristle of their nose, and colour their lips blue with indigo, and go always bare-legged and bare-footed, with plates or rings of brass above their ankles, and bracelets of brass about their hands. They are people which can and do endure great hardness and misery, both for diet and lodging. Their women are skilful in mourning and crying by art, and therefore they are hired to cry at the funerals of Turks and Moors oftentimes, tearing their hair, and making all their face blue with indigo.

. . . Besides all these Mahometans (which I have already named) there are many Jews in Constantinople, Aleppo, Damascus, Babylon, Grand Cairo, and every great city and place of merchandise, throughout all the Turks' dominions, who are known by their hats: for . . . they are constrained to wear hats of blue cloth, because red was accounted too stately, and princelike a colour for them to wear. They are of more vile account in the sight of Turks than Christians; insomuch that if a Jew would turn Turk, he must first turn Christian before they will admit him to be a Turk. Yea, it is a word of reproach amongst the Turks, and a usual protestation amongst them, when they are falsely accused of any crime, to clear themselves they use to protest in this manner, *If this be true, then God grant I may die a Jew.* And the Jews in like cases use to say, *If this be not a false accusation; then God grant I may die a Christian*, praying better for themselves than they believe, and as all of them must be that shall be saved. And the poor Christians sojourning and dwelling in these parts, do hate them very uncharitably and irreligiously. . . .

[The Jews] observe still all their old ceremonies and feasts, sacrifices only excepted. Yet some of them have confessed that their physicians kill some Christian patient or other, whom they have under their hands at that time, instead of a sacrifice. . . . Many of them are rich merchants, some of them dragomen, and some brokers. Most of them are very crafty and deceitful people. They have no beggars amongst them, but many thieves, and some who steal for necessity, because they dare not beg. . . .

[B]oth at Constantinople, Aleppo, and other places of Turkey, where there is trafficking, and trading of merchants, it is no rare matter for popish Christians of sundry other countries, to *cut cabine*, (as they call it) that is, to take any woman of that country where they sojourn (Turkish women only excepted, for it is death for a Christian to meddle with them), and when they have bought them, and enrolled them in the *Cadies* book, to use them as wives so long as they sojourn in that country, and maintain them gallantly, to the consuming of their wealth, diminishing of their health, and endangering of their own souls. And when they depart out of that country, they shake off these their sweethearts, and leave them to shift for themselves and their children. And this they account no sin, or at leastwise such a sin as may be washed away, with a little holy water. And these are the virtues which many Christians learn by sojourning long in heathen countries. . . .

Figure 7 Maternal impression, from Ambroise Paré, *The works of that famous chirurgeon Ambrose Parey* (London, 1630). From the collections of The Rare Book & Manuscript Library, University of Illinois at Urbana-Champaign.

This picture shows a black child born to white parents as a result of the mother gazing upon the image of a black man during pregnancy, along with a hairy woman. Both are examples of monstrous births appearing in French Royal Surgeon Ambroise Paré's *The works of that famous chirurgeon* (London, 1630). A similar image earlier appeared in Pierre Boaistuau's *Certaine secrete wonders of nature* (1569), extracted in this volume.

Figure 8 Pict man, from Theodore de Bry, *Amiranda Narratio Fida Tamen, de Commodis et Incolarum Ritibus Virginiae* (Frankfurt, 1590). From the collections of The Rare Book & Manuscript Library, University of Illinois at Urbana-Champaign.

Figure 9 Pict woman, from Theodore de Bry, *Amiranda Narratio Fida Tamen, de Commodis et Incolarum Ritibus Virginiae* (Frankfurt, 1590). From the collections of The Rare Book & Manuscript Library, University of Illinois at Urbana-Champaign.

These pictures of painted Picts were juxtaposed with those of painted bodies of Virginian natives in *A briefe and true report of the new found land of Virginia,* the first of de Bry's America series that made such images visible all over Europe. Thomas Hariot wrote the text and John White supplied the illlustrations. Both were members of Sir Walter Raleigh's Roanoke colony. The comparison between Native Americans and ancient Britons was hinted at by many writings of the period.

Figure 10 "Virginian matron with baby," from Theodore de Bry, *Amiranda Narratio Fida Tamen, de Commodis et Incolarum Ritibus Virginiae* (Frankfurt, 1590). Reproduced by permission of the University of Illinois Urbana-Champaign Library.

The pictures of Native Americans in de Bry's volumes are examples of early ethnographic images. This woman with her baby is painted from different angles, front and back.

Figure 11 Cannibalism, from Theodore de Bry, *America,* Vol. 3 (German edn: *Britte Buv Americae,* 1593). From the collections of The Rare Book & Manuscript Library, University of Illinois at Urbana-Champaign.

Inhabitants of the New World were frequently pictured as violent cannibals, and sometimes as devouring white men. Although cannibalism was imagined to exist in Africa and Asia as well, and seen to define all savages, it was most frequently deployed in descriptions of the Americas. Some writers such as Las Casas (in this volume) suggested that European brutality often forced Native Americans into cannibalism.

Figure 12 Jew as Native American, frontispiece from Lancelot Addison, *The present state of the Jews* (London, 1675). Reproduced by permission of the Folger Shakespeare Library.

This picture of a Jew as a feathered Native American is a graphic instance of the confusions and cross-overs imagined in relation to both peoples.

MORO DI
CONDI-
TIONE.

Figure 13 "Moor of High Quality," from Cesare Vecellio, *Degli habiti antichi et moderne* (Venice, 1598). From the collections of The Rare Book & Manuscript Library, University of Illinois at Urbana-Champaign.

In the 1590s, the printmaker Cesare Vecellio compiled two anthologies of woodcuts exhibiting costumes from "the diverse nations of the world." Vecellio gathered information from travel books as well as first hand from international visitors to Venice.

Figure 14   "Mehomet II," from Richard Knolles, *The generall historie of the Turkes* (London, 1603). Reproduced by permission of the Haverford College Library.

This image of Mehmet (or Mahomet) II (1432–81), the Ottoman Sultan known as the Conqueror after the 1453 Ottoman conquest of Constantinople, appeared in Richard Knolles's *The generall historie of the Turkes* (London, 1603). Republished six times in the seventeenth century, Knolles's work draws on translated Turkish texts to provide richly detailed accounts of "the lives and conquests of the Ottoman Kings and Emperors."

Figure 15   Men and women of China, from Theodore de Bry and Johannes Israel de Bry, *India Orientalis,* Volume 2 (Frankfurt, 1598). From the collections of The Rare Book & Manuscript Library, University of Illinois at Urbana-Champaign.

Partly in response to the success of Linschoten's *Itinerario,* the de Bry family issued a series illustrating voyages and travels to the East Indies. Published in a slightly smaller page size than the *America* volumes, the two parallel sets subsequently became known among bibliophiles as de Bry's *Petits Voyages* and his *Grands Voyages,* respectively.

IX.

Dᵃfunere in demortui cremandique Brachmani honorem inftituto:ın
quo fimul corum vxores viuæ in rogum ardentem
infiliunt.

Os eſt Brachmanis, vt aliquo ex ipſis demortuo,propin-
qui foueam parent, in quam ligna Sandali, herbas odo-
ratas, cibaria, oriʒam, filiginem atque oleum inflam-
mando rogo infundant, quibus incenfis cadauer fuper-
imponunt. mox procedit vidua, comitata inſtrumentis
muſicis, quam cognatæ alacres exhortantur, vt virum fideliter inſequa-
tur, quo in altero mundo cum ipſo inter mille gaudia exultet. ipſa vero a-
nimo paratiſſimo, lætabunda veſtes & clenodia depofita inter pro -
ximas diſtribuit, mox ridens rogum infilit viua cum
mariti cadauere concremanda.
vid.cap.36.

C ²   Rɪᴛᴠꜱ

Figure 16   Widow burning in India, from Theodore de Bry and Johannes Israel de Bry, *India Orientalis*, Vol. 2 (Frankfurt, 1599). Reproduced by permission of the Folger Shakespeare Library.

This picture of a high-caste widow ascending the funeral pyre of her husband captures the fascination widow burning held for European visitors to India, who viewed it both as a barbaric Eastern practice as well as an ideal of wifely devotion.

WILLIAM CAMDEN (1551–1623)

*Britain, or A chorographical description of the most flourishing
kingdomes, England, Scotland, and Ireland* (London:
George Bishop and Joannis Norton, 1610), 26, 31, 63.

In this book, the schoolmaster and historian William Camden
tried to document the pre-Roman British past using every kind of
historical evidence imaginable, from written records, inscriptions,
and mythology, to testimony drawn from the physical landscape.
Immediate recognition of the first Latin edition of 1586 led to
five expanded editions prior to an English translation by Philemon
Holland in 1610. Camden was a major force in discrediting the
myth of Britain's Trojan origins and emphasizing instead the civilizing force of Roman colonization.

Keywords: Englishness—Body-painting—Body-carving—Ancient
Roman Colonialism—Civility

The Name of Britain

[T]he most sufficient authors that be, as Caesar, Mela, Pliny, and the rest do
show that the Britons coloured themselves with woad, called in Latin *glastum*
(and *glass* at this day with them signifieth blue). What if I should conjecture
that they were called Britons of their depainted bodies? For whatsoever is thus
painted and coloured, in their ancient country speech they call *Brith*. . . .

The Manners and Customs of the Britons

That they enameled or branded themselves (as it were) with certain marks
which Tertullian termeth *Britannorum stigmata*, that is, the Briton's mark,
Solinus showeth. The country (sayeth he) is partly peopled with barbarians,
who by the means of artificial incisions of sundry forms, have from their
childhood diverse shapes of beasts incorporate upon them. . . .

Romans in Britain

This yoke of the Romans, although it were grievous, yet comfortable it proved
and a saving health unto them. For that healthsome light of Jesus Christ shone
withal upon the Britons . . . and the brightness of that most glorious empire
chased away all savage barbarism from the Britons' minds, like as from other
nations whom it had subdued. . . .

For, to say nothing of the rest of the provinces, the Romans having brought
over colonies hither, and reduced the natural inhabitants of the island unto the
society of civil life, by training them up in the liberal arts, and by sending them
into Gaul for to learn perfectly the laws of the Romans . . . governed them with
their laws and framed them to good manners and behavior so, as in their diet and
apparel they were not inferior to any other provinces, they furnished them also
with goodly houses and stately buildings, in such sort that the relics and rubbish
of their ruins do cause the beholders now exceedingly to admire the same.

BARNABE RICH (1540?–1617)

A new description of Ireland wherein is described the disposition of the Irish (London: William Jaggard, 1610), 12–15, 18, 23, 32.

Rich served in campaigns in Ireland, participating in the colonization of Ulster and writing several works on Ireland, including *Allarme to England* (1578), *A new description of Ireland* (1610), and *The Irish Hubbub, or, The English hue and crie* (1617). Of particular interest is Rich's assertion that Irish are "wild" not because of nature but due to their education in Catholic doctrine.

Keywords: Irish Clothing and Bodies—Popery—Cruelty—Irish
        Lamentations

Chapter 3

. . . I think it would be admired in any part of Christendom, to see the manners of the Irish, how they use to carry their dead to their graves, in the remote parts of the country. . . . [A] stranger that had never seen the sight before, at the first encounter, would believe that a company of hags or hellish fiends, were carrying a dead body to some infernal mansion; for what with the unseemliness of their show, and the ill-faring noise they do make, with their howling and crying, an ignorant man would sooner believe they were devils of hell than Christian people. . . . [It is] pitiful indeed that a people so many years professing Christianity, should yet show themselves more heathen like, than those, that never heard of God. . . . [I]n cities and towns where any deceaseth that is of worth or worthiness, they will hire a number of women to bring the corpse to the place of burial, that for some small recompense given them, will furnish the cry, with greater shrieking and howling, than those that are grieved indeed, and have greatest cause to cry; and hereupon ariseth this proverb, to weep Irish, that is to say, to weep at pleasure, without cause, or grief. . . .

Chapter 4

To speak now of the Irish more at large, I say they are beholden to nature, that hath framed them comely personages, of good proportion, well limbed, and to speak truly, the English, Scottish, and Irish are easy to be discerned from all the nations of the world . . . by all the rest of their lineaments, from the crown of the head, to the sole of the foot. And although that in the remote places, the uncivil sort so disfigure themselves with their glibs, their trowes, and their mis-shapen attire, yet they appear to every man's eye to be men of good proportion, of comely stature, and of able body.[65] Now to speak of their dispositions, whereunto they are addicted and inclined. I say, besides they are rude, uncleanly, and uncivil, so they are very cruel, bloody minded, apt and ready to commit any kind of mischief. I do not impute this so much

[65] Glib = A thick mass of matted hair on the forehead and over the eyes. Trowes = Beliefs, superstitions.

to their natural inclination, as I do to their education that are trained up in treason, in rebellion, in theft, in robbery, in superstition, in idolatry, and nuzzled from their cradles in the very puddle of popery.

This is the fruit of the Pope's doctrine. . . . From hence it doth proceed, that the Irish cannot endure the English, because they differ so much in religion.

Chapter 5

The wild uncivil Scythians, do forbear to be cruel the one against the other. The cannibals, devourers of men's flesh, do leave to be fierce amongst themselves, but the Irish, without all respect, are evermore cruel to their very next neighbours. . . .

SAMUEL RID (fl. 1612)

The art of jugling or legerdemaine (T. Bushell, 1612), B1ᵛ–B2ʳ.

Nothing is known about Samuel Rid, and he has been confused with other authors such as Samuel Rowlands and Reginald Scot. *The art of jugling* is largely a plagiarized and abridged version of Scot's *The discoverie of witchcraft*. Rid made the crucial change of reframing Scot's text so that gypsies, or "Egyptian wanderers," replaced what were originally witches.

Keywords: Gypsies—Egyptians—Deceit—Clothing and Identity— Body Painting—Englishness—Vagabonds

Certain Egyptians banished their country . . . arrived here in England, who being excellent in quaint tricks and devices, not known here at that time among us, were esteemed and had in great admiration, for what with strangeness of their attire and garments, together with their sleights and legerdemains, they were spoke of far and near, insomuch that many of our English loiterers joined with them, and in time learned their craft and cozening. The speech which they used was the right Egyptian language, with whom our Englishmen conversing with, at last learned their language. These people continuing about the country in this fashion . . . purchased to themselves great credit among the country people, and got much by palmistry, and telling of fortunes: insomuch they pitifully cozened the poor country girls, both of money, silver spoons, and the best of their apparel, or any good thing they could make, only to hear their fortunes.

. . . [I]t pleased the council to look more narrowly into their lives, and in a parliament made in the first and second years of Philip and Mary, there was a strict statute made, that whosoever should transport any Egyptians into this realm, should forfeit forty pounds: moreover, it was then enacted, that such fellows as took upon them the name of Egyptians, above the age of fourteen, or that shall come over and be transported into England, or any other persons, and shall be seen in the company of vagabonds, calling themselves Egyptians, or counterfeiting, transforming, or disguising themselves

by their apparel, speech, or other behaviours like unto Egyptians, and so
shall continue, either at one or several times, by the space of a month, they
should be adjudged fellows, not allowed their book or clergy. These acts and
statutes now put forth, and come to their hearing, they divide their bands
and companies into diverse parts of the realm: for you must imagine and
know that they had above two hundred rogues and vagabonds in a regiment:
and although they went not altogether, yet would they not be above two or
three miles one from the other, and now they dare no more be known by the
name of Egyptians, nor take any other name upon them than poor people.
But what a number were executed presently upon this statute, you would
wonder; yet notwithstanding all would not prevail; but still they wandered,
as before up and down, and meeting once in a year at a place appointed. . . .
Then it pleased Queen Elizabeth to revive the statute before mentioned, in
the twentieth year of her happy reign, endeavoring by all means possible to
root out this pestiferous people, but nothing could be done, you see until
this day: they wander up and down in the name of Egyptians, colouring their
faces and fashioning their attire, and garment like unto them, yet if you ask
what they are, they dare no otherwise than say, they are Englishmen, and of
such a shire, and so are forced to say contrary to that they pretend.

WILLIAM STRACHEY (1572–1621)

*For the colony in Virginea Britannia. Lawes divine, morall and
martiall . . .* (London: W. Stansby, 1612)

Source: *The historie of travaile into Virginia Britannia* . . . , ed.
R.H. Major (London: Hakluyt Society, 1849), 17–19, 44–45,
51–53, 63–66, 110.

William Strachey was secretary to the English ambassador at
Constantinople and a member of the Virginia Company. His
report of the wreck of the *Sea Venture* on Bermuda may have
been a source for Shakespeare's *Tempest*. *For the colony in Virginea Britannia. Lawes divine, morall and martiall . . .* is an
eyewitness account of life in Virginia, even as it draws on earlier
works. Though suppressed for its critical stance, Strachey's narrative presents several key arguments in defense of expansionism, in
particular the comparison of English settlers to Roman colonizers
in ancient Britain.

Keywords: Ancient Roman Colonialism—Civility—Sons of Noah—
Tyranny—Polygamy—Lust—Skin Color—Body Painting—
Childbirth

But yet [settlement in the New World] is injurious to the natural inhabitants,
still say [some Englishmen]. Wherefore? Is it . . . a great piece of injury to
bring [the Indians] . . . out of the warm sun, into God's blessing; to bring

them from bodily wants, confusion, misery, and these outward anguishes, to the knowledge of a better practice, and improving of those benefits . . . which God hath given unto them, but evolved and hid in the bowels and womb of their land (to them barren and unprofitable, because unknown); nay, to exalt, as I may say, mere privation to the highest degree of perfection, by bringing their wretched souls (like Cerberus, from Hell) from the chains of Satan to the arms and bosom of their Saviour: here is a most impious piece of injury. Let me remember what Mr. Simondes, preacher of St. Saviour's, sayeth in this behalf: It is as much, sayeth he, as if a father should be said to offer violence to his child when he beats him to bring him to goodness. Had not this violence and this injury been offered to us by the Romans . . . who reduced the conquered parts of our barbarous island into provinces, and established in them colonies of old soldiers, building castles and towns, and in every corner teaching us even to know the powerful discourse of divine reason (which makes us only men, and distinguisheth us from beasts, amongst whom we lived as naked and as beastly as they). We might yet have lived overgrown satyrs, rude and untutored, wandering in the woods, dwelling in caves, and hunting for our dinners, as the wild beasts in the forests for their prey, prostituting our daughters to strangers, sacrificing our children to idols, nay, eating our own children, as did the Scots in those days. . . .[66]

It were perhaps too curious a thing to demand how these people might come first, and from whom, and whence, to inhabit these so far remote, westerly parts of the world, having no intercourse with Africa, Asia, or Europe? . . . As also to question how that it should be that they (if descended from the people of the first creation) should maintain so general and gross a defection from the true knowledge of God, with one kind, as it were, of rude and savage life, customs, manners, and religion, it being to be granted that (with us), infallibly they had one and the same descent and beginning from the universal deluge, in the scattering of Noah, his children, and nephews, with their families (as little colonies), some to one, some to other borders of the earth, to dwell. . . .

But it is observed that Cham and his family were the only far travellers and stragglers into diverse and unknown countries, searching, exploring, and sitting down in the same; as also it is said of his family, that what country soever the children of Cham happened to possess, there began both the ignorance of true godliness and a kind of bondage and slavery to be taxed one upon another. . . .

It is strange to see with what great fear and adoration all [the Indians] do obey this Powhattan, for at his feet they present whatsoever he commandeth, and at the least frown of his brow the greatest will tremble, it may be, because he is very terrible, and inexorable in punishing such as offend him. . . . Howbeit his ordinary correction is to have an offender whom he

---

[66] The distance between the English and the natives was not always imagined as temporal. In *A true discourse of the present estate of Virginia.* . . . (London, 1615), Ralph Hamor remarks that William Parker, captured three years before by the Powhatan, had "grown so like both in complexion and habit to the Indians, that I only knew him by his tongue to be an Englishman" (44).

will only punish and not put to death, to be beaten with cudgels as the Turks do. . . .

According to the order and custom of sensual heathenism, in the allowance of polygamy, he may have as many women as he will, and hath (as is supposed) many more than one hundred, all which he doth not keep, yet as the Turk, in one seraglio or house, but hath an appointed number, which reside still in every their several places. . . .

[The Indians] are generally of a colour brown or rather tawny, which they cast themselves into with a kind of arsenic stone, like red patise or orpiment, or rather red tempered ointments of earth, and the juice of certain scrused roots, when they come unto certain years, and this they do (keeping themselves still so smudged and besmeared) either for the custom of the country or the better to defend them (since they go most what naked) from the stinging of mosquitoes.[67] . . . Captain Smith (living sometimes amongst them) affirmeth how they are from the womb indifferent white, but as the men, so do the women, dye and disguise themselves into this tawny colour, esteeming it the best beauty to be nearest such a kind of murrey as a sodden quince is of (to liken it to the nearest colour I can), for which they daily anoint both face and bodies all over with such a kind of fucus or unguent as cast them into that satin . . . as the Britons dyed themselves red with woad; howbeit . . . after their anointing (which is daily) they dry in the sun, and thereby make their skins (besides the colour) more black and spotted, which the sun kissing oft and hard, adds to their painting the more rough and rugged.[68]

Their hair is black, gross, long, and thick; the men have no beards; their noses are broad, flat, and full at the end, great big lips, and wide mouths, yet nothing so unsightly as the Moors; they are generally tall of stature, and straight, of comely proportion, and the women have handsome limbs, slender arms, and pretty hands, and when they sing they have a pleasant tang in their voices.

For their apparel they are sometimes covered with the skins of wild beasts, which in winter are dressed with the hair, but in the summer without, the better sort use large mantles of deer's skins, not much differing from the Irish falings . . . but the common sort have scarce wherewithal to cover their

[67] Patise = a red pigment made from white lead and red ochre. Orpiment = arsenic trisulphide, a bright yellow mineral formerly used as a dye or artist's pigment.

[68] Fucus = Paint or cosmetic for beautifying the skin; a wash or coloring for the face. René Laudonniere's "Description of the West Indies," also reproduced by Hakluyt, writes that "Indians which take pleasure in painting their skins know very well how to use the same. . . . The most part of them have their bodies, arms, and thighs painted with very fair devices, the painting whereof can never be taken away, because the same is pricked into their flesh. . . . They paint their faces much, and stick their hair full of feathers or down, that they may seem more terrible. . . . The women are . . . painted as the men be. Howbeit when they are born, they be not so much of an olive colour and are far whiter. For the chief cause that maketh them to be of the colour proceeds of anointings of oil which they use among them" (*The Principal Navigations*, 3: 306–307).

nakedness, but stick long blades of grass, the leaves of trees, or such like, under broad baldrics of leather, which covers them behind and before. . . .

True it is sometimes in cold weather, or when they go a hunting, or seeking the fruits of the woods, or gathering bents for their mats, both men and women (to defend them from bushes and shrubs) put on a kind of leather breeches and stockings, all fastened together, made of deer skins, which they tie and wrap about the loins, after the fashion of the Turks or Irish trousers. . . .

They are a people most voluptuous; yet the women very careful not to be suspected of dishonesty, without the leave of the husbands; but he giving his consent they are like Virgil's *scrantiae*, and may embrace the acquaintance of any stranger for nothing, and it is accounted no offense; and incredible it is, with what heat both sexes of them are given over to those intemperances, and the men to preposterous Venus, for which they are full of their country disease (the pox) very young. . . .[69]

The women are said to be easily delivered of child; yet do they love children very dearly.[70] To make the children hardy, in the coldest mornings they wash them in the rivers, and by paintings and ointments so tan their skins that, after a year or two no weather will hurt them. . . .

JOHN DOVE (1560/61–1618)

The conversion of Salomon (London: W. Stansby, 1613), 29–30, 35–36.

> The London clergyman John Dove wrote seven tracts defending the Reformed theology of the Church of England. His exegesis on the Song of Solomon stands out for its assertion that the outward blackness of the bride of the Canticles was not a mark of tribulation, but due to her being Ethiopian.

Keywords: Song of Songs—Blackness—Washing an Ethiope—Beauty

Verse 4, 5, 6, 7

According to the allegory in these four verses . . . her need of purification: *I am black as the tents of Kedar*. Seven maids to attend upon her: *ye daughters of Jerusalem*. Her purification: *I am comely as the curtains or tents of Salomon*. Her blackness was natural; she was an Ethiopian, as black *as the tents of Kedar*, the second son of Ishmael, whose posterity dwelt in tents, and not in

---

[69] Scrantiae = An epithet of an unchaste woman, actually from Plautus, not Virgil. Laudonniere writes, "They have their priests . . . serve in stead of physicians and surgeons. They carry always about them a bag full of herbs and drugs to cure the sick diseased which for the most part are sick of the pox, for they love women and maidens exceedingly, which they call the daughters of the sun. And some of them are sodomites. They marry, and every one hath his wife, and it is lawful for the king to have two or three. . . . There are in all this country many hermaphrodites, which take all the greatest pain, and bear the victuals when they go to war" (*The Principal Navigations*, 3: 307).

[70] Early modern authors including Richard Jobson, William Wood, George Sandys, and Richard Ligon regularly attributed pain-free childbirth to African and Native American women.

any certain mansion places; her blackness was also accidental, being tanned with the scorching heat of the sun, always abroad keeping the vines, and therefore subject to the violence and injury of the weather. . . .

According to the moral exposition . . . she is infected with sin: I am black; yet her righteousness by imputation of the righteousness of Christ her husband: I am comely. . . .[71]

But comely as the curtains of Salomon: If she be an Ethiopian, how can she be made fair? To wash a black-a-more with us, is to labour in vain, as much as to plough the rocks, to sow the sands, to milk the ram-kind goats, to yoke the foxes together in the plough. *A blackemore sayeth Jeremie cannot wash away his blackness.* S. Augustine sayeth: . . . Ethiopia surpasseth Judaea by putting off the blackness of sin, and putting on the beauty of faith. As she is . . . black through sin which is inward and dwelleth in her, so she is . . . beautiful by outward righteousness, not of her own, but of Jesus Christ which is imputed unto her. As Jacob put on Esau his clothes to get his father's blessing, so we must put on the righteous garments of Jesus Christ, that we may appear righteous before God.[72]

ALEXANDER WHITAKER (1585–1617)

Good newes from Virginia (London: Felix Kyngston, 1613), 23–25.

Alexander Whitaker, the minister at Henrico, published his letters in order to combat the "falsehoods devised by the enemies of the plantation." Although Whitaker described native priests as "a generation of vipers," he also argued that the Powhattans had had knowledge of the Judaeo-Christian God in the past and retained "many footsteps of God's image." As evidence, he claimed to have converted the famed Powhattan princess, Pocahontas.

Keywords: Native Americans—Idolatry—Monogenesis—Conversion

. . . [L]et the miserable condition of these naked slaves of the devil move you to compassion toward them. They acknowledge that there is a great good God, but know him not, having the eyes of their understanding as yet blinded: wherefore they serve the devil for fear, after a most base manner, sacrificing sometimes (as I have here heard) their own children to him. I have sent one image of their god to the Counsel in England, which is painted

[71] In *A Christian dictionary* published one year before *The Conversion of Salomon*, Thomas Wilson offers the following definition: "Blackness fig. Afflictions, or persecutions, which diminish the outward beauty and glory of the church."
[72] In *Solomon's Song of songs . . . with annotations* (Amsterdam, 1623) Henry Ainsworth carefully partitions the phrase, "I am black but comely," so that the bride's comeliness "is in the parts, features, and proportion of the body, which the Church hath by her creation or new birth, as she is the workmanship of God. . . . Thus was she *black* in herself, but comely in Christ. . . ." (B4v–C1v).

upon one side of a toad-stool, much like unto a deformed monster. Their priests . . . are no other but such as our English witches are. They live naked in body, as if their shame of their sin deserved no covering. Their names are as naked as their body: they esteem it a virtue to lie, deceive, and steal as their master the devil teacheth them. . . . If this be their life, what think you shall become of them after death? but to be partakers with the devil and his angels in hell forevermore. Wherefore my brethren, put on the bowels of compassion, and let the lamentable estate of these miserable people enter in your consideration: One God created us, they have reasonable souls and intellectual faculties as well as we; we all have Adam for our common parent: yea, by nature the condition of us both is all one, the servants of sin and slaves of the devil. Oh remember (I beseech you) what was the state of England before the Gospel was preached in our country. How much better were we then, and concerning our souls health, than these now are?

GEORGE SANDYS (1578–1664)

A relation of a journey begun an: Dom: 1610 . . . Containing a description of the Turkish Empire, of Aegypt, [and] of the Holy Land (London: Richard Field, 1615)

Source: Samuel Purchas, Purchas his Pilgrimes in Five Bookes. (London: Printed by William Stansby for Henrie Fetherstone, 1625), 899–900, 912–13, 1287–90, 1294–95, 1297–301, 1306–8.

Sandys traveled to Constantinople, Cairo, and Jerusalem, producing *Relation of a Journey*, which included an extended description of the Ottoman Empire. It was consulted by Ben Jonson, Francis Bacon, Robert Burton, Sir Thomas Browne, and John Milton, among others. In attributing blackness to "the curse of Noah upon Cham," Sandys specifically delinks color from "seed" while suggesting that blackness originates in sinful behavior and transmits itself over the generations.

Keywords: Egypt—Tatooing—Childbirth—Hygiene—Gender Inversion—Sons of Noah—Turkish Empire and Sultan—Turkish Family and Women—Skin Color—Veiling—Baths—Women's Desire for Women—Slavery—Jews

[Of Egypt]

The Egyptian Moors . . . are men of a mean stature, tawny of complexion, and spare of body, shrill tongued, and nimble footed; naturally industrious, affecting more their profit than their ease; yet know they not how to live of a little, as in nothing riotous. Rather crafty they are than wise; more observant than faithful, by much more devout than the Turks in the Mahometan religion. . . . Diverse of the women have I seen with their chins distained into knots and flowers of blue, made by pricking of the skin with needles, and rubbing it over with ink and the juice of an herb, which will never wear out again.[73] They have quick and easy labour, bearing heretofore often two, and sometimes three at a burden: those also born in the eighth month living, rarely if elsewhere heard of. . . . A people breathes not more savage and nasty, crusted with dirt, and stinking of smoke, by reason of the fuel, and their houses which have no chimneys. . . .

But the Coptics are the true Egyptians. . . . These . . . are Christians, notwithstanding they are circumcised, whereof they now begin to be ashamed; saying, that in the country they are thereunto compelled by the Moors; and in cities where secure from violence, they use it not; howbeit, doing it rather in . . . ancient custom of their nation . . . than out of religion. . . .

. . . All of a trade keep their shops in one place, which they shut about the hour of five, and solace themselves for the rest of the day, cooks excepted, who keep theirs open till late in the evening. For few, but such as have great families dress meat in their houses, which the men do buy ready dressed; the women too fine fingered to meddle with housewifery, who ride abroad upon pleasure on easy-going asses, and tie their husbands to the benevolence that is due; which if neglected, they will complain to the magistrate, and procure a divorcement. . . .

Upon the fourth of March we departed from Cairo, in the habits of pilgrims, four of us English, consorted with three Italians, of whom one was a priest, and another a physician. . . . The merchants brought with them many Negros; not the worst of their merchandizes. These they buy of their parents, some thirty days journey above, and on the west side of the river. As the wealth of others consists in multitudes of cattle; so theirs in the multitude of their children, whom they part from with as little passion; never after to be seen or heard of: regarding more the price than condition of their slavery. These are descended of Chus, the son of cursed Cham, as are all of that complexion. Not so by reason of their seed, nor heat of the climate: Nor of the soil as some have supposed; for neither haply, will other races in that soil prove black, nor that race in other soils grow to better complexion: but rather from the curse of Noe upon Cham in the posterity of Chus.

The Turkish Empire is the greatest that is, or perhaps that ever was from the beginning. . . . But the barbarous policy whereby this tyranny is sustained, doth differ from all other: guided by the heads, and strengthened by the hands of his slaves, who think it as great an honour to be so, as they do with us that serve in the courts of princes: the natural Turk (to be so called a reproach) being rarely employed in command or service, amongst whom there is no nobility of blood, no known parentage, kindred, nor hereditary possessions, but are as it were of the Sultan's creation, depending upon him only for their sustenance and preferments. . . . These are the sons of Christians (and those the most completely furnished by nature) taken in their childhood from their miserable parents, by a levy made every five years . . . throughout the whole

[73] Distayned = Discolored, stained, or dyed.

empire, (excepting certain privileged places, amongst which are Sio and Constantinople) who are bestowed in several seminaries, instructed in the Mahometan religion (changing their names upon their circumcision), taught the use of their several weapons, and made patient of hunger and labour, with inured abstinence, and continual exercise. These they call *jemoglans*, who have their faces shaven (the token of servitude), wearing long coats and cropped caps, not unlike to our idiots. The choicest of them for spirit and feature, are after a while received into the Grand Signor's seraglio . . . where all are brought up in the discipline of war; and not a few, acquainted with the secrets of state: such as by the excellency of their gifts do assure the expectation of a future eminency. . . .

But it is to be considered, that all these before named, are not only of that tribute of children. For not a few of them are captives taken in their childhood, with diverse renegados, that have most wickedly quitted their religion and country, to fight against both, who are to the Christians the most terrible adversaries. . . .

. . . And surely it is to be hoped, that their greatness is not only at the height, but near an extreme precipitation: the body being grown too monstrous for the head, the sultans unwarlike, and never accompanying their armies in person; the soldier corrupted with ease and liberty, drowned in prohibited wine, enfeebled with the continual converse of women, and generally lapsed from their former austerity of life, and simplicity of manners. . . .

So much the continuance of honors in families are avoided, that when a bassa is given . . . to the sister or daughter of a sultan for an husband, the children begotten on them, do most rarely rise above the degree of a private captain. But more severe are these tyrants to their own, who lop all the branches from the bole;[74] the unnatural brother solemnizing his father's funerals, with the slaughter of his brothers. So fearful are they of rivality, and so damnably politic; making all things lawful that may secure the perpetuity of their empire. Yet they mourn for those being dead, whom they murdered; honoring them with all dues of burial, and customary lamentations. . . .

[The Turks] be generally well complexioned, of good statures, and full bodies, proportionably compacted. They nourish no hair about them, but a lock on the crown, and on their faces only; esteeming it more cleanly, and to be the better prepared for their superstitious washings. But their beards they wear at full length, the mark of their affected gravity, and token of freedom (for slaves have theirs shaven), insomuch that they will scoff at such Christians as cut, or naturally want them, as if suffering themselves to be abused against nature. All of them wear on their heads white sashes and turbans, the badge of their religion. . . .

[The Turks] are by their law in general exhorted to marry, for the propagation of their religion, and he ill reputed of, that forbeareth so to do until the age of five and twenty. Every man is allowed four wives, who are to be of his own religion, and as many concubine slaves as he is able to keep, of what religion soever. For God (sayeth the Alcoran) that is good and gracious, exacteth

---

[74] Bole = The stem or trunk of a tree.

not of us what is harsh and burdensome, but permits us the nightly company of women, well knowing that abstinency in that kind is both grievous, and impossible. Yet are they to meddle with none but their own peculiars: the offending woman they drown, and the man they gansh.[75] . . . Now, he is to entertain his wives with an equal respect, alike is their diet, alike is their apparel, alike his benevolence. . . . They give him the reverence of a master; they are at no time to deny him their embracements, whom he toucheth not again until they have been at the bannias. They receive chastisement from him, and that they hold to be an argument of his affection. They feed apart, and intermeddle not with household affairs. All that is required at their hands is to content their husbands, to nurse their own children, and to live peaceably together, which they do (and which is strange) with no great jealousy, or envy. No male accompanies them above twelve years old, except they be eunuchs: and so strictly are they guarded, as seldom seen to look out at their doors.

the top of their heads a cap not vnlike the top of a sugar lofe, yet a little flat, of paſt-boord, and couered with cloth of ſiluer or tiſhue. Their vnder-garments (which within doores are their vppermoſt) do little differ from thoſe that be worne by the men, which we will preſent to the eye to auoide repetition.

The better ſort about the vpper part of their armes, and ſmalls of their legs weare bracelets, & are elſewhere adorned with iewels. When they go abroad they weare ouer all long gownes of violet cloth, or ſcarlet, tied cloſe before, the large ſleeues hanging

Figure 17   Turkish damsel, from George Sandys, *A relation of a journey* (1615). From the collections of The Rare Book & Manuscript Library, University of Illinois at Urbana-Champaign.

[75] Gansh = Variant of "ganch." To impale (a person) upon sharp hooks or stakes as a mode of execution.

They be women of elegant beauties, for the most part ruddy, clear, and smooth as the polished ivory. . . . When they go abroad they wear over all long gowns of violet cloth, or scarlet, tied close before, the large sleeves hanging over their hands, having buskins on their legs, and their heads and faces so mabbled in fine linen that no more is to be seen of them than their eyes, nor that of some, who look as through the sight of a beaver.[76] For they are forbidden by the Alcoran to disclose their beauties unto any, but unto their fathers and husbands. They never stir forth, but (and then always in troupes) to pray at the graves, and to the public bannias. . . .

[In the baths] the men are attended upon by men, and the women by women; in the outermost room they put off their clothes, and having aprons of stained linen tied about their waists, then entering the baths to what degree of heat that they please. . . . Much unnatural and filthy lust is said to be committed daily in the remote closets of the darksome bannias: yea, women with women; a thing uncredible, if former times had not given thereunto both detection and punishment.[77] They have generally the sweetest children that ever I saw; partly proceeding from their frequent bathings, and affected cleanliness. As we bear ours in our arms, so they do theirs astride on their shoulders.

Now, next to their wives we may speak of their slaves: for little difference is there made between them who are Christians taken in the wars, or purchased with their money. Of these there are weekly markets in the city, where they are to be sold as horses in fairs: the men being rated according to their faculties, or personal abilities, as the women for their youths and beauties, who are set out in best becoming attires, and with their aspects of pity and affection, endeavour to allure the Christians to buy them, as expecting from them a more easy servitude, and continuance of religion: when being thrall to the Turk, they are often enforced to renounce it for their better entertainment. Of them there be many of excellent outward perfection; and when the buyer hath agreed of the price (but yet conditionally) they are carried aside into a room, even to the search of her mouth, and assurance (if so she be said to be) of her virginity. Their masters may lie with them, chastise them, exchange, and sell them at their pleasure. But a Christian will not lightly sell her whom he hath lain with, but give her liberty. If any of their slaves will become Mahometans, they are discharged of their bondage: but if a slave to a Turk, he only is the better entreated. . . .

[The Sultan] is, in this year 1610 about the age of three and twenty, strongly limbed, and of a just stature, yet greatly inclining to be fat: insomuch as sometimes he is ready to choke as he feeds, and some do purposely attend to free him from that danger. His face is full and duly proportioned, only his eyes are extraordinary great, by them esteemed (as is said before) an excellency in beauty. Phlegm hath the predominancy in his complexion. He

---

[76] Mabbled = Wrapped or muffled up.

[77] Sandys here renders perverse a practice by which Muslims distinguished themselves from the relatively filthy European Christians. See also Africanus on the baths of Fez in this volume.

hath a little hair on his upper lip, but less on his chin, of a darksome colour. His aspect is as haughty as his empire is large. . . . [He is] an unrelenting punisher of offences, even in his own household: having caused eight of his pages, at my being there, to be thrown into the sea for sodomy (an ordinary crime, if esteemed a crime in that nation). . . .

[H]is virgins, of whom there seldom are so few as five hundred, are kept in a seraglio by themselves, and attended on only by women, and eunuchs. They all of them are his slaves, either taken in the wars, or from their Christian parents, and are indeed the choicest beauties of the Empire. . . . She that beareth him the first son is honoured with the title of sultana. But for all his multitude of women, he hath yet begotten but two sons and three daughters, though he be that way unsatiably given (perhaps the cause that he hath so few), and useth all sorts of foods that may enable performance. . . .

[The Holy Land]

It is for the most part now inhabited by Moors and Arabians. . . . Turks there be few, but many Greeks, with other Christians, of all sects and nations, such as impute to the place an adherent holiness. Here be also some Jews, yet inherit they no part of the land, but in their own country do live as aliens; a people scattered throughout the whole world, and hated by those amongst whom they live. . . . Although they agree with the Turk in circumcision, detestation of images, abstinency from swine's-flesh, and diverse other ceremonies: nevertheless, the Turks will not suffer a Jew to turn Mahometan, unless he first turn a kind of Christian.[78] As in religion they differ from others, so do they in habit, in Christendom enforcedly, here in Turkey voluntarily. . . . They shave their heads all over; not in imitation of the Turk, it being their ancient fashion. . . . Their only studies are divinity and physic, their occupations brokage and usury; yet take they no interest of one another, nor lend but upon pawns; which once forfeited, are unredeemable. . . .

THOMAS TUKE (d. 1657)

A discourse against painting and tincturing of women (London: Thomas Creed and Bernard Alsop, 1616), B3ʳ–B4ᵛ, 17, 24.

The London curate Thomas Tuke's *A discourse against painting and tincturing of men and women* is a biblically inspired attack on cosmetics. Not only are painted women here compared with demons and barbarians, Tuke goes so far as to argue that

[78] This idea is a commonplace of the period; see William Biddulph in this volume. Also commonplace is the idea of overlaps between Jews and Christians, as in the anonymous *The policy of the Turkish Empire* (1597), which compares Jews and Muslims at some length. Both ideas can also be found in the extracts from Nicolas de Nicolay's *The Navigations . . . made into Turkey* extracted in this volume.

7

anatomical alterations might generate biological difference and
be passed on to a woman's progeny.

Keywords: Cosmetics—Original Sin—Transmission of Sin—Ancient
Britons

The Invective of Doctor Andreas de Laguna, a Spaniard and Physician to
Pope Julius the Third, against the painting of women.

The ceruse or white lead wherewith women use to paint themselves was,
without doubt, brought in use by the devil, the capital enemy of nature,
therewith to transform human creatures, of fair, making them ugly enormous and abominable. . . . What shall God say to such in the Last Judgment,
when they shall appear thus masked before him with these antifaces: Friends,
I know you not, neither do I hold you for my creatures. For these are not
the faces that I formed. Thus the use of this ceruse, besides the rotting of the
teeth, and the unsavory breath which it causeth, being ministered in paintings, doth turn fair creatures into infernal furies. . . .

The excellency of this mercury sublimate (sayeth he) is such, that the
women, who often paint themselves with it, though they be very young, they
presently turn old with withered and wrinkled faces like an ape, and before
age come upon them, they tremble (poor wretches) as if they were sick of the
staggers . . . being applied to the face, it is true, that it eateth out the spots
and stains of the face, but so, that withal, it drieth up, and consumeth the
flesh that is underneath, so that of force the poor skin shrinketh. . . . [T]he
infamous inconveniences which result from this mercury sublimate might be
somewhat the more tolerable if they did stick and stay only in them who use
it, and did not descend to their offspring. For this infamy is like to original
sin, and goes from generation to generation, when as the child born of them,
before it is able to go, doth shed his teeth one after another, as being corrupted and rotten, not through his fault, but by reason of the viciousness and
taint of the mother that painted her self, who, if she were loath and abhor to
hear this, let her forebear to do the other.[79]

Of Painting of the Face

Some write of some barbarous people, which delight in painting their skin.
Saint Jerome writes that Maximilla Montanus, his prophetess, a woman
devil-driven did use to paint. . . . Caesar likewise writes that the Britons used
to colour their faces with their woad, but this was not out of pride, or wantonness, but to strike terror in their enemies. . . .

[79] A toxic recipe for a "mineral fucus for the face" appears in Hugh Plat's *Delightes for ladies
to adorne their persons* (1602). See also *The secretes of the reverend Mayster Alexis of Piemont* in
this volume.

. . . Holinshed in his description of Scotland, tells how the Picts used to paint over their bodies and some write that Medea, a notable sorceress, devised these arts. And sure it is that the heathen and infidels did first and most usurp them. Seeing therefore we have cast off their barbarism and infidelity, let us also lay aside their other vanities and adulterous devices.

FYNES MORYSON (1565/66–1630)

An itinerary . . . containing his ten yeeres travell . . . (London, John Beale, 1617), I: 219, III: 37–39, 44, 49, 149, 161–64.

An extensive traveler through Europe and the Ottoman Empire, Moryson was employed by Sir Charles Blount, Lord Mountjoy, to write a journal of Irish affairs, published as *An itinerary . . . .* Moryson dismisses climatic theory to argue that "wisdom and wit, rather than heat or cold, make men to be valiant"; he describes the Irish as beasts whose ways also infect the English to become like them.

Keywords: Nature and Culture—Faith—Women of Different Nations Compared—English-Irish—Degeneracy—Hygiene—Irish Bestiality—Humors and Diet

Part 3, Book 1, Chapter 3

Old writers affirm that the northern men, in respect of their heat kept in by the cold, are generally greater eaters than southern men. Thus they prove it: because all men have a better stomach in the winter than in summer, because northern men passing towards the south daily lose their appetite, and because both men and beasts of the south are more lean than those of the north. This opinion is of itself true, but the arguments for proof admit some exceptions, for the Turks towards the south be fatter generally than our men of the north, not that they eat more, but that they are eunuchs, and given to idleness. I say therefore, that the opinion is generally true, but by many accidents proves false. . . .

[I]t were fitter to say that wisdom and wit, rather than heat or cold, make men to be valiant. . . .[80] Nature hath his force, as the eagle begets not a dove, but reason, rather than nature, is the cause, that when common soldiers run away, yet gentlemen choose rather to die, than escape by flight. Not so much because they are born of a noble race, as because they will not be a reproach to themselves, and their race. Not because gentlemen die with less

[80] This passage follows a section where Moryson borrows from Bodin a discussion of characteristics of the mind and body peculiar to northern and southern men as a consequence of their differing climates.

pain then the common sort, but because they better understand that the soul is immortal, that he dies in a good cause who fights for his country, and that an honorable death is to be preferred before a disgraceful life. . . .

Bodin affirms that northern men, because they are fat, are less prone to the extremities of good or evil, and so concludes them to be less cruel. . . . For my part . . . I am induced to conclude . . . [that] not the north, nor the south, but philosophical precepts, godly laws, and the knowledge of God's word, or otherwise the wants thereof, make men good or ill, and where knowledge, religion, and good laws flourish, there virtues are practiced, but among barbarous and superstitious people, living in Cimerian darkness, all vices have ever, and will forever flourish. . . .

Old writers affirm that northern men have softer skins than southern men, as women have them in general softer than men . . . . yet the Ethiopians and other people of Africa dwelling near the extreme south on this side the line, as they have properly white teeth, so is their skin (howsoever tanned) far softer than the skins of any nation whatsoever, by the common consent of all men. . . .

The Italian women are said to be sharp witted, the Spanish blunt (I should hardly think it), the French simple (I should rather say most crafty, as most women are everywhere), the Germans good mothers of family (yea exceeding good). . . . The Spanish women are said to be painted, the Italians somewhat less painted, the French seldom painted, and sometimes the German virgins (never that I observed, except those of Prussians have perhaps borrowed this vice of the Muscovites their neighbours). . . . She is said to be a fair woman that hath the face of an English woman, the body (from the neck to the navel) of the French, the other parts of the Flemish. . . . England in general is said to be the hell of horses, the purgatory of servants, and the paradise of women.

Part 3, Book 3, Chapter 5.

. . . Many of the English-Irish, have by little and little been infected with the Irish filthiness, and that in the very cities, excepting Dublin, and some of the better sort in Waterford, where the English continually lodging in their houses, they more retain the English diet. The English-Irish after our manner serve to the table joints of flesh cut after our fashion, with geese, pullets, pigs and like roasted meats, but their ordinary food for the common sort is of whitemeats, and they eat cakes of oats for bread, and drink not English beer made of malt and hops, but ale.[81] At Cork I have seen with these eyes, young maids stark naked grinding of corn with certain stones to make cakes thereof, and striking off into the tub of meal, such relics thereof as stuck on their belly, thighs, and more unseemly parts. And for the cheese or butter commonly made by the English-Irish, an English man would not touch it with his lips, though he were half starved; yet many English inhabitants make very good of both kinds. . . .

[81] The term "whitemeats" refers to all foods produced from dairy animals.

The Irish aqua-vitae, vulgarly called usquebaugh, is held the best in the world of that kind.[82] . . . These drinks the English-Irish drink largely, and in many families (especially at feasts) both men and women use excess therein. And since I have in part seen, and often heard from others' experience, that some gentlewomen were so free in this excess, as they would kneeling upon the knee, and otherwise [carouse] health after health with men; not to speak of the wives of Irish lords, or to refer it to the due place, who often drink 'til they be drunken, or at least 'til they void urine in full assemblies of men. . . .

The wild and (as I may say) mere Irish, inhabiting many and large provinces, are barbarous and most filthy in their diet. They skim the seething pot with a handful of straw, and strain their milk taken from the cow through a like handful of straw, none of the cleanest, and so cleanse, or rather more defile the pot and milk. They devour great morsels of beef unsalted, and they eat commonly swine's flesh, seldom mutton, and all these pieces of flesh, as also the entrails of beasts unwashed, they seethe in a hollow tree, lapped in a raw cow's hide, and so set over the fire, and therewith swallow whole lumps of filthy butter. Yea (which is more contrary to nature) they will feed on horses dying of themselves, not only upon small want of flesh, but even for pleasure. . . .

The foresaid wild Irish do . . . willingly eat the herb shamrock, being of a sharp taste, which as they run and are chased to and fro, they snatch like beasts out of the ditches. . . . Many of these wild Irish eat no flesh, but that which dies of disease or otherwise of itself, neither can it scape them for stinking. . . . Yet will they upon hunger in time of war open a vein of the cow, and drink the blood, but in no case kill or much weaken it. A man would think these men to be Scythians, who let their horses' blood under the ears, and for nourishment drink their blood, and indeed (as I have formerly said), some of the Irish are of the race of Scythians, coming into Spain, and from thence into Ireland. . . .

These wild Irish never set any candles upon tables; what do I speak of tables? since indeed they have no tables, but set their meat upon a bundle of grass, and use the same grass for napkins to wipe their hands. . . .

I trust no man expects among these gallants any beds, much less featherbeds and sheets, who like the nomads removing their dwellings, according to the commodity of pastures for their cows, sleep under the canopy of heaven, or in a poor house of clay, or in a cabin made of the boughs of trees, and covered with turf, for such are the dwellings of the very lords among them. . . . To conclude, not only in lodging passengers, not at all or most rudely, but even in their inhospitality towards them, these wild Irish are not much unlike to wild beasts, in whose caves a beast passing that way, might perhaps find meat, but not without danger to be ill-entertained, perhaps devoured of his insatiable host.

[82] Usquebaugh = Whiskey.

Source: *Shakespeare's Europe: A Survey of the Condition of Europe at the End of the 16th Century*, 2nd edition (New York: Benjamin Bloom, 1903), 408–9, 418–19.

. . . For fleshly lusts, the very Turks (whose carnal religion alloweth them) are not so much transported therewith, as the Italians are (in their restraint of civil laws and the dreadful law of God). A man of these northerly parts can hardly believe without the testimony of his own eyes and ears how chastity is laughed at among them, and hissed out of all good company, or how desperate adventures they will make to achieve disordinate desire in these kinds. . . . The women of honour in Italy, I mean wives and virgins, are much sooner inflamed with love, be it lawful or unlawful, than the women of other nations. For being locked up at home, and covered with veils when they go abroad, and kept from any conversation with men . . . they are more stirred up with the sight of and much more with the flattering and dissembling speeches of men, and more credulous in flattering their own desires . . . than the women of other nations having free conversation with men.[83] In general the men of all sorts are carried with fierce affections to forbidden lusts. . . .

ROBERT BURTON (1577–1640)

The anatomy of melancholy (Oxford: Printed by John Lichfield and James Short, for Henry Cripps, 1621)

Source: Robert Burton, *The Anatomy of Melancholy*, ed. Holbrook Jackson (New York: New York Review Books, 2001), I: 211–13, 382–83, II: 61, III: 61–62, 264–65, 283–84.

Robert Burton's *The anatomy of melancholy* was revised many times before his death; a sixth edition was published posthumously in 1651. Burton ranges across vast and disparate areas, covering theories about the workings of the human mind and its relation with the body, as well as with geographic location, history, and politics. Of particular interest is his notion that exogamy is not only necessary but also a matter of divine providence.

Keywords: Heredity—Complexion—Crossbreeding—Environmental Influences—Lust—Jealousy—Humors—Turkish Patriarchy

---

[83] Moryson's description here of Italian women employs the same terms that are elsewhere used for Turkish women, i.e., that they are locked up and therefore given to excess when let out.

Parents a cause by propagation

That other inward inbred cause of melancholy is our temperature, in whole
or part, which we receive from our parents . . . it being an hereditary disease; for . . . such as the temperature of the father is, such is the son's, and
look what disease the father had when he begot him, his son will have after
him. . . . And where the complexion and constitution of the father is corrupt, there (sayeth Roger Bacon) the complexion and constitution of the
son must needs be corrupt, and so the corruption is derived from the father
to the son. Now this doth not so much appear in the composition of the
body, according to that of Hippocrates, "in habit, proportion, scars, and
other lineaments; but in manners and conditions of the mind," *Et patrum
in natos abeunt cum semine mores* [the character of the parents is transmitted
to the children through the seed]. . . .

. . . For these reasons, belike, the church and commonwealth, human
and divine laws, have conspired to avoid hereditary diseases, forbidding
such marriages as are any whit allied; and as Mercatus adviseth all families
to . . . make choice of those that are most differing in complexion from
them; if they love their own, and respect the common good. And sure, I
think, it hath been ordered by God's especial providence, that in all ages
there should be (as usually there is) once in 600 years, a transmigration
of nations, to amend and purify their blood, as we alter seed upon our
land, and that there should be as it were an inundation of those northern
Goths and Vandals, and many such like people which came out of that
continent of Scandia and Sarmatia (as some suppose) and over-ran, as a
deluge, most part of Europe and Afric, to alter for our good, our complexions, which were much defaced with hereditary infirmities, which
by our lust and intemperance we had contracted. A sound generation of
strong and able men were sent amongst us, as those northern men usually are, innocuous, free from riot, and free from diseases, to qualify and
make us as those poor naked Indians are generally at this day; and those
about Brazil . . . in the isle of Maragnan, free from all hereditary diseases,
or other contagion. . . .

Air rectified. With a digression of the air

. . . The Egyptians by all geographers are commended to be . . . a conceited
and merry nation: which I can ascribe to no other cause than the serenity of
their air. They that live in the Orcades are registered by Hector Boethius and
Cardan, to be of fair complexion, long-lived, most healthful, free from all manner of infirmities of body and mind, by reason of a sharp purifying air, which
comes from the sea. The Boeotians in Greece were dull and heavy . . . by
reason of a foggy air in which they lived. . . . The clime changes not so much
customs, manners, wits (as Aristotle, . . . Plato, [and] Bodin, hath proved at
large) as constitutions of their bodies, and temperature itself. In all particular
provinces we see it confirmed by experience, as the air is, so are the inhabitants,
dull, heavy, witty, subtle, neat, cleanly, clownish, sick, and sound. . . .

Causes of heroical love, temperature, full diet, idleness, place, climate, &c.

. . . Your hot and southern countries are prone to lust, and far more incontinent than those that live in the north, as Bodin discourseth at large . . . , so are Turks, Greeks, Spaniards, Italians, even all that latitude; and in those tracts, such as are more fruitful, plentiful, and delicious. . . . Solomon of old had a thousand concubines; Ahasuerus his eunuchs and keepers; Nero his Tigillinus, panders, and bawds; the Turks, Muscovites, Mogors [Moguls], Xeriffs [Sharifs] of Barbary, and Persian Sophies, are no whit inferior to them in our times. . . . [T]hey press and muster up wenches as we do soldiers, and have their choice of the rarest beauties their countries can afford, and yet all this cannot keep them from adultery, incest, sodomy, buggery, and such prodigious lusts. . . .

Causes of jealousy

Bodin . . . ascribes a great cause to the country or clime, and discourseth largely there of this subject, saying, that southern men are more hot, lascivious, and jealous, than such as live in the north; they can hardly contain themselves in those hotter climes, but are most subject to prodigious lust. Leo Afer [Africanus] telleth incredible things almost, of the lust and jealousy of his countrymen of Africa, and especially such as live about Carthage, and so doth every geographer of them in Asia, Turkey, Spaniards, Italians. . . . In the most northern countries young men and maids familiarly dance together, men and their wives, which, Siena only excepted, Italians may not abide. [A]s Bodin observes . . . "the Italians could never endure this," or a Spaniard, the very conceit of it would make him mad: and for that cause they lock up their women, and will not suffer them to be near men, so much as in the church, but with a partition between. . . . [W]e are far from any such strange conceits, and will permit our wives and daughters to go to the tavern with a friend . . . and suspect nothing, to kiss coming and going, which, as Erasmus writes in one of his epistles, they cannot endure. England is a paradise for women, and hell for horses: Italy a paradise for horses, hell for women, as the diverb goes. . . .[84]

Symptoms of Jealousy

See but with what rigour those jealous husbands tyrannize over their poor wives . . . [i]n Greece, Spain, Italy, Turkey, Africa, Asia, and generally over all those hot countries. . . . Mahomet in his Alcoran gives this power to men, your wives are as your land, till them, use them, entreat them fair or foul, as you will yourselves. . . . [T]hey lock them still in their houses, which are so many prisons to them, will suffer nobody to come at them, or their wives to be seen abroad. . . . They must not so much as look out. And if they be great persons,

---

[84] This was a commonplace in the period; see Moryson in this volume.

they have eunuchs to keep them, as the Grand Signor among the Turks, the Sophies of Persia, those Tartarian Mogors, and Kings of China. . . . The Turks have I know not how many black, deformed eunuchs (for the white serve for other ministries) to this purpose sent commonly from Egypt, deprived in their childhood of all their privities, and brought up in the seraglio at Constantinople to keep their wives; which are so penned up they may not confer with any living man, or converse with younger women, have a cucumber or carrot sent into them for their diet, but sliced, for fear, & c. and so live and are left alone to their unchaste thoughts all the days of their lives. The vulgar sort of women, if at any time they come abroad, which is very seldom, to visit one another, or to go to their baths, are so covered, that no man can see them. . . .

RICHARD JOBSON (fl. 1620)

The golden trade, or A discovery of the river Gambra, and the golden trade of the Aethiopians (London: Nicholas Okes, 1623), 33–38, 44–45, 51–53.

In 1620 Richard Jobson accompanied an expedition of London entrepreneurs up the Gambia River. Although it did not help to fund future expeditions, *The golden trade* was the first account of the area in English and was published by Samuel Purchas in his *Hakluytus Posthumus* or *Purchas his Pilgrimes*. Jobson inaccurately proclaimed that the English were "a people who did not trade in [slaves]." His account compares Africans to animals and identifies them as the descendants of Ham.

Keywords: African Brutishness—African Women's Beauty—Diet— Africans and Irish Compared—Concubinage—Sons of Noah—Outsized Genitalia

The wandering Fulbie

[The] Fulbies . . . [are] a tawny people, and have a resemblance right unto those we call Egyptians. The women amongst them are straight, upright, and excellently well bodied, having very good features, with a long black hair, much more loose than the black women have, wherewith they attire themselves very neatly, but in their apparel they go clothed and wear the same habit, the black women do; the men are not in their kinds, so generally handsome, as the women are, which may be imputed to the course of lives, whereof I proceed to tell you. . . .

This is the poor Fulbie's life, whereunto he is so inured that in a manner he is become bestial, for I have noted diverse times . . . when we have called for the m[aste]r, or chief of them, to make a bargain for a beef, or beeves, as we had occasion, he would come unto us, from forth the middle of the herd, and those parts of him which were bare, as his face and hands, but especially his face, would stand so thick of flies . . . which the Fulbie would let alone, not offering to put up his hand to drive them away, therein seeming more senseless, than our country beasts, who will whisk with their tails, and seek any other defense, to avoid or be rid of them. . . . The women are our chiefest customers, for in most places, within the ebbing and flowing, where we did lie for trade, we should be sure to have their custom every day, which was to bring us new milk, sour milk, and curds, and two sorts of butter, one new and white, the other hard and of an excellent colour, which we called refined butter, and it is without question, but for a little freshness, as good as any we have at home. All which they brought unto us in great and small gourds like dishes, made up very handsomely, and one thing let me not forget to give them due praise in, that in whatsoever you received from them, you should have it so neat and clean that in your milk you should not perceive a mote, nor in her butter any uncleanliness. . . .

In noting of which, I have diverse times said, there was a great difference between them, and the Irish calios, although their manner of lives had great resemblance in following of their cattle, and as they were out of heart in one ground, to remove whole towns together, which but few years since was the Irish kern's true course of life; but with cleanliness your Irish woman hath no acquaintance. . . .[85]

The Mandingo or Ethiopian, being the natural Inhabitants

The people, who are lords, and commanders of this country, and profess themselves the natural inhabitants, are perfectly black, both men and women. The men for their parts, do live a most idle kind of life, employing themselves . . . to no kind of trade nor exercise, except it be only some two months of the year, which is in tilling and bringing home their country corn, and grain. . . . All other times of the year, they live wandering up and down, from one to another, having little understanding, either to hunt in the woods, or fish in the waters. . . .

To countenance [the king's] state, he hath many times two of his wives sitting by him, supporting his body, and laying their hands upon his naked skin, above the waist, stroking, and gently pulling the same, wherein he seems to receive content. . . . The king hath an orderly allowance of seven women, which are called wives . . . distinguished from other women which he hath use of . . . for he hath the use of other women, who are not of that esteem, but rather as we may term them concubines . . . and these . . . are rather taken for necessity than that it is a settled course amongst them, which word *necessity* I must better explain, and therefore tell you, that it may and doth diverse times fall out, that of his seven wives he hath none to accompany him in the nature of a wife. For undoubtedly these people originally sprung from the race of Canaan, the son of Ham, who discovered his father

[85] See Fynes Moryson's description of Irish butter in this volume.

Noah's secrets, for which Noah awakening cursed Canaan as our holy scripture testifieth. The curse, as by schoolmen hath been disputed, extended to his ensuing race, in laying hold upon the same place, where the original cause began, whereof these people are witnesses, who are furnished with such members as are after a sort burdensome unto them, whereby their women being once conceived with child, so soon as it is perfectly discerned, accompanies the man no longer, because he shall not destroy what is conceived to the loss of that, and danger of the bearer . . . until she hath brought up the child, to a full and fitting time to be weaned, which every woman doth to her own child . . . so that many times it falls out, he hath not a wife to lie withal; and therefore as I said, hath allowance of other women, for necessity's sake, which may seem not over-strange unto us, in that our holy writ doth make mention thereof, as you may read in the twenty-third chapter of the Prophet Ezekiel, where Jerusalem and Samasia, being called by the names of the two sisters, Aholah and Aholibah, being charged with fornication, are in the twenty verse of the same chapter, said to dote upon those people, whose members were as the members of asses, and whose issue was like the issue of horses, therein right and amply explaining these people.[86]

ANTHONY KNYVETT (1577–1626)

"The admirable adventures and strange fortunes of Master Antonie Knivet, which went with Master Thomas Candish in his second voyage to the South Sea. 1591," in Samuel Purchas ed., *Purchas his Pilgrimes* (London: William Stansby, 1625) VOL. 4, 1212, 1227, 1229, 1233–34.

Anthony Knyvett or Knivet accompanied Thomas Cavendish on his second voyage around the world in 1591. Knyvett was taken captive by Portuguese settlers off the coast of Brazil and enslaved for a decade. During this time he traveled to Congo and Angola. In the 1614 edition of his *Pilgrimage*, Samuel Purchas described some of Knyvett's adventures, publishing a longer account in his 1625 *Pilgrimes*. Knyvett distinguishes between different types of "savages" and "cannibals," describing how Portuguese colonists brand Angolans like animals, and concluding that the English can take Angola if they wish.

Keywords: Cannibalism—Clothing and Identity—Slavery—
        Brazilians and Europeans Compared—Branding of
        Africans—Colonialism

[86] In his *Anthropometamorphosis,* John Bulwer replicates this discussion of large penises as a mark of a curse on Canaan. In the marginalia he added to his 1625 reprint of Jobson, Samuel Purchas emphasized the monstrosity of the genitals of the black men he called "Priapian Stallions" (1571).

[Of Brazil]

Although the danger of going into the country of wild man-eaters where I never had been was no less than the value of my life, yet considering with myself that my offense deserved death among the Portugals, I chose once again rather to stand to the heathen mercy of savage man-eaters, than at the bloody cruelty of Christian Portugals. . . . With me there went one of their own nation, by the name Morosoeii, who had been taken by the Wayanasses, and they sold him to the Portugals. . . . The two cannibals that we took in the boat were amazed to see men apparelled insomuch that they knew not their own countryman that was with me, when they saw him apparelled like a Portugal. If they were amazed at us, I was no less at them, for in all my travel I never saw the like fashion of cannibals. For when I saw them first I thought they had been born with feathers on their heads and bodies, like fowls of the air, they had anointed their bodies with gum of the oiletusees of balsome, and covered themselves so artificially with feathers of diverse colours, in such order, that you could not have seen a spot of their skins but their legs. . . .[87]

The Waytaquazes inhabit at Cape Frio . . . in low marish grounds. . . . They wear their hair long like wild Irish; the women do war with their bows and arrows as well as the men. Their houses are very low and little. . . . These cannibals have no peace with any kind of nation, but do eat all kind of people, Frenchmen, Portugals, and Blackamoores. . . .

After you have passed the famous River of Paraiba, you shall come into a country of cannibals called Molpaques. They are much like unto Dutchmen in bigness, very fair of complexion, they have all beards like other men . . . . Most of them do cover their privy parts. They are very civil in their behavior. Their towns are very strong, all circled with walls made of earth and great logs. They have houses several every man with his family. . . . The women are goodly of person, fair of complexion, as our English women are, they are very modest and civil in their behavior. You shall never see them laugh. They are people very capable to conceive anything. They have their hair so long that they tie it about their middles with the bark of a tree, wherewithal they cover their nakedness. . . . Their hair is of colours like our English women, some yellow, some white, some brown.

[Of Angola]

. . . The Portugals do mark [the Moors] as we do sheep with a hot iron, which the Moors call crimbo. The poor slaves stand all in a row one by another and sing *Mundele que sumbela he Carey ha belellle*, and thus the poor rogues are beguiled, for the Portugals make them believe that they that have not the mark is not accounted a man of any account in Brazil or in Portugal, and thus they bring the poor Moors to be in a most damnable

[87] Balsome = An obscure form of "balsam," an aromatic oily or resinous medicinal preparation, usually for external application, for healing wounds or soothing pain.

bondage under the colour of love. . . . Angola may be very easily taken: for the Portugals have no Forts to defend it of any strength.

EDMUND SCOT (fl. 1602)

A Discourse of Java, and of the first English factories there . . . ,
in Samuel Purchas, ed., *Purchas his Pilgrimes* (London: William
Stansby, 1625)

Source: Robert Kerr, *A General History and Collection of Voyages and Travels*, Vol. VIII (Edinburgh: W. Blackwood, 1811–24). Free online edition via http://www.gutenberg.org/files/13366/13366-h/13366-h.htm#chapter3-10.

Edmund Scot accompanied Sir James Lancaster, the first director of the East India Company, on his voyage to Java in 1602. Scot's account of Indonesian culture features many of the qualities associated with "Asian despotism"—from tyranny and pride, to idleness and frailty. Because he cannot describe the Chinese in these terms, Scot instead denigrates their industriousness as comparable to the greed and cunning of Jews.

Keywords: Tyranny—Javanese Indolence and Poverty—Lust—
Polygamy—Chinese Craftiness and Industry

The King of Bantam is an absolute sovereign, and . . . uses martial law on any offender he is disposed to punish. If the wife or wives of any private individual are guilty of adultery, upon good proof, both the woman and her paramour are put to death. They may put their slaves to death for any small fault. For every wife that a free Javan marries he must keep ten female slaves, though some keep forty such for each wife, and may have as many more as they please, but can only have three wives; yet may use all their female slaves as concubines. The Javanese are exceedingly proud, yet very poor, as hardly one among them of a hundred will work. The gentry among them are reduced to poverty by the number of their slaves, who eat faster than their pepper and rice grow. The Chinese plant, dress, and gather all the pepper, and sow the rice, living as slaves under the Javanese proprietors; yet they absorb all the wealth of the land by their industry, from the indolent and idle Javanese. All the Javanese are so proud that they will not endure an equal to sit an inch higher than themselves. They are a most blood-thirsty race, yet seldom fight face to face, either among themselves or with other nations, always seeking their revenge after a cowardly manner, although stout men of good stature. . . .

The principal people are very religious, yet go seldom to church. They acknowledge Jesus to have been a great prophet, calling him Nabu Isa, or the prophet Jesus, and some of them entertain Mahometan priests in their houses, but the common people have very little knowledge of any religion, only saying that there is a God who made heaven and earth and all things. They say that God is good, and will not hurt them, but that the devil is bad, and will do them harm; wherefore many of them are so ignorant as to pray to him, for fear he should harm them.[88] Assuredly, if there were here men of learning, and having a sufficient knowledge of their language to instruct them, many of these ignorant people might be drawn over to the true Christian faith, and civilized; for many with whom I have conversed upon Christian laws have liked all very well, except the prohibition of a plurality of wives, as they are all very lascivious, both men and women. . . .

They are all much given to stealing, from the highest to the lowest; and surely they were, in times past, cannibals or man-eaters, before they had trade with the Chinese, which some say is not above a hundred years ago. . . .

The Javanese are a very dull and blockish people, very unfit for managing the affairs of a commonwealth, so that all strangers who come to their land get beyond them. . . . The Chinese especially, who live crouching under them like Jews, rob them of their wealth, and send it to China.

The Chinese are very crafty in trade, using every conceivable art to cheat and deceive. They have no pride in them, neither will they refuse any labour, except they turn Javans when they have committed murder or some other villainy, when they become every whit as proud and lazy as a Javan. They follow several different sects of religion, but are mostly atheists; many of them believing, that if they lead good lives, they will be born again to great riches, and be made governors; whereas those who lead bad lives will be changed to some vile animal, as a frog or toad. They burn sacrifices every new moon, mumbling over certain prayers in a kind of chanting voice, tingling a small bell, which they ring aloud at the close of each prayer. . . . I have often asked them, to whom they burn their sacrifices? When they always said, it was to God; but the Turks and Guzerates who were there, alleged it was to the devil: If so, they are ashamed to confess. . . .

PIETER DE MAREES (fl. 1602)

"A description and historicall declaration of the golden Kingdome of Guinea, otherwise called the golden coast of Myna . . . ," translated by G. Artic Dantise, in *Purchas his Pilgrimes* (London: William Stansby, 1625), 930–44.

Pieter de Marees' history of Guinea is one of the earliest European descriptions of Luso-African society. Primarily about the Gold Coast (Ghana), De Marees' account also treats modern-day Senegal, Benin, and Gabon. Its interest in Luso-African interbreeding allowed both the Dutch (who read it in Theodor De Bry's *India Orientalis* of 1604) and the English (who read the

[88] William Biddulph makes the same claim in regards to the religious practice of tribes between Aleppo and Scanderone.

translation appended by Purchas to his extract from Richard Jobson's *Voyage to Gambra*) to distinguish their own involvement in the West African slaving for which Africans are here figured as physically suitable.

Keywords: Childbirth—Suckling—Skin Color—Nakedness—Lust—
Interracial Sex—Scarfication—Slavery—Fetishes—Europeans
and Africans compared

. . . [A]nd now you shall read of the coast of Mina. And first of the iron people in this golden coast.

Being with child, when their time of deliverance, and bringing forth of their child into the world cometh, when she is in labour, both men, women, maids, young men & children, run unto her, and she in most shameless manner is delivered before them all. I would say much more hereof, but in respect of the credit of women, I will leave it. When the child is born, she goes to the water to wash & make clean herself, not once dreaming of a month's lying in, nor of making caudles of ipocras, and other wines, as women here with us use to do: they use no nurses to help them when they lie in child-bed, neither seek to lie dainty and soft; but they presently take a spoonful of oil, and a handful of manigette or grain, whereof they make a drink, and drink it up.[89]

The next day after, they go abroad in the streets to do their business as other women do. They give their child such a name as they think good to themselves, and bless the same with their fetissos, and other witchcrafts, and when time serveth, circumcise both boys and girls, at which time they make a great feast, whereof they make great account.[90] But where the women are most shameless at the time of the birth of their children, the men in three months after lie not with that wife, nor once have the use of her body, which . . . I think they do not for any shame or regard that they have to deal with that woman, but only because they have other wives enough. They take the young child as soon as it is born, and wrapping a clean cloth about the middle thereof, lay it down on a mat upon the ground, and not in a cradle, and there let it turn and sprawl about and do what it will, and when it is two or three months old, the mother ties the child with a piece of cloth at her back, and so lets it hang there, as the high Dutch wives use to follow their husbands in the wars. When the child crieth to suck, the mother casteth one of her dugs backward over her shoulder, and so the child sucks it as it hangs. . . .

Every woman bringeth up her own children, and each child knoweth the mother, and remaineth with her until the father either buyeth it of her or that it goeth away from the mother. It oftentimes falleth out that the husband taketh the child from the mother & selleth it to other men for a slave. When

[89] Caudles of ipocras (hippocras) = Warm drinks made of wine flavored with spices and given frequently to women in childbed.

[90] Fetisso = An obscure form of "fetish." Originally, any of the objects used by the inhabitants of the Guinea coast and the neighboring regions as amulets or means of enchantment, or worshipped on account of their supposed inherent magical powers, or as being animated by a spirit.

they begin to go, they presently learn to swim and to run into the water, and when they are first born they are not black, but reddish as the Brazilians are; and then by little and little begin to be black; and at last, to be as black as pitch, and growing bigger, run up and down like savage men, boys and girls together, fighting one with another, taking each other's meat from them, and from their childhood upwards, begin to be envious one against the other, and so grow bigger and exercise all kind of villainy and knavery, their parents not once teaching them any civility, nor showing them what they should do, suffering both boys and girls to go stark naked as they were born, with their privy members all open, without any shame or civility. . . .

The men in those countries are of a very good proportion, with fair members, strong legs, and well-shaped bodies, which is easily to be seen, for that they go almost naked of their bodies, they have round faces, and no great lips, nor wide mouths, as the barbarian Moors have, but their noses are flat, which they make flat when they are young, for they esteem a flat nose to be a great ornament unto them, and to say truth, it doth not amiss in them, for that according to the proportion of body, it beautifieth their faces: their ears are small, their eyes white, their eye brows very great, white teeth in their mouths, (for they keep their teeth very clean, scouring them with small sticks, and thereby make them very smooth, and shining like ivory) they have little beard, and are at least thirty years of age, before they have any. They have broad shoulders, thick arms, great hands, and long fingers, and let their nails grow very long, which they keep very clean with scraping, for some of them let them grow as long as the joint of a man's finger, which they esteem for a great ornament, for that cause thinking themselves to be gentlemen. . . . They have small bellies, long legs, broad feet, and long toes, little hair upon their bodies, curled hair upon their heads, but not so much curled as the tawny Moores, for theirs is almost like bristles, and not like wool. In the palms of their hands, under their feet, and under their lips, they are very white, their skins are as soft as velvet, and smooth, which they raze not, they likewise have a great privy member, whereof they make great account, therein they much surpass our countrymen.[91]

As they grow in years, they become blacker and blacker, at thirty years of age being in their best time, but when they are seventy or eighty years old, then their blackness begins to decay, and their bodies become yellowish, and their skins begin to be rugged, and to wrinkle like Spanish leather; they exceed all other Moores in Africa, for proportion and stature of body. . . .

They are very lecherous, and much addicted to uncleanness; especially with young women, whereby they are much subject to the pox, and other unclean diseases, that are gotten thereby, which they make small account of, and are nothing ashamed of them. They are no less given to drinking; for they are great drunkards, and dainty mouthed, and can eat and drink of the best. In their feeding, they are very greedy. . . .

[91] Reports of black men's oversized penises go back as far as the Greek historian Ctesias Indica's fifth-century BCE account of black, Indian pygmies; see Jobson and Bulwer in this volume.

The Portugals in Mina marry mullato women, half white, half black, because white women cannot live there. These wear their hair short, as the men, wear many corals, and are bravely appareled. But of the native women of these parts, first I will tell you of their natures, complexions, and conditions: From their youths upwards, they are given to lust and uncleanness. For a great while they go with their privy members uncovered, as I said before; and as they had no shame at all, so when they begin to wear some thing upon their bodies, they begin to express shamefastness, but then begin to be lecherous, which they naturally learn from their youth upwards. And before the Netherlanders and Portugals dwelt among them, and traffic in that country, the women were not so proud nor curious, as they are now; but that they have learned much of us by seeing that we rather desire a handsome, than an evil favoured wench; and for that cause, they give themselves thereunto, that they might be beloved of us; for they esteem it to be good fortune for them to have carnal copulation with a Netherlander, and among themselves, brag and boast thereof. . . . Upon their foreheads they cut three or four slashes in the flesh, about the length of the joint of a man's finger, and also on their cheeks not far from their ears, which they suffer to swell and rise up, about the breadth of a knife, which they cover over with painting, and under their eye brows, they also make white strikes, and on their faces they set white spots, which afar off show like pearls. They also race their arms and their breasts with diverse kinds of cuts, every morning putting diverse colours upon them, whereby they show like black silk doublets cut and pinked, or like a woman's satin stomacher. . . .

They hang many straw wisps upon their heads, and think thereby to be free and safe as long as they wear them, and that their fetissos can do them no harm. In the morning betimes when they have washed their bodies clean, they stroke their faces with white stripes, made of earth like chalk, which they do in honour of their fetisso, and use it in stead of prayers in a morning; when they eat any thing they present their fetisso (the straw wisps which they wear about their legs) the first bit, and also the first draught that they drink, giving him to drink, which if they do not, they think they shall have no good luck that day, for they persuade themselves that their fetisso would not otherwise suffer them to be quiet. . . .

. . . But when the Netherlanders saw them use such vain toys, which were so foolish, and laughed and jested at them, they were ashamed, and durst make no more fetissos in our presence, but were ashamed of their own apishness. . . .

But the Negros which dwell among the Portugals, know much of God, and can speak of his commandments, as I have found some among them, that could tell of the birth of Christ, of the Lord's Supper, of his bitter passion, and death of his resurrection, and diverse other such like points, concerning our Christian faith; specially, one whom I knew well, and that was my good friend: for he could write and read Portugal, and was indifferent well learned in the scriptures . . . but it seemeth, that it hath not pleased God to call them to the understanding of the Christian faith, and therefore we are much bound to praise and thank God, that it hath pleased him to

---

vouchsafe us the knowledge of his holy word, and to understand and know what belongeth unto our salvation. . . .

SIR ANTHONY WELDON (d. 1649?)

A discription of Scotland (Netherlands, 1626)

Source: *A Perfect Description of the People and Country of Scotland* (London: Richard Lownds, 1659), 1–2, 16–19.

Clerk of the Green Cloth in the royal court, Anthony Weldon was knighted by King James but subsequently dismissed in 1617 after James found racist writings by Weldon about the King's native Scotland. This was likely the manuscript for Weldon's *A Discription* . . . , which would not be published until 1626, after James's death. Weldon is remembered not only for his vitriolic attack comparing the Scots to animals, but also for first suggesting that James had an effeminate interest in men.

Keywords: Scottish Brutishness—Hygiene—Acquisition of Culture—Jealousy

First, for the country, I must confess it is good for those that possess it, and too bad for others, to be at the charge to conquer it. The air might be wholesome for some but for the stinking people that inhabit it. The ground might be fruitful had they wit to manure it.

Their beasts be generally small, women only excepted, of which sort there are none greater in the whole world. There is great store of fowl too, as foul houses, foul sheets, foul linen, foul dishes and pots, foul trenchers and napkins. . . . They have good store of fish too, and good for those that can eat it raw; but if it come once into their hands, it is worse than if it were three days old. For their butter and cheese, I will not meddle withal at this time, nor no man else at any time that loves his life. . . .

For the lords temporal and spiritual, [they are] temporizing gentlemen, if I were apt to speak of any, I could not speak much of them; only I must let you know they are not Scottishmen, for as soon as they fall from the breast of the beast their mother, their careful sire posts them away for France, which as they pass, the sea sucks from them that which they have sucked from their rude dams; there they gather new flesh, new blood, new manners, and there they learn to put on their clothes, and then return into their countries to wear them out. There they learn to stand, to speak, and to discourse, and congee, to court women, and to compliment with men. . . .[92]

The country, although it be mountainous, affords no monsters but women, of which the greatest sort (as countesses and ladies) are kept like

[92] Congee = To bow in courtesy or obeisance.

lions in iron gates; the merchants' wives are also prisoners, but not in so strong a hold; they have wooden cages, like our boar-franks, th[r]ough which, sometimes peeping to catch the air, we are almost choked with the sight of them. The greatest madness among the men is jealousy; in that they fear what no man that hath but two of his senses will take from them.

The ladies are of opinion, that Susanna could not be chaste, because she bathed so often. Pride is a thing bred in their bones, and their flesh naturally abhors cleanliness. Their breath commonly stinks of pottage, their linen of piss, their hands of pig turds, their body of sweat, and their splay feet never offend in socks. To be chained in marriage with one of them, were to be tied to a dead carcass, and cast into a stinking ditch. . . .

And therefore to conclude, the men of old did no more wonder that the great Messiah should be born in so poor a town as Bethlehem in Judea, than I do wonder that so brave a prince as King James, should be born in so stinking a town as Edinburgh in lousy Scotland.

SIR FRANCIS BACON (1561–1626)

Sylva sylvarum: or, A naturall historie (London: John Haviland and Augustine Mathewes, 1627)

Source: *The Works of Francis Bacon*, edited by James Spedding, Robert Leslie Ellis, and Douglas Denon Heath (Boston: H. O. Houghton and Company, 1878), Vol. II, 473.

Widely regarded as a key figure of the scientific revolution, Bacon's best known works include *Of the proficience and advancement of learning* (1605); *New Atlantis* (1627), envisioning a scientific utopia in an island community; and his natural historical work, *Sylva sylvarum*, a compilation of one thousand paragraphs consisting of extracts from many books as well as his own experiments. In the following extract, Bacon returns to the argument that dark skin is produced by the heat of the sun.

Keywords: Skin Color—Environmental Influence—Heliotropism

Experiment solitary touching the colouration of black and tawny Moors.

The heat of the sun maketh men black in some countries, as in Aethiopia and Guinea, &c. Fire doth it not, as we see in glass-men that are continually about the fire. The reason may be because the fire doth lick up the spirits and the blood of the body, so as they exhale; so that that it ever maketh men look pale and sallow; but the sun, which is a gentler heat, doth but draw the blood to the outward parts, and rather concocteth it than soaketh it; and therefore we see that all Aethiopes are fleshy and plump, and have great lips; all that betoken moisture retained, and not drawn out. We see also, that the Negroes are bred in countries that have plenty of water, by rivers or otherwise; for

Meroë, which was the metropolis of Aethopia, was upon a great lake; and Congo, where the Negroes are, is full of rivers. And the confines of the river Niger, where the Negroes also are, are well watered, and the region about Cape Verde is likewise moist, insomuch as it is pestilent through moisture; but the countries of the Abyssenes, and Barbary, and Peru, where they are tawny and olivaster, and pale, are generally more sandy and dry. As for the Aethiopes, as they are plump and fleshy, so (it may be) they are sanguine and ruddy coloured, if their black skin would suffer it to be seen.

HENRY BYAM (1580–1669) AND
EDWARD KELLET (1580–1641)

A returne from Argier A sermon preached at . . . the re-admission of a relapsed Christian into our Church (London: T. Harper, 1628), 2–3, 19–20, 35, 74–75.

A returne from Argier is the published version of two sermons preached in Minehead in 1627 on the occasion of the readmission into the Church of England of an English sailor who had converted to Islam while enslaved by Turkish pirates. The sermons indicate that English churchmen were concerned not only with the fidelity of their congregations, but also with the fact that religious difference was not visibly recognizable.

Keywords: Religious Conversions—Turning Turk—Clothing and
        Identity—Muhammad

Byam

. . . I am informed, many hundreds are Musselmans in Turkey and Christians at home, doffing their religion as they do their clothes, and keeping a conscience for every harbour where they shall put in. And those apostates and circumcised renegadoes they have discharged their conscience wondrous well if they can return, and (the fact unknown) make profession of their first faith. These men are cowards and flexible before the fall, careless and obstinate after it. . . .

When I think upon your Turkish attire, that emblem of apostasy, and witness of your woeful fall, I do remember Adam and his fig-leaf breeches; they could neither conceal his shame, nor cover his nakedness. . . . How could you hope in this unsanctified habit to attain heaven? How could you, clad in this unchristian weed, how could you but with horror and astonishment think on the white robe of the innocent martyrs which you had lost?

Kellet

Briefly, to our purpose, thus *Acts 15.1, Certain men came down from Judea, and taught the Brethren, saying, Except ye be circumcised after the manner of Moses, ye cannot be saved.* What sort of men these seducers were is mentioned, *Acts 15.5, They were of the sect of the Pharisees which believed* these Christian-Jews, or

Jewish Christian, would join Moses and Christ, the Law and the Gospel, for-getting the substance of the precepts given unto them, *Levit. 19.19, Thou shalt not let thy cattle gender with a diverse kind; Thou shalt not sow thy field with a mingled seed, neither shall a garment of linen and woollen come upon thee.* And *Deut. 22.9, Thou shalt not sow thy vineyard with diverse seeds, nor plow with an ox and an ass together.* Nor would they remember what was written in the gospel, *Matt 9.16, No man putteth a piece of new cloth upon an old garment; neither do men put new wine into old bottles.* All which places do in their moral forbid min-gling of religions as the fathers expound them, so whilst they would be both Jews and Christians, they were neither true Jews, nor perfect Christians. . . .

. . . Thy offense was greater than diverse of the Jews who put our redeemer unto death; for they did it through ignorance, as did also their rulers, *Acts 3.17.* But you wittingly against your own conscience forsook your saviour; and though they preferred Barabbas (who was a robber, *John 18.40,* a mur-derer, *Acts 3.14,* a mutineer, *Luke 23.19*) yet you have adhered to one every way worse than Barrabas; before the most holy, just, and innocent Christ, you have esteemed Mahomet, that rake-shame of the world . . . the ravisher of his mistress; the known adulterer with one Zeid, which he himself con-fesseth in his law, and sayeth, God made it sinless, and exemplary for ever; a murderer of the emperor's brother; a rebel against Heraclius, who was his benefactor; a gentile in some points, a Jew in others, a Christian in others, a Manichee, Nestorian, and Arrian; a very compound of heresies; a com-pounder of vanities . . . and in whose Alcoran, there is such an hotch-potch of errors palpable as the Egyptian darkness; nasty, as bred in the lap of lust; so brutish, so blockish, that knowing all his vanities would be easily confuted, he cutteth off all disputations with the sword, and instead of Persuasion, the child of Truth displayed, he hath set Death before them to keep them in fast blindness. Yet in spite of worldly policy there have broke forth seventy-two principal Mahometan sects, sayeth Johannes Leo in his third book of his *African History.* And Leo was sometime himself a learned Mahumetan; but seeing with the eyes of his mind their abominable errors, and with the eyes of his body such villainy as ever was heard of, to be upheld by their superstitious belief, contrary to sight & sense, at one open market in Cairo (as in the same third book) he bathed himself in the laver of regeneration, and detesting their religion became a Christian. . . .

Others change faith for gain; and here the treacherous villainy of factors is notorious; who being entrusted with much goods of their master, turn Turk to be masters of those goods; destroying their souls to cozen the honest brave merchant-adventurers. Among all the revolters in Africa, you cannot name one who, whilst he was of our profession, served God daily, honored Christ duly, lived consciously, evidencing his fruitful faith, by multitude of charitable works. But, such as are among us, such as are to choose religion: ambo-dexters, nullifidians, such amphibia, as can live both on land and water, or such as have stained their souls with some black sins. These are the chameleons which will change colour with every air, and their belief, for matters of small moment.

RICHARD BRATHWAITE (1588?–1673)

The English gentlewoman (London: B Alsop and
T. Fawcet, 1631), 7–10, 67–68.

Better known for his poetry and satirical writing, Brathwaite was
a wealthy landowner whose conduct books *The English gentleman* (1630) and *The English gentlewoman* went through several
editions. Whereas gentlemen are advised about education and
their management of public or private affairs, the sequel is more
concerned with women's appearance and obedience, as well as
the relationship between their internal and external qualities.

Keywords: Cosmetics—Face-painting—Foreign Commodities—
    Infection—Washing a Moor—Humors—Clothing and
    Identity

Our life consists in the perfection or temperate infusion of natural or radical
humour, or in the conservation of natural heat. To preserve this, to increase
that, nature hath provided means inwards and outwards. To invert the use,
is to pervert the ordinance itself. So use the outward that you darken not the
inward; so dispose of the inward that you may rectify the outward. . . .

O but the misery and levity of this age is such as that becomes generally
least affected which adorns us most . . . that valued most which becomes us
least. Time was . . . when the only flower to be loved of women was a native
red, which was shamefastness. The face knew not then what painting was,
whose adulterate shape takes now acquaintance from the shop. Then were
such women matter of scandal to Christian eyes, which used painting their
skin, powdering their hair, darting their eye. Our commerce with foreign
nations was not for fashions, feathers, and follies. There was a distinction
in our attires; differences of ranks and qualities; a civil observance of decent
habits; which conferred no less glory on our isle at home than victorious
managements by the prowess of our inhabitants did abroad.

The infection of vice leaves a deeper spot or speckle on the mind, than
any disease doth on the body. The Blackmoor may sooner change his skin,
the leopard his spots, than a soul deep dyed in the grain of infection can put
off her habituate corruption.

WILLIAM LITHGOW (1582–1645)

*The totall discourse of the rare adventures, and painefull peregrinations
of long nineteene yeares travayles, from Scotland, to the most
famous kingdomes in Europe, Asia, and Affrica . . .*
(London: Nicolas Okes, 1632)

Source: *The totall discourse* . . . (London, I. Okes, 1640), 141–43,
    145–47, 152–56, 161–64, 169–70.

The Scotsman William Lithgow traveled widely in Europe and around the Mediterranean, and was well known at the English court. Lithgow's account of the Ottoman world is representative of a widespread tendency to denigrate the Turks as lascivious and tyrannical, while at the same time admiring their discipline.

Keywords: Turkish Polygamy, Prostitution, Concubinage, and Lust—
        Turkish-Christian Liaisons—Lineage of Jews and Turks—
        Persian-Turkish Difference

. . . It is a common thing with [the Turks] to kill their servants for a very small offence, and when they have done, throw them like dogs in a ditch. . . . Their wives are not far from the like servitude, for the men by the Alcoran are admitted to marry as many women as they will, or their ability can keep. And if it shall happen that any one of these women (I mean either wife or concubine) prostituteth herself to another man besides her husband, then may he by authority bind her hands and feet, hang a stone about her neck, and cast her into a river, which by them is usually done in the night.

But when these infidels please to abuse poor Christian women against their husbands' will, they little regard the transgression of the Christian law who as well deflower their daughters as their wives; yet the devout Mahometans never meddle with them, accounting themselves damned to copulate . . . with the offspring of dogs. The Turks generally, when they commit any copulation with Christians or their own sex, they wash themselves in a south running fountain before the sun rising, thinking thereby to wash away their sins. . . .

The Turks in general, whensoever they loath or dislike their wives, use to sell them in markets, or otherwise bestow them on their men-slaves. And although their affection were never so great towards them, yet they never eat together, for commonly the women stand and serve their husbands at meat, and after that, [they] eat apart by themselves, secretly, without admission of any mankind in their company, if they be above fourteen years of age. They go seldom abroad, unless it be each Thursday at night, when they go to the graves to mourn for the dead, always covering their faces very modestly with white or black masks, which are never uncovered till they return to their houses. . . . And notwithstanding of all this external gravity . . . there are in Constantinople above 40,000 brothel-houses . . . in any of which, if a Christian (especially Franks) be apprehended, he must either turn Turk, or slave all his life. But the women by policy apply a counterpoison to this severity, for they accustomably come to the chambers of their benefactors and well-willers, or other places appointed secretly. . . .

As for the Great Turk's concubines, they are of number eight hundred, being the most part emirs', bashaws', and timariots' daughters. The third and inmost part of the seraglia is allotted for their residence, being well attended at all times with numbers of eunuchs and other gelded officers.

Every morning they are ranked in a great hall and set on high and open seats, where when he cometh, and, selecting the youngest and fairest, he toucheth her with a rod; and immediately she followeth him into his cabin of lechery, where if any action be done, she receiveth from the head-clerk her approbation thereupon, which ever afterwards serveth her for a conditional dowry to her marriage, with much honour and reputation besides. And if any of them conceive, and the child born, it is suddenly dispatched from this life. . . . The oldest and last hundred that are every month dismissed, they depart from the Galata home to their parents and several countries, rejoicing that they were counted worthy to be chosen and entertained to be their Emperor's concubines. . . .

The Sarazens are descended of Esau, who, after he had lost the blessing, went and inhabited in Arabia Petrea; and his posterity, striving to make a clear distinction between them—the Ismaelites and Jews—called themselves (as come of Sara) Sarazens; and not of Hagar, the handmaid of Abraham, of whom came the Ismaelites, neither of the race of Jacob, of whom came the Jews. But now the Sarazens being joined with the Turks, their conquerors, have both lost their name and the right of their descent.

. . . The Turks, being naturally descended of the Scythians or Tartars, are of the second stature of man, and robust of nature, circumspect and courageous in all their attempts, and no way given to industry or labour, but are wonderful avaricious and covetous of money above all the nations of the world. They never observe their promises, unless it be with advantage, and are naturally prone to deceive strangers, changing their conditional bargains as time giveth occasion to their liking. They are humble one to another, but especially to their superiors, before whom they do not only great homage, but also keep great silence, and are wonderful coy during the time of their presence. They are extremely inclined to all sorts of lascivious luxury, and generally addicted, besides all their sensual and incestuous lusts, unto sodomy, which they account as a dainty to digest all their other libidinous pleasures. . . .[93]

. . . Their armies in marching or camping (notwithstanding infinite multitudes) keep modesty and silence, and are extremely obedient unto their captains and commanders. . . .

Amongst the Turks there is no gentility nor nobility, but are all as ignoble and inferior members to one main body: the Great Turk, lineally descending of the House of Ottoman, whose magnificence, puissance, and power is such

---

[93] Nicolas de Nicolay complained that the Turks had turned "the incomparable temple of S. Sophia" into "a stable and a brothel for buggerers and whores" (48–49, 99–102). Henry Blount's *A Voyage into the Levant* (1636) claims that "each basha hath as many, or likely, more catamites, which are their more serious loves; for their wives are used . . . but to dress their meat, to laundress, and for reputation" (79). In his *Political Reflections upon the Government of the Turks* (1662), Francis Osborne connects the Turkish seraglio to climatic theory, arguing that the Turks kept concubines in order to prevent "sodomy and bestiality, sins infesting these hot countries" (81).

that the most eloquent tongue cannot sufficiently declare. . . . The inhumane policy of the Turks to avoid civil dissension is such that the seed of Ottoman (all except one of them) are strangled to death. . . . His daughters or sisters are not so used, but are given in marriage to any bassa, whom so they affect; yet with this condition: the King sayeth to his daughter or sister: I give thee this man to be thy slave, and if he offend thee in any case, or be disobedient to thy will, here I give thee a dagger to cut off his head; which always they wear by their sides for the same purpose.

The Persians differ much from the Turks in nobility, humanity, and activity, and especially of religion; who by contention think each other accursed, and notwithstanding both factions are under the Mahometanical law. Neither are the sons of the Persian kings so barbarously handled as theirs, for all the brethren (one excepted) are only made blind, wanting their eyes, and are always afterward gallantly maintained like princes.

EDMUND SPENSER (1552–99)

A Veue of the present state of Irelande (Dublin: James Ware, 1633)

Source: Edmund Spenser, "A View of the State of Ireland" (Part 1),
     from Henry Morley ed., *Ireland Under Elizabeth and James
     the First* (London: Routledge, 1890), 74–76, 80–82, 87–92,
     94, 96, 98–107, 110–11. Crucial words and passages omitted
     by Morley have been added in square brackets following the
     1596 manuscript version available at http://darkwing.uoregon.
     edu/~rbear/veue1.html.

Best known as the author of poetic masterpieces such as *The
Faerie Queen* (1590), *Amoretti, Epithalamion* (both 1595), and
Prothalamion (1596), Edmund Spenser was also deeply involved
in the English colonization of Ireland, where he went in 1580 as
private secretary to the Lord Deputy and remained for most of
his life. Spenser probably completed *A Veue of the present state of
Irelande* in 1596, although it was not published until 1633. *A
Veue* is written as a dialogue between two Englishmen (Irenius,
an expert on Irish affairs; and Eudoxes, a newcomer to them)
who justify and discuss the strategies for an effective and long-
lasting English rule in Ireland.

Keywords: Irish Lineage and Customs—Irish Barbarism—Scythians—
     Spain—Mingling of Nations—Clothing and Identity—Irish
     Women—Wet-nurses—English-Irish—Degeneracy—Irish
     Soldiers

Eudox: How cometh it then to pass, that the Irish do derive themselves from Gathelus the Spaniard?

Iren: They do indeed, but . . . the Irish do herein no otherwise than our vain Englishmen do in the tale of Brutus, whom they devise to have first conquered and inhabited this land. . . . But surely the Scythians . . . at such time as the northern nations overflowed all Christendom came down to the seacoast . . . and getting intelligence of this country of Ireland . . . passed thither, and arrived in the north part thereof, which is now called Ulster; which first inhabiting, and afterwards stretching themselves forth into the land, as their numbers increased, named it all of themselves Scuttenland, which more briefly is called Scutland, or Scotland.

Eudox: I wonder, Irenius, whither you run so far astray; for whilst we talk of Ireland, methinks you rip up the original of Scotland; but what is that to this?

Iren: Surely very much, for Scotland and Ireland are all one and the same. . . . After this people thus planted in the north or before, . . . another nation, coming out of Spain, arrived in the west part of Ireland, and finding it waste, or weakly inhabited, possessed it; who whether they were native Spaniards, or Gauls or Africans, or Goths, or some other of those northern nations which did overspread all Christendom, it is impossible to affirm. . . .

Eudox: Whence cometh it, then, that the Irish do so greatly covet to fetch themselves from the Spaniards, since the old Gauls are a more ancient and much more honourable nation?

Iren: Even of a very desire of newfangledness and vanity; for they derive themselves from the Spaniards, as seeing them to be very honorable people, and next bordering unto them: But all that is most vain . . . for the Spaniard that now is, is come from as rude and savage nations as they, there being, as there may be gathered by course of ages and view of their own history, though they therein labored much to ennoble themselves, scarce any drop of the old Spanish blood left in them; for all Spain was first conquered by the Romans, and filled with colonies from them. . . . Afterwards the Carthaginians . . . subdued it wholly unto themselves . . . [a]nd lastly, the Romans, having again recovered that country . . . so that betwixt them both, to and fro, there was scarce a native Spaniard left, but all inhabited of Romans. . . . [T]here long after arose a new storm, more dreadful than all the former, which overran all Spain, and made an infinite confusion of all things; that was, the coming down of the Goths, the Huns, and the Vandals; and lastly, all the nations of Scythia, which, like a mountain flood, did overflow all Spain, and quite drowned and washed away whatever relics there were left of the land-bred people; yea and of all the Romans too. . . . And yet, after all these, the Moors and the Barbarians, breaking over out of Africa, did finally possess all Spain, or the most part thereof, and did tread down under their foul heathenish feet whatever little they found there yet standing. The which, though afterwards they were beaten out by Ferdinand of Aragon, and Isabella his wife, yet they were not so cleansed but that, through the marriages which they had made and mixture of the people of the land during their long continuance there, they had left no pure drop of Spanish blood, no more than of Roman or Scythian. So that of all nations under heaven, I suppose the Spaniard is the most mingled and most uncertain. . . .

Eudox: You speak very sharply, Ireneus, in dispraise of the Spaniard, whom some other boasts to be the only brave nation under the sky.

Iren: So surely he is a very brave man; neither is that anything which I speak to his derogation; for in that I said he is a mingled people it is no dispraise, for I think there is no nation now in Christendom nor much further but is mingled and compounded with others. For it was a singular providence of God, and a most admirable purpose of his wisdom, to draw those northern heathen nations down into those Christian parts where they might receive Christianity, and to mingle nations so remote, miraculously to make, as it were, one blood and kindred of all people, and each to have knowledge of him. . . .

I will begin, then, to count [Irish] customs in the same way that I counted their nations, and first with the Scythian or Scottish manners, of the which there is one use amongst them, to keep their cattle and to live themselves the most part of the year in boolies, pasturing upon the mountain and waste wild places, and removing still to fresh land as they have depastured the former. . . .[94]

They have another custom from the Scythians; that is, the wearing of mantles and long glibs, which is a thick curled bush of hair hanging down over their eyes, and monstrously disguising them; which are both very bad and hurtful. . . . [F]or [the mantle] is a fit house for an outlaw, a meet bed for a rebel, and an apt cloak for a thief. . . . [A]nd surely for a bad housewife it is no less convenient; for some of them that be wandering women. . . . [I]n summer you shall find her arrayed commonly but in her smock and mantle, to be more ready for her light services: in winter, and in her travail, it is her cloak and safeguard, and also a coverlet for her lewd exercise; and when she hath filled her vessel, under it she can hide both her burden and her blame; yea, and when her bastard is born it serves instead of swaddling [clothes]. And as for all other good women which love to do but little work, how handsome it is to lie in and sleep. . . .

[F]or the Irish glibs, they are as fit masks as a mantle is for a thief. For whensoever he has run himself into that peril of law that he will not be known, he either cutteth off his glib quite, by which he becometh nothing like himself, or pulleth it so low down over his eyes that it is very hard to discern his thievish countenance. . . .

. . . Of which the next that I have to treat of is the manner of raising their cry in their conflicts, and at other troublesome times of uproar; the which is

---

[94] A temporary fold or enclosure.

very natural Scythian, as we may read in Diodorus Siculus and in Herodotus, describing the manner of the Scythians and Parthians coming to give the charge at battles, at which . . . they come running with a terrible yell as if heaven and earth would have gone together; which is the very image of the Irish hubbub which their kerns use at their first encounter. . . .

There be other sorts of cries also used amongst the Irish which savour greatly of the Scythian barbarism; as their lamentations at their burials with despairful outcries and immoderate wailings, the which Mr. Stanihurst might also have used for an argument to prove them Egyptians. . . . Others think this custom to come from the Spaniards, for that they do immeasurably like-wise bewail their dead. But the same is not proper Spanish, but altogether heathenish, brought in first thither either by the Scythians, or the Moors that were Africans, and long possessed that country. For it is the manner of all pagans and infidels to be intemperate in their wailings of their dead, for that they had no faith nor hope of salvation . . . and is yet among the northern Scots at this day, as you may read in their chronicles. . . .

Eudox: But have you, I pray you, observed any such customs amongst them, brought likewise from the Spaniards or Gauls, as these from the Scythians? . . .

Iren: . . . [T]he women amongst the old Spaniards had the charge of all household affairs, both at home and abroad, as Boemus writeth, though now these Spaniards use it quite otherwise. And so have the Irish women the trust and care of all things, both at home and in the field. . . . Moreover, the manner of their women's riding on the wrong side of the horse, I mean with their faces toward the right side, as the Irish use, is, as they say, old Spanish, and some say African, for amongst them the women, they say, used so to ride. Also the deep smock-sleeve which the Irish women use, they say, was old Spanish, and is used yet in Barbary. . . .

Eudox: . . . But have you any customs remaining from the Gauls or Britons?

Iren: . . . [T]he Gauls used to drink their enemies' blood and paint them-selves therewith. So also they write that the old Irish were wont; and so have I seen some of the Irish do, but not their enemies but friends' blood, as, namely at the execution of a notable traitor at Limerick, called Murrogh O'Brien, I saw an old woman, which was his foster-mother, take up his head, whilst he was quartered and suck up all the blood running thereout, saying that the earth was not worthy to drink it, and therewith also steeped her face and breast and tore her hair, crying out and shrieking most terribly.

Eudox: . . . It now remaineth that you now take in hand the customs of the old English which are amongst the Irish. . . .

Iren: . . . [T]he chiefest abuses which are now in that realm are grown from the English, and some of them are now much more lawless and licentious than the very wild Irish; so that as much care as was by them had to reform the Irish, so and more must now be used to reform them; so much time doth alter the manners of men.

Eudox: That seemeth very strange which you say, that men should so much degenerate from their first natures as to grow wild.

Iren: So much can liberty and ill examples do. . . . From which disorder . . . they are almost now grown to be like the Irish—I mean of such English as were planted above towards the west; for the English Pale hath preserved itself through nearness of the state in reasonable civility; but the rest which dwelt in Connaught and in Munster, which is the sweetest soil of Ireland, and some in Leinster and Ulster, are degenerate; yea, some of them have quite shaken off their English names and put on Irish, that they might be altogether Irish. . . . [M]any other of them which were mere English, . . . joined with the Irish against the king, and termed themselves very Irish, taking on them Irish habits and customs, which would never since be clean wiped away; but the contagion hath remained still amongst their posterities. . . .

Eudox: It seemeth strange to me that the English should take more delight to speak that language than their own, whereas they should, me thinks, rather take scorn to inure their tongues thereto. For it hath ever been the use of the conqueror to despise the language of the conquered and to force him by all means to learn his. . . .

Iren: I suppose that the chief cause of bringing in the Irish language amongst them was specially their fostering and marrying with the Irish, the which are two most dangerous infections. For first, the child that sucketh the milk of the nurse must of necessity learn his first speech of her, the which being the first inured to his tongue, is ever after most pleasing unto him; insomuch as, though he afterwards be taught English, yet the smack of the first will always abide with him; and not only of the speech, but of the manners and conditions. For, besides that young children be like apes, which affect and imitate what they have seen done before them, specially by their nurses whom they love so well, they moreover draw into themselves together with their suck, even the nature and disposition of their nurses; for the mind followeth much the temperature of the body, and also the words are the image of the mind; so as, they proceeding from the mind, the mind must be . . . affected with the words; so that, the speech being Irish, the heart must needs be Irish. . . . The next is the marrying with the Irish, which how dangerous a thing it is in all commonwealths appeareth to every simplest sense. . . . And indeed, how can such matching succeed well [but bring forth an evil race] seeing that commonly the child taketh most of his nature of the mother, besides speech, manners, and inclination, which are, for the most part, agreeable to the conditions of their mothers? For by them they are first framed and fashioned, so as what they receive once from them, they will hardly ever after forgo. . . .[95]

Iren: [The Irish soldiers live in] the most barbarous and loathly conditions of any people, I think, under heaven; for, from the time that they enter into that course they do use all the beastly behaviour that may be, they oppress all men; they spoil as well the subject as the enemy; they steal, they are cruel and bloody, full of revenge, and delighting in deadly execution, licentious, swearers and blasphemers, common ravishers of women, and murderers of children. . . . Yet sure they are very valiant, and hardy, for the most part great endurers of cold, labour, hunger, and all hardiness, very active and strong of hand, very swift of foot, very vigilant and circumspect in their enterprises, very present in perils, very great scorners of death. . . .[96]

Iren: [T]hroughout all that country . . . they be all Papists by their profession, but in the same so blindly and brutishly informed, for the most part, as that [you would rather think them atheists or infidels] for not one amongst a hundred knoweth any ground of religion and any article of his faith, but can perhaps, say his *Paternoster* or his *Ave Maria,* without any knowledge or understanding what one word thereof meaneth. . . .

[I do not blame the Christendom of them: for to be sealed with the mark of the Lamb, by what hand so ever it be done rightly, I hold it a good and gracious mark, for the general profession which (they) then take upon them at the cross and faith in Christ. . . . But nevertheless since they drank not of the pure spring of life, but only tasted of such troubled waters as were brought unto them, the dregs thereof have brought a great contagion in their souls, the which daily increasing and being still more augmented with their own lewd lives and filthy conversation, hath now bred in them this general disease that cannot, but only with very strong purgations, be cleansed and carried away.]

SIR THOMAS HERBERT (1606–82)

A relation of some yeares travaile begunne anno 1626. Into Afrique and the greater Asia, . . . and some parts of the orientall Indies (London: William Stansby and Jacob Bloom, 1634), 10, 14–16.

Thomas Herbert traveled extensively in Asia and Africa; many editions, revisions, and translations of his book of travels appeared all over Europe, and the book continued to be reprinted after his

[95] Spenser imagines only the possibility of Irish women marrying English men, and seems unwilling to countenance the possibility of Irish men marrying English women.

[96] Spenser borrows selectively from the discourse of humoral theory, representing the Irish as hardy northerners, but also exhibiting qualities commonly associated with "southern" cultures, such as lechery and vengefulness; see Bodin in this volume.

death. With each expansion, Herbert elaborated upon his comparison of certain African peoples to primates, a practice central to nineteenth-century racist discourses.

Keywords: Cannibalism—African Brutishness and Lust—Ape-like Africans—Scarification—Diet—Nursing of Infants—African-Amazonian Difference—Female Circumcision—Descent from Apes

[Of Southwestern Africa–Zaire and Angola]

Next these inhabit the Anzigues, a nation endowed with many temporal benefits, as wealth, health, gold, strength, valor, and the like, yet want these the virtue to make them civil, for though they abound with nature's blessings, yet they delight in eating man's flesh more than other food. And whereas other people infesting them content their appetites with the flesh of their enemies, these barbarous Anzigui covet their friends, whom they embowel with a greedy delight, saying they can no way better express a true affection than to incorporate their dearest friends and cousins into themselves, as in love before, now in body uniting two in one, a bloody sophistry. They have shambles of men's and women's flesh, jointed and cut in several morsels and some (weary of life) voluntarily proffer themselves unto the bloody butchers, who accordingly are sod and eaten. . . .[97]

These and other black-faced Africans are much addicted to rapine and thievery.[98] They will commit a villainy sooner in the day than night, lest the Moon and stars give testimony against them. The Devil is no stranger amongst them, whose oracles they use to offend an Amazonian people near them, valiant, though naked, and not fearing them.

A Description of the Savage Inhabitants

[T]he people are of a swarthy dark colour (I cannot say complexion) well limbed and proper, nor want they courage (though discretion) to their limbs. Their heads are long, their hair curled, and seeming rather wool than hair, 'tis black and knotty. . . . Their ears are long and made longer by ponderous baubles, they hang there, extending the holes to a great capacity, so put a link of brass or iron, others chains, glass, blue stones or bullets in them. Such as want that treasure make use of singles of deer, beaks of birds, bells, stones of dogs, or wild cats, of which fopperies these Troglodites esteem so much, as we of gold, pearl, amber, or the like. About their necks (for I omit their flat noses, and blubberd lips, big enough without addition) they

[97] Sod = Boiled. Spenser attributes the same quality to the Irish in *A View,* exemplifying how markers of extreme difference were regularly transplanted, particularly in making connections between Africans and the Irish.

[98] Herbert expands on this idea in the 1638 edition entitled *Some yeares travels into divers parts of Asia and Afrique,* suggesting of all the "black skinned wretches" he has seen in Africa, "Let one character serve them all: they look like chimney sweepers, are of no profession, except rapine and villainy makes one" (9).

are ornified with long brass chains or hoops of iron, such as mariners afford them. . . .[99]

Their arms are laden with pride, such make the iron shackles, beads, twigs of trees, and brass rings. . . . Both men and women hideously cut and slash their flesh in sundry forms, their brows, noses, cheeks, arms, breast, back, belly, thighs, and legs and pinked and cut in more admirable (than amiable) manner. . . .

Their clothing at best is a stinking beast skin, the hair inverted reaching from head to waist. And as a cover to their modest parts they gird themselves with a piece of raw leather, and fasten a square piece like the back of a glove to it, which almost hangs so low as their pendants. Most have but one stone, the other is forced away in their infancy, that Venus allure them not more than Pallas. Their bums and legs are naked, some only have a broad piece of leather which, helped by a small string, is fastened to their feet, which too, when they come into a stranger's company, they usually hold them in their hands, whereby their feet may have the greater liberty to steal, which with their toes, they practice and can perform most cunningly. . . .

These well-bred people descend each morning from the mountains adorned with two or three raw guts of cats or lions, serving for chains or necklaces, and breakfast too, and in their active compliments salute, eating and speaking both together. They are very ceremonious in thanksgivings, for, wanting requitals, if you give a woman a piece of bread, she will immediately pull by her flap and discover her pudenda. A courtesy commanded them, I suppose, by some Dutch-ill-bred sailor, for taught it they are, they say, by Christians. And English men, I know, have greater modesty. The female sex are for the greater sort excised in their hidden parts, but the men know no such custom, for in place of circumcision, they pull away one stone, fearing to beget too many children. . . .

These Troglodites live sometimes under ground, at other, in mansions like to ovens, round and without furniture. A whole tribe usually live associate, commit villainies, feed and sleep together, the ablest in force swaying over the other. . . . Their words are sounded rather like that of apes than men, whereby it's very hard to sound their dialect, the antiquity of it, whether from Babel or no. For the reader's content I have noted some of their language, which I have writ so near as I could pronounce it, their pronunciation is like the Irish, their customs not much unlike the rude ones of antique times. . . .[100]

[99] Ornify = To adorn, ornament.

[100] In the 1638 edition, Herbert goes further in bestializing the natives of southern Africa, claiming, "Their language is apishly sounded (with whom 'tis thought they mix unnaturally), the idiom very hard to be counterfeited . . . being voiced like the Irish . . ." (18). By the 1665 edition, this tendency was even more pronounced: "[T]hey have a voice 'twixt human and beast, [which] makes that supposition to be of more credit, that they have a beastly copulation or conjuncture. So as considering the resemblance they bear with baboons, which I could observe kept frequent company with the women . . . what philosophers allege concerning the function of the soul may be made applicable to these animals, saying, that the soul of man gradually rather than specifically differenced from the souls of beasts. . . . Upon which account, the Spaniard of late years made it the subject of their dispute. Whether the Indians were of descent from Adam, or no? or whither they were not rather a middle species of men and apes" (19).

One word of their food, tis dead whales, seals, grease, raw puddings, or man's flesh, which rather than want they will dig Christians out of their graves. They delight to daub and make their skin glister with grease and charcoal beat together, which when half dried, they then indent it with their fingers. In a word, they have all tricks possible to disfigure themselves, and to prove their patrimony and reversions in Acheron.

And comparing their imitations, speech, and visages, I doubt many of them have no better predecessors than monkeys, which I have seen there of great stature. The women give their infants suck as they hang at their backs, the uberous dug stretched over her shoulder.[101] And though these savages be treacherous, yet doubtless they esteem more of an Englishman than of Portugal or Flemming.

GOVERNOR AND COUNCIL OF VIRGINIA

Statutes (1630–70)

Source: William Waller Henning, ed., *The Statutes at Large: Being a Collection of All the Laws of Virginia, from the First Session of the Legislature in the Year 1619*, 13 vols. (Richmond, 1809–23), I: 146, 410, 552; II: 139–40, 170, 260, 280.

Modeled after the assembly of Virginia Company stockholders in London, the first legislative assembly in Jamestown met in April 1619. From the very beginning, legislation was discussed concerning the rights and baptisms of native peoples, and concerning relations between colonists and Indians. Similar statutes regulating relations with black slaves soon followed.

Keywords: Interracial Sex—Slavery—Property Rights—Conversion of Indians and Slaves

1630

September 17th, 1630, Hugh Davis to be soundly whipped, before an assembly of Negroes and others for abusing himself to the dishonor of God and shame of Christians, by defiling his body in lying with a Negro; which fault he is to acknowledge next Sabbath day.

1640

Robert Sweet to do penance in church according to the laws of England, for getting a Negro woman with child and the woman whipt.

---

[101] Uberous = Supplying milk or nourishment in abundance. Said (a) of animals, etc.; or (b) of the breasts.

1655
Act 2

. . . and be it further enacted that . . . all Indian children by leave of their parents shall be taken as servants for such term as shall be agreed on by the said parents and master as aforesaid, provided that due respect and care be had that they the said Indian servants be educated and brought up in the Christian religion and the covenants for such service or services to be confirmed before two justices of the peace. . . .

1661–62
Act 138

. . . that the Indians proprieties of their goods be hereby assured and confirmed to them, and their persons so secured that whoever shall defraud or take them from their goods and do hurt and injury to their persons shall make such satisfaction and suffer such punishment as the laws of England or this country do inflict, if the same had been done to an Englishman. . . .

   . . . and if any Englishman shall presume to take from the Indians . . . any of their goods, or shall kill, wound, or maim any Indian, he shall suffer as if he had done the same to an Englishman, and be fined for his contempt.

1662
Act 12

Whereas some doubts have arisen whether children got by any Englishman upon a Negro woman should be slave or free, be it therefore enacted and declared by this present grand assembly that all children born in this country shall be held bond or free according to the condition of the mother, and that if any Christian shall commit fornication with a Negro man or woman, he or she so offending shall pay double the fines imposed by the former act.

1667
Act 3

Whereas some doubts have risen whether children that are slaves by birth, and by the charity and piety of their owners made partakers of the blessed sacrament of baptism, should by virtue of their baptism be made free, it is enacted and declared by this grand assembly, and the authority thereof, that the conferring of baptism doth not alter the condition of the person as to his bondage or freedom; that diverse masters, freed from this doubt, may more carefully endeavor the propagation of Christianity by permitting children, though slaves, or those of greater growth if capable to be admitted to that sacrament.

1670
Act 5

Whereas it hath been questioned whether Indians or Negroes manumitted, or otherwise free, could be capable of purchasing Christian servants, it is enacted that no Negro or Indian though baptized and enjoined their own freedom shall be capable of any such purchase of Christians, but yet not debarred from buying any of their own nation

WILLIAM WOOD (fl. 1630)

New Englands Prospect (London: Thomas Cotes, 1634), 62–63.

William Wood lived in Massachusetts from 1629 until 1633. New Englands Prospect describes the topography, flora, and fauna of New England, its difference from England, and its bounty and beneficence. Vigorous natives of New England are presented here as evidence of the healthfulness of the land.

Keywords: Comparison of Indians and Europeans—Health and Diet of Indians—Nakedness—Skin Color

Of the Aberginians or Indians Northward

First of their stature, most of them being between five or six foot high, straight bodied, strongly composed, smooth-skinned, merry countenanced, of complexion something more swarthy than Spaniards, black haired, high foreheaded, black eyed, out-nosed, broad shouldered, brawny armed, long and slender handed, out breasted, small waisted, lank bellied, well thighed, flat kneed, handsome grown legs, and small feet. In a word, take them when the blood brisks in their veins, when the flesh is on their backs and marrow in their bones, when they frolic in their antic deportments and Indian postures, and they are more amiable to behold (though only in Adam's livery) than many a compounded fantastic in the newest fashion. It may puzzle belief to conceive how such lusty bodies should have their rise and daily support-ment from so slender a fostering, their houses being mean, their lodging as homely, commons scant, their drink water, and nature their best clothing. . . . I have been in many places, yet did I never see one that was born either in redundance or defect a monster, or any that sickness had deformed, or casu-alty made decrepit, saving one that had a bleared eye and another that had a wen on his cheek. The reason is rendered why they grow so proportion-able and continue so long in their vigour (most of them being fifty before a wrinkled brow or gray hair bewray their age) is because they are not brought down with suppressing labor, vexed with annoying cares, or drowned in the excessive abuse of overflowing plenty, which oftentimes kills them more than want, as may appear in them. For when they change their bare Indian com-mons for the plenty of England's fuller diet, it is so contrary to their stom-achs that death or a desperate sickness immediately accrues, which makes so few of them desirous to see England. Their swarthiness is the sun's livery, for they are born fair. Their smooth skins proceed from the often anointing of their bodies with the oil of fishes and the fat of eagles, with the grease of raccoons, which they hold in summer the best antidote to keep their skin from blistering with the scorching sun. . . .

ROGER WILLIAMS (1606–83)

A Key into the Language of America (London: Gregory Dexter, 1643), A4R–A5R, 49, 52–53. 113, 143.

The clergyman Roger Williams traveled to Plymouth Plantation in 1629, where he became a controversial figure for his belief that that native land rights had not been taken seriously enough by English colonists. After challenging the validity of the colonial charter and rejecting the notion that the King of England had the right to bestow Indian land on his own subjects, Williams was sentenced to be sent back to England. Instead, he fled south, taking refuge with the Narragansett in what is now Rhode Island. In his writings, Williams emphasizes that Native Americans and Europeans are of one blood, all derived from Adam.

Keywords: Monogenesis—Conversion—Migration—Childbirth—Degeneracy—Blood—Adorning of Bodies—Marriage—Skin Color—Unlettered Natives—Clothing and Identity

From Adam and Noah that [the Indians] spring, it is granted on all hands. But for their later descent, and whence they came into those parts, it seems as hard to find, as to find the wellhead of some fresh stream, which running many miles out of the country to the salt ocean, hath met with many mixing streams by the way. They say themselves that they have sprung and grown up in that very place, like the very trees of the wilderness.

. . . They have no clothes, books, nor letters, and conceive their fathers never had: and therefore they are easily persuaded that the God that made English men is a greater God, because he hath so richly endowed the English above themselves. But when they hear that about sixteen-hundred years ago England and the inhabitants thereof were like unto themselves, and since have received from God, clothes, books, &c., they are greatly affected with a secret hope concerning themselves.

Wise and judicious men, with whom I have discoursed, maintain their original to be northward from Tartaria. And at my now taking ship at the Dutch plantation, it pleased the Dutch governor, in some discourse with me about the natives, to draw their line from Iceland; because the name Sackmakan, the name for an Indian prince about the Dutch, is the name for a prince in Iceland.

Other opinions I could number up. . . . First, others and myself have conceived some of their words to hold affinity with the Hebrew. Secondly, they constantly anoint their heads, as the Jews did. Thirdly, they gave dowries for their wives, as the Jews did. Fourthly, and which I have not so observed

amongst other nations as amongst the Jews and these, they constantly separate their women, during the time of their monthly sickness. . . . Yet again I
have found a greater affinity of their language with the Greek tongue.

1. As the Greeks and other nations and ourselves call the seven stars, or
   Charles' wain, the bear; so do they, Mosk, or Paukunnawaw, the bear.
2. They have many strange relations of one Wetucks, a man that wrought
   great miracles amongst them, walking upon the sea, &c. with some kind
   of broken resemblance to the Son of God.

Chapter 7: Of their Persons and Parts of Body

[S]ome cut their hair round, and some as low and as short as the sober English. Yet I never saw any so to forget nature itself, in such excessive length
and monstrous fashion, as to the shame of the English nation, I now with
grief see my countrymen in England are degenerated unto. . . .[102]

For the temper of the brain, in quick apprehensions and accurate judg-
ments, to say no more, the most high and sovereign God and Creator hath
not made them inferior to the Europeans. . . .

. . . [T]hey call a blackamore (themselves are tawny by the sun and
their anointings, yet they are born white) *suckautacone,* a coal-black man.
For *sucki* is black, and *wautacone,* one that wears clothes: whence English,
Dutch, French, Scotch, they call *wautaconauog,* or *coat-men.* . . .

Nature knows no difference between Europe and Americans in blood,
birth, bodies, &c. God having of one blood made all mankind, Acts 17, and
all by nature being children of wrath, Ephes. 2. . . .

Chapter 21: Of Marriage

> When Indians hear that some there are,
>   (that men the Papists call)
> Forbidding marriage bed and yet,
>   to thousand whoredomes fall;
> They ask if such do go in clothes
>   and whether God they know?
> And when they hear they're richly clad,
>   know God, yet practice so.
> No sure they're beasts not men (say they),
>   men's shame and soul disgrace.
> Or men have mixt with beasts and so,
>   brought forth that monstrous race.

---

[102] In *The unlovelinesse of love-lockes* (1628), William Prynne similarly complains of "this our
English climate; which like another Africa, is always bringing forth some new, some strange,
misshapen, or prodigious forms, and fashions, every moment" (1).

SIR THOMAS BROWNE (1605–82)

Pseudodoxia epidemica: or, Enquiries into very many received tenents, and commonly presumed truths (London: Printed by T.H. for E. Dod, 1646), 201–4, 323–33.

Thomas Browne's encyclopedic *Pseudodoxia epidemica*, commonly known as "Vulgar Errors," addressed what he considered widespread misconceptions about a variety of subjects as well as offering new knowledge about the same. His discussion of blackness testifies to the popularity of theories of the curse of Ham as well as climate in understanding blackness. Widely cited by medical men and philosophers, Dutch, German, French, and Italian editions appeared through the eighteenth century.

Keywords: Jews—Nature and Culture—Body Odor—Blood Libel—Skin Color—Heliotropism—Climatic Influence—Jacob and Laban—Maternal Impression—Theories of Generation and Descent—Sons of Noah—Song of Songs—Beauty

The Fourth Book. Chapter 10: Of the Jews

That Jews stink naturally, that is, that in their race and nation there is an evil savour is a received opinion we know not how to admit; . . . that an unsavoury odour is gentilitious or national unto the Jews, if rightly understood, we cannot well concede, nor will the information of reason or sense induce it.[103]

For first upon consult of reason, there will be found no easy assurance for to fasten a material or temperamental propriety upon any nation; there being scarce any condition (but what depends upon clime) which is not exhausted or obscured from the commixture of . . . nations either by commerce or conquest; much more will it be difficult to make out this affection in the Jews, whose race how ever pretended to be pure, must needs have suffered inseparable commixtures with nations of all sorts, not only in regard of their proselytes, but their universal dispersion. . . .

Now having thus lived in several countries, and always in subjection, they must needs have suffered many commixtures, and we are sure they are not exempted from the common contagion of venery contracted first from Christians; nor are fornications unfrequent between them both, there commonly passing opinions of invitement, that their women desire copulation with them, rather than their own nation, and affect Christian carnality above circumcised venery. . . .

[103] Gentilitious = Of, pertaining to, or characteristic of, a nation; national. This is the first usage of the word noted by the Oxford English Dictionary.

. . . [I]f we concede a national unsavouriness in any people, yet shall we find the Jews less subject hereto than any, and that in those regards which most powerfully concur to such effects, that is, their diet and generation. As for their diet, whether in obedience unto the precepts of reason, or the injunctions of parsimony, therein they are very temperate, seldom offending inebriety or excess of drink, nor erring in gulosity or superfluity of meats, whereby they prevent indigestion and crudities, and consequently putrescence of humors. . . .

As for their generations and conceptions (which are the purer from good diet), they become more pure and perfect by the strict observation of their law; upon the injunctions whereof, they severely observe the times of purification, and avoid all copulation, either in the uncleanness of themselves, of impurity of their women; a rule, I fear, not so well observed by Christians. . . .

Lastly, experience will convict it, for this offensive odor is no way discoverable in their synagogues where many are, and by reason of their number could not be concealed . . . ; And lastly, were this true, our opinion is not impartial, for unto converted Jews who are of the same seed, no man imputeth this unsavoury odor; as though aromatized by their conversion, they admitted their scent with their religion. . . .

Now the ground that begat or propagated this assertion might be the distasteful averseness of the Christian from the Jew, from their corruptness, and the villainy of that fact, which made them abominable and stink in the nostrils of all men; which real practice and metaphorical expression did after proceed into a literal construction. . . .

The Sixth Book. Chapter 10: Of the Blackness of Negroes[104]

. . . [W]hy some men, yea and they a mighty and considerable part of mankind, should first acquire and still retain the gloss and tincture of blackness? Which who ever strictly enquires, shall find no less of darkness in the cause than blackness in the effect itself, there arising unto examination no such satisfactory and unquarrellable reasons, as may confirm the causes generally received, which are but two in number; that is the heat and scorch of the Sun, or the curse of God on Cham and his posterity.

The first was generally received by the ancients. . . . It hath been doubted by several modern writers, particularly by Ortelius, but amply and satisfactorily discussed as we know by no man; we shall therefore endeavour a full delivery hereof.

And first, many which countenance the opinion in this reason, do tacitly and upon consequence overthrow it in another. For whilst they make the river Senaga to divide and bound the Moores, so that on the south-side they are black, on the other only tawny; they imply a secret causality herein from the air, place or river, and seem not to derive it from the Sun; the effects of

---

[104] Browne's lengthy discussion of blackness is digested in John Bulwer's *Anthropometamorphosis*.

whose activity are not precipitously abrupted, but gradually proceed to their cessations.[105]

Secondly, if we affirm that this effect proceeded, or . . . may be advanced and fomented from the fervor of the Sun, yet do we not hereby discover a principle sufficient to decide the question concerning other animals; nor doth he that affirmeth the heat makes man black afford a reason why other animals in the same habitations maintain a constant and agreeable hue unto those in other parts. . . .

Thirdly, if the fervor of the Sun, or intemperate heat of clime did solely occasion this complexion, surely a migration or change thereof might cause a sensible, if not a total mutation; which notwithstanding experience will not admit. For Negroes transplanted, although into cold and phlegmatic habitations continue their hue both in themselves, and also their generations; except they mix with different complexions . . . and if they preserve their copulations entire they still maintain their complexions, as is very remarkable in the dominions of the Grand Signior, and most observable in the Moors in Brasilia, which transplanted about an hundred years past, continue the tinctures of their fathers unto this day: and so likewise fair or white people translated into hotter countries receive not impressions amounting to this complexion, as hath been observed in many Europeans who have lived in the land of Negroes. . . .

Fourthly, if the fervor of the Sun were the sole cause hereof in Aethiopia or any land of Negroes, it were also reasonable that inhabitants of the same latitude subjected unto the same vicinity of the Sun, the same diurnal arch, and direction of its rays, should also partake of the same hue and complexion, which notwithstanding they do not. For the inhabitants of the same latitude in Asia are of a different complexion, as are the inhabitants of Cambodia and Java. . . . But this defect is more remarkable in America, which although subjected unto both the Tropics, yet are not the inhabitants black. . . .

Fifthly, we cannot conclude this complexion in nations from the vicinity or habitude they hold unto the Sun, for even in Africa they be Negroes under the southern tropic, but are not all of this hue either under or near the Northern. So the people of Gualata, Agades, Garamantes, and of Goaga, all within the northern tropics are not Negroes, but on the other side about Capo Negro, Cefala, and Madagascar, they are of a jetty black. . . .

Sixthly . . . there are Negroes in Africa beyond the southern tropic, and some so far removed from it, as geographically the clime is not intemperate, that is, near the Cape of Good Hope, in thirty-six [degrees] of southern latitude. Whereas in the same elevation northward, the inhabitants of America are fair, and they of Europe in Candy, Sicily, and some parts of Spain deserve not properly so low a name as tawny.

Lastly, whereas the Africans are conceived to be more particularly scorched and torrified from the Sun, by addition of dryness from the soil, from want and

---

[105] John Pory's introduction to Africanus suggests that the river Senaga forms a natural barrier between tribes of varying skin colors.

defect of water, it will not excuse the doubt. For the parts which the Negroes possess are not so void of rivers and moisture, as is herein presumed. . . . Beside, in that part of Africa, which with all disadvantage is most dry . . . the people are not esteemed Negroes; and that is Libya, which with the Greeks carries the name of all Africa . . . yet is this country accounted by geographers no part of *Terra Nigritarum,* and Ptolemy placeth herein the *Leuco Aethiopes,* or pale and tawny Moors.

. . . It may be therefore considered whether the inward use of certain waters or fountain of peculiar operations might not at first produce the effect in question. For of the like we have records in story related by Aristotle, Strabo, and Pliny. . . .

Secondly, it may be perpended whether it might not fall out the same way that Jacob's cattle became speckled, spotted and ringstraked, that is, by the power and efficacy of imagination, which produceth effects in the conception correspondent unto the fancy of the agents in generation, and sometimes assimilates the idea of the generator into a realty in the thing engendered. For, hereof there pass for current many indisputed examples; so in Hippocrates we read of one, that from the view and intention of a picture conceived a Negro. And in the history of Heliodore of a Moorish Queen, who upon aspection of the picture of Andromeda, conceived and brought forth a fair one. . . .

Thirdly, it is not indisputable whether it might not proceed from such a cause and the like foundation of tincture, as doth the black jaundice, which meeting with congenerous causes might settle durable inquinations, and advance their generations unto that hue.[106] . . . And this transmission we shall the easier admit in colour, if we remember the like hath been effected in organical parts and figures, the symmetry whereof being casually or purposely perverted, their morbosities have vigorously descended to their posterities.[107] . . . This was the beginning of Macrocephali or people with long heads. . . . Thus have the Chinese little feet, most Negroes great lips and flat noses and thus many Spaniards, and Mediterranean inhabitants, which are of the race of Barbary moors, (although after frequent commixture) have not worn out the Camoys nose unto this day.[108]

Lastly, if we must still be urged to particularities, and such as declare how and when the seed of Adam did first receive this tincture, we may say that men became black in the same manner that some foxes, squirrels, lions first turned of this complexion, whereof there are a constant sort in diverse countries. . . . All which mutations, however they began, depend on durable foundations, and such as may continue for ever. . . .

[106] Inquinations = Defilements, or defiling agents.

[107] Morbosity = Illness, diseased condition. Also: a morbid or unhealthy characteristic.

[108] Camoys = Possibly a form of camois which in relation to noses means "low and concave" and when applied to persons "pug-nosed." See John Bulwer in this volume for a description of two children borne by a Portuguese woman after coupling with an ape, whom they resembled in the face "especially in the nose, which is very flat and Camoyse."

However therefore this complexion was first acquired, it is evidently maintained by generation, and by the tincture of the skin as a spermatical part
traduced from father unto son, so that they which are strangers contract it
not, and the natives which transmigrate omit it not without commixture, and
that after diverse generations. And this affection (if the story were true) might
wonderfully be confirmed, by what Maginus and others relate of the Emperour
of Aethiopia, or Prester John, who derived from Solomon is not yet descended
into the hue of his country, but remains a mulatto, that is, of a mongrel complexion unto this day. Now although we conceive this blackness to be seminal,
yet are we not of Herodotus's conceit, that is, that their seed is black, an opinion long ago rejected by Aristotle, and since by sense and enquiry. . . thus may
it also be in the generation and sperm of Negroes; that being first and in its
naturals white, but upon separation of parts, accidents before invisible become
apparent; there arising a shadow or dark efflorescence in the outside, whereby
not only their legitimate and timely births, but their abortions are also dusky,
before they have felt the scorch and fervor of the Sun.

Chapter 11: Of the same

A second opinion there is, that this complexion was first a curse of God
derived unto them from Cham, upon whom it was inflicted for discover-
ing the nakedness of Noah. Which notwithstanding is sooner affirmed than
proved, and carrieth with it sundry improbabilities. For first, if we derive the
curse on Cham, or in general upon his posterity, we shall benegroe a greater
part of the earth then ever was, or so conceived . . . we may introduce a
generation of Negroes as high as Italy, which part was never culpable of
deformity, but hath produced the magnified examples of beauty.
    Secondly, the curse mentioned in Scripture was not denounced upon
Cham, but Canaan his youngest son. . . . Thirdly, although we should place
the original of this curse upon one of the sons of Cham, yet were it not known
from which of them to derive it. For the particularity of their descents is imper-
fectly set down by accountants. . . . For, whereas these of Africa are generally
esteemed to be the issue of Chus, the elder son of Cham, it is not so easily made
out. For the land of Chus, which the Septuagint translates Aethiopia, makes
no part of Africa, nor is it the habitation of blackmoors, but the country of
Arabia. . . . Fourthly . . . the curse is plainly specified in the text, nor need we
dispute it, like the mark of Cain; *Servus servorum erit fratribus suis,* Cursed be
Canaan, a servant of servants shall he be unto his brethren. . . .
    Lastly, whereas men affirm this colour was a curse, I cannot make out the
propriety of that name, it neither seeming so to them, nor reasonably unto us;
for they take so much content therein, that they esteem deformity by other
colours, describing the devil, and terrible objects white. And if we seriously
consult the definitions of beauty, and exactly perpend what wise men determine thereof, we shall not reasonably apprehend a curse, or any deformity
therein. For first, some place the essence thereof in the proportion of parts,
conceiving it to consist in a comely commensurability of the whole unto

the parts, and the parts between themselves, which is the determination of the best and learned writers: and whereby the Moors are not excluded from beauty; there being in this description no consideration of colours, but an apt connexion and frame of parts and the whole. Others there be, and those most in number, which place it not only in proportion of parts, but also in grace of colour. . . . And by this way likewise the Moors escape the curse of deformity, there concurring no stationary colour, and sometimes not any unto beauty.

. . . [B]eauty is determined by opinion, and seems to have no essence that holds one notion unto all. . . . Thus flat noses seem comely unto the Moor, an aquiline or hawked one unto the Persian, a large and prominent nose unto the Roman, but none of all these are acceptable in our opinion. . . . Thus we that are of contrary complexions accuse the blackness of the Moors as ugly. But the spouse in the Canticles excuseth this conceit, in that description of hers[elf], I am black, but comely. And howsoever Cerberus, and the furies of Hell be described by the poets under this complexion, yet in the beauty of our Saviour blackness is commended, when it is said his locks are bushy and black as a raven. So that to infer this as a curse, or to reason it as a deformity, is no way reasonable. . . .

THOMAS CALVERT (1605/6–79)

The blessed Jew of Marocco: or, A Blackmoor Made White . . . by Rabbi Samuel, a Jew turned Christian . . . to which are annexed a diatriba of the Jews sins (York: T. Broad, 1648), 15–21, 31, 33, 42–43.

Thomas Calvert translated into English the testimony of the eleventh-century Fezzan Jew Samuel Marochitanus in *The blessed Jew of Marocco*. First published in Latin in the year 1339, the authenticity of the epistle of Samuel of Morocco has never been confirmed. However, its presentation of a converted Jew and its justification, excerpted here, of Jewish tribulations, may explain why it appeared in more than 20 printings prior to 1500, and 11 more before Calvert's edition.

Keywords: Jews—Blood Libel—Poisoners—Body Odor—Male
          Menstruation

Now if any ask what is [the Jews'] misery, and what is the cause, I shall unfold it:

First, there is the judgment of God upon them, they prayed Christ's blood might be upon them, and upon their children, it is so, it follows and haunts them wherever they go; few states and kingdoms entertain them, and where they are entertained, they are kept under, and made to endure very hard things, the state serving their own ends by them. . . . Now besides this great sin of murdering Christ once, they have other notorious vices that will make any Christian commonwealth first or last vomit them out, unless they leave their Jewish pranks. . . . They used by craft and by coin to buy and get of the consecrated bread which was left at a Christmas sacrament of the Lord's supper, and prick it, burn it, and very basely and scornfully abuse it, because they heard Christians call it the body of Christ. . . .

Sometimes they were accused for poisoning of wells and springs to make an end of Christians, sometimes for beggaring Christians by excessive usury and extortion; sometimes for clipping of coin, for magic, for cozenage, etc. But their cursing of Christ and Christians, their imprisoning of their dearest friends, and laying some foul false accusations against them, if they smell, that they intend to turn Christians, makes them oftentimes intolerable, some of their rabbis reading such lectures as these, "A Jew may murder or stay a baptized Jew without sin." So much are they bent to shed the blood of Christians that they say a Jew needs no repentance for murdering a Christian; and they add to that sin to make it sweet and delectable, that he who doth it, it is as if he had offered a corban to the Lord, hereby making the abominable sin an acceptable sacrifice.[109] But beyond all of these they have a bloody thirst after the blood of Christians. In France and many kingdoms they have used yearly to steal a Christian boy, and to crucify him, fastening him to a cross, giving him gall and vinegar, and running him in the end through with a spear, to rub their memories afresh into sweet thoughts of their crucifying Christ, the more to harden themselves against Christ, and to show their curst hatred to all Christians. . . . Our diligent Foxe hath given us notice that when England gave Jews harbour, they got our English children, and sometimes crucified them in diverse places, as you may find in *Acts and Monuments*, and he publishes it withal in his Latin sermon at the baptism of a Jew. There is an excellent relation, if it can be proved to bear its weight with truth, to show the original of child-crucifying among the Jews. . . . [A] certain prophet of theirs when he was at point of death, did prophesy of the Jews thus: "Know ye (sayeth he) this for a most certain truth, that you can never be healed of this shameful punishment wherewith you are so vexed, but only by Christian blood." This punishment so shameful, they say, is that Jews, men as well as females, are punished *cursu menstruo sanguinis*, with a very frequent blood-flux. These words (sayeth the converted Jew) the Jews did take with a mistake, for hereupon to heal themselves they every year get the blood of some Christian child, whom they murder; whereas if they had understood aright, this *sanguine Christiano*, was Christ's blood that they should get, which in the sacrament we receive, to the healing and saving of sinners, we are presently healed of our father's curse. . . .

I would not charge the Jews falsely, but I think they are often charged with things that truth gives warrant for. . . . Some will aver it that all Jews yield a stink and filthy savour to them that converse with them, and that they judge this cannot be helped better than by the drinking of the blood of Christians. . . . I leave it to the learned to judge and determine by writers or

---

[109] Corban = An offering.

travelers, whether this be true or no, either that they have a monthly flux of blood, or a continual mal-odoriferous breath. . . .

JOHN BULWER (1606–56)

Anthropometamorphosis: man transform'd, or, The artificial changeling historically presented . . . (London: J. Hardesty, 1650)

Source: *Anthropometamorphosis* (London: William Hunt, 1653), 20, 30, 260–62, 311–12, 317, 354–57, 363–65, 378–80, 386, 398–403, 437, 440, 466–69, 529–32, 534–35, 543–44, 558.

The London physician John Bulwer published four volumes exploring the theme of the human body as a medium of communication. *Anthropometamorphosis* offers a global survey of artificial deformations of the body. Drawing on numerous travelogues and scientific treatises included in the present volume, *Anthropometamorphosis* features a moralistic attack on those who artificially alter the body, warning that cultural practices can generate biological traits. A concluding section on "The Pedigree of the English Gallant" discusses the possibility that English people will be transformed as a result of their imitating foreign fashions.

Keywords: Artifice and Nature—Monstrous Races—Cosmetics—
       Suckling—Men with Outsized Breasts—Eunuchs—
       Circumcision—Degeneracy Genitalia—Crossbreeding—
       Monogenesis—Castration—Hermaphrodites—
       Jewish Women

Ancient writers have spoken of Acephali, or a headless nation. . . . For these strange histories of monstrous nations, which in Pliny and other ancient authors I have heretofore counted vain, do now require and deserve some credit; since in these times there is a new nature revealed, new miracles, a new world, full of strange varieties and sincere novelties. . . . St. Augustine, where he speaks of these Acephali and other monstrous nations's men . . . concludes, that whatsoever he begot that is man, that is, a mortal reasonable creature, be his form, voice, or whatever, never so different from any ordinary man's, no faithful person ought to doubt that he is Adam's progeny. . . . But St. Augustine speaks more like a divine than a philosopher for . . . the final cause of these prodigious aberrations may be the anger of God, who is no way bound to the law of nature and who, in revenge for some crime committed, may transform a man as he did Nebuchadnezzar. . . .[110]

[110] Nebuchadnezzar was a ruler of Babylon who conquered Judah and Jerusalem in the seventh century BCE. The transformation mentioned here is probably a reference to Nebuchadnezzar's dream that he would be "driven away from human society" (*Daniel* 4:25), develop bestial qualities, and live among the animals for seven years, until he accepted God's sovereignty (Daniel 4:32–33).

. . . But for my own part I much suspect some villainous artifice and affectation to have been concurrent causes of this non-appearance of the head. . . . And I conceive that they are not so much headless as that their heads by some violent and constant artifice are pressed down between their shoulders. . . .

That horns may be engrafted upon the head appears possible by the report too we have read of some nations who are wont to cut off the spurs from the heels of cocks new gelt, and to insert them so cut off into their own foreheads, which afterwards increase there and grow in a wonderful manner.

Now whether this cornuted nation was the offspring of horned monsters suffered to propogate themsleves and so to become national, or whether they are first affecting such a badge of bestial strength engrafted them and so it became natural to them, I leave to my masters of the jury to find out. . . .

Our English ladies who seem to have borrowed some of their cosmetical conceits from barbarous nations are seldom known to be contented with a face of God's making, for they are either adding, detracting, or altering continually. . . . Sometimes they think they have too much colour, then they use art to make them look pale and fair. Now they have too little colour, then Spanish paper, red leather, or other cosmetical rubrics must be had. Yet for all this, it may be, the skins of their faces do not please them; off they go with mercury water, and so they remain like peeled ewes, until their faces have recovered a new epidermis.

Our ladies here have lately entertained a vain custom of spotting their faces, out of an affectation of a mole to set off their beauty, such as Venus had. . . . This is as odious and as senseless an affectation as ever was used by any barbarous nation in the world. . . . Painting is bad in both a fair and foul woman, but worst of all in a man. . . . These fantastical correctors of their natural forms . . . seem to do nothing else than to reprehend the power of their maker, who as a most wise artificer hath so framed and coloured them. . . . For as St. Augustine sayeth, his works should not seem to be such unto thee as if he transformed natures, or in the creation of anything had ever turned white into black, or black into white. . . .

The women of Mexico so love to have great dugs, that they strive to have their children suck over their shoulders. In the island Arnobon, the nurses have so long dugs, that they cast them over their shoulders. The women of Guinea, when their children cry to suck, they cast their dugs backward over their shoulders, and so the child sucketh as it hangs. So also do the Irish-women at this day, whose breasts (as one says) were fit to be made money bags for East or West Indian merchants, being more than half a yard long, and as well wrought as any tanner with the like charges could ever mollify such leather. . . . A fault therefore it is in the women of Ireland, and others who never tie up their breasts, but they sin with a higher hand against the law of nature who forcibly endeavour to break these bonds drawing them out unto a monstrous and ugly greatness. . . .

Figure 18   Irish woman suckling her baby, from John Bulwer, *Anthropometamorphosis* (1650). From the collections of The Rare Book & Manuscript Library, University of Illinois at Urbana-Champaign.

In Egypt the men have greater breasts than the biggest of our women.[111] . . . But if I should say that men in some countries have not only great breasts, bearing out like unto women which give suck, but that many men have given suck unto their own children, it would sound very strange and somewhat against kind, yet upon credible witnesses it appears to be very true. For one Peter, a Christian Cafar at Sofula, his wife dying after travail of a daughter, nourished the same with milk from his own breast for a whole year. . . . A poor Jew of Ormuz nourished his son with his breast, the mother dying when it was young in the cradle.[112] . . . In particular we read of the Cumacaiaros, a nation of Brazil, that the men are endowed with large breasts, swelling with milk, which are sufficient for the suckling and nursing up of infants; their women on the contrary being endowed with small and manlike breasts. . . .

Many fantastical reasons have been framed and ends propounded to introduce eunuchism, and this way of degrading men from their manhood. Semiramis was the first that caused young male children to be made eunuchs,

[111] Bulwer attributes this to their having become fat, but still this is an extension of the Herodotean idea of gender reversal in Egypt.

[112] Here Bulwer faithfully reproduces Joao Dos Sanctos's *Aethiopia Orientalis* (1597), which describes the Portuguese occupation of Africa at the end of the sixteenth century, when Portugal was at the height of her power there.

therein offering violence to nature, and turning from her appointed course, by a tacit law, as it were stopping the primagenial fountains of seed, and those ways which nature had assigned for the propagation of posterity, that so she might make them have small voices, and to be more womanish that conjoined with her, she might the better conceal her usurpation and counterfeit manhood. . . .

. . . Some have practised this artifice to introduce a necessary chastity and purity of body. . . . But the main design in this business originally was to make them more fit to keep their women; the name eunuch imposed upon them, as if it were a cloak, wherewith they covered the injury done to nature . . . yet in some countries where eunuchs have religious women in keeping, because they shall not be loved, they also have their noses and lips cut off.

And as the genital parts put a difference between nation and nation, so between one religion and other: for the priests of Cybele (the great mother of the Gods) used to cut off their own members, and so geld themselves without danger of death. . . .

. . . But the eunuchs in the Great Turk's seraglio, who are in number about two hundred, they are all of them not only gelt, but have their yards also clean cut off, and are chosen of those renegado youths which are presented from time to time to the Grand Signior: few or none of them are gelt against their will. . . . The Turks that dwell in Europe and Asia do use the very same castration on such young boys as they can seize in Christian countries, and then make sale of them in manner aforenamed. . . . And it is so manifestly against the law of nature to tamper with the witnesses of man's virility, that our laws have made it felony to geld any man against his will. . . .

The extravagant invention of man hath run so far as the castration of women; Andramistes the king of Lydia, as the report goes, was the first that made women eunuchs, whom he used instead of male eunuchs, after whose examples the women of Egypt were spaded. . . . And a friend of mine told me he knew a maid in Northampton-shire that was thus spaded by a sow-gelder, and escaping the danger grew thereupon very fat. . . . [T]his last maid's name was Margaret Brigstock, but the Judges were much confounded how to give a sentence upon an act against which they had no law; for, although the castration of men was felony by law, yet there was nothing enacted against the spading of women. . . .

. . . [I]t is thought . . . that Jewish women desire copulation with the Christians rather than their own nation, and affect carnality before circumcised venery, as the ingenious examiner of popular errors well notes.[113] And yet it is noted, that the Turks, Persians, and most Oriental nations use opium to stimulate them to venery. . . . And therefore Mahomet well knowing this their beastly and inordinate affection, promiseth them that the felicity of their paradise should consist in a jubilee of conjunction, that is, a coition of one act prolonged into fifty years. . . .

---

[113] Marginal note: "D. Browne. Pseudoxia Epidem."

In Arabia there is a kind of people called Creophagi, amongst whom they were not wont to circumcise (judaically) the men only, but the women also. The women of the Cape of Good Hope also circumcise themselves, not from a notion of religion, but as an ornament. In Ethiopia, especially in the dominion of Prester John, they circumcise women. These Abassines have added error upon error, and sin upon sin, for they cause their females to be circumcised, whom they call *Cophles*. A thing which was never practised in Moses law, neither was there ever found any express commandment to do it; I know not where the noseless Moors learned it, for they cut their females, although they be of marriage estate, taking away a certain apophosis, or excrescence of musculous skin that descended from the superior part of the matrix, which some call nympha or hymenea.

Munster (indeed) shows the original of this invention, attributing it to the Queen of Sheba, whose proper name was Maqueda, who ordained that women should be circumcised, led to it by this reason, that as men have a prepuce, so women also after the same manner have a glandular flesh in their genitals, which they call nympha, not unfit to receive the character of circumcision, this being used to the males and females upon the eighth day. . . .

In Florida and Virginia there is a nation of hermaphrodites, which have the generative parts of both sexes. . . . There is a book in French, called *The Hermaphrodite,* which does notably set forth the effeminacy and prodigious tenderness of this nation.[114] But let us a little examine the causes of their generation. Andernacus Mathetis, inquiring why nature in human bodies doth so mock and laugh a man to scorn, answers, and says, he knows no other cause besides the influx of the stars, intempestive copulation, and evil diet, since at this time of day, there is such corruption of life and manners, and so great lust, that it is no wonder if men altogether degenerate into beasts. . . .

They of Guinea have a great privy member, much surpassing our countrymen, whereof they make great account. . . . [The size of the penis] varies much according to the race of families and course of life; for there are certain families, (and as you see) nations, who have an ill or a good report according to this very thing. . . . But it may be that these Guineans, tamper not with nature, but have this prerogative from the subtle indulgency of their midwives. For it is thought it will be longer, if the navel-strings be not close knit by the midwives when the child is new-born, and that because of a ligament which cometh to the navel from the bottom of the bladder, which they call *urachos;* for, the straighter that is tied to the navel, the more the bladder, and the parts adjoining are drawn upward. . . . Now if the supposition be true, we are all at the mercy of the midwives for our sufficiency. . . .

The *Floridians* so love the feminine sex that, for to please them the more, they busy themselves very much about that which is the primary sign of

---

[114] This discussion of hermaphrodites follows from that of female circumcision without a break or transition.

unclean desires; and that they may the better do it, they furnish themselves with ambergris, which they have in great store, which first they melt at the fire, then inject it (with such pain that it maketh them to gnash their teeth) even so far as to the *os sacrum,* and with a whip of nettles, or such like thing, make that idol of *Maacha* to swell.[115] . . .

In the isle of Hermes the men's members hang down to their shanks, insomuch that the men of that country, who knew better manners, do bind them straight, and anoint them with ointments, made there for to hold them up, whereby they may live more civilly, which is supposed to be by reason of the heat of the climate dissolving the body.

Ctesias sayeth, that the Negro Pigmies who dwell in the midst of India, who are saddle-nosed and deformed, have a *veretrum* so great and long, that it hangs down even unto their ankles.[116] . . . From this it is to be asked regarding dwarves and pigmies, why they have larger penises? Or whether, perhaps, it is, as Aristotle writes, just as in man, lacking a tail, that same material is changed into the buttocks, similarly, the material that does not serve to augment the stature of a dwarf is transmuted into the penis.

In some places of the region of Peru, there be certain great apes inhabiting, with whom the inhabitants, by the suggestion of the devils are mingled, whence there ariseth monsters, with the head and privities of men, but with the hands and feet of apes, the rest of their bodies all hairy, which speak not but with howling, after a manner emulate devils.

. . . Of which monster [a Guinea drill baboon which Bulwer saw near Charing Cross], I may say . . . that it proceeded from the wicked copulation of man and beast, the devil cooperating, and divine revenge (without all doubt) ensuing thereupon: of the same tribe and original were those two children which the Portugal woman bore to the great ape, when she was exposed into a desert island inhabited only by such apes. . . .

Why some men, and they a mighty and considerable part of mankind, should first acquire and still retain the gloss and tincture of blackness they who have strictly enquired into the cause, have found no less darkness in it, than blackness in the effect itself, there arising unto examination no such satisfactory and unquarellable reasons as may confirm the causes generally received, which are but two in number, that is, the heat and the scorch of the Sun, or the curse of God on Cham and his posterity. . . .[117] To omit (therefore) the other conjectures of our ingenious author, we shall take leave in the tenor of his own words to say, that it may be the seed of Adam first receive this tincture, and became black by an advenient and artificial way of denigration, which at first was a mere affectation arising from some conceit they might have of the beauty of

---

[115] In 1 Kings 15 of the Vulgate Bible, Maacha is a queen whose worship of a priapic idol is stopped by her grandson Asa, the King of Judah.
[116] Veretrum = The male sexual organ.
[117] Bulwer here follows Browne in a passage included earlier in this volume.

blackness, and an apish desire which might move them to change the complexion of their bodies into a new and more fashionable hue, which will appear somewhat more probable by diverse affectations of painting in other nations, mentioned in this treatise; and that they take so much content therein, that they esteem deformity by other colours, describing the devil, and terrible objects white, for they think and verily persuade themselves that they are the right colour of men, and that we have a false and counterfeit colour: And so from this artifice the Moors might possibly become Negroes, receiving atramentitious impression, by the power and efficacy of imagination. And this complexion, first by art acquired, might be evidently maintained by generation, and by the tincture of the skin, as a spermatical part traduced from father to son. For thus perhaps this which at the beginning of this complexion was an artificial device, and thence induced by imagination, having once impregnated the seed, found afterwards concurrent productions, which were continued by climes, whose constitution advantaged the artificial into a natural impression. . . .

An Appendix, Exhibiting the Pedigree of the English Gallant

. . . it were not impossible to prove, that there was never any conceit so extravagant, that ever forced the rules of Nature; or fashion so mad, which fell into the imaginations of any of these indited nations, that may not meet with some public fashion of apparel among us. . . .[118]

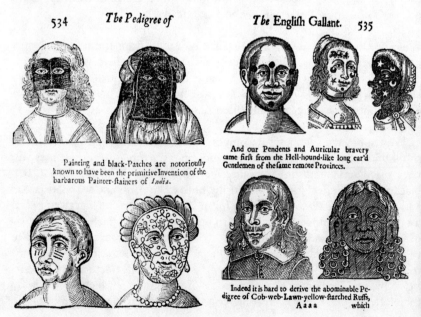

534   *The Pedigree of*   *The English Gallant.*   535

Painting and black-Patches are notoriously known to have been the primitive Invention of the barbarous Painter-ftainers of *India.*

And our Pendents and Auricular bravery came firft from the Hell-hound-like long ear'd Gentlemen of the fame remote Provinces.

Indeed it is hard to derive the abominable Pedigree of Cob-web-Lawn-yellow-ftarched Ruffs,
                    A a a a   which

Figure 19 English imitating foreign fashions, from John Bulwer, *Anthropometamorphosis* (1650). From the collections of The Rare Book & Manuscript Library, University of Illinois at Urbana-Champaign.

[118] Indited = Described.

I pray, what were our sugar-loaf hats, so mightily affected of late both by men and women, so incommodius for use. . . ? Was it not the same conceit that the Macrones of Pontus and the Macrocephali once had . . . ?

What were the square-caps, which Montaigne gives us amongst the most phantastical inventions, but the same fancy with those square-headed gallants of India? Painting and black-patches are notoriously known to have been the primitive invention of the barbarous painter-stainers of India. . . . Masks perchance were derived first from the Numidians who cover their faces with a black cloth with holes, made mask-like to see through. . . .

Painting and black-patches are notoriously known to have been the primitive invention of the barbarous painter-stainers of India. . . . And our pendants and auricular bravery came first from the hell-hound like long ear'd gentlemen of the remote provinces. . . .

That upstart impudence and innovation of naked breasts, and cutting and hallowing down the neck of women's garments below their shoulders, an exorbitant and shameful enormity and habit, much worn by our semi-Adamites, is another mere piece of refined barbarism . . . to facilitate an accommodation with those American ladies in the court of King Atabiliba or Pocahuncas; and having once bandied there, it hazard upon them a shrewd project of heresy. . . . This very fantasticality being a reproach even unto Christianity. . . .

ALEXANDER ROSS (1591–1654)

Arcana microcosmi, or, The hid secrets of mans body disclosed . . .
(London: Thomas Newcombe, 1651), 185–86.

The Scots-born Church of England clergyman Alexander Ross produced biblical scholarship, as well as the first English translation of the Qur'an, published in 1649. A steadfast defender of scholasticism, he dismissed the revisions or refutations of contemporaries such as William Harvey, Thomas Browne, Johann Kepler, Petrus Ramus, and Thomas Hobbes. Written in this vein, *Arcana Microcosmi* argues against Browne that the sun in fact causes blackness in those "disposed to receive his impression."

Keywords: Skin Color—Heliotropism—Causes of Blackness

Book 3. Part 2. Chapter 6

. . . Dr. Brown's book . . . will not have the sun to be the cause of the Negro's blackness . . . I answer, that . . . [the sun] doth work upon each subject according as it is disposed to receive his impression, and accordingly produceth diversity of colours. Hence in the same hot climate men are black, parrots and leaves of trees are green, the emmets as some report, are white, the gold is yellow·and every thing there hath its own peculiar colour, and yet all are produced by the same sun; nay, the same man that hath a black skin, hath white teeth . . . it is observed, that the sun whiteneth those things which are inclined to be hard, and blackeneth soft things; so he makes the Ethiopians teeth white, the skin black. . . .

. . . He objects again, that Negroes transplanted into cold countries continue their hue, therefore the sun is not the sole cause of this blackness. Answer: The question is not if the sun be the sole cause, but whether a cause at all; which the doctor in his former objections seemed to deny. 2. I say, that the sun is the sole primary cause; if there be any other causes, they are secondary and subordinate to the sun's heat and influence. 3. He may as well infer, the sun is not the cause of greenness in leaves, grass, or plants in the Torrid Zone, because these being transplanted into cold climates, retain their hues. . . . 4. If the impression of black, which the sun causeth in a hot clime, must alter in a cold, then may the other qualities also which the sun by his heat procureth, be lost in a cold country; and so what is hard in Ethiopia, must be soft in England, and the heat of Indian spices must here grow cold. He objects again, that there are Negroes under the southern tropic, and beyond which are colder countries. I answer, that these Negroes were colonies out of hotter countries, and not aborigines or natives at first: And he confesseth there be plantations of Negroes in Asia, all which retain their original blackness. . . .

SEBASTIAN MÜNSTER (1489–1552)

The Messias of the Christians and the Jewes held forth in a discourse between a Christian, and a Jew (London: Printed by William Hunt, 1655), 1–9.

A convert to Lutherism and a leading German geographer, Sebastian Münster published an edition of Ptolemy supplemented with many new maps of Europe. His *Cosmographia*, which represented the pinnacle of his labor, was published in England in the 1570s. Münster's work on Hebrew and the Jews is less known, but as its publication in English more than eighty years later attests, *The Messias of the Christians and the Jewes* remained an important source for the notion that Jews were physically distinct from Christians.

Keywords: Jews—Skin Color—Beauty of Jewish Women—Jacob and Laban—Maternal Impression

A Disputation of a Christian with an obstinate Jew

Christian: Is that man who comes to meet me a Jew? Truly his face & form show him to be a man. . . . I will salute him in Hebrew, and I shall easily know whether he be a Jew or not. If he be a Jew, he will answer in Hebrew, but if he be not a Jew, he will hold his peace, not knowing what I say. God save you, O Jew.

Jew: And God save you; how know you me to be a Jew, that you speak so in Hebrew with me? Art thou a Jew and one of our people?

Christian: I am not a Jew, neither of thy people, neither am I acquainted with you; but from the form of your face, I knew you to be a Jew: For you Jews have a peculiar colour of face, different from the form and figure of other men; which thing hath often fill'd me with admiration, for you are black and uncomely, and not white as other men.

Jew: It is a wonder, if we be uncomely, why you Christians do so love our women, and they seem to you more beautiful than your own.

Christian: Your women indeed are more comely than your men, but you seduce them most corruptly.

Jew: Nay, seeing we are the elect people of God, and his inheritance, we are more comely than all the nations of the earth; as it is written in Daniel, that the countenances of the Jewish children appeared fairer and fatter in flesh than all the other children. . . .The Israelites who are free from menstruous blood, have not in their original any drop of redness; but the Gentiles, who do not dread that uncleanness, nor abstain from women in the time when they ought to abstain, they in their original contract a certain redness, and for that cause their fruit, namely their children, are white. Moreover the unchaste Gentiles in the day time do generate, and do behold images and beautiful shapes, and beget sons like them, such as we read was done by Jacob, in Genesis, where it is said, and the sheep conceived when they came to drink, & c. Gen. 30. 39.

Christian: Your arguments do not well answer the proposed business; . . . whereas you add, that you are more comely than any people, that is proved false in our time, forasmuch as not one amongst a thousand is found in the nation, who is of a comely countenance; the reason whereof know, is this, because you no longer are God's inheritance, and beloved people, but rather ye are an abomination in his eyes, and a stink in his nostrils, wherefore he hath left you, so that you go wandering up and down as sheep which are without a pastor, and have no certain dwelling in any place.

Jew: I see you manage your business with reproaches and rebukes, as you were wont commonly to do with us. Have you not read what Isaiah wrote concerning us? Isa. 52. 14 namely, his form is estranged from men, and his countenance unlike the sons of men. We are unlike men by reason of our many tribulations and injuries which we suffer by the Gentiles, amongst whom we are disperst.

Christian: You have not yet told me, why the women amongst you are more beautiful than the men, and are not so easily known as the men.

Jew: Because you Christians do not so much reproach them, as the men; moreover we adorn them with excellent apparel, that they may find favour in your eyes, and we by them obtain what we desire, and it may be well with us by reason of them, and our souls may live for their sakes among the Gentiles; as it is written, and they entreated Abraham well for Sarah's sake, because she was a woman of a comely countenance, Gen. 12. 16. But I am ashamed to speak with thee in public, in the sight of those that pass by and repass. If you please come with me into my chamber, and there we will speak together more concerning these things.

Christian: Go and I will follow you; for I have many things in my heart to speak to you, and now for a long time I have not entered the house of any Jew. . . .

EDWARD TERRY (1590–1655)

A voyage to East-India (London: Printed by T.W., 1655), 16–23,
127, 132, 134–36, 158–59, 162–63, 252–53, 256–58, 450–51.

As a chaplain to the East India Company, Edward Terry went to Surat, India, in 1616. He joined the English ambassador Sir Thomas Roe in following the Mughal Emperor Jahangir on his travels south. An abridged version of Terry's account was published by Samuel Purchas in 1625; the fuller *A voyage to East-India* featured more extended religious commentary. The passages here record Terry's observations of natives at the Cape of Good Hope on the journey out. He argues that only unalterable brutishness can explain the unhappiness of an African who is taken captive to England.

Keywords: Brutishness—Diet—Nursing—Idleness—Clothing and
          Identity—Degeneracy—Native Ingenuity—The Great
          Mogol—Conversion

We saw in this Bay of Souldania . . . beasts in the skins of men, rather than men in the skins of beasts, as may appear by their ignorance, habit, language, diet, with other things, which make them most brutish.

First for God, the great God of heaven and Earth, whom generally all the people in the world, heathen as well as Christians do confess, they . . . acknowledge none. For their speech, it seemed to us an inarticulate noise rather than language, like the clucking of hens, or gabbling of turkeys; and thus making a very strange confused noise, when they walk here or there: if there be two, or three, or five, or ten, or twenty, or very many more in company, it is their manner to walk in rank one after the other, in small paths they have made by their thus walking; as kine in summer many times do, when they come home to the pale. . . . Their habits are their sheeps-skins undressed, thonged together, which cover their bodies to the middle, with a little flap of the same skin tied before them, being naked downward. . . .Their ornaments and jewels, bullocks, or sheeps-guts full of excrement, about their necks; and therefore when we bought their cattle, they would take (and we were content they should) their skins, guts, and garbage, which plentifully furnished them with that rich attire, and gay ornaments; and when they were hungry, they would sit down upon some hillock, first shaking out some of that filthy pudding out of the guts they wore about their necks, then bowing and bringing their mouths to their hands, almost as low as their knees, like hungry dogs would gnaw, and eat the raw guts. . . . The women as the men are thus adorned, thus habited, and thus dieted, only they wear more about their lower parts than the men. And . . . these carry their sucking infants under their skins upon their backs, and their breasts hanging down like bag-pipes, they put up with their hands to their children, that they may suck them over their shoulders.[119] Both sexes make coverings for their heads like to skull-caps, with cow-dung, and such-like filth, mingled with a little stinking grease, with which they likewise besmear their faces, which makes their company unsufferable, if they get the wind of you. I observed, that some of the rest of their diet was agreeable to the former; for they would eat any refuse thing, as rotten and moldy biscuits, which we have given them, fit indeed for nothing but to be cast away; yea, they will eat that which a ravenous dog in England will refuse . . . which makes me almost to believe, that those wretched creatures have but three senses, wanting the benefit both of smelling and tasting. They lodge upon the earth in hovels, so ill-covered that they keep not out the weather, made like to those we call summer-houses, with boughs and sticks. . . .

Methinks when I have seriously considered the dresses, habitations and the diet of this people, with other things, and how these beasts of mankind live all like brutes, nay worse, I have thought that if they had the accommodations we enjoy (to make our lives more comfortable) by good dwelling, warm clothing, sweet lodging, and wholesome food, they would be abundantly pleased with such a change of their condition. . . .

But I shall here insert a short story: . . . [one of these natives] was brought to London, and there kept for the space of six months in Sir Thomas Smith's house (then Governor of the East-India Company), where he had good diet, good clothes, good lodging, with all other fitting accommodations; now one would think that this wretch might have conceived his present, compared

---

[119] African women's ability to suckle children over their shoulder, a supposed indication of their distinct ability to both labor and nurture future laborers, is likewise attributed in Bulwer to Native American, Irish, and South Pacific Islands women. Related to this is the tendency to describe the childbirth of African and Native American women as relatively easy, as in De Marees, Jobson, Strachey, Sandys, Wood, and Ligon.

with his former condition, an heaven upon earth; but he did not so, . . . for
never any seemed to be more weary of ill usage, than he was of courtesies;
none ever more desirous to return home to his country than he: For when
he had learned a little of our language, he would daily lie upon the ground,
and cry very often thus in broken English, *Cooree home go, Souldaniago, home
go;* And not long after, when he had his desire, and was returned home, he
had no sooner set footing on his own shore, but presently he threw away his
clothes, his linen, with all other covering, and got his sheeps skins upon his
back, guts about his neck, and such a perfumed cap (as before we named)
upon his head; by whom that Proverb mentioned, 2 Pet 2. 22 was literally
fulfill'd, *Canis ad vomitum;* The dog is return'd to his vomit, and the swine
to his wallowing in the mire. . . .

   'Tis most strange that a creature who hath any thing of reason in him should
thus degenerate . . . but it is most true in these, as of millions more of brutish
heathens in the world, who live as if they had nothing of man left in them.

   After this fellow was returned, it made the natives most shy of us when
we arrived there . . . fearing belike we would have dealt with some more of
them, as formerly we had with Cooree. . . . It was here that I asked Cooree
who was their God? He lifting up his hands answered thus, in his bad English,
England God, great God, Souldania no God.

Section 5: Of the Inhabitants of East-India

The inhabitants in general of Indostan were all anciently gentiles, called in
general Hindoos, belonging to that very great number of those which are
called heathens, which take up almost two thirds of the number of the people
who inhabit the face of the whole Earth. . . .

   For the stature of the natives of East-India, they are like us, but generally
very straight; for I never observed nor heard of any crooked person amongst
them. . . .

   Now for the complexion of this people, they are all of them of a sad tawny
or olive-colour; their hair black as a raven, very harsh, but not curl'd. They
like not a man or woman that is very white or fair, because that (as they say)
is the colour of lepers, common amongst them. . . . The people there often
wash their bodies, and keep their feet as clean and as sweet as their hands.
The better sort annoint themselves very much with sweet oils, which makes
their company . . . very savoury.

   The natives there . . . show very much ingenuity in their curious manufac-
tures; as in their silk-stuffs which they most artificially weave, some of them
very neatly mingled either with silver or gold, or both. As also in making
excellent quilts of their stained cloth, or of fresh coloured taffeta lined with
their pintadoet, or of their satin lined with taffeta, betwixt which they put
cotton-wool, and work them together with silk.[120] . . . They make likewise

[120] Pintadoet = Probably a version of "pintado," which referred to Eastern printed cloths,
such as chintz.

excellent carpets of their cotton-wool, in fine mingled colours, some of them more than three yards broad, and of a great length. . . .

They are excellent at limning, and will copy out any picture they see to the life. . . . The truth is, that the natives of that monarchy are the best apes for imitation in the world, so full of ingenuity that they will make any new thing by pattern, how hard soever it seem to be done; and therefore it is no marvel, if the natives there make shoes, and boots, and clothes, and linen, and bands and cuffs of our English fashion, which are all of them very much different from their fashions and habits, and yet make them all exceeding neatly. . . .

Section 7

[T]he Mogol is a master of unknown treasure, having silver, as 'tis written of Solomon, 1 Kings 10. 27, like stones in the streets. And certainly in far greater abundance than ever Solomon had. . . . Now he that can command what treasure he will, may likewise command what men he please, as the Mogol doth besides his own people. . . .

Yet, however the people here in general are cowardly, they appear men of very terrible aspects, having great long mustachios upon their upper lips, their chins continually kept bare by the razor, which makes them all to look like the pictures of our old Britains; or like those our rude painters daub upon clothes, and call them the Nine-Worthies.[121] And further, to make them the more formidable, they will appear on horse-back as if they were surrounded with an armory, or carrying an whole armory about them, thus appointed; . . . For they dare not look a man of courage in the face, though they be thus fortified with such variety of weapons for their defence. Nay, a man of resolution will beat one of these out of all his weapons, with a small stick or cane. So that I shall do the natives of that country no wrong, if I say of them, that they are *sola libidine fortes*, most strong and valiant in their base lusts, and not otherwise.

The base cowardice of which people hath made the great Mogol sometimes to use this proverb, that one Portugal would beat three of his people; and (because the English there have prevailed at sea against those Portugals) he would further add, that one Englishman would beat three Portugals.

The truth is that the Portugals, especially those which are born in those Indian colonies, most of them a mixed seed begotten upon those natives, are a very low, poor-spirited people, called therfore *galijnes deli mar*, the hens of the sea.

Section 30

. . . When I lived in those parts it was my earnest desire and daily prayer, to have put my weak hands unto that most acceptable, but hard labour of

---

[121] Devised by the fourteenth-century French author Jean de Longuyon, the Nine Worthies were a set of champions including three pagans and three Christians who were supposed to embody the height of chivalry.

washing Moors, that the name of Jesus Christ might have been there enlarged (if God had pleased to honour me so far) by my endeavours. But there are three main and apparent obstacles . . . that hinder the settlement and growth of Christianity in those parts. First, the liberty of the Mahometan religion given the people there in case of marriage. Secondly, the most debauched lives of many coming thither, or living amongst them who profess themselves Christians . . . by whom the Gospel of Jesus Christ is scandalized, and exceedingly suffers. And lastly, the hearts of that people are so confirmed and hardened in their own evil old ways, their ears so sealed up, their eyes so blinded with unbelief and darkness . . .

RICHARD LIGON (fl. 1647–50)

A true & exact history of the island of Barbados (London: Peter Parker, 1657), 12–13, 15–16, 46–47, 50–51, 53–55.

A royalist who lost his fortune in the Civil War, Ligon fled in 1647 to Barbados, where he lived for three years, before falling sick and returning to England. Ligon's interest in the religion of African slaves looks forward to the argument of Morgan Godwyn (also in this volume) for the conversion of slaves, while his account of the Indian "Yarico" was Steele's source for his tale of "Inkle and Yarico" in *The Spectator*. Variously reimagined and even re-raced (sometimes Indian, sometimes African), Yarico and her lover, the Englishman Inkle, were the subject of several romances.

Keywords: Black Beauty—Slavery—Native Bodies—Nakedness and Clothing—Easy Childbirth—Negroes compared to Native Americans—Interracial Romance—Conversion

[On St. Iago, Cape Verde Islands]

Dinner being ended, and the [Portuguese] Padre so well near weary of his waiting, we rose, and made room for better company; for now the Padre, and his black mistress were to take their turns. A Negro of the greatest beauty and majesty together that ever I saw in one woman. . . . In her ears she wore large pendants, about her neck; and on her arms fair pearls. But her eyes were her richest jewels, for they were the largest and most oriental that I have ever seen.

. . . Yet a word or two would not be amiss to express the difference between these [women of the Cape Verde Islands] and those of high Africa as of Morocco, Guinea, Benin, Cacheu, Angola, Ethiopia, and Mauritania, or those that dwell near the River of Gambia, who are thick lipped, short nosed, and commonly [with] low foreheads. But these are composed of such features as would mar the judgment of the best painters to undertake to mend. Wanton as the soil that bred them, sweet as the fruits they fed on, for being come so near as their motions, and graces might perfectly be discerned, I guessed that nature could not, without help of art, frame such accomplished beauties not only of colours, and favour, but of motion too, which is the highest part of beauty.

[In Barbados]

When [Negro slaves] are brought to us, the planters buy them out of the ship, where they find them stark naked, and therefore cannot be deceived in any outward infirmity. They choose them as they do horses in a market; the strongest, youthfullest, and most beautiful yield the greatest prices. Thirty pound sterling is a price for the best man Negro; and twenty-five, twenty-six, or twenty-seven pounds for a woman; the children are at easier rates. And we buy them so, as the sexes may be equal, for if they have more men than women, the men who are unmarried will come to their masters and complain that they cannot live without wives. And he tells them that the next ship that comes he will buy them wives, which satisfies them for the present. And so they expect the good time, which the master performing with them, the bravest fellow is to choose first, and so in order, as they are in place, and every one of them knows his better, and gives him the precedence, as cows do one another, in passing through a narrow gate, for the most of them are as near beasts as may be, setting their souls aside. Religion they know none, yet most of them acknowledge a God, as appears by their motions and gestures. . . . Chaste they are as any people under the sun, for when the men and women are together naked, they never cast their eyes towards the parts that ought to be covered; and those amongst us that have breeches and petticoats, I never saw so much as kiss or embrace, or a wanton glance with their eyes between them.

[The author is asked by a slave if "he might be made a Christian"]

I promised to do my best endeavor, and when I came home, spoke to the master of the plantation and told him that poor Sambo desired much to be a Christian. But his answer was that the people of that island were governed by the laws of England, and by those laws we could not make a Christian a slave. I told him my request was far different from that, for I desired him to make a slave a Christian. His answer was that it was true, there was a difference in that, but, being once a Christian, he could no more account him a slave, and so lose the hold they had of them as slaves, by making them Christians; and by that means should open such a gap as all planters in the island would curse him. So I was struck mute, and poor Sambo kept out of the Church, as ingenious, as honest, and as good natured poor soul as ever wore black or eat green. . . .

I have been very strict in observing the shapes of these people; and for the men they are very well timbered, that is, broad between the shoulders, full breasted, well filleted, and clean legged, and may hold good with Albert Durer's rules, who allows twice the length of the head to the breadth of the shoulders, and twice the length of the face to the breadth of the hips, and according to this rule, these men are shaped.[122] But the women not. For the same great master of proportion allows to each woman twice the length of the face to the breadth of the shoulders, and twice the length of her own head to the breadth of her hips. And in that these women are faulty. For I have seen very few of them whose hips have been broader than their shoulders, unless they have been very fat. The young maids have ordinarily very large breasts, which stand strutting out so hard and firm, as no leaping, jumping, or stirring will cause them to shake any more than the brawns of their arms. But when they come to be old, and have had five or six children, their breasts hang down below their navels, so that when they stoop at their common work of weeding, they hang almost down to the ground, that at a distance you would think they had six legs. And the reason of this is, they tie the clothes about their children's backs, which comes upon their breasts, which by pressing very hard, causes them to hang down to that length. Their children, when they are first born, have the palms of their hands and soles of their feet, of a whitish colour, and the sight of their eyes of a bluish colour, not unlike the eyes of a young kitling; but, as they grow older, they become black. . . .[123]

As for the Indians, we have but few, and those fetched from other countries, some from the neighboring islands, some from the main, which we make slaves. . . . They are very active men, and apt to learn anything sooner than the Negroes, and as different from them in shape almost as in colour, the men very broad shouldered, deep breasted, with large heads, and their faces almost three square, broad about the eyes and temples, and sharp at the chin, their skins some of them brown, some a bright bay. They are much craftier and subtler than the Negroes, and in their nature falser; but in their bodies more active. Their women have very small breasts, and have more of the shape of the European than the Negroes, their hair black and long, a great part whereof hangs down upon their backs as low as their haunches, with a large lock hanging over either breast, which seldom or never curls. Clothes they scorn to wear, especially if they be well shaped. . . . We had an Indian woman, a slave in the house, who was of excellent shape and colour, for it was a pure bright bay and small breasts with the nipples of porphyry colour. This woman would not be wooed by any means to wear clothes. She chanced to be with child by a Christian servant, and lodging in the Indian house, amongst other women, of her own country, where the Christian servants, both men and women came, and being very great, and that her time was come to be delivered, loath to fall in labor before the men, walked down to a wood, in which was a pond of

[122] Albrecht Durer (1471–1528), a German printmaker, painter, draughtsman, and writer, considered one of the greatest figures in Northern Renaissance art and especially known for his highly developed technique of wood-cutting.

[123] Kitling = The young of any animal; a cub, a whelp. A young cat, a kitten.

water, and there by the side of the pond, brought herself abed, and presently washing her child in some of the water of the pond, lap'd it up in such rags as she had begged of the Christians, and in three hours time came home, with her child in her arms, a lusty boy, frolic and lively.

This Indian dwelling near the sea-coast, upon the main, an English ship put in to a bay and sent some of her men ashore to try what victuals or water they could find, for in some distress they were. But the Indians perceiving them to go up so far into the country, as they were sure they could not make a safe retreat, intercepted them in their return and fell upon them, chasing them into a wood, and being dispersed there, some were taken, and some were killed, but a young man amongst them straggling from the rest was met by this Indian maid, who upon the first sight fell in love with him, and hid him close from her countrymen (the Indians) in a cave, and there fed him till they could safely go down to the shore where the ship lay at anchor, expecting the return of their friends. But at last seeing them upon the shore, [they] sent the long boat for them, took them aboard, and brought them away. But the youth, when he came ashore in the Barbados, forgot the kindness of the poor maid that had ventured her life for his liberty, and sold her for a slave, who was as free born as he. And so poor Yarico for her love, lost her liberty.

Miso-Spilus

A wonder of wonders: or, A metamorphosis of fair faces voluntarily transformed into foul visages. or, an invective against black-spotted faces (London: J.G., 1662), A2^v–A3^v, 1–3, 6, 14, 17–19.

No identity has been assigned to the pseudonym Miso-Spilus, Latin for "I hate spots (or deformities)." In the author's condemnation of paint and black patches, Miso-Spilus expands on John Bulwer's anxiety over the extent to which culture can penetrate the human anatomy, and joins authors like Thomas Tuke in seeing cosmetics as a sin against God. In addition to its likening of certain cosmetic fashions to crossbreeding, *A wonder of wonders* offers an extended gloss on the biblical Song of Songs.

Keywords: Cosmetics—Blackness and Beauty—Blood—Jacob and
Laban—Song of Songs

On Painted and Black-Spotted Faces

> . . . Your paint resembleth you to posts and signs,
> Under such visors thieves obscure their crimes.
> The breast-shop windows open, and patcht skin,
> Are signs hung out to sell the wares within.
> Your spots are Pluto's marks, who much do please
> To send such tokens to his friends as these;

> But none of the good shepherd's ear-mark this,
> This spot (sayeth he) none of my children is:
> If you be sheep at all, these speckling tricks,
> Like Jacob's ewes, show where you love to mix. . . .

Others on the Same

> . . . The white and red did Eve in Eden wear;
> But now (God's image lost) black fiends appear:
> Complexion speaks you mongrels, and your blood
> Part Europe, part America, mixt brood;
> From Britains and from Negroes sprung, your cheeks
> Display both colours, each their own there seeks. . . .

There is now of late in this brazen-fac'd age of ours, started up a foolish
and fantastical generation of young lasses (yea of some old crones also) who
having good complexions of their own, out of an apish humor of following all fashions (though never so ridiculous) without regard of their own
credit, or of the good advice or counsel of the most sober and discreet sort
of people, under pretence of making themselves more lovely than God hath
made them, foolishly blemish and deform their otherwise comely visages
with uncomely and loathsome black spots and patches. . . .

. . . But albeit that this kind of black-spotting and patching of faces be
not commendable, yet we must grant, that in some sort it may prove available and advantageous unto them, namely, that when they have a desire to
go unto any brothel-houses, or other infamous places, these antics may with
these disguised faces and disfigured favours more freely and securely prosti-
tute themselves and take their pleasure, unknown and undiscovered, desiring
perhaps that their names and qualities might for their reputation (though
it be little) be concealed. And this privilege also they may peradventure say,
jestingly, that they may enjoy hereafter, to wit, that when their appearance
shall be, after their life ended in another world, before their black prince
(being conscious to themselves that he is to be their sovereign, whom they
have chiefly obeyed in this world) they may be taken for his natural children,
they so much resembling him in their black hue, and thereby to their comfort may be the more favoured as the devil's darlings. . . .

[H]ear what the sacred scriptures write both concerning spots, as also
touching black colours and blackness. . . .

Cant. 1. 5, 6. *I am black, but comely.* Here the Church of Christ calls her
self black, not (as some may think) for any comeliness in that colour, for black
is there distinguished from comely in these very words, *I am black, but comely;*
but she calls herself black because she was brought into such a sorrowful
and doleful condition by the tribulations and afflictions she lay under by her
persecutors, who obscured and denigrated her glory and renown, and made
her as it were seem black and contemptible, . . . and therefore confessing her
deformity, signified by her black colour, she willeth her flock, 5. 6 not to look

upon her; *Look not upon me,* sayeth she, *because I am black,* meaning deformed outwardly (accounting external black a deformity) but internally comely. . . .

By these places of the holy Scriptures we may learn that black colours and blackness itself oft-times have been hideous signs and tokens of God's heavy displeasure, and therefore not always without exception are they generally to be approved or commended, nor fit in such respect to be imitated, but rather to be dreaded. . . . Yet I grant, that . . . all black colours in beasts, fowl, or other living creatures, being natural, are in their kinds commendable, being such as God hath ordained them; likewise the natural black complexions of Black-Moors is more respected by them than the white, for the abuse and not the good use of colours is condemned; for colours fitly applied is a grace, and unfitly applied turn to the disgrace of the subject unto which they are applied. . . .

But if there be no remedy but that they will still continue in their old courses, and sit in the seat of scorners, despising all good admonition, though for their own welfare, I shall not then endeavor to make a blackmoor white, but must leave them to the care and correction of the magistrate, who foreseeing the danger of the contagious infection of their disease . . . will speedily take such a course to reduce them to a conformity with civil people . . . which I conceive may properly be by way of indictment of high treason, for that they having not the fear of God before their eyes, but moved by the instigation of the Devil, did abuse, counterfeit, and deface God's image in their faces. . . .

ANONYMOUS

The Maidens complaint against coffee (London, J. Jones, 1663), 6.

The first coffee-house opened in London around 1652, and within a decade coffee was as popular as English ale. Pamphlets soon appeared translating Arabic testimonials to coffee's salubrious qualities and its popularity among the Turks. Yet in response to those publications lauding coffee for its stimulative qualities, other writers warned that the "Mahometan berry" had the power to disturb the mind and sought to associate coffee with renegadism, arguing that it was the devil's drink, proferred by the Turks to corrupt Christendom.

Keywords: Coffee—Sickness—Blackness

The Mountebank's Postscript to the Reader

> Reader, this drink called Coffee, it is good
> To dry the brains, and purify the blood.
> It cures the body of its health, no doubt
> The sight also, if that it put not out
> The eye, its full of gravel, and there's none
> That use it, but may soon obtain the stone,

The palsy, dropsy, gout, fever, and prisick,[124]
So that in fine, they'll come to see me for physick.
It dries up moisture, shortens precious life,
And makes a man unkind unto his wife.
It makes a Christian blacker far within,
Than ever was the Negar's outward skin.
It's of a berry, men, this liquor make,
Which is transported from the Stygian lake,
Upon the banks of it these bushes grows,
The which the Stygian waters overflows,
(Like Nilus) and so nourished is the weed,
That now hath gained the name of coffee seed,
If it be not brought from Styx, no man can tell,
(It be so black) except it grew in Hell.

ROBERT BOYLE (1627–91)

Experiments and considerations touching colours
(London: Henry Herringman, 1664)

Source: Free online edition via http://www.gutenberg.org/files/14504/
14504-h/14504-h.htm.

The scientist and philosopher Robert Boyle invested in the East
India Company, the Hudson Bay Company, and the Turkey Company. Despite his life-long commitment to an empirical investiga-
tion of the natural world, Boyle's *Experiments and considerations
touching colours* is largely a compilation of various and sometimes
contradictory theories concerning the cause of blackness; although
Boyle cites recent dissections of bodies to discuss new ideas about
blackness, he also endorses many older notions, including that of
maternal impression.

Keywords: Blackness—Skin Color—Sunburn—Sons of Noah—
        Seminal Impression—Maternal Impression—Polygenesis—
        Crossbreeding

Experiment 11

The cause of the blackness of those many nations, which by one common
name we are wont to call Negroes, has been long since disputed of by
learned men, who possibly had not done amiss, if they had also taken into
consideration, why some whole races of other animals besides men, as foxes
and hares, are distinguished by a blackness not familiar to the generality of

---

[124] Prisick = Likely a misspelling of "phtisic," a common early modern term for a consump-
tive cough.

animals of the same species. . . . It is commonly presumed that the heat of
the climate wherein they live is the reason why so many inhabitants of the
scorching regions of Africa are black; and there is this familiar observation
to countenance this conjecture, that we plainly see that mowers, reapers,
and other country-people, who spend the most part of the hot summer days
exposed to the Sun have the skin of their hands and faces, which are the parts
immediately exposed to the Sun and air, made of a darker colour than before,
and consequently tending to blackness; and contrariwise we observe that the
Danes and some other people that inhabit cold climates, and even the English
who feel not so rigorous a cold, have usually whiter faces than the Spaniards,
Portuguese and other European inhabitants of hotter climates. But this argument I take to be far more specious than convincing; for though the heat of
the Sun may darken the colour of the skin, by that operation, which we in
English call sun-burning, yet experience doth not evince, that I remember,
that that heat alone can produce a discolouring that shall amount to a true
blackness, like that of Negroes, and we shall see by and by that even the
children of some Negroes not yet 10 days old (perhaps not so much by three
quarters of that time) will notwithstanding their infancy be of the same hue
with their parents. Besides, there is this strong argument to be alleged against
the vulgar opinion, that in diverse places in Asia under the same parallel, or
even of the same degree of latitude with the African regions inhabited by
blacks, the people are at most but tawny; and in Africa itself diverse nations
in the Empire of Ethiopia are not Negroes, though situated in the Torrid
Zone, and as near the Æquinoctial, as other nations that are so. . . . Moreover . . . I find not by the best navigators and travellers to the West-Indies,
whose books or themselves I have consulted on this subject, that excepting
perhaps one place or two of small extent, there are [not] any blacks originally
natives of any part of America (for the blacks now there have been by the
Europeans long transplanted thither) though the New World contain in it so
great a variety of climates, and particularly reach quite cross the Torrid Zone
from one tropic to another. . . . But if the case were the same with men, and
those other kinds of animals I formerly named, I should offer something as
a considerable proof that cold may do much towards the making men white
or black, and however I shall let down the observation as I have met with it,
as worthy to come into the history of whiteness and blackness, and it is, that
in some parts of Russia and of Livonia it is affirmed by Olaus Magnus and
others, that hares and foxes . . . which before were black, or red, or gray, do
in the depth of winter become white by reason of the great cold; (for that it
should be, as some conceive, by looking upon the snow, seems improbable
upon diverse accounts). . . .

There is another opinion concerning the complexion of Negroes, that is
not only embraced by many of the more vulgar writers, but likewise by that
ingenious traveler Mr. Sandys, and by a late most learned critic, besides other
men of note, and these would have the blackness of Negroes an effect of
Noah's curse, ratified by God's, upon Cham; but though I think that even a
naturalist may without disparagement believe all the miracles attested by the

holy scriptures, yet in this case to fly to a supernatural cause, will, I fear, look like shifting off the difficulty, instead of resolving it; for we enquire not the first and universal, but the proper, immediate, and physical cause of the jetty colour of Negroes. And not only we do not find expressed in the scripture, that the curse meant by Noah to Cham, was the blackness of his posterity, but we do find plainly enough there that the curse was quite another thing, namely that he should be a servant of servants. . . . Nor is it evident that blackness is a curse, for navigators tell us of black nations, who think so much otherwise of their own condition, that they paint the devil white. Nor is blackness inconsistent with beauty, which even to our European eyes consists not so much in colour, as an advantageous stature, a comely symmetry of the parts of the body, and good features in the face. So that I see not why blackness should be thought such a curse to the Negroes, unless perhaps it be, that being wont to go naked in those hot climates, the colour of their skin does probably, according to the doctrine above delivered, make the Sun-beams more scorching to them, than they would prove to a people of a white complexion.

Greater probability there is that the principal cause (for I would not exclude all concurrent ones) of the blackness of Negroes is some peculiar and seminal impression, for not only we see that blackamoor boys brought over into these colder climates lose not their colour, but good authors inform us that the off-spring of Negroes transplanted out of Africa, above a hundred years ago, retain still the complexion of their progenitors, though possibly in tract of time it will decay. As on the other side, the white people removing into very hot climates, have their skins by the heat of the Sun scorched into dark colours; yet neither they, nor their children have been observed, even in the countries of Negroes, to descend to a colour amounting to that of the natives; whereas I remember I have read in Piso's excellent account of Brazil, that betwixt the Americans and Negroes are generated a distinct sort of men, which they call Cabocles, and betwixt Portuguese and Æthiopian women, he tells us, he has sometimes seen twins, whereof one had a white skin, the other a black; not to mention here some other instances he gives, that the productions of the mixtures of differing people, that is (indeed), the effects of seminal impressions which they consequently argue to have been their causes; and we shall not much scruple at this, if we consider, that even organical parts may receive great differences from such peculiar impressions, upon what account soever they came to be settled in the first individual persons, from whom they are propagated to posterity, as we see in the blobber-lips and flat-noses of most nations of Negroes.[125] And if we may credit what learned men deliver concerning the little feet of the Chinese, the Macrocephali taken notice of by Hippocrates will not be the only instance we might apply to our present purpose. . . . And this recalls into my memory

---

[125] Cabocle = Perhaps a variant of Caboclo, a civilized Amerindian descended from aboriginals of Brazil. Also applied to others of mixed Indian and Negro or Indian and white parentage. Gulielmus Piso, was physician to the Dutch settlement in Brazil from 1633–44 and wrote *De Medicina Brasiliensis Libri Quatuor* (Leiden, 1648).

what a very ingenious physician has diverse times related to me of a young lady, to whom being called, he found that though she much complained of want of health, . . . that scrupling to give her physic, he persuaded her friends rather to divert her mind by little journeys of pleasure, in one of which going to visit St. Winifred's well, this lady, who was a Catholic, and devout in her religion, and a pretty while in the water to perform some devotions, and had occasion to fix her eyes very attentively upon the red pipple-stones, which in a scattered order made up a good part of those that appeared through the water, and a while after growing big, she was delivered of a child whose white skin was copiously speckled with spots of the colour and bigness of those stones, and though now this child have already lived several years, yet she still retains them. I have but two things to add concerning the blackness of Negroes, the one is that the seat of that colour seems to be but the thin epidermis, or outward skin, for I knew a young Negroe who having been lightly sick of the small pox or measles, . . . I found by enquiry of a person that was concerned for him, that in those places where the little tumors had broke their passage through the skin, when they were gone, they left within specks behind them. And the lately commended Piso assures us, that having the opportunity in Brazil to dissect many Negroes, he clearly found that their blackness went no deeper than the very outward skin, which cuticula or epidermis being removed, the undermost skin or cutis appeared just as white as that of European bodies. And the like has been affirmed to me by a physician of our own, whom, hearing he had dissected a Negroe here in England, I consulted about this particular. The other thing to be here taken notice of concerning Negroes is that having enquired of an intelligent acquaintance of mine (who keeps in the Indies about 300 of them as well women as men to work in his plantations,) whether their children come black into the world, he answered, that they did not, but were brought forth of almost the like reddish colour with our European children; and having further enquired, how long it was before these infants appeared black, he replied, that 'twas not wont to be many days. . . . But more pregnant is the testimony of our country-man Andrew Battel, who being sent prisoner by the Portuguese to Angola, lived there, and in the adjoining regions, partly as a prisoner, partly as a pilot, and partly as a soldier, near 18 years, and he mentioning the African Kingdom of Longo, peopled with blacks, has this passage: "The children in this country are born white, and change their colour in two days to a perfect black. As for example, the Portuguese which dwell in the Kingdome of Longo have sometimes children by the Negroe-women, and many times the fathers are deceived, thinking, when the child is born, that it is theirs, and within two days it proves the son or daughter of a Negroe, which the Portuguese greatly grieve at." And the same person has elsewhere a relation, which . . . shows a possibility that a race of Negroes might be begun, though none of the sons of Adam, for many precedent generations were of that complexion. For I see not why it should not be at least as possible that white parents may sometimes have black children, as that African Negroes should sometimes have lastingly white ones, especially since concurrent causes may easily more befriend the productions of the former kind, than under the scorching heat of Africa those of the latter. . . . But let us hear our author himself: "Here are . . . born in this country white children, which is very rare among them, for their parents are Negroes; And when any of them are born, they are presented to the king, and are called dondos; these are as white as any white men. These are the king's witches, and are brought up in witchcraft, and always wait on the king. There is no man that dare meddle with these dondos, if they go to the market they may take what they list, for all men stand in awe of them. The King of Longo hath four of them." And yet this country in our globes is placed almost in the midst of the Torrid Zone (four or five degrees southward of the line).

JANE SHARP (fl. 1671)

The midwives book, or The whole art of midwifry discovered
(London: Simon Miller, 1671), 44–45.

Sharp's is the first book of midwivery written by an English woman. It draws on her thirty-year experience as a midwife and eschews Latin anatomical language. Her efforts to legitimate English midwives and challenge male-dominated medical knowledge (and particularly men's disgust concerning female genitalia) can, as in the passage included here, result in a tendency to displace onto foreign women physical anomalies and non-normative sexual behaviors.

Keywords: Hermaphrodites—Clitoris—Indies—Egypt

. . . Some think that hermaphrodites are only women that have their clitoris greater, and hanging out more than others have, and so show like a man's yard, and it is so called, for it is a small exuberation in the upper, forward, and middle part of the share, in the top of the greater slit where the wings end. It differs from the yard in length, the common pipe, and the want of one pair of the muscles which the yard hath, but is the same in place and substance . . . and it will swell and stand stiff if it be provoked, and some lewd women have endeavoured to use it as men do theirs. In the Indies and Egypt they are frequent, but I never heard of one in this country, if there be any they will do what they can for shame to keep it close.

WILLIAM HUGHES (fl. 1665–83)

The American physician, . . . whereunto is added a discourse of the cacao-nut-tree and the use of its fruit, with all the ways of making of chocolate
(London: Printed by J.C. for William Crook, 1672), 109.

This is one of the first English books on the horticulture of the New World. It includes ways of making chocolate, the planting and harvesting of the plant, and "the virtues of the drink called chocolate." Along with coffee, tea, tobacco, and sugar, chocolate was a lightweight, high-value commodity. Hughes joins authors like Brathwaite and Miso-Spilus in worrying over degeneracy resulting from the consumption of foreign goods.

Keywords: Chocolate—Complexion—Degeneracy

These [Jamaican] cacaos, when they be well cured, are bitterish in taste, and are also fat or oily; and in quality moderately cold and dry, as some think; because, say they, the Indian women and others coming thither, and eating them dry, without either grinding or beating, or any other alteration, they then prove to be of an astringent nature, causing obstructions; and thereby those women (say they) become leucophlegmatical, and look of a whitish colour. But in this I conceive there is a great mistake; for it is natural to those regions (by reason of heat) for all women (how ruddy soever they are when they first come there) to alter their complexions, and in short time become pale or yellowish: and doubtless women in England might eat a long time of these cacaos before they would find any alterations or change thereby in themselves.

ANONYMOUS

A broad-side against coffee, or, The marriage of the Turk
(London: John Hancock, 1672), 58–59.

As coffee-houses grew popular, authors attacked the "Maho-metan berry" as endangering good health and warned against the cultural and economic consequences of coffee consumption. To drink coffee was seen an act of apostasy, traitorous to English brewers and tavern-keepers, and a sign of the English vulnerability indicated elsewhere in this volume. Here coffee is compared to Othello, who will overcome and destroy English water.

Keywords: Coffee—Interracial Romance—Skin Color—Slavery—
    Englishness—Othello

Coffee, a kind of Turkish renegade,
Has late a match with Christian water made;
At first between them happen'd a demur,
Yet joined they were, but not without great stir.
For both so cold were, and so saintly meet,
The Turkey Hymen in his turban sweet.
Coffee was cold as Earth, water as Thames,
And stood in need of recommending flames.
For each of them steers a contrary course,
And of themselves they sue of a divorce.
Coffee so brown as berry does appear,
Too swarthy for a nymph so fair, so clear:
And yet his sails he did for England hoist,

Though cold and dry, to court the cold and moist.
If there be ought we can, as love admit;
'Tis a hot love, and lasteth but a fit.
For this indeed the cause is of their stay,
Newcastles's bowels warmer are than they.
The melting nymph distills herself to do't,
Whilst the slave Coffee must be beaten to't;
Incorporate him close as close may be,
Pause but a while, and he is none of he;
Which for a truth, and not a story tells,
No faith is to be kept with infidels.
Sure he suspects, and shuns her as a whore,
And loves, and kills, like the Venetian Moor;
Bold Asian brat! With speed our confines flee;
Water, though common, is too good for thee.
Sure Coffee's vext he has the breeches lost,
For she's above, and he liest undermost;
What shall I add but this? (and sure 'tis right)
The groom is heavy, cause the bride is light.
This canting Coffee has his crew enriched,
And both the water and the men bewitched.

SIR MATTHEW HALE (1609–76)

The primitive origination of mankind (London: William Bodbid, 1677), 182–85, 189, 196–97.

Matthew Hale became Chief Justice of the King's Bench in 1671. Best known as an authority on English criminal law, Hale was also the author of several religious treatises, including *The primitive origination of mankind* (1677). While arguing for the creation of the human race by an intelligent agent, Hale here takes issue with the polygenetic arguments of Isaac de la Peyrère while himself speculating about the origins of Native Americans.

Keywords: Native Americans—Polygenesis—Migration—Degeneracy

The late discovery of the vast continent of America and islands adjacent, which appears to be as populous with men, and as well stored with cattle almost as any part of Europe, Asia, or Africa, hath occasioned some difficulty and dispute touching the traduction of all mankind from the two common parents supposed of all mankind, namely Adam and Eve; but principally concerning the storing of the world with men and cattle from those that the sacred history tells us were preserved in the ark. And the objection runs thus:

It seems . . . that the whole continent of America and the adjacent isles thereof are no way contiguous to any parts of Asia, Europe, or Africa, but disjointed from the same by huge and vast oceans. . . .

The inhabitants of this continent as they greatly differ among themselves, so they extremely differ from the Asiaticks, Europeans, and Africans in their language and customs, they recognize no original from these parts. . . .

And upon these premises, they thus argue:

That since by all circumstances it is apparent that America hath been very long inhabited, and possibly as long as any other continent in the world, and since it is of all hands agreed that the supposed common parents of the rest of mankind, Adam, Noah and his three sons, had their habitations in some parts of Asia, and since we have no probable evidence that any of their descendents traduced the first colonies of the American plantations into America, being so divided from the rest of the world, the access thither so difficult, and navigation the only means of such a migration being of a far later perfection than what could answer such a population of so great a continent; that consequently the Americans derive not their original either from Adam, or at least not from Noah; but either had an eternal succession, or if they had a beginning, they were aborigines, and multiplied from other common stocks than what the Mosaical history imports. . . .

The author of the book called *Preadamitæ* hath set down certain supposi- tions, which though they salve the difficulties, yet they cross the tenor of the Mosaical history, viz.[126]

1. That Moses in the history of the creation of man doth not set down the original of mankind, but only the original or common parent of the Jewish nation: that Adam was not the first man that was created, but there were many ages of men before him that peopled the greater part of the world long before the creation of Adam. And consequently, though Adam was the common parent of the inhabitants of Palestine and many of the countries adjacent, yet those that peopled the far greater part of the world, especially the parts of America, were not descended from him.

2. That the flood in Noah's time, though it drowned the descendents from Adam and the countries inhabited by them, namely, Palestine and some of the adjacent countries, yet it was no universal deluge, but the far greater part of the world and the inhabitants thereof were free from that deluge. . . . And in favor of his opinion allegeth the long computations of the Egyptians, Babylonians, and Chineses; the vast armies of Ninus, Semiramis, Zoroaster, and others, and the great extent of their monarchies suddenly after the flood, which could not, as he supposeth, be so suddenly propagated from Noah and his three sons. But especially insists upon the greatness of the continent of America and the islands thereof, the populousness and great store of men and animals, which could not be in any tolerable probability transported from countries divided by such great seas from it. . . .

I shall not in this place undertake a particular answer of all that this man said, it is besides my intention in this place to make so large an excursion,

---

[126] Hale refers here and responds throughout to the controversial work of the French mil- lenarian Isaac de La Peyrère, published first in Latin in 1655 and translated into English a year later as *Men before Adam.*

and many others have done it to my hand. Only I may say thus much, that
a man that gives so much credit to the Egyptian, Chaldean, and Grecian
prodigious traditions, in derogation of that very scripture which this man
in complement at least seems to venerate, might have remembered that the
tradition of the universal flood hath obtained in all places, even among the
Americans themselves. . . .

The means of transmigration of the children or descendents of Adam and
Noah from Asia into America must be either by land or by sea, or by both. . . .

Upon these and the like probabilities it may seem reasonable to conclude,
1. That the Americans had their original from the inhabitants of Europe,
Asia, and Africa, that transmigrated into that continent either intentionally,
or casually, or both. 2. That those migrations were not of any one single
nation or people, but from many or diverse nations. 3. That these migrations were not altogether at one time, but successively in several ages, some
earlier, some later. 4. That therefore it is impossible to determine the time or
first epochs of such migrations but only that they were all since the universal
deluge, which is now above 4000 years since. . . . 5. That if we should admit
that the first migration thither were above 2000 years since, of an hundred
pairs they might easily propagate a number competent enough to people all
that vast continent. 6. That it seems that since the last of these ancient migrations, supposed that of Madoc and his Britons, until our late migrations by
the Spaniards, French, English, Dutch, and Scots, there probably interceded
an interval of at least four or five hundred years, in all which interval the
commerce and communication between Europe or Asia, and America, hath
as it were slept, and been forgotten both by them and us.[127] 7. That in the
interval of 500 years or thereabouts in all parts, but in some parts far greater,
there must in all probability happen a great forgetfulness of their original, a
great degeneration from the primitive civility, religion, and customs of those
places from whence they were first derived; a ferine and incestuous kind of
life, a conversation with those that having been long there were fallen into
a more barbarous habit of life and manners, would easily assimilate at least
the next generation to barbarism and fereneness. It is true, where a colony
comes and keeps it self in a body, as the Roman colonies anciently, and our
plantations in Virginia and New England do, and the new accessions incorporate and join themselves unto that body, customs, both religious and civil,
and the original language are kept entire. But where the accessions are but
thin and sparing, and scattered among the natives of the country where they
come, and are driven to conform themselves unto their customs for their
very subsistence, safety, and entertainment, it falls out that the very first
planters do degenerate in their habits, customs, and religion, as a little wine

---

[127] Madoc ap Owain Gwynedd was a twelfth-century Welsh prince who, according to
legend, led a group of Welshmen to the Americas where they integrated with a tribe of natives
known as the Mandans. The first written account of Madoc's story is in George Peckham's
A true reporte of the late discoveries . . . of the new-found landes (1583), and it later appeared
in Richard Hakluyt's *The Principall Navigations, Voyages and Discoveries of the English Nation*
(1589), propping up the notion of a long history of British voyaging.

poured into a great vessel of water loseth it self. But if they escape a total assimilation to the country where they thus are mingled, yet the next generation in such a mixture is quickly assimilated to the corrupt manners and customs of the people among whom they are thus planted. . . .

MORGAN GODWYN (1640–ca. 1686)

The Negro's & Indian's advocate, suing for their admission into the church, or, A persuasive to the instructing and baptizing of the Negro's and Indians in our plantations
(London: J.D, 1680), 9, 12–15, 20–23, 35–36, 142, 155.

The Anglican clergyman and missionary Morgan Godwyn provoked controversy in Virginia by preaching that planters should promote the spiritual welfare of their slaves by converting them to Christianity. He was obliged to flee to Barbados, where he faced similar resistance. There he began composing the works that would later inspire the formation, in 1701, of the Society for the Propagation of the Gospel in Foreign Parts: *The Negro's & Indian's advocate* (1680), *A supplement to the Negro's & Indian's advocate* (1681), and a sermon entitled *Trade preferr'd before religion* (1685).

Keywords: African Slaves—Native Americans—Conversion—
Slavery—Humanity—Intelligence of Slaves—Sons of
Noah—Skin Color—Blackness—Crossbreeding—Irish—
Slavery—Degeneracy

I betake myself to my first general assertion, which I shall divide into three propositions.

1. First, that naturally there is in every man an equal right to religion.
2. Secondly, that Negroes are men, and therefore are invested with that same right.
3. Thirdly, that being thus qualified and invested, to deprive them of this right is the highest injustice.

. . . And as to this, there wanting not irrational creatures, such as the ape and drill, that do carry with them some resemblances of men. The too frequent unnatural conjunctions (as Tavernier discourseth in his *Voyages*[128]) of some Africans with those creatures (though not so as to unpeople that

---

[128] John Baptiste Tavernier (1605–89), author of *Le Six Voyages de J. B. Tavernier* (Paris, 1676), traveled across Europe, to Constantinople, Persia, and Baghdad, among other places in the Levant, and, finally, to India.

great continent), giving occasion for such surmises as to some few there, though never of any that were brought hither, our factors being too worldly wise to commit such gross oversights in their civil affairs, whatever greater may escape them in the spiritual. And the Spaniards's question (which the same Tavernier also mentions) touching the brutality of the Americans, (and which I have heard was held in the affirmative in one of the universities of Spain) serving not a little to make my report more credible, and to acquit me of all fictitious romancing herein. Wherefore it being granted for possible that such wild opinions, by the inducement and instigation of our planters' chief deity, Profit, may have lodged themselves in the brains of some of us, I shall not fear to betake myself to the refuting of this one which I have spoken of. For the effecting of which, methinks, the consideration of the shape and figure of our Negroes' bodies, their limbs and members, their voice and countenance, in all things according with other men's, together with their risibility and discourse (man's peculiar faculties) should be a sufficient conviction. How should they otherwise be capable of trades, and other less manly employments, as also of reading and writing; or show so much discretion in management of business eminent in diverse of them; but wherein (we know) that many of our own people are deficient, were they not truly men? . . . Or why should their owners, men of reason not doubt, conceive them fit to exercise the place of governors and overseers to their fellow slaves, which is frequently done, if they were but mere brutes?

Their objections against this are poor and trivial. . . . The first whereof are certain impertinent and blasphemous distortions of scripture, out of which they would fain bribe four places, to wit, in *Genesis 1.27, 28* and *2.7*, and *4.15*, and lastly *9.25, 26* , to give in evidence for them. Now in the two first of these they strain hard to derive our Negroes from a stock different from Adam's, but by the third they bespeak them as descendants from Cain, and to carry his mark. And yet by the last, as if condemned to contradictions, they make them the posterity of that unhappy son of Noah, who, they say, was together with his whole family and race, cursed by his father. Of which curse 'tis worth the observing what blessed use they to themselves do make, and what variety of advantages they thereby reap. For from thence, as occasion shall offer, they'll infer their Negro's brutality, justify their reduction of them under bondage, disable them from all rights and claims, even to religion itself, pronounce them reprobates, and upon a sudden (with greater speed and cunning than either the nimblest juggler or witch) transmute them into whatsoever substance the exigence of their wild reasonings shall drive them to. . . .

. . . Their specious reasons on which this pious belief is grounded, do seem to have been drawn from these four pretenses: the complexion, bondage, pretended stupidity, and barbarousness of our Negro's manners, because different from ours. Of the second of which they make this two-fold use, first to brutify them, and then, that proving defective, to deprive them of all both temporal and spiritual rights, which their manhood, notwithstanding their being slaves, would otherwise infer. . . .

I shall begin with the first, and that is their complexion, which being most obvious to the sight . . . is apt to make to slight impressions upon rude minds, already prepared to admit of anything for truth which shall make for interest, especially if supported with but the least shadow of argument. . . .

For it is well known that the Negroes in their native country, and perhaps here also, if they durst speak their inward sentiments, do entertain as high thoughts of themselves and of their complexion, as our Europeans do, and at the same time holding the contrary in equal disdain. . . . But the determination of this point will much depend upon the right understanding and knowledge of real beauty, a true standard thereof the nations have not yet pitched upon. That being deformity with others which amongst us is the only perfect and complete figure. . . . So that if the other part of the world should once come to agree upon 'tis particular, without consulting us here (which 'tis possible, whenever they go about it, they may omit), and like unto us, maliciously determine the matter in favor of themselves, and they only may be the men, and ourselves but beasts.

. . . [T]he largest proportion of people, perchance five out of six parts of the world, will, upon a due survey, be found of a more dull and sable complexion than the Europeans. . . . And those of our own nation, or our neighbors, who have betaken themselves to these hotter climes, do in a short time after their setting foot here, discover a very discernable alteration, not only from those at home, but from themselves also as to what they were at their first arrival. Whose offspring, after the succession of some few ages, may, (judging by what is already visible of many of them) become quite black, at least very dusky and brown, like our brindle mullatos and Indians. . . . Now if the like should happen here to our English offspring, we should one day have too much cause to repent of our large discoveries in these parts, which of men (by their being transplanted hither) must so inevitably make them degenerate into brutes.

This fiction of the brutality of the Negroes doth contradict that maxim in common observation concerning the non-generation of monsters, for these being no part of the first creation, did not obtain from God that blessing of being fruitful and multiplying, and of replenishing the earth (*Gen. 1. 28 & 8.17*) which other created animals then did. According to which our mulattos and mestizos (the production of Negro or Indian mixtures with other less swarthy people) would want this prolific faculty, and never be able to procreate their like, the contrary whereof is daily seen in this and in the other colonies. . . .

And though Ireland in times past . . . be reported to have been a place of learning . . . yet so much are they degenerated . . . that the natives of that kingdom, who have been imported hither, are observed to be, in diverse respects, more barbarous than the Negros. And this in its kind is so notorious in some of them, as to fall under even the Negro's observation; by whom this petulant taunt hath comptemptuously, and in reproach of their doltish stupidity, been returned upon them, viz. "That if the Irishman's country had first lighted in the Englishman's way, he might have gone no further to look for Negros." That is slaves, such as the Negros here generally are. (These two words, Negro and slave, being by custom grown homogeneous and convertible; even as Negro and Christian, Englishman and heathen, are by the like corrupt custom and partiality made opposites; thereby as it were implying that the one could not be Christians, nor the other infidels.) . . .

Bondage is not inconsistent with Christianity. . . . Some few of [our planters] being discoursed already into this acknowledgement, that in regard religion would be apt to create a conscience in their slaves, it might be convenient, in order to make them the truer servants.

FRANÇOIS BERNIER (1620–88)

"A New Division of the Earth, according to the Different Species or Races of Men who Inhabit It," *Journal des Scavans* 12 (1684), 148–55.[129]

Source: J.S. Slotkin, *Readings in Early Anthropology* (Chicago: Aldine Publishing Company, 1965), 94–95.

François Bernier traveled to Egypt and to India, where he served as physician to the Mughal Emperor Aurangzeb. Back in France, he published the very successful *Travels in Moghul India* and became part of a circle that included Racine and Boileau. Observations made during his residence in India laid the groundwork for his anonymous essay, excerpted below, in which can be found what is ostensibly the first use of the term "race" to classify peoples according to their physiognomy and skin color.

Keywords: Physiognomy—Humans as a Species—Skin Color

Geographers up to this time have only divided the earth according to its different countries or regions. The remarks which I have made upon men during all my long and numerous travels, have given me the idea of dividing it up in a different way. Although in the exterior form of their bodies, and especially of their faces, men are almost all different from one another, according to the different districts of the earth which they inhabit, so that those who have been great travelers are often never mistaken in distinguishing each nation in that way; still I have remarked that here are four or five species or races of men in particular whose difference is so remarkable that it may properly be used as the foundation for a new division of the earth. . . .

I comprehend under the first species France, Spain, England, Denmark, Sweden, Germany, Poland, and generally all Europe, except a part of

---

[129] The French title was "Nouvelle division de la terre, par les différentes espèces ou races d'hommes qui l'habitent." It was translated into English by T. Bendyshe (London, 1863–64).

Muscovy [Russia]. To this may be added a small part of Africa, that is, from the kingdoms of Fez, Morocco, Algiers, Tunis, and Tripoli up to the Nile; and also a good part of Asia, as the empire of the Grand Seignior [the Turkish sultan] with the three Arabias, the whole of Persia, the states of . . . [India], . . . [Southeast Asia] and . . .[Indonesia]. For although the Egyptians, for instance, and the Indians are very black, or rather copper-coloured, that colour is only an accident in them, and comes because they are constantly exposed to the sun; for those individuals who take care of themselves, and who are not obliged to expose themselves so often as the lower class, are not darker than many Spaniards. It is true that most Indians have something very different from us in the shape of their face, and in their colour which often comes very near to yellow; but that does not seem enough to make them a species apart, or else it would be necessary to make one of the Spaniards, another of the Germans, and so on with several other nations of Europe.

Under the second species I put the whole of Africa, except the coasts I have spoken of. What induces me to make a different species of the Africans, are, 1. . . . thick lips and squab noses . . .; 2. . . . blackness . . . which is not caused by the sun, as many think; for if a black African pair be transported to a cold country, their children are just as black, and so are all their descendants until they come to marry with white women. The cause must be sought for in the peculiar texture of their bodies, or in the seed, or in the blood–which last are, however, of the same colour as everywhere else; 3. Their skin [texture] . . . 4. . . . [lack] of beard.; 5. Their hair . . . ; and, finally, their teeth whiter than the finest ivory, their tongue and all the interior of their mouth and their lips as red as coral.

The third species comprehends a part of the kingdoms of Aracan and Siam, the islands of Sumatra and Borneo, the Philippines, Japan, . . . [Vietnam] . . . Georgia and Muscovy, . . . [Central Asia,] . . . a small part of Muscovy, the little Tartars and Turcomans who live along the Euphrates towards Aleppo. The people of all those countries are truly white; but they have broad shoulders, a flat face, a small squab nose, little pig's-eyes long and deep set, and three hairs of beard.

The Lapps make the fourth species. They are little stunted creatures with thick legs, large shoulders, short neck, and a face elongated immensely; very ugly and partaking much of the bear. I have only seen two of them at Danzig [Gdansk]; but, judging from the pictures I have seen, and the account which I have received of them from many persons who have been in the country, they are wretched animals.

As to the [Native] Americans, they are in truth most of them olive-coloured, and have their faces modeled in a different way from ours. Still I do not find the difference sufficiently great to make of them a peculiar species different from ours. Besides, as in our Europe, the stature, the turn of the face, the colour and the hair are generally very different, as we have said, so it is the same in other parts of the world; as for example, the blacks of the Cape of Good Hope (the Bushmen) seem to be of a different species to those from the rest of Africa. They are small, thin, dry, ugly, quick in running, passionately fond of carrion . . . and speaking a language altogether strange, and almost inimitable by Europeans. . . .

EDWARD TYSON (1650–1708)

Orang-outang, sive Homo sylvestris, or The anatomy of a pygmie compared with that of a monkey, an ape, and a man
(London: Thomas Bennet and Daniel Brown, 1699),
unsigned preface and 1–2, 91.

A member of the Royal Society, Tyson was a physician best remembered as a pioneer of comparative anatomy. His first major publication, *Phocaena, or, The anatomy of a porpess dissected at Gresham College* (1680), looked at the porpoise as a transitional structure between fish and land animals, and stressed the importance of comparative anatomy for medicine. Drawing on the same methods, *Orang-outang* addresses the cadaver of a chimpanzee, which was alleged by some to be a pygmy.

Keywords: Comparative Anatomy—Chimpanzees—Pygmies—Africa

'Tis a true remark, which we cannot make without admiration, that from minerals to plants, from plants to animals, and from animals to men, the transition is so gradual that there appears a very great similitude, as well between the meanest plant and some minerals, as between the lowest rank of men, and the highest kind of animals. . . .

Figure 20 Comparative anatomies, from Edward Tyson, *Orang-outang, sive Homo sylvestris* (1699). Reproduced by permission of the University of Pittsburgh Health Sciences System, Falk Library of the Health Sciences.

That the pygmies of the ancients were a sort of ape, and not of human race, I shall endeavor to prove in the following essay. And if the pygmies were only apes, then in all probability our ape may be a pygmy; a sort of animal so much resembling man, that both the ancients and the moderns have reputed it to be a puny race of mankind, call'd to this day, *homo sylvestris*, the wild man, orang-outang, or a man of the woods. . . .

What I shall most of all aim at in the following discourse will be to give as particular an account as I can of the formation and structure of all the parts of this wonderful animal; and to make a comparative survey of them with the same parts in a human body, as likewise in the ape and monkey-kind. For tho' I own it to be of the ape kind, yet, as we shall observe, in the organization of abundance of its parts, it more approaches to the structure of the same in men. But where it differs from a man, there it resembles plainly the common ape, more than any other animal. . . .

Now notwithstanding our pygmy does so much resemble a man in many of its parts, more than any of the ape-kind, nor any other animal in the world that I know of, yet by no means do I look upon it as the product of a mixt generation; 'tis a brute-animal *sui generis*, and a particular species of ape. For when I was dissecting it, some sea-captains and merchants who came to my house to see it assured me that they had seen a great many of them in Borneo, Sumatra, and other parts, tho' this was brought from Angola in Africa.

. . . Our pygmy is no man, nor yet the common ape; but a sort of animal between both; and tho' a biped, yet of the quadrumanus-kind, though some men too have been observed to use their feet like hands, as I have seen several.

APPENDIX: EARLY MODERN DICTIONARIES

John Palsgrave (d. 1554)

Lesclarissement de la Langue Francoyse (London?: Richard Pynson, 1530)

Colour for a horse, licol (m); colier (m)[1]

Colour, the complexion in a man, colere (f), cole (f)

Fayrnesse, beaulté, formosité, speciosité

Hethynesse, sarazinesme (f)

Infydele nat christened, payn (m)

Jue, a man of Jurye, Juif (m)

Rase as the rase of Bretayne, ras (m)

Tawyny colour, tanny (m)

Thomas Elyot (1490?–1546)

The Dictionary of Sir Thomas Elyot, Knight
(London: Thomae Bertheleti, 1538)

Apostata, a Rebel. It is now used for them, which do forsake the religion, that they have once received.

Barbari, in the old time were all people, except Greeks, properly it be they, which do speak grossly, without observing of congruity, or pronounce not perfectly, specially Greek or Latin. Also they that abhor all elegancy. Moreover it signifieth them, which be without letters, fierce or cruel, of manners or countenance, barbarous.

Barbaria, The country where dwelleth people rude or beastly.

---

[1] In this and several other dual-language dictionaries in this volume, gendered nouns and adjectives are noted as in the originals, with *m* denoting masculine and *f* feminine terms.

Converto, uerti, tere, to convert, or turn.

Ethnicus, a gentile.

Gens, gentis, a people, sometime a kindred.

Gentilis, a kinsman of the same name and stock. Sometimes it signifieth a gentile or paynyme, sometimes a country man.

Infidus, da, dum, unfaithful.

Infici, feci, ficere, to dye cloth, to stain or infect.

Morus, a mulberry tree, and a bramble that beareth black berries.

Natales, is taken for progeny or descent, or blood. *Generosi natales,* gentyl blood, *Obscuri natales,* a poor descent or low birth, sometime it is used for years.

Natio, a nation.

Niger, gra, grum, black, foul. Also it is sometime used for dead.

THOMAS COOPER (1517?–94)

Thesaurus Linguae Romanae et Brittannicae (London: Henry Wykes, 1565)

Apostata, A rebel or renegade: he that forsaketh his religion.

Barbarus, Barbarous, rude in doing or speaking: fierce: cruel: ignorant: rustical: churlish: without eloquence: uncivil. In old time all saving Greeks were called Barbari.

Color, huius, A. colour, the external face or beauty of a thing B. cloak or pretence.

Converto, convertis, conversum, convuertere, To return: to convert or turn: to change or transform: to translate.

Ethnicus, An ethnic: a gentile.

Genus, The beginning of one's birth, either at the person that begot him, or at the place, where he was engendered: a kindred: a stock: a lineage: a race: a parentage: Also a manner or fashion.

Generosus, Noble: coming of a noble race: a gentleman born: excellent: courageous: of a gentle and good kind.

Gentilis, & hoc gentile, Proper or familiar to that people or kindred: of the same name, ancestry, and stock.

Natio, nationis, A nation: a people having their beginning in the country where they dwell.

Nativus, natural: That is naturally engendered in a thing.

Nativus, color. Plin. A natural colour, as is black or white.

Niger, nigra, nigrum, Black, purple, dark.

THOMAS THOMAS (1533–88)

Dictionarium Linguae Latinae et Anglicanae (Cantibrigiae: John Legatt, 1587)

Apostasia, A rebellion, apostasy, a backsliding, a revolting: a forsaking or falling away from one's own religion, captain, allegiance, or purpose.

Barbare, Barbarously, unmannerly, grossly, rudely, strangely, without eloquence.

Niger, gra, gru, Black, purple, dark, shadowed with many trees. Also dead, hurtful, perilous, ill, naughty.

JOHN MINSHEU (1560–1627)

A Dictionary in Spanish and English (London: William Stansby and Melchisidec Bradwood, 1617)

Convertir, to turn, to convert, to alter, to translate.

Limpieza, cleanness, purity, neatness, fineness.

Mestizo, that which is come or sprung of a mixture of two kinds, as a black-Moore and a Christian, a mongrel dog or beast.

Mora, a Mulberry. Also a woman black-More.

Moro, a black Moore of Barbary, or a Negar that followeth the Turkish religion.

Morisco, a black Moore made or become a Christian.

Mulata, the daughter of a blackmoore, and one of another nation [also Mulato (m)]

Mular, pertaining to a mule.

Negro, black. Also a black Moore of Ethiopia.

Ráça, a ray or beam shining thorough a hole. Also a race, stock, kind, or breed.

ROBERT CAWDREY (1538–?)

A Table Alphabetical (London: I. Roberts, 1604)

Complexion, nature, constitution of the body

Converse, company with

Convert, turn, change

Ethnick, an heathen or gentile

Hebrew, from Heber's stock[2]

JOHN COWELL (1554–1611)

The Interpreter (Cambridge: John Legate, 1607)

Barbaries (*Oxycantha*) is a thorny shrub known to most men to bear a berry or fruit of a sharp taste. These berries (as also the leaves of said tree) be medicinable, as Gerard in his herbal showeth, Lib 3. Cap. 21. You find them mentioned among drugs to be garbled, anno I. Jacob. Cap. 19.

Apostata capiendo is a writ that lyeth against one, that having entered and professed some order of religion, breaketh out again, and wandereth the country, contrarily to the rules of his order.

Egyptians (*Egyptiani*) are in our statutes and laws of England, a counterfeit kind of rogues, that being English or Welsh people, accompany themselves together, disguising themselves in strange robes, blacking their faces and bodies, and framing to themselves an unknown language, wander up and down, and under pretence of telling of fortunes, curing diseases, and such like, abuse the ignorant common people, by stealing all that is not too hot or too heavy for their carriage. . . . These are very like to those, whom the Italians call *Cingari,* of whom Franciscus Leo, in his records of the ecclesiastical court (first part, chapter 13), thus writeth:[3] Gypsies are people, who, from a corrupted word, since they are also called Saracens, wander throughout Italy by permission of princes and other lords, yet never pass through the lands of those lords in Italy; nor have they ever seen the lands of the infidels—much less do they know the law of Mahomet: But they are almost all Italians, and they live wickedly by theft, crooked commerce, and trickery, by which means they commit the greatest crimes, and they are baptized [as Christians].

Gentleman, (*generosus*) seemeth to be made of two words the one French (*gentil.* I. *honestus vel honesto loco natus*) the other Saxon (*mon*) as if you would say, a man well born.[4] The Italian followeth the very word, calling those (*gentil homini*) whom we call gentlemen. The Spaniard keepeth the meaning, calling him *hidalgo,* or *hyo dal go,* that is, the son of some man, or of a man of reckoning. The Frenchmen call him also *gentil homme:* so that gentlemen be those whom their blood and race doth make noble and known . . . under this name are all comprised that are above yeomen, so that noblemen be truly called gentlemen. But by the course and custom of England, nobility is either major or minor: the greater contains all titles and degrees from knights upward: the

---

[2] Heber = or "Eber"(as it is spelled in The King James), a descendent of Shem and an ancestor of Abraham (See Genesis 11:10–26).

[3] In the original, the passage which follows is in Latin.

[4] Honestus vel boncuo loco natus = Noble or born in a noble position.

lesser all barons downward. . . . The reason of the name, as I take it, groweth from this, that they observe *gentilitatem suam,* that is, the race and propagation of their blood, by giving of arms, which the common sort neither doth, nor may do.

RANDLE COTGRAVE (d. 1634)

A Dictionary of the French and English Tongues
(London: Adam Islip, 1611)

Barbare: Barbarous, rude, uncivil, rustical, ignorant.

Barbaresque: As barbare; Or, clown-like, like a barbarous fellow.

Barbarie: A part or province of Affricke; also, barbarism; also, the trade of a barber.

Convers: un con. A convertite; one that hath turned to the faith; or is won unto a religious profession; or hath abandoned a loose to follow a godly, a vicious to lead a virtuous life.

Conversion: f. A conversion; alteration, change; a turning, revolution, compass, or course of things.

Converti: m. ie: f. Converted, altered, changed, turned, transformed, translated.

Convertier: To convert; alter, change, transform, turn; translate.

Race: A race; lineage, family, kindred, house, blood; litter, brood; sort, kind; also as Race. Fair race. To get children; also, to begin or set up, a race, or brood, of horses, dogs, etc.

JOHN FLORIO (1553?–1625)

Queen Anna's New World of Words (London: Melch. Bradwood and William Stansby, 1611)

Amazona, in Greek signifies, without a dug, or teat or pap-less.

Cingani, rogueing Egyptians.

Conversabile, sociable, conversable.

Conversione, a conversion, a change, a transformation.

Ethiopa, an Ethiopian, a Black-more.

Negro, black, swart, dark. Also sable in armory. Also vicious, foul, or unclean in conscience.

Pagano, a pagan, a heathen, an infidel.

Razza, a race, a brood, a stock, a descent, a lineage, a pedigree.

THOMAS BLOUNT (1618–79)

Glossographia (London: Thomas Newcomb, 1656)

Mussulmans (Arab), the Turks or Mahumetists so called; the word signifies as much as a people faithful in their law or religion.

Negro (Italian and Spanish), a Neger or Blackmoor, whom the Dutch call a Swart.

EDWARD PHILLIPS (1630–96?)

New World of English Words (London: E.Tyler, 1658)

Barbarisme, (Greek) a rudeness of behaviour, a clownish pronunciation of words.

Black-buried, gone to hell.

Conversion, (lat.) a changing from one state to another, especially from bad to good.

Ethnick, (Greek) belonging to the heathens or gentiles.

INDEX

CPSIA information can be obtained at www.ICGtesting.com
Printed in the USA
LVOW130206051212

310127LV00011B/294/P